The publisher gratefully acknowledges the generous support of the African American Studies Endowment Fund of the University of California Press Foundation, which was established by a major gift from the George Gund Foundation.

Stealing the Show

Stealing the Show

Stealing the Show

*African American Performers and
Audiences in 1930s Hollywood*

Miriam J. Petty

UNIVERSITY OF CALIFORNIA PRESS

University of California Press, one of the most
distinguished university presses in the United States,
enriches lives around the world by advancing scholarship
in the humanities, social sciences, and natural sciences. Its
activities are supported by the UC Press Foundation and
by philanthropic contributions from individuals and
institutions. For more information, visit www.ucpress.edu.

University of California Press
Oakland, California

Library of Congress Cataloging-in-Publication Data

Petty, Miriam J., author.
  Stealing the show : African American performers and
audiences in 1930s Hollywood / Miriam J. Petty.
     p.   cm.
  Includes bibliographical references and index.
  ISBN 978-0-520-27975-9 (cloth : alk. paper)
  ISBN 978-0-520-27977-3 (pbk. : alk. paper)
  ISBN 978-0-520-96414-3 (ebook)
  1. African American motion picture actors and
actresses—California—Los Angeles—History—20th
century.   2. African Americans in motion pictures.
I. Title.
  PN1995.9.N4P45   2016
  791.43'652996073—dc23   2015032357

Manufactured in the United States of America

24   23   22   21   20   19   18   17   16
10   9   8   7   6   5   4   3   2   1

The paper used in this publication meets the minimum
requirements of ANSI/NISO Z39.48–1992 (R 2002)
(*Permanence of Paper*).

For Naomi E. Jackson Petty, my Mama,
the Queen who loved me so

For Esther Merle Jackson, the Brave Forerunner

For Rudolph P. Byrd, the Rough Diamond Cutter

For Jim Clark, the Angel who said "grow, grow"

For Clement A. Price, the Great Heart of the
Brick City

Contents

Illustrations

Acknowledgments

INSTITUTIONAL THANKS

Portions of this book were presented at the Chicago Film Seminar, the Society for Cinema and Media Studies national conference, the Princeton University Society of Fellows' colloquium series, the Northwestern University Performance Studies Institute, the DuSable Museum of African American History, and the American Studies Association national conference.

This book could not have been completed without the support I received as a postdoctoral fellow with the Princeton Society of Fellows, in residence with Princeton's Department of English and Center for African American Studies.

This book was also completed with the support of Kerry Ann Rocquemore and the National Center for Faculty Development and Diversity's faculty bootcamp program.

I wish to thank the Crisis Publishing Co., Inc., the publisher of the magazine of the National Association for the Advancement of Colored People, for the use of the image of Nina Mae McKinney first published in the March 1930 issue of *The Crisis*.

I wish to thank the *Defender*, for the use of the image of Bill "Bojangles" Robinson first published in the October 15, 1927 issue of the *Chicago Defender*.

Thanks are due to the Northwestern University Research Grants Committee for their generous grant providing subvention funds for this book.

Many librarians, collectors and archivists helped to make this book possible. I wish to extend my thanks to:

Barbara Hall, at the Margaret Herrick Library of the Academy of Motion Picture Arts and Sciences

Camille Billops and James Hatch, at the Hatch-Billops Collection in New York City

Julie Graham and Lauren Buisson, at the University of California, Los Angeles, Arts Special Collections

Mark Quigley, at the University of California, Los Angeles, Archive Research and Study Center

Ned Comstock, at the University of Southern California, Cinema Special Collections

Sandra Lee, at the Warner Brothers Archive at the University of Southern California,

Renea Henry, at the Amistad Collection

The Connecticut Historical Society

Karen Nangle and Anne Marie Menta, at Yale University's Beinecke Library

Steve Wilson and Albert Palacios, at the University of Texas at Austin's Harry Ransom Center's (the David O. Selznick Collection)

The Will Rogers Memorial Museum in Claremore, Oklahoma

The Eastman House in Rochester, New York

SPECIAL THANKS

I used to wonder why book acknowledgment pages were so long; now I know better. The village that builds a scholar from scratch, creates context and history, and actively offers love, encouragement, tough talk, more love, reading, writing on site-ing, friendship, consumption of strong drink, intellectual honesty, and hope in the long road to build a book is indispensible; their essentiality to this project cannot be underestimated. I am certain that I've lost some names along the way here, and for any glaring omissions, I do sincerely beg pardon.

I am a proud product of the Chicago public school system; my mother, Naomi E. Jackson Petty, was a public school teacher for over thirty years herself. So I would be less than honorable if I did not thank and acknowledge my teachers at Beulah Shoesmith Grammar School, especially Ms. Dolores Snyder, Ms. Joanna (Papageorgiou) Lalos, Ms. Hunter, Ms. Mican, and Ms. Haynes; my teachers at Louis Wirth Experimental Middle School, especially Mr. Freeman Willis, Ms. Selby, Ms. Webster, Mr. James Mooney, and Mr. James Johnson; and my teachers at Kenwood Academy High School, especially Ms. Bonnie Tarta.

As an undergraduate at Carleton College in Northfield, Minnesota, I was taught by a faculty of dedicated and generous teachers, whose model I still hold up before myself in the classroom. My thanks go out to Harry M. Williams, Diethelm Prowe, Mary Moore Easter, Jewelnel Davis, Cherif Keita, Kofi Owusu, John Ramsay, and Richard Crouter. And I am also thankful to my Carleton friends, who formed my first intentional intellectual circles, in the Gold Room, in Sayles-Hill, on the Bald Spot, in We Speak, at the Rueb, in Faribault, and wherever else we gathered to argue, agree, protest, pray, teach, cry, learn, laugh, and take care of each other: Maurice Lee, Audra Watson, Julia Baker, Chris Navia, Demetrius Bagley, Darwin Conner, Karen Thompson, Stephen Taylor, Stace Burnside, Lisa Bass, Cyrus Farmer, Truscee Dorham, Anjula Prasad, Ben Gill, Dara Moskowitz, Pam Rahmings, Lucy Vilankulu, Johanna Hinman, Margaret Henry, Angelina Carrillo, Alex Bannerman, Michael Bazzett, Read Winkelman, Paul Gore, Eliot Wajskol, Pat Carriere, Nate Turner, John Podezwa, David A. Johnson, Lance McCready, Beverly Boxhill, Cheryl Johnson, and Kristene Maxie.

Stealing the Show began as a dissertation written during my graduate school years at Emory University's interdisciplinary Graduate Institute of the Liberal Arts. I am fully indebted to the late Rudolph P. Byrd, whose mentorship, friendship, and love changed my path in life indelibly. My warmest and most especial thanks are due to the living members of my doctoral committee, Matthew Bernstein, Mark A. Sanders, and Kimberly Wallace-Sanders, for the many hours of help and encouragement that they gave me during my years at Emory. I also had a particularly amazing set of colleagues and friends at Emory, who were crucial to my intellectual growth, and to the maintenance of my sanity: Calinda N. Lee, Mimi Kirk, Michael Antonucci, Trystan Cotton, Rhea Combs, Kimberly Springer, Frances Wood, Lynell Thomas, Marsha Ford, Tony "the ladies' man" de Velasco, Donna Troka, Eddie Gamarra, Lina Buffington, John Willis, Yanique Hume, Aldo Valmon-Clark, Stuart Patterson, and Petrina Dacres. At Emory I was also fortunate enough to have a number of professors and administrators who supported and mentored me from outside my committee and my department, and who deserve my gratitude: Randall Burkett, Leroy Davis, Leslie Harris,

Nathan McCall, Paula Gomes, Charlie Shepherdson, Chris Levenduski, Robert Paul, Dana White, Karen Fulton, and Virginia Shadron.

In my years in New Jersey, as a postdoc at Princeton University, and as a postdoc and later a member of the faculty of Rutgers University-Newark, I had the benefit of extensive support from a vibrant community of colleagues. First and foremost among them is the late Clement A. Price, whose scholarship, activism, kindness, and humanity were an incredible model for me as a newly minted PhD. In New Jersey, I was also lucky enough to meet and be befriended by the brilliant and audacious Noliwe Rooks and Bill Gaskins, eternal and loving friends whose support, generosity, and joyful fellowship has never wavered. Heartfelt thanks are also due to my colleagues at Rutgers-Newark, especially Sherri-Ann Butterfield, Ian Watson, Aimee Meredith Cox, Nick Kline, Tim Raphael, Ruth Feldstein, and Frances Bartkowski.

My time as a postdoc in the dynamic community of the Princeton Society of Fellows was especially fruitful for my work on *Stealing the Show*. From that time I owe a real debt to the Society of Fellows' brilliant, patient, and clear-sighted executive director, Mary Harper, as well as to my colleagues Mendi Obadike, Gayle Salamon, Margot Canaday, Amin Ghaziani, Eduardo Canedo, Graham Jones, Ricardo Montez, Andrew Quintman, Jennifer Rubenstein, and Sarah Ross. Major thanks are due to my Princeton colleague and fellow 1930s film scholar Judith Weisenfeld, for her camaraderie and support, and to the phenomenal Valerie Smith, for her consistent encouragement, mentorship, and enthusiasm. It was also nothing short of a blessing to meet the late Jim Clark at Princeton; his joy, shining good spirit, and generosity lifted me, as they did so many others.

At Princeton, I worked up significant portions of this book with the wonderful Black women's writing group Fire and Wine; besides Noliwe Rooks and Mendi Obadike, this group's members Amada Sandoval and MR Daniel were some of my best and most honest critics, with whom I shared laughter and tears.

My many visits to California for the use of archives included kind hosting, especially by my San Pedro cousins, John and Marjar Childs, and their beautiful daughter, Ava. I owe them many times over for their hospitality and good humor. And I thank my extended Adams/Orton/Childs family-in-love for their enthusiasm, encouragement, and even for just remembering to ask "Is it done yet?" Thank you Karen Adams, Gayle McKeown, Tracie McKeown, Kim Abercrombia, Brandon Daniel, John Childs, Michael Childs, and Brian Childs.

At Northwestern University, I have benefited from the gracious support of the School of Communication, my home department of Radio/Television/Film, and the program in Screen Cultures. I have also been befriended by a group of scholars and colleagues whose feedback, criticisms, and encouragement were vital to the completion of *Stealing the Show*. I owe great thanks to mentors and friends Hamid Naficy, Mimi White, Jacob Smith, Susie Phillips, E. Patrick Johnson, Thomas Bradshaw, Jasmine Cobb, and C. Riley Snorton. Found friend Nick Davis's wise counsel and innately gentle and incisive readings of nearly the entire manuscript has been invaluable; his contribution to this book cannot be overstated. (Mary J. Blige would be proud.) Long-lost brother, road dog and fellow coffeehouse rat Joshua Chambers-Letson's generous sharing of his sharp mind, infectious wit, and truth-telling made the days spent working through *Stealing the Show* far more joyous and profound.

Thanks are also due to Northwestern Screen Cultures alumnae Jocelyn Szepaniac-Gillece, who was my wonderful RA through much of the completion of this manuscript, and Maureen Ryan who did such careful and methodical work on the photographic permissions for *Stealing the Show*.

There are also the friends and colleagues who helped make *Stealing the Show* possible, even as they defy straightforward categorization and location. I thank Jacqueline Stewart for being a model scholar, and a friend and true ally no matter where she is; her well-grounded suggestions and criticisms are always incredibly prescient and timely. I thank Paula Massood for her amazing, eleventh-hour coaching as this manuscript took what was to be its final shape(s). My profound thanks also go to such dear and cherished friends as Jamie Rosman, Daniel O. Black, Karen Bowdre, Terri Francis, Marcia Sinclair, Angela Jackson, Bambi Haggins, Sabrina Miller, Theri Pickens, Beretta Smith-Shomade, Carina Ray, Camille Billops, James Hatch, Raena Osizwe Harwell, Christine Acham, Anna Everett, Racquel Gates, and Kristen Warner. And thanks of every kind go to Mary Francis, my patient, able, and steadfast editor at the University of California Press, not to mention the Press staff who put all of this book's disparate pieces together: the kind and patient Kate Hoffman and Zuha Khan, and freelance copyeditor Caroline Knapp.

Finally, my gratitude is most unbounded for my family: thank you to my late mother, Naomi Elizabeth Jackson Petty, for a lifetime of music and worrying, for your bottomless love of teaching, for your love and pride in your children.

Thank you to my father, Joe Louis Petty, for coming to my talks, for answering my questions about going to the movies as a child, and for being a steady, kind, and openhearted presence in my life, all my life.

Thank you to my beautiful and brilliant big sisters, Jill and Audrey Petty, for being unparalleled friends, models, therapists, editors, and life coaches. Thanks too, to my sweet brothers-in-love, Evan Lyan and Maurice Rabb, for their support of my support system. To my niece, Ella Esther, and my nephew, Malcolm Rowland: I love you both, and no, this book is not going to make us rich.

And thanks, thanks, thanks to my husband, Steven Michael Azikiwe Adams: with your graceful, gracious, contemplative, and patient self, your humor and your wisdom, you have kept me going all this time. Thank you for knowing when a play ain't being played right.

For my beautiful, joyful, wonderful son, Saul Wole Petty Adams—we prayed for you and you came home to us. This is for you, with love.

Introduction

Stealing the Show . . . or the Shoat?

Indeed, nothing more effectively burlesqued the entire notion
of ownership in human beings than the incessantly told story
of the slave who was caught killing and eating one of his
master's pigs, and who mockingly rationalized his act by
arguing that since both the animal and the slave were the
master's possessions nothing was lost: "Yes, suh, Massah,
you got less pig now but you sho' got more nigger."[1]

—Lawrence Levine, *Black Culture and Black Consciousness:
  Afro-American Folk Thought from Slavery to Freedom*

In the second of his autobiographical slave narratives, *My Bondage and
My Freedom,* American statesman Frederick Douglass describes his
various white owners and handlers, over the twenty years of his life in
which he was enslaved. In Thomas Auld, a ship's captain who owned
Douglass for nearly a decade, the "stinginess" that the man evinced
with respect to keeping his slaves fed was only one aspect of his cruelty.
Desperate to keep himself nourished, Douglass and the three other
slaves owned by Auld "were compelled either to beg, or to steal, and we
did both." He recalls:

> I frankly confess, that while I hated everything like stealing, *as such,* I never-
> theless did not hesitate to take food, when I was hungry, wherever I could
> find it . . . . this practice . . . was, in my case, the result of a clear apprehen-
> sion of the claims of morality . . . . Considering that my labor and person
> were the property of Master Thomas, and that I was by him deprived of the
> necessaries of life—necessaries obtained by my own labor—it was easy to
> deduce the right to supply myself with what was my own . . . . In the case of
> my master, it was only a question of *removal*—the taking of his meat out of
> one tub, and putting it into another; the ownership of the meat was not

I

affected by the transaction. At first, he owned it in the *tub,* and last, he owned it in *me.*[2]

Douglass's description mirrors the "burlesque" joke of the epigraph above. And his three autobiographies, like so many other narratives and firsthand accounts of slavery from the point of view of African Americans, support the point that historian Lawrence Levine makes about slave humor, that in effect it "stripped the actors bare revealing the ludicrousness of the white man's puffery and the black man's situation. It was on this plane of absurdity that much of Afro-American humor took place."[3] The thefts that Levine and Douglass describe in these passages are, on one level, committed in secret as a matter of survival against the hardships of slavery. Yet they are also enacted as protest that nearly invites detection, to be registered and acknowledged by its target, the slaveholder who enforces and benefits from the slave system, while keeping his or her slaves in a state of poverty and want. Levine's reference to the "actors" in this scenario is fortuitous for my purposes; all the better to bridge these instances of literal theft with a collection of dramatic and cinematic analogues that are the preoccupation of *Stealing the Show.*

The seemingly offhand phrase "stealing the show" is often used to describe and praise acts of performance that "steal" our attention, managing to detract from the ostensible center of attention of a film, scene, or sequence. Through these acts, skilled performers pull a viewer's eye and interest away, sometimes even into the margins. The phrase may be used in a distinctly American spirit of celebrating the underdog, the scrappy second-string player who works harder for recognition than anyone guaranteed the spotlight. But considering "stealing the show" in terms of its historical utility and implications for African American performers in the context of early Hollywood also provides an opportunity to reconsider specific Black histories and experiences. Of course the central notion of theft is overdetermined in relationship to Black bodies in the United States, and to those same bodies on cinema screens in particular, in images dating back to some of the earliest representations of Blacks in motion pictures.[4] The longstanding stereotypical assumption of Black illicitness complicates the meaning of stealing the show in this way. But the phrase—as informed by Douglass, Levine, and others, to indicate theft as an act of survival and protest—also invokes the skewed power relations between African American performers and Hollywood's essentially white major studios during the 1930s. The thirties were an era of normative Jim Crow segregation throughout America, a decade that was only beginning to see any dwindling in the number of routine lynchings, rapes, and other forms of racist terrorism against African Americans that became prevalent and even routine after the end of the Civil War. What is more, the thirties also found America less than a century removed from the end of formal and legal slavery, and somewhat enamored of an idealized slave-owning past as manifest in the popularity of the plantation setting in period films like *Dixiana* (RKO, 1930), *Carolina* (Fox Film Corporation, 1934), *The Littlest Rebel* (Twentieth Century Fox, 1935), *The Gorgeous Hussy* (MGM, 1936), *Jezebel* (Warner Bros, 1938), and *Gone with the Wind* (Selznick International/MGM, 1939). Perhaps the staging and restaging of America's antebellum tableaux in such media texts best confirms just how relevant the charged context of slavery is for an analysis of the personae of the era's Black film performers. The past, after all, is prologue.

Toni Morrison's 1987 novel *Beloved* provides an eloquently customized version of the tale of slaves stealing food from their masters. Morrison's interpretation highlights the theft's significance both as a means of survival and as a critical commentary upon the inhuman practice of buying, selling, and owning other human beings. She imagines a standoff between African American slave Sixo and his white master, "Schoolteacher," who has discovered Sixo in the slave quarters in possession of a cooked and partially eaten young suckling pig, or a "shoat." Schoolteacher immediately presses Sixo for an explanation, demanding,

"Did you steal that shoat?" . . . . Schoolteacher was quiet but firm . . . .
  "You stole that shoat, didn't you?"

"No. Sir," said Sixo, but he had the decency to keep his eyes on the meat.

"You telling me you didn't steal it, and I'm looking right at you?"

"No, sir. I didn't steal it."

Schoolteacher smiled. "Did you kill it?"

"Yes, sir. I killed it."

"Did you butcher it?"

"Yes, sir."

"Did you cook it?"

"Yes, sir."

"Well, then. Did you eat it?"

"Yes, sir. I sure did."

"And you telling me that's not stealing?"

"No, sir. It ain't."

"What is it then?"

"Improving your property, sir."[5]

Following this exchange, Morrison notes, "clever, but Schoolteacher beat him anyway to show him that definitions belonged to the definers—not the defined."[6] This bleak postscript disrupts the tale's humor, and displaces the triumphal slave hero/trickster of the African American folkloric cosmology, revealing his vulnerability to the harsh realities of slavery itself. Morrison's historically accurate use of the archaic term *shoat* in her retelling of the fable is serendipitous, as its convenient sonic proximity to the word *show* allows for a productive wordplay. The historical and cultural implications of "stealing the shoat," introduced here, significantly illuminate this text's approach to African American film performers and their attempts at "stealing the show" in 1930s Hollywood. The comparison to slavery is meaningful, given the predominance of the slave and servant roles allotted to Black actors and actresses, as well as their repetitive, menial, marginal, and essential presences in Hollywood films.

Abolitionist Theodore Dwight Weld's *American Slavery As It Is: Testimony of a Thousand Witnesses,* begins the chapter detailing "Privations of the Slaves" with a section simply entitled "Food." Weld explains that "we begin with the food of the slaves, because if they are ill treated in this respect . . . they will be ill treated in other respects, and generally in a greater degree."[7] One particularly damning allegation that Weld makes is that "the slaves are allowed, in general, *no meat* . . . [and even] in the [two] slave states which regulate the slaves' rations by law . . . the *legal ration* contains *no meat*." Like other critics of slavery, Weld connects the scanty food provisions allowed to slaves to any acts of theft that they commit against their masters, especially considering the demanding nature of their labor. Metaphorically speaking, one might rightfully allege that in the 1930s African American performers were only infrequently allowed any "meat" in terms of their appearances in Hollywood films. A speaking role with any significant screen time, or a character who could boast any depth or dimensionality, was an exceptional, phenomenal occurrence, one that happened just frequently enough to stoke the hopes of the very ambitious. Far more routine were the roles which required performers to follow some version of what Langston Hughes called "the standard form of direction for Negro actors," which ran as follows: "Upon opening the car door for one's white employer in any film, the director would command: 'Jump to ground . . . Remove cap . . . Open car door . . . Step back and bow . . . Come up smiling . . . Now bow again . . . Now straighten up and grin.'"[8] As a decade often dominated by cinematic representations of Blacks as menial and domestic workers, the 1930s nevertheless provided more opportunities for Black actors and actresses to be cast in distinct, visible roles than ever before.[9] But given the nature of these roles, Black performers' opportunities to "steal" anything more substantial were risky and few and far between. More to the point, individual "attention grabbing" performances in this context were ultimately constrained by the larger racialized structure of the American film industry itself. However successful such performances may have been in increasing a single actor's visibility, or in engaging Black audiences in celebration or critique, they ultimately served primarily to "improve the property" of the Hollywood studios for which these performers worked.

African American actors were continually confronted with the question of whether these acts of stealing the shoat could be significant to anyone beyond the indirectly enriched master and the temporarily sated slave. Their individual, limited access within Hollywood's economy of power and resources created an emphasis upon the difference between artistry and survival, revealing it to be a narrow and uneasy divide. Their performances were generally confined to this liminal space, and exceeding it too far in either direction generally meant the end of a career. Thus, "stealing the shoat" acts as a kind of shadow figuration for "stealing the show"—it is always there, undermining the phrase's celebratory connotations and reminding one of the specific social, political, cultural, and historical terms of Black cinematic performance. Even when African American players received mainstream kudos as "picture stealers," such acclaim carried with it the implicit understanding that most possibilities in the cinema arts were wholly closed to them.

"PICTURE STEALERS" IN DEMAND
Show Stealing, Stardom, and Cinematic Performance

In the spring of 1935, the *Los Angeles Times* carried a puff piece about Hollywood casting practices entitled "'Picture Stealers' More in Demand Than Costly Stars." *Times* reporter John Scott detailed an extensive group of actors "who appear in support of the stars and, through the excellence of their 'type' portrayals, often save pictures and frequently steal them."[10] Scott profiled popular character actors like Berton Churchill and Una

Merkel, explaining that in their portrayals of "banker types," "dignified tipplers," "homewrecking females," et cetera, they could "command good salaries, may only work a week on a picture, but are considered indispensable by casting directors."[11]

The article closed with a short paragraph quoting Columbia casting director William Pearlberg, who identified African American comedian Lincoln "Stepin Fetchit" Perry as "the Negro most in demand," adding that Pearlberg feared "that at least three ebony-faced gentlemen will yell their heads off [in protest of Fetchit]. They are Slickem [Clarence Brown], Oscar Smith, and Henry Martin, the boot-black-actors at M-G-M, Paramount, and Columbia Studios, respectively."[12] Though Scott incorporates a section about frequently cast comedians and comediennes in the article, Fetchit's nearly postscripted inclusion identifies him only as an in-demand "Negro," which Scott clearly thought of as an equally uncomplicated type as a "dignified tippler" or "homewrecking female." In terms of race, the hierarchy of "stars" versus "scene stealers" is all but meaningless given that "the Negro most in demand" is effectively one of the *only* Negroes in demand, as "star" or anything else. It is rendered even less significant when one considers that Fetchit's biggest acting competition in his category, according to the reporter, are simply the Negroes closest to hand, a trio of shoeshine men who work the studio lots.

Still, though the article touts "picture stealers" as everyday paragons in terms of their relative merit as measured against "costly" stars, the writer implicitly reinforces the understanding that stars exist at the top of the Hollywood food chain. *Stealing the Show* complicates this schematic for African Americans in particular, arguing for the cultural significance of performers who would likely be considered character actors at most, and scene stealers at best. In the 1930s, a decade in which stardom was such a potent cultural and industrial force, many African American viewers took "their" stars as they found them, even when they were contained and marginalized in Hollywood offerings. Cotemporary Black critics like the NAACP's Loren Miller railed against the African American press for "pumping some Negro bit actor up to the dimensions of a star," decrying the practice as "the abjectness of a beggar fawning over a penny tossed him by his lord."[13] Yet as present-day scholar Arthur Knight asserts in his critical essay "Star Dances," the counterargument, then as now, is that these bit actors "are (or may become) stars in a different, Black universe."[14] *Stealing the Show*'s subjects are largely performers who inhabit what Knight labels a "problematic stardom": regularly cast and highly visible despite their usual narrative marginalization,

significantly well known for a limited and stereotyped set of performances. Yet these performers were put to a surprisingly wide variety of
ideological uses by Black moviegoers. *Stealing the Show* explores the
ways in which 1930s Black performers and African American audiences
expressed agency and negotiated ideas about their lives and identities
through acts of performance and discourse that incorporated and
exceeded the cinematic frame.

The *Times'* reporter is correct insofar as Lincoln Perry, in the guise of
his cinematic persona Stepin Fetchit, was a near-virtuoso scene stealer
with an idiosyncratic presence and performance style that made it difficult to look at anyone else in the frame. Perry's stylized performance
of Stepin Fetchit was initially so mesmerizing as to provoke Fox Studios
to put him under contract twice between 1929 and 1937. His slurred
drawl, slumped posture, alternately open and collapsing facial expressions, clean-shaven head, and unsustainably lazy spirit, made him the
apotheosis of the 1930s chief African American racial stereotype—as
well as a blatant parody thereof, for those able and willing to see his
performance as such.

In one of Perry's earliest movie appearances, in the 1929 Fox Movietone film *Salute,* his performance as Stepin Fetchit is arresting enough
that he even distracts the white actors with whom he shares his scenes.
Directed by John Ford (who would work with Stepin Fetchit throughout
the 1930s in popular Will Rogers movies), *Salute* is a softhearted story
about sibling rivalry between two brothers, one enrolled as an army
cadet at West Point, the other as a midshipman at the U.S. Naval Academy. As Stepin Fetchit, Perry is cast as "Smoke Screen," the erstwhile
valet of the younger, Navy-bound brother, Paul (William Janney). Family
rivalry provides the device for the film's attention to the Army-Navy
football game, in which the brothers compete against one another.

Salute has a thin, slow plot, which gives Perry significant latitude to
indulge himself as a performer. The role is one of the most blatant examples of his deployment of the lazy, incoherent Stepin Fetchit persona as
a way to draw out his screen time. During the film's fateful Army-Navy
game, Smoke Screen is on the sidelines, languorously hurling an extem-
porized hex at the Army team, while the Navy coach (David Butler) and
his assistants look on. He drawls: "Navy goat, the way you smell . . .
beat that Army mule I know darn well. Oh hoo-*doooo* the Army! Hoo-
dooo them *all!* Win this game for Massa Paul. *(sings)* Naaaaa—vy goat
. . . an' awayyyy we go . . ." He also performs a sleepy, ersatz set of
"hoo-doo" gestures (e.g., picking up soil from the ground and listlessly

flinging it at the football field as he shambles offscreen). Here as else-where, Perry's performance is in direct tonal contrast with the straitlaced manner of most of the film's white performers. He clearly unsettles many of them in a way that only creates more time, space, and attention for Stepin Fetchit. The men on the sidelines patiently gawk, unsure of when he will finish his obviously unscripted and equally unclear speech.

Even in a context where abject, stereotyped African American per-formance was the rule, Perry was exceptional. His over-the-top per-formance style is a testimony to the bizarre lengths to which a Black performer might expect to go in order to attract a white audience's attention in the context of the 1930s. After flawlessly embodying the dominant stereotype of Blackness as lazy and idiotic, Perry added odd details (like the strange doggerel of his speech) that made his performance fully baroque. As he concludes his monologue in *Salute*, he leaves a somewhat stunned silence in his wake, as the white male actors who have been watching him attentively, chuckle, mystified. Being the center of such dubious attention was the paradoxical hall-mark of African American cinematic performance in the classical Hol-lywood era.

Stealing the Show examines the impact of cinematic performance, extra-cinematic dynamics, and performer-audience discourse upon African American presences in Hollywood film. I also consider the dec-ade of the 1930s itself, an era in which marginalized, "problematic stars" transformed Black audiences' expectations of Hollywood films, acting as lightning rods for praise, critique, blame, identification, and interrogation. The 1930s saw these and other Black film performers cast for the first time in distinct, recognizable roles with screen credit. Black film performers' newfound visibility allowed them to negotiate an unprecedented set of questions around the impact and significance of their own racialized performances. Bounded on one end by the coming of sound technology to the cinema, on the other by Hattie McDaniel's 1940 Oscar win for her performance in *Gone with the Wind* (*GWTW*), and between those markers, characterized by a highly visible, well con-solidated Hollywood star system that largely ignored Black performers and audiences altogether, the 1930s witnessed a subtle yet profound cultural shift in the relationships among African American performers, audiences, and Hollywood.

The images of Blacks in 1930s film were controlled and influenced by industrial factors, including the experiment with Black-cast sound films at the start of the sound era, the well-worn myth of the Southern box office among major studios, and the dominance of the option contract as the primary mode of regular employment with any one studio.[15] The images were also overwhelmingly influenced by white audience expectations that further reinscribed what Black performers' screen presences could mean. My notion of their "stealing the show" in such a context owes much to James Baldwin's observation that "what the black actor has managed to give are moments—indelible moments, created, miraculously, beyond the confines of the script: hints of reality, smuggled like contraband into a maudlin tale, and with enough force, if unleashed, to shatter the tale to fragments."[16] As Baldwin implies, only rarely, if ever, were such moments "unleashed" to reveal the reality that lay beneath them. Still, these are moments in which Black performers take distinct advantage of the peculiar and fleeting high-relief visibility afforded to them by racial difference. They create performances that are bounded by the strictures of American racism, yet that resonate and Signify in ways that exceed these same boundaries.[17]

Stereotyped and repetitive as the roles given Black actors were, the 1930s was a decade of some representational gains. The previous era of silent films typically saw the greatest use of Black performers for the creation of "scenery" or "atmosphere," as groups of slaves, African or "island" natives, and the like. Yet in the thirties, a small set of Black performers became widely known, and five of these performers—Louise Beavers, Fredi Washington, Hattie McDaniel, Lincoln "Stepin Fetchit" Perry, and Bill "Bojangles" Robinson—constitute the foci for the analysis in *Stealing the Show*. The increase in Black performers' visibility certainly owed something to the highly functioning star system in place for white stars in major studios. Film industry practices that had developed a decade and a half before, such as the assigning of screen credit, the promotion of recognizable stars, and the contracting of stars to specific studios, now began to "trickle down" to African Americans.

Out of the small colony of African American performers working in Hollywood in the 1930s, I have chosen the quintet of Beavers, McDaniel, Perry, Robinson, and Washington because of their collective and individual screen prominence. For Louise Beavers and Hattie McDaniel, such prominence was partially due to being cast in so many films as to become recognizable faces to screen audiences and readily known names to studio casting agents. Between 1930 and 1940, Beavers appeared in nearly one hundred films, McDaniel in more than seventy. Moreover, Beavers, McDaniel and Washington had major performances in two of the decade's most significant and popular Hollywood films dealing with race: *Imitation of Life* (John Stahl, 1934, featuring Beavers and Washington), and *Gone with the Wind* (Victor Fleming, 1939, featuring McDaniel). Likewise, Perry, as Stepin Fetchit, had a sizable role in *Hearts in Dixie* (Fox, 1929), one of the historic Black-cast "talkies" that inaugurated the technical advance of sound films. He went on to appear in more than thirty films during the 1930s. His character and performance style made him one of the most recognizable Black performers of the thirties, and arguably one of the most popular with white audiences. Finally, Bill Robinson's mainstream film fame, and his significance to cinema history, can be attributed not to any single movie but to his multiple onscreen appearances alongside the decade's most popular child star, Shirley Temple, in films like *The Little Colonel* (1935), *The Littlest Rebel* (1935), and *Rebecca of Sunnybrook Farm* (1938). Robinson was already an accomplished and well-known tap dancer by the 1930s, and brought several trademarks to his film appearances, including his "stair dance."[18] These actors are central to *Stealing the Show* because of the sheer number of films in which they appeared, the impact of the particular films in which they appeared, or a combination of both. They are, at the same time, part of a larger coterie of Black actors of the era who worked steadily and with some modicum of success in Hollywood films. This cohort includes Nina Mae McKinney, Ethel Waters, Clarence Muse, Willie Best, Gertrude Howard, Sam McDaniel, and Libby Taylor.

Perhaps the most conspicuous absence from the list of performers discussed in *Stealing the Show* is Paul Robeson. Robeson was for many the personification of the African American "renaissance man," a legal and intellectual scholar, singer, actor, writer, and political activist whose *starring* appearances in mostly British-made films like *The Emperor Jones* (1933), *Song of Freedom* (1936), *Jericho* (1937), and *The Proud Valley* (1940) complicated and even defied the conventions of race that otherwise dominated the Black presence in American film. I omit him from this study primarily because when it comes to the notion of "stealing the show," Robeson's exceptional presence proves the rule. His status as the unambiguous star of the majority of the films in which he appeared meant that he was not required to do as much calculated upstaging. His fellow African American actors, with their limited characters and transient screen times, were obliged to engage in these practices as a matter of visibility and survival. Robeson's top-billed roles in international films point to his stature as a performer with enough celebrity to go outside the Hollywood system in order to obtain substantial parts. On a strictly economic level, Robeson also had other sources of fame—his singing, for one—that made him less beholden to Hollywood and the film industry for his mainstream celebrity than were his counterparts.

Yet Robeson is singularly important to the 1930s. The first major Black performer to find comparable popularity among Black and white audiences over more than one medium, he was an early, even prototypical exemplar of the crossover star.[19] Indeed, his unique status is equally clear today, in terms of the amount of scholarly ink devoted to the man. Symbolically, Robeson works as a popular cultural foil to the quintet of actors I've chosen to examine in *Stealing the Show*. Ultimately, the concept of "show stealing" fundamentally illustrates how exceptional Robeson was, as a Black performer to whom the show actually occasionally belonged. This is not to overly simplify the terms of Robeson's stardom, which was a tenuous and unquestionably vexed phenomenon. Nor is it to overstate the control he had over "his" films. Indeed Robeson was consistently disappointed with the conservatism of the films in which he appeared, which more often than not reinforced a racist and colonialist vision of race, nation, empire, and the relationships among them. Nevertheless, Robeson was regularly placed in the narrative center of his films in ways that gave him minutes and hours, instead of moments, in which to capture an audience's attention.

THE BLACK PRESS
"Stealing the Show" as African American Discursive Critique

In the 1930s, both the mainstream media and the Black press frequently referenced Black actors' performances in terms of "scene stealing," "show stealing," or other variants on the theme. On the surface, Black and white reviewers alike sought to commend actors who, performing on the margins of films, managed to command sustained viewer interest. Yet in these two different contexts, the phrases took on distinct, even oppositional meanings. In the white press, the notion of Black performers stealing the show generally served as a kind of backhanded compliment, a species of praise that was both limiting and limited. By contrast, the Black press frequently used the phrase to instantiate an oblique critique of Hollywood and American racial politics. The distinction between these two discursive modes underscores the significant cultural fault line upon which these performers and their cinematic presences rested.[20]

Media coverage of Hattie McDaniel, and specifically of her performance in the 1939 film *Gone with the Wind* (as well as her Oscar nomination and subsequent win for Best Supporting Actress in that film), usefully illustrates these different interpretations of stealing the show, and supports the idea that, like the other African American performers explored in this book, McDaniel's Hollywood career was suspended between poles of spectatorial projection, pleasure, frustration, and desire, even as it was assessed distinctly by Black audiences and white audiences.

Anna Everett has described the prominent strains of African American film criticism in the 1930s as engaged with a modernist dialectical model, that "bifurcates along familiar lines in African American political thought, that duality of accommodation and radicalism."[21] It is the more mainstream Black press that typically evinces the accommodationist line, and it is within this school of thought that the critical discourse of "stealing the show" most frequently surfaces. Mainline African American newspapers like the *Chicago Defender,* the *Baltimore Afro-American,* the *New York Amsterdam News,* and the *Pittsburgh Courier* evidenced ambivalence regarding McDaniel's casting and performance in *GWTW,* as well as for her Oscar nomination and win.[22] Their coverage frequently sought to reconcile a fundamental inclination to support an African American public figure who had "made good" so publically, with an equally strong impulse to reject the ideological commitments to white supremacy and pro-slavery thought that the film, and McDaniel's "Mammy" character, plainly represented.[23] The rhetoric of "stealing the show" was sometimes employed as a near-surgical procedure, amputating the talented actress from the character she played. In one such instance, McDaniel was defended by a fellow African American actor, Clarence Muse. Muse wrote a regular and nationally syndicated show business column, "What's Going On in Hollywood." His December 23, 1939 column ran in the *Chicago Defender* soon after *GWTW*'s Atlanta and New York premieres, on December 15 and 19, respectively.

Though Muse wrote the piece long before the February 11 announcement of McDaniel's Best Supporting Actress nomination, McDaniel's casting as Mammy and her performance in the film had already created significant interest, and concern from various quarters. Muse clearly hoped that his column would represent and influence a favorable African American reception for the film's Black players as early as possible, even in the light of objections to the film as a whole. Noting how "sensational" it was "that three NEGRO ARTISTS [McDaniel, Butterfly

McQueen, and Oscar Polk] finished 'NECK AND NECK' with the 'STARS,'" Muse declared that

> HATTIE McDANIEL as the overbearing, devoted 'MAMMY' steals scene after scene. HOLLYWOOD almost cheered her every ENTRANCE .... There are many THINGS about the story that will not SATISFY our people. BUT IT MEANS a great DEAL when our THESPIANS can rise above distasteful things and turn in a FINE PERFORMANCE. I think it is more difficult, because I AM SATISFIED these artists would have enjoyed DOING SOMETHING more uplifting. HOWEVER their PROFESSION is ACTING and they ACT. Please give these fellow CRAFTSMEN all the praise you can, they are VICTIMS like you of the AMERICAN habit of 'UNCLE TOM.' I'm glad they will be seen by MILLIONS AND MILLIONS [who] must recognize NEGRO ARTISTRY. It is SENSATIONAL to rise to the TOP with a 'BIT OF MEAT' in your mouth, YOU DON'T LIKE.[24]

Muse's prose is profoundly haunted by the specter of the stolen shoat, the purloined provisions that offer temporary satiety for the eater but do nothing to alter the conditions that make the theft necessary. His allusion to the metaphorical bit of meat that one doesn't like outlines the clear schism between the acclaim and visibility of stealing "scene after scene" and the price of the theft, both for Black audiences ostensibly left unsatisfied and far from nourished (hence the critiques against which he seems eager to defend McDaniel and company), and for Black performers for whom such "stealing" as this was the only, dubious opportunity for exhibiting "Negro artistry." What is more, with his attempt at a laudatory column, Muse himself made do with a bit of meat—*Gone with the Wind's* relatively sizable yet unimaginative African American roles—which he plainly found less than savory.

Muse reflected a sensitive set of insights about the limited options available for Blacks in the motion picture industry. In his 1934 essay, "The Dilemma of the Negro Actor," he lamented the popularity of "Uncle Tom" characters with white audiences, whose demand for such one-note characterizations essentially resulted in Black actors finding themselves permanently "stopped with the slave period."[25] Muse reflected upon the dilemma of Black actors' dependence on white audiences' disproportionate economic power, juxtaposed against their wishes to perform beyond the frame of white-sanctioned characterizations, for the benefit and entertainment of Black audiences. Anticipating his defense of McDaniel's *Gone with the Wind* performance, he acknowledged that the Negro artist is flexible. He will do well that which is demanded of him, but he never loses his desire to do bigger things. Every chance he has he warms up this artistic expression on his colored hearers. He is ready for the day when they will permit him to be himself.[26]

From his perspective, the show-stealing performances that he and other actors offered were "sensational" in their ability to hint at prodigious talent in a context that forbade its full expression. He suggests that these performances met an unreasonable challenge, in which all the standard labor of acting was compounded by the ideological duress of making oneself over into "Uncle Tom." Muse closes his review of *Gone with the Wind* by observing that "IT'S a business, they say in HOLLY-WOOD, and COLORED ACTORS must EAT," foregrounding the question of how actors like McDaniel could ever make a meal of the scanty offerings available to them in the movies.

Another article lauding McDaniel's show stealing appeared in the African American press one week after she won the Best Supporting Actress Oscar. The *Norfolk Journal and Guide,* a Virginia newspaper, ran an editorial entitled "Hattie McDaniel: Landmark of an Era." Like Muse in his earlier column, the *Journal and Guide's* editors attempted to celebrate the individual distinction of the Oscar for McDaniel, and for "the race," while at the same time criticizing the role and the larger Hollywood and American contexts that desired primarily to see her cast as "Mammy." They reasoned that

if 'Gone with the Wind' was to be produced, there had to be "Mammy"—and Miss McDaniel did it so thoroughly and so touchingly that critics, both colored and white, credit her with stealing the honors from an all-star cast that was in the making fully two years. That is the important present point to remember.[27]

Concluding that McDaniel and other African American actors had essentially done their part "to get in to movies at all and convince producers that they were acceptable . . . to advance from the bit parts . . . to the dignity of principal or star roles," the *Journal and Guide* exhorted its readership to do *its* part, with "a continual campaign to have our actors and actresses provided with sounder . . . more realistic . . . less offensive roles . . . by writing producers when they offend AND when they please us in this connection."[28] Like Muse, the *Journal and Guide* advocated Black audiences' engagement with Hollywood's power structure, through writing to producers, as an effective means of transforming African American images in mainstream films. From this perspective, the "stealing" that McDaniel and others effected within the limited, racist means offered them, was rendered an honorable sacrifice made for the good of the race as a whole, requiring a correspondent action on the part of the race for the fullness of its promise to be realized.[29] That "stealing the honors" in this way was the only way Black actors were likely to obtain them was itself indicative of the racism and discrimination endemic to the motion picture industry and to America at large. "As producers reason," the editors wrote, "the Negro being a racial and a box office minority, the least risk is in offending him by pandering to tradition-fixed social patterns."[30]

While this discursive strategy of celebrating Black performers "stealing the show" was most pronounced in mainline African American newspapers, Black leftist media sources espousing a more radical perspective likewise attempted "to negotiate the thorny problem of condemning damaging black stereotypes without pillorying black performers of them."[31] Many of the African American press's more radical voices still shared the mission of "uplift" common to the Black middle class of this time, and in this context, direct attacks on Black stars could be seen as counterproductive to the agenda of racial unity. African American "writer-poet-scholar-professor-political activist" Melvin Tolson penned two separate columns reviewing and analyzing *Gone With the Wind* in 1940.[32] Tolson, who identified himself "publicly as a radical and, occasionally, to close friends as a Marxist" used these columns to expose what he saw as both the superficial and the deep structural propagandistic functions of *GWTW*.[33]

In the first piece, "*Gone with the Wind* Is More Dangerous than *Birth of a Nation*," Tolson objected to the cultural and commercial marking of the film as "the" story of the Old South, given its many historical inaccuracies with respect to slavery, the Civil War and its causes, and the Reconstruction era. He also remarked acerbically that its appeal for African Americans was rooted in these audiences' conditioned, low expectations of Hollywood representations of Blacks. Tolson argues that these two factors combined, regrettably, in the acceptance of the film by Blacks who should have protested and rejected it, and its celebration by whites, who praised its upholding of southern pro-slavery and "Lost Cause" ideology:

> Since *Gone with the Wind* didn't have a big black brute raping a white virgin in a flowing white gown, most Negroes went into ecstasies . . . . The tragedy is this: Negroes went to see one thing; whites went to see another. Negroes asked: "Were there any direct insults to the race?" The white folk wanted to know: "Was the North justified in freeing black men?" Both questions were

answered in this picture. Negroes were not directly insulted. The North was wrong in freeing the Negroes. For seventy years Negro-hating white men have tried to prove with arguments and lynchings that the North was wrong in freeing the Negroes. And some Negro fools have agreed with the white Negro-haters. If the North was wrong, old Frederick Douglass and the Abolitionists were idiots.[34]

Yet even with such a trenchant analysis, Tolson opens the column with a nod to the film's aesthetic merits, and to McDaniel's performance in particular, asserting that

the acting in *Gone with the Wind* is excellent. The photography is marvelous. Miss Hattie McDaniel registered the nuances of emotion, from tragedy to comedy, with the sincerity and artistry of a great actor. Some of my friends declare that the picture is fine entertainment. So were the tricks of Houdini. So is a circus for children."[35]

Tolson is clearly preparing to launch his argument that these aesthetic considerations are essential to *Gone with the Wind*'s ability to trick Black audiences and delight white ones. Still, his description of McDaniel's performative "sincerity and artistry" is conspicuous for its own seeming sincerity in complimenting the actress. Perhaps Tolson was influenced by the fact that McDaniel had actually won the Best Supporting Actress Oscar by the time he published this column. Whether Tolson felt personal sympathy towards her, or wanted to acknowledge her importance, even as a vexed cultural symbol of African American talent and skill, admitting the ostensibly "objective" truth of McDaniel's exceptional performance did nothing to undermine his criticisms, and even strengthened them in significant ways. The idea of "stealing the show"—of a Black performer who contributes such a notably distinguished performance to a problematic motion picture that their performance becomes a point of reference in and of itself—is certainly communicated in Tolson's review.

In a second column, "The Philosophy of the Big House," Tolson advances an even more stridently Marxist critique, arguing that *GWTW* is consistent with other celebratory and quasi-historical representations of the South in its depiction of a symbolic "Big House" (in this case, Tara, Twelve Oaks, and the resplendent life of the Southern planter classes). He identifies the "Big House" as an icon that functions to focus our vision upon excessive, lavish splendor ("its sweeping green lawns, its magnolia blossoms, its high-ceilinged rooms, its magnificent staircases, its waltzing couples, its mellow aristocracy, and the stables of fine horses") while distracting viewers from the oppressed, exploited people who make such pleasures possible ("below the Big House . . . the poverty of the cabins, the half-fed and ragged slaves and serfs . . . . The Big House represents exploitation, Jim Crowism, disfranchisement, chauvinistic superiority").[36] In this piece, Tolson references McDaniel only indirectly, alluding to her character, Mammy, as someone who "loved the Big House, for she received the crumbs that fell from the Big House table." However, he asserts, "a man's body may have to accept crumbs, but a man's soul can demand his share of the dinner."[37] As we will see in chapter 1's analysis of McDaniel, the gender split in Tolson's rhetoric, discussing the *Mammy* who loves and the *man* who demands, is itself important to the South's glorification of Mammy in particular.

As a whole, Tolson's meditation on the "Big House" illuminates the exploitative power dynamics of slavery that McDaniel's performance as Mammy obscures. Mammy is, after all, an icon designed to mask these very problems behind a veneer of familial affection and sentimentality. Moreover, the tension that Tolson articulates here between the realities of the body and the strivings of the soul reaffirms the importance of the dual notions of stealing the show and stealing the shoat for African American performers of this era. He implies that a demand for a proper "share" is always potentially contained within the seeming acceptance of crumbs—that sampling the master's dinner creates an appetite for greater, fuller satisfaction. This furtive "sampling" is an apt analogy for the experience that McDaniel and others were having in Hollywood throughout the 1930s; their screen credits, their casting as named (albeit marginal) characters with lines and plot significance, their budding contractual relationships with major studios, and their initiation into the possibility of industrial recognition held out by McDaniel's nomination and award, all signified an unprecedented access to the film industry that set the scene for greater Black hopes and expectations. Despite the ideological distance between Tolson and Clarence Muse, Tolson's notion of the impatient appetite created by "crumbs" echoes Muse's sentiment about the "flexible" Negro artist who "will do well that which is demanded of him, but . . . never loses his desire to do bigger things."[38]

Tolson's writing about *Gone with the Wind* is a tangible example of the way that the discursive concept of "stealing the show" and its critical corollary "stealing the shoat" manifested in the more radical wing of the African American press. Though the phrase "stealing the show" does not appear in Tolson's writing, the idea is plainly present beneath its surface. By contrast, the mainstream white press's awareness of

African Americans "stealing the show" typically hewed toward the notion of an illegitimate African American presence, kindly tolerated by a "progressive" Hollywood film industry. The mainstream white press's response to McDaniel, especially once she had achieved the recognition of her Academy Award nomination and win, well reflected this attitude.

THE MAINSTREAM PRESS
"Stealing the Show" as Discourse of Tolerance and Containment

The *Los Angeles Times* included two pieces about McDaniel that celebrated her performance as Mammy as a show-stealing phenomenon. They address her from two markedly different perspectives, yet both demonstrate the distinct difference that race made in audience conceptions of the significance of Black presences in Hollywood films. One feature story on the actress appeared in February 1940, after McDaniel had been nominated for the Oscar, but before she had been chosen as 1939's Best Supporting Actress. The lengthy profile, penned by *Times* reporter Don Ryan, lauds McDaniel's breakthrough performance while touting her common sense and her pragmatic, hard-working ethos. Ryan's rhetoric also draws upon a distinctly raced discourse of "show stealing." In a telling passage, he asserts that "in the part of Scarlett O'Hara's colored mammy Hattie just about stole *Gone with the Wind*. The fan mail stacked up on her piano is almost as high as the stack Clark Gable got."[39] On the one hand, Ryan favorably compares a supporting player with a lead. Yet his comparative rhetoric takes a pointed and patronizing tone when describing the predominantly African American community in Los Angeles in which McDaniel lived and worked. According to Ryan, Black men and women in the Central Avenue film colony proudly used and coveted the second-hand material goods of white stars. Black Central Avenue is described as "the Great White Way of the East Side colored district."[40] Ryan consistently compares Black and white achievements, communities, and standards of living, all with tongue planted firmly in cheek. He renders for the reader the picture of an entire African American community eagerly competing for white material and cultural castoffs, and his praise of McDaniel's performance in *Gone with the Wind* as "show stealing" can also be understood in this light.

In a description of a scene in which McDaniel encounters a group of African American men who loiter on Central Avenue, Ryan writes that these idlers, "toil not, neither do they spin—except to make those educated dice revolve—yet Solomon in all his glory was not arrayed as one of these on a Saturday afternoon." He continues:

> It's natural that anybody with a new second-hand car is going to drive past the Dunbar [Hotel], preferably with the cut-out open. On a bright afternoon last summer a brilliant sidewalk assemblage stood watching the parade . . . There's Bill Pierce got his old flivver all purpled up. Here come Sally Smith in a 'most new Chevy . . .
>
> "Say, look!" . . .
>
> "Comin' down the avenue—that big Packard. Boy, is that sumpin'!"
>
> "I know that car. That's Nelson Eddy's. I used to drive for him. He musta just done sold it."
>
> "Yeah—looky who's drivin' it now."
>
> "Well, I'll be—it's Hattie—Hattie McDaniel!"
>
> "Sure 'nough—Hattie. Hi'ya, Hattie!"
>
> "Yoohoo!" . . .
>
> But the inscrutable dark-brown face surmounting 200 odd pounds of buxom colored girl ensconced behind the Packard's wheel vouchsafed her sudden admirers merely the ghost of a polite smile.
>
> "Sorry, gentlemen," she said, shifting into high. "Got no time to socialize. They're waiting for me at the studio. We're starting to shoot that 'Gone with the Wind' today."
>
> The sidewalk Romeos stared after her with dropping jaws, each thinking what a cheesehead he'd been to disregard the attractions of Hattie McDaniel for any miss, however slender, but lacking Hattie's brains—and Hattie's Packard.
>
> "Ain't gone but seven thousand miles," the one-time driver for Nelson Eddy muttered sadly. "Just fair broke in."[41]

Ryan uncritically conjures the raced power dynamics governing the fable of the stolen shoat, given the folk tale's antebellum plantation context, where nothing that Black slaves possessed—from their labor to their children—truly belonged to them. He is simultaneously matter-of-fact and romantic about racial inequalities, at best suggesting their seeming inevitability, at the most extreme implying African Americans' contentedness with such hierarchical arrangements. Ryan's prose also implies a general illegitimacy of Black presences in Hollywood, given that the Blacks of his narrative primarily ride the coattails of "real," white stars to make their living. The double edge of his praise is cutting indeed.

The story also emphasizes McDaniel's "natural" affiliation with cooking and cleaning as a Black woman, in a way that implicitly renders her status as an actress incongruous. In one photo of McDaniel that accompanies the article she wears a "Mammy"-style headtie while running laundry through a wringer; the photo is accompanied by the caption, "Nothin' wrong with washin'. I do it." Another photo depicts her smiling over a stove, above a caption reading "Hattie McDaniel a cook? Sure. She cooks, washes and irons. But she also found a goal."[42] Given the primacy of domestic work for McDaniel's star persona, that she "also found a goal" becomes both ancillary and unusual, connected to the high degree of discipline that also implicitly sets her apart from the average Negro to be found loafing on Central Avenue. But the slippage between McDaniel's natural domesticity and her goal inheres in the fact that her roles as an actress so inflexibly mirror this servile life. McDaniel's oft-cited declaration that she would rather play a maid than be one was, by and large, "a literal delineation of her options."[43] From the perspective of white viewers especially, the screen was simply another potential place for McDaniel to "be" a maid.

The story also includes quotes from McDaniel about the possibility of her marrying (for a third time); her commentary reifies the notion that for her, acting is a luxury, extraneous in ways that potentially require balance:

> I don't want a man with money. I wouldn't have anybody in the acting line—we'd fight ourselves crazy. Most men would want to run my business. But I'd get 'em told quick, anybody tried that. No, I'd rather have a workingman. Maybe a mail carrier, somebody working for the city, that's got a steady job. Then, if pictures get slack, we'd still have income.[44]

Following this quote, Ryan chalks up another point to McDaniel's level-headedness, claiming that "if other actresses who make a success in the cinema had half of Hattie's common sense the Screen Actors' Guild would save itself a lot of trouble giving benefits." According to Ryan, part of what makes Hattie exceptional—an actress who mixes pragmatism with an artistic temperament—is the fact that she is African American, since: "for all except the most gifted and determined . . . a child of Negro blood can only go so far. The colored individual in the higher brackets has to be made of something like steel, asbestos and 500-kilowatt energy to be a success."[45]

However, he neglects to mention the origins of this "handicap"; thorny and uncomfortable issues of American racism and Jim Crow are carefully sidestepped. He also avoids any question of whether race has anything to do with why, for McDaniel, the potential hazard of "pictures getting slack" is one that must always be anticipated and planned for. The same slippage that exists between McDaniel's "cooking and cleaning" and "her goal" applies here; being Black is the central reason that McDaniel is not like other, white, actresses, ultimately because it means that she is not in fact really an actress, but is simply what she seems to be onscreen—a nurturing, feisty, levelheaded, Black Mammy who can "get 'em told quick" when the need arises. Here as in other mainstream media contexts, the phrase "stealing the show" carries raced overtones about whether Black performers have a legitimate claim to a place in Hollywood. Ryan's article is also familiar in its uncritical assumption that the compliment of "stealing the show" is ample accolade for African American performers, and in its reduction of these performers to the sum of the parts they played onscreen.

The second *Times* article, a December 1939 "Jimmie Fidler in Hollywood" column, is a borderline case of sorts; at first glance, it substantially echoes the ironic and critical tone of the African American press. A popular gossip columnist and radio personality, Fidler was best known as a rival to Hollywood gossip queen Louella Parsons. The column commences with Fidler's pensive musings on McDaniel's performance in *GWTW*. He asserts that, fundamentally, McDaniel had given a sterling class, "breakout" performance, and now had nowhere to go.

> Consider the case of Hattie McDaniel, the rotund, middle-aged Negress who plays Scarlett O'Hara's Mammy in "Gone with the Wind." You've seen her often on the screen these past 10 years in incidental comedy roles, laughed at her and dismissed her from mind without a second thought. I defy you to treat her as casually in viewing "Gone with the Wind." For Hattie, with one of the greatest dramatic performances of all time, steals that picture.[46]

Assuming that the white reader he addresses would typically have forgotten McDaniel in other films, he asserts that in this case, McDaniel's performance renders the admittedly fine work of *Gone with the Wind*'s white stars less than memorable. "Long after I've forgotten their work," he writes, "I'll still see the emotion-wracked, ebony face of Hattie, tears coursing down her cheeks . . . . The most prejudiced critic alive could not watch her work without admitting that it is acting at its artistic best."[47]

Though Fidler laments McDaniel's tragedy—"a very great artist, whose skin unfortunately happens to be black, is being wasted"—he is nevertheless unwilling to straightforwardly address Hollywood's responsibility for maintaining and promoting the racism that made the color of McDaniel's skin an issue. Bitterly forecasting that the talented McDaniel would ultimately be relegated "to playing incidental comedy maids, of course," Fidler disingenuously asserts that "no one's to blame, least of all the producers who would ask nothing better than to capitalize on her ability." His attempt to characterize the institutionalized and culturally accepted racism that restricts McDaniel's chances as a kind of perpetratorless crime ultimately presupposes that nothing can be done to change it; a force of nature, it is merely the way of things. He offers no commentary on what precisely is stopping Hollywood's very eager producers, nor does he issue any call for his readers to boycott a particular film or studio, or to mount a letter-writing campaign. Instead his remarks are personal and sentimental, sighing, for example, that "I don't think it will be easy for me to laugh at Hattie's comedy in the future."[48] Despite his unambiguously critical stance, the paralysis and impotence of Fidler's frustration stands in marked contrast to the passionate criticisms, pragmatic prescriptions, and urgent calls to action offered to Blacks by assorted voices from the African American press.

Fidler's praise for McDaniel's show-stealing performance as one that displaces and outmatches the film's white characters is itself complicated by the power of white supremacist iconography and mythology as codified in the symbol of the mammy. Even as African American reporters and reviewers attempted to separate McDaniel's acting ability from her role in *Gone with the Wind,* reviews like Fidler's suggested that for white viewers, such a task was nigh impossible. Though he is not as patronizing as Ryan, and though he strikes a critical tone with respect to "race prejudice," his own bemused description of McDaniel as a "rotund, middle-aged Negress," and his reference to the staircase scene, emphasizing McDaniel's "emotion wracked, ebony face [with] tears coursing down her cheeks," underscores the way that for white viewers, admiration of African American performers was often positively bound up with racial objectification of Black bodies onscreen. And Fidler's sentimental, individual lionizing of McDaniel is of a piece with the ideological work that the mammy icon performed so prominently in this era of American culture; white people's personal love for their individual mammies did not obligate them to see or oppose racism at work in its myriad forms. Ultimately, even as distinct points on the map of white viewership perspectives, both Ryan and Fidler assess McDaniel's ability to steal the show—her ostensible performance and ability—in terms simultaneously magnified and eclipsed by the mammy that so many white viewers wanted badly to see and believe in.

As the foregoing suggests, the divergent discursive functions of "stealing the show" in mainstream and African American press accounts provide one example of the layered and polysemic significance of Black performers who have often been discounted and dismissed as marginal. Something less than "real" stars, these performers nonetheless occupied a symbolic and ideological position that revealed much about the contemporary meanings of Blackness and the future of Black stardom. Ultimately, in the 1930s, a handful of Black actors were rendered spectacular by the visual, cultural, and mythic significance of racial difference, and simultaneously deprived of the full benefit of their visibility, which instead accrued to the white performers they supported and the studios that employed them. This paradox suspended them in an oddly liminal position, especially with respect to stardom as a cultural phenomenon and an essential economic asset for the movie business. The frequency with which mainstream and white reviews and media accounts referenced them as "stealing the show" was, from one perspective, a codified articulation of this liminality. The metaphor's very illicitness also referenced the carefully contained, but no less concrete threat of African American presences in Hollywood films, the felt threat that Blackness carried in its potential to disrupt and undercut the film industry's "maudlin tales."[49] These actors' marginality and limited screen time contained but did not erase their star power, the power to mediate the meanings of race in early twentieth-century America.

ABOUT THIS BOOK

The stardom that dominated the 1930s owed much of its development to the notion of the star as market strategy, to use Cathy Klaprat's phrase.[50] Moreover, as Adrienne McLean has noted, the 1930s saw "a greater number [of stars] than . . . any other decade of the twentieth century."[51] But given the capitalistic function of Hollywood and the relative minoritarian status of African American audiences, the marketability of African American stars was clearly a lesser consideration for major Hollywood studios. As such, this study is decidedly skewed toward the semiotic meaning and function of the Black "proto-stars" that make up its focus. The runaway box-office success of *Gone with the Wind* is the premise and precondition for all of chapter 1's contemplation of Hattie McDaniel's alternately celebrated and condemned turn as the film's iconic "Mammy." In the chapter, I argue for the *monumental* impact and significance of McDaniel's Mammy character, owing to the way that her strong performance converged with *Gone with the Wind*'s cultural juggernaut and the preexisting, historically, and politically rooted appeal of the mammy as an American icon. I offer an extended close reading of her performance in a somber staircase scene that she shares with Olivia de Havilland in the second half of *GWTW,* as central to this claim. Yet in her engagements with African American audiences especially, McDaniel attempted to steal the show from Mammy's totalizing cultural presence, by discursively reframing both the performance and the character in terms of a racially progressive narrative of Mammy's history. In these opposed permutations, McDaniel's Mammy was emblematic of larger political struggles around the meaning of Black womanhood in the early twentieth century. As I discuss in the chapter, Black and white women reformers engaged the meaning, representation, and presence of Black women's bodies within the American body politic as a site of significant contestation, with mammy the icon in particular serving as a key point of reference. These contests serve as informative context for McDaniel's mammy monument—and for her own attempts to complicate and refute Mammy's iconographic power.

Chapter 2, "Every Kid in Colored America Is His Pal," consists of two overlapping and intersecting subjects. The first is Bill "Bojangles" Robinson's filmic star persona, especially as informed by notions of children and childhood. The second is African American children as moviegoers in the 1930s and the early 1940s. Although Robinson's serial cinematic association with child star Shirley Temple between 1934 and 1935 initially served as the impetus for the chapter's youth focus, Robinson's celebrity among African American audiences in fact incorporates and exceeds Temple's influence. The chapter explores the valences of the Robinson/Temple dyad, as well as the way that Robinson's image can be read in terms of an equally significant cinematic and extra-cinematic association with Black children in particular. I identify a trio of elements—play, mentorship, and philanthropy—that recur throughout Robinson's star persona over the course of his career as an entertainer. Shifting its focus to Black children's spectatorship, the chapter next draws upon works of autobiography and memoir penned by African Americans who were children in the 1930s and early 1940s. The analysis begins with their accounts of watching Robinson, then moves beyond him to other stars who were subjects of their viewership, to more fully theorize Black children's complex raced and gendered acts of spectatorship, identification, and play as moviegoers.

Like chapter 2, chapter 3's consideration of Louise Beavers and Fredi Washington is primarily interested in the semiotic function of Black proto-stars for the Black audiences who watched them. Building on scholarship that ponders the profound appeal of John Stahl's 1934 film *Imitation of Life* for African American audiences, the chapter posits the power of Beavers's "Delilah" character and Washington's "Peola" character as two sides of the same culturally specific coin. As their characters and as themselves, on the screen and off, each woman ultimately acted as one half of a "perfect double act" of race, gender, class, and color that was extremely relevant and powerful for Black moviegoers of the era. The pronounced visual, narrative, thematic, and performative opposition between Beavers/Delilah and Washington/Peola evoked the gendered opposition between the notions of the "Old Negro" and of the "New Negro," and bound the two together, making them indispensible to one another for the ways that they signified for Black viewers. Beavers and Washington are perhaps the most intriguing example of stealing the show in the thirties, as the de facto stars of a film that on the one hand relegated them to the background, yet on the other, offered little else beside their storyline to make its plot compelling to audiences irrespective of race.

Chapter 4 provides an extended analysis of Lincoln "Stepin Fetchit" Perry as a provocative symbol of the convergence of cultural, technological, and industrial forces in 1930s Hollywood. Much of the appeal of Perry's character rested upon his oddly distinctive vocalizations; Perry himself articulated a performance philosophy regarding Stepin Fetchit's indecipherable speech that emphasized the importance of his emergence as a Black "talkies" star. As such, Hollywood's industrial transition from silent film to sound is an essential aspect of Perry's success and his "problematic stardom." As one of the first African American performers to sign a standard option contract with a major studio, Perry became subject to the industry's publicity machine, which zealously promoted Stepin Fetchit as a cinematic racial curio, while at the same time satirizing Lincoln Perry's antics and failings offscreen. And to the extent that Perry proved a cantankerous and "difficult" talent for studio executives to manage, the very popularity of his screen image and performance style, as well as the equation of that style with typical Blackness, meant that major studios readily sought out imitators and pretenders to furnish the cultural commodity that the actor so successfully popularized. In the end imitations and imitators helped to render Perry fully redundant to the production of "Stepin Fetchit." Perry may then be this text's most poignant object lesson regarding the constraints that the historical frame of stealing the shoat placed upon stealing the show. The public persona that he styled, refined, practiced, and improved was shown, in the end, never to have belonged to him in the first place.

As a collection of case studies, *Stealing the Show* raises a host of critical questions about the nature of stardom as inflected by American racial ideologies. And in turning to Black audiences to assess their stakes in the phenomenon of movie stardom, it provides an unprecedented and much-needed opportunity for the centering of a set of perspectives that go largely unheard in conventional film and media history. At first glance it seems commonsense to define stardom in terms that reify the zero-sum, "bright, brighter, brightest" logic of the metaphor of the star itself. After all, one either can see a star, or one cannot. Yet an exploration of the phenomenon of stardom from the margins of race begins to suggest that the seeing and not-seeing that initially seem so absolute as to be scientific, depend on a plethora of factors, including where one is looking, how much of the picture one can see, what elements are allowed into the frame together or separately, and which other images one has or has not seen before. Such fundamental shifts in perspective and framing provide the needed reorientation for the intervention that commences (and continues) in *Stealing the Show.*

ONE

Hattie McDaniel

"Landmark of an Era"

Hattie McDaniel's biggest Hollywood success—her performance in and Oscar for the American epic *Gone with the Wind* (1939)—occurred at the very end of the 1930s, bringing the decade to a close on a decidedly mixed note with respect to African American performances and presences in Hollywood film. McDaniel's work in *Gone with the Wind* both catapulted her to fame and simultaneously reinforced her "unfitness" for any other kind of role (not that any other sort was ever offered her). As "Mammy," McDaniel embodied a historical and cultural myth of slavery and its interpersonal racial relations, as well as a contemporary social reality: the post-slavery predominance of domestic work as the way many African American women earned a living. Her win would also set the model for a vexed tradition of Black Academy Awardees whose roles reinforced the parameters of well-worn racialized, gendered, and sexual-cultural stereotypes.

Born in Wichita on June 10, 1893, Hattie McDaniel was the youngest of her parents' seven children. Throughout her young life, her family was serially dogged by poverty. McDaniel's father, Henry, was a disabled veteran of the Civil War, with injuries that made it difficult for him to maintain a paying job. Moreover, the U.S. government refused his repeated applications for a pension for nearly twenty years, despite his military service to the Union Army from 1863 until 1866.[1] The family left Wichita for Denver when Hattie was five years old, but their privations continued. Hattie's mother, Susan McDaniel, also suffered ongoing ill health, such that all of the McDaniel children were needed to work in order to augment the family's income. McDaniel biographer Jill Watts writes that as early as Hattie's toddling years, "her mother took her along to work in white homes. There she learned to cook, clean, tend children, do laundry, and serve meals properly."[2] From Susan McDaniel's perspective, it was likely that "her daughter's life would not be much different from her own ... society would compel Hattie McDaniel to follow her into domestic service someday. It was imperative that little Hattie McDaniel have the proper skills."[3]

Yet Hattie, like her siblings Sam, Otis, and Etta, had a talent for entertaining. A lively dancer, she was also a speaker and a singer with a ringing alto voice. A recitation that she performed at fifteen for an oratorical contest staged by the Women's Christian Temperance Union is often cited as a point of origin for her flair for the dramatic arts.[4] And McDaniel did make her own way onto the minstrel and vaudeville stages before audiences in Denver, both with her family members and as the head of her own all-woman troupe, the McDaniel Sisters Company. Their performances were extremely popular, drawing predominantly African American crowds and receiving positive notices in Denver's Black newspapers.[5] Like her brothers and sisters, McDaniel hoped that entertaining might provide her with an escape from the cycles of poverty and menial work that blighted her childhood and entrapped so many other African Americans. Yet because of her race and her gender, she found that she could not expect steady work as a performer, and always relied upon the domestic work she had been schooled in so young to sustain her when no other options were available. Clearly, she had ample experience to back up the declaration so often attributed to her, about her preference for playing a maid to being a maid. When her performances were left to her own imagination, she crafted other, far different worlds to inhabit and enact. But on Hollywood screens, the distance between "playing" and "being" probably seemed somewhat semantic—other than the substantial difference in pay.

Over the course of her Hollywood career, McDaniel worked to manage the impact and meaning of her star persona in ways that anticipated the struggle for visibility and relevance with which later Black would-be stars would find themselves saddled.[6] Her efforts reflect the complex implications of stealing the show for African American performers and audiences. As a result of her performance as Mammy in *Gone with the Wind,* McDaniel was caught between competing cultural conversations about Black performers in general, and about African American womanhood in particular. I argue that as *GWTW*'s Mammy, McDaniel created a kind of filmic monument to the mammy figure as glorified by the southern white women who propagated the popular "Lost Cause" ideology of the early twentieth century. Yet in public discourse, McDaniel attempted to reimagine the character along ideological lines that reflected notions of respectability as articulated by African American church- and clubwomen who wanted to claim autonomy over their own lives and public images. For this latter half of the chapter's work, I explicate McDaniel's *Gone with the Wind* performance in the context of Siegfried Giedion's theories of monumentality as well as Evelyn Brooks Higginbotham's work on African American clubwomen and the phenomenon she terms "the culture of respectability."[7] Thinking in terms both of how others characterized McDaniel, and of how she attempted to influence such interpretations in the interest of her success and reputation, provides a layered and polyvalent sense of the images and import of Black performers of this era.

Performance and ability are at the center of what stealing the show has traditionally meant for actors of stage and screen. Indeed, among *Gone with the Wind*'s talented and celebrated cast, the bar for what constituted a credible performance was significantly elevated, and McDaniel's own initiative and agency were evident throughout the film's production. David O. Selznick's perfectionistic tweaking of the script and incessant last-minute changes gave performers like McDaniel far more latitude to improvise and self-direct. The film's on-set historian, Wilbur Kurtz, recalled McDaniel's dramatic independence and autonomy in the face of such continuous alterations, noting that "Selznick could hand her a part of the script and count on her to know exactly what to do with it . . . . She even threw in certain *business* without any direction from the script or from the director."[8] Turning specifically to the very last scene featuring Mammy in *GWTW*, I argue that as McDaniel's Mammy ushers Melanie up an ornate flight of stairs to intervene with Rhett and Scarlett after their daughter Bonnie has died, she performs her role with a degree of power and finesse that intersects with the myth of the mammy figure and the diegesis of *GWTW* itself to create a dynamic, medium-specific mammy monument.

A MONUMENTAL PERFORMANCE
Up the Stairs with Mammy

The palatial staircase of Scarlett and Rhett's Atlanta home is the site of a handful of pivotal moments in *GWTW*. This is the staircase up which an angry Rhett carries Scarlett to their bedroom, for a rape scene that occurs offscreen. When Scarlett becomes pregnant from the rape, she inadvertently tumbles down this same staircase, miscarrying the pregnancy, just after Rhett has made an ugly joke about her "having an accident." Yet when viewers refer to *GWTW*'s "staircase scene," more often than not they are referencing a scene that takes place a scant twenty minutes before the end of the film, which features neither Scarlett nor Rhett, but instead Mammy and Melanie Wilkes. It is a scene that takes place directly after Scarlett and Rhett's only daughter, Bonnie, has been killed in a riding accident. Mammy has asked Melanie for her help, and as they climb the stairs from the foyer to the living rooms upstairs, Mammy relates to Melanie the tragic aftermath of Bonnie's death, stressing its impact upon "Mister Rhett." For contemporary viewers and critics, the staircase scene was the clear standout of McDaniel's work on *GWTW*. Margaret Mitchell herself was quoted in the *Atlanta Constitution* declaring that "the scene in which Mammy walked up the stairs with Melanie after Bonnie's death was one of the finest I ever saw." When she wrote a personal note to McDaniel nearly two years later, she admitted that "I do not weep easily but now I have wept five times at seeing you and Miss de Havilland go up the long stairs."[9] Hollywood columnist Jimmie Fidler's oft-reprinted lament about the limits that race placed upon McDaniel's future prospects referenced this sequence.[10] Similarly *Variety*'s reviewer asserted that as she climbed the stairs with de Havilland, McDaniel "contributed the most moving scene in the film." In the *Los Angeles Times,* film critic Edwin Schallert declared that this scene especially made "a deep impress."[11] *GWTW* producer David O. Selznick concurred, calling McDaniel's Mammy "one of the great supporting performances of all time," and pronouncing the staircase sequence "easily the high emotional point of the film."[12]

For an understanding of the power of McDaniel's performance in this sequence, it is important to consider that the staircase scene joins together three elements: a powerful watershed moment of the film's narrative, a formal and performative tour de force from McDaniel, and a central American symbol of race, class and gender—Mammy—through which Black women's bodies and lives had been consistently objectified and obfuscated. In the pages that follow, I argue that all three of these elements converge to give the staircase scene its potency, and to make it an essential part of McDaniel's filmic mammy monument.

As Selznick's comment suggests, Mammy and Melanie meet at a crucial narrative juncture—an expositional moment in which we learn of the depth of Rhett Butler's devastation at losing his daughter, Bonnie, and the shattering effect that the child's death has had upon Scarlett and Rhett's already estranged relationship. As Mammy remarks, "It like to turn my blood cold, the things they say to one another." This scene also provides the occasion for us to learn of Melanie's own grave illness. Though Mammy successfully importunes her to intervene with the grief-crazed Rhett, Melanie subsequently emerges from his room-turned-sepulcher, ashen-faced and thoroughly drained from her efforts at convincing him to allow Bonnie's funeral to take place. When she faints away at Mammy's feet, Melanie's death is effectively foreshadowed, especially given Mammy's declaration to Melanie—meant as praise—that "the angel flies on your side, Miss Mellie." This four-minute exchange between Mammy and Melanie sets the stage for the story of *Gone with the Wind* to slide from denouement to conclusion. The tragedy of Bonnie's death will in short order give way to a succession of others: Melanie's death, the death of Scarlett's dream that Ashley ever really loved her—or anyone but Melanie—and finally, the death of Scarlett and Rhett's marriage, complete with Rhett's abandonment of Scarlett and his now-famous declaration that he does not "give a damn" about her any longer. The plot of the film turns heavily on this mournful exchange, which communicates the calamity of Bonnie's death and heralds the losses to follow.

There can be no doubting that McDaniel recognized how significant this scene was to the film's narrative, and that she especially understood it as Mammy's most important dramatic moment. She spent most of the day of filming and the day before repeatedly rehearsing it offstage, while the crew set up the intricate crane and lighting.[13] McDaniel uses this very key, solemn, *legato* walking scene to showcase her nuanced, powerful acting. As she invites Melanie into the house, cloaked from its doorsills in blue mourning for the much-loved Bonnie Blue Butler, Mammy herself becomes a physical and performative symbol of grief. She is fully costumed in jet black clothing from head to toe, with her dark face shining beneath the black headtie that neatly caps her head. When she is fully lit, her image nevertheless gives the effect of being cast in heavy shadow. Even the handkerchief that Mammy carries is an exceptionally large black piece of cloth that she fretfully presses to her face to staunch her tears.[14] The monochromatic, dark visual of Mammy's image is strongly contrasted by Melanie's white skin and by the long ivory lace scarf that Melanie wears draped over the front of her dark dress.

McDaniel also makes Mammy's voice tremulous, faltering and more treble than usual, not the gruff alto shout she has used to chasten and order the residents of Tara in past encounters. Even as she ages through the latter part of the film, Mammy's voice maintains its authority and grandiosity, for instance, when she proclaims the "happy day" of Bonnie's birth. By contrast, in this scene McDaniel adds a sense of both strain and restraint to her voice, which wavers as she begins to explain why she has called for Melanie's help. This tense quality underscores Mammy's anxiety about revealing intimacies about "her" family. The bitter recriminations that have raged between Rhett and Scarlett since Bonnie's death are shameful, yet Mammy is determined to share them with Melanie, the only person decent and trustworthy enough to hear them without judgment, and with the capacity to soften both Rhett and Scarlett's hearts.

McDaniel's labored tread on the staircase also reminds us of Mammy's advanced age, and of the heavy burden that she carries in this final act of supporting "her" family. McDaniel charges her voice with emotion, emphasizing particular words with adjustments of volume, pitch, and intensity. For instance, when Mammy recounts that "when Dr. Meade say her [Bonnie's] neck broke, Mr. Rhett grab his gun, and run out there and shoot that po' pony," McDaniel stifles a sob, her voice raising in pitch and breaking somewhat on the word "broke." She manages the same effect on the word "shoot," and stresses "po' pony" as though to emphasize Mammy's empathy for both the animal as an innocent casualty of the tragedy, and for the anguish behind Rhett's senseless lashing out. Melanie attempts to check the torrent of terrible revelations midway through the sequence, saying softly, "Stop, Mammy. Don't tell me any more." McDaniel pauses at length, punctuating the beat with choked sobs; Mammy is seemingly resigned to tell as she must, in this effort to restore some semblance of sanity and decency to the household. As they near the top of the stairs, and the terrible height of her story, McDaniel delivers her lines breathlessly—perhaps Mammy is winded from the long walk up, but also fighting her own distress and horror at what has taken place. "And then *this evening*," she gasps raggedly, in a voice uncharacteristically high and tremulous, "Miss Scarlett, she shout through the door, and she say the funeral set for tomorrow morning. And he says 'You try that, and I *kills* you tomorrow.'" As she reports this, McDaniel effects a subtly accurate imitation of the voice of Clark Gable as Rhett Butler. Even through her mandated use of Hollywood-ized Black dialect, her appropriation of Gable's manner and intonation is evident and adds an element of pathos and gloom that communicates the seriousness of the situation and of Butler's very real threat. She repeats the same action with Vivian Leigh/Scarlett's voice in this sequence, when she tells Melanie that Scarlett has called Rhett a murderer, demanding, "You gimme my baby what you kilt!"

Charlene Regester has perceptively observed that as Mammy, McDaniel "articulates multiple voices" in *GWTW*.[15] Yet ironically, McDaniel's understated appropriation of these voices reinforces Mammy's narrative function as a medium, a channel through which the concerns and interest of the family for which she works are delivered. This function is not solely or even primarily due to the expository nature of this sequence; indeed, this channeling is Mammy's role throughout the film, a role sometimes characterized as the film's "Greek chorus," or even, as Regester argues, as a ventriloquist for Scarlett's "conscience."[16]

But Mammy might more accurately be called a *cipher*—using the definition of the word as "a method of transforming a text in order to conceal its meaning"—for a particular politics and sensibility.[17] Fundamentally, the mammy icon takes a Black female character with the potential for individual personality, ideas, and agenda and empties these out to be replaced with Lost Cause ideology and rhetoric. That they come encased in a Black female body is the aspect of the mammy cipher intended to transform and conceal. Through mammy, the slavery of the American South is transformed from a vicious and brutal system of human trafficking into a harmonious, familial ecosystem. McDaniel's acting in *GWTW*, as fine as it is, is ultimately always already contained by this function. Thus even as she emerges in the staircase scene as an exceptional actress, her fine performance creates a moving, walking, and talking monument to the Lost Cause. Mammy enriches the ideological property of what African American cultural commentator Melvin Tolson called the "Big House," *Gone with the Wind*'s spectacular fetishization of the ease, wealth, and finery made possible by the exploitation of slaves.[18]

McDaniel's voice alternately rises and falls throughout the speech, building to a suppressed yet intense crescendo marked by Melanie's awed realization of the truth of Mammy's conclusion about Rhett, "Oh Mammy, Mammy, he *has* lost his mind." With her persuasion of Melanie complete, Mammy lowers her voice and diminishes its intensity in a way that suggests she has been fatigued by the effort, and that she is relieved that Melanie believes her. Bodily, Mammy's full concentration upon Melanie as she relates these events only reinforces how urgent her task of persuasion is; as they march solemnly upwards, she studies Melanie's face intently, as though she is measuring whether her words are having the effect they must. The camera, which has been tracking their slow progress up the stairs from the side since they began the climb, now cuts to a medium shot directly in front of Melanie and Mammy, the new angle reflecting the change in Melanie's mind, as Mammy replies, "Yes'm that's the God's truth. He ain't gwine let us bury that child. You got to help us, Miss Mellie." She deflects Melanie's initial demurral, an attempt to return to the world of southern manners and etiquette in which she "can't intrude," by rejoining that "if you can't help us, who can? Mister Rhett always set great store by your opinion." McDaniel's recitation of the latter sentence is made especially poignant by the way that it comes out sounding rote, like a truism of the household often heard and repeated. McDaniel concludes with a soft, deflated, "Please, Miss Mellie," trailing off this final plea, sobbing quietly and continuing to peer watchfully at Melanie, indicating that Mammy is out of words, at a loss as to any other possible persuasion, and potentially defeated, should Melanie refuse to help.

Despite the overwhelming significatory presence of Mammy, somehow McDaniel delivers a signature performance, on the stairs and throughout *Gone with the Wind*. Her interpretation is one of the sort that makes it difficult to imagine anyone else playing the role; think Orson Welles as Charles Foster Kane, Judy Garland as Dorothy Gale, Peter Sellers as Inspector Clouseau, or Whoopi Goldberg as Celie Johnson. As the foregoing suggests, McDaniel's use of her distinctive, husky voice was one important hallmark of her performance; her use of her eyes was another. Indeed, the artful series of shot-reverse-shots that transpire between Scarlett and Mammy in another signature *GWTW* scene, when Mammy "dresses" Scarlett for the barbecue at Twelve Oaks, rely on McDaniel's alternately reckless and coquettish eyeballing for much of their humor and tempo. When Scarlett threatens to not "eat a bite" if Mammy informs her mother of the inappropriate dress she wishes to wear to the party, McDaniel's well paced over-the-shoulder glower expresses Mammy's frustration that Scarlett has got the upper hand, and then resignation to the terms of Scarlett's bargaining. Just moments later, the visual tables turn, as Mammy insists that Scarlett eat before the event, so that she won't "eat like a field hand and gobble like a hog" in front of the eligible gentlemen at Twelve Oaks. To Scarlett's dismissive "fiddle-dee-dee," Mammy notes meaningfully, "I ain't notice Mr. Ashley asking to marry you." Scarlett, who has started out of the room happily, is stopped in her tracks. She slowly turns, giving an angry and malicious over-the-shoulder glance of her own. In the corresponding reverse shot, McDaniel's Mammy, smiling at the point she has scored against Scarlett's weakness for Ashley, slowly lowers her eyes in a gesture of girlish modesty, even as she exerts control over her strong-willed charge.

McDaniel's face is treated to its share of close-ups, and she makes the most of them, using her eyes to amplify or underscore feelings of tension, joy, or upset. Indeed, the film's many reaction shots of Mammy's nonverbal judgments, mostly in response to Scarlett acting out, are significantly accentuated by McDaniel's expressive eyes, as she scowls deeply, narrowing them and creasing her forehead, or lifts and widens her eyes to look outward or upward in joy. McDaniel's so-called "Greek chorus" is given greater dimension by this aspect of her performance.

McDaniel also brings an energy and intensity to Mammy that is affected by her bodily presence as a woman of size. She bustles about Tara in an early scene in the film, alternately dispensing orders and muttering to herself under her breath. As she makes her way down the house's (less grand) back staircase, she quick steps from room to room announcing "Miss Ellen's home" to slaves, masters, and young mistresses alike. McDaniel hustles around nimbly, with the rolling camera following her around a dizzying, complete circle that ends at the front door, which she opens to send Pork (Oscar Polk) out to help "Miss Ellen" out of her horse-drawn coach. Here, as elsewhere in the film, McDaniel's brisk manner invests her large body with a characteristic vigor, a trait marked by its contrast with the expectations conjured by heavyset body types in visual and popular culture.

McDaniel's strong acting forms an important part of how she makes Mammy into an endearing and enduring cinematic monument. That Mammy evinces her deepest sorrow (and McDaniel performs most memorably) on account of the untimely death of Scarlett and Rhett's daughter, Bonnie, reinforces the mythological role of the mammy in the antebellum South as "a white child's best friend, a secure refuge against the world."[19] Her openly shed tears provide a site of identification for the audience, whom the film intends should be moved by Bonnie's tragic death and its shattering effect upon Scarlett, and especially upon Rhett. But her tears also solidify this cinematic mammy as the apotheosis of the Lost Cause mythology that "claimed for the white family the ultimate devotion of black women, who reared the children of others as if they were their own."[20]

These tears take on even greater relevance when considered in the light of the way that bossiness and irascibility are otherwise the dominant emotional notes of both McDaniel's performance style in general and of *GWTW*'s Mammy character in particular. Though Mammy has her moments of pride—at Bonnie's birth—and even of coquetry—as Rhett demands to see the red silk petticoat hidden beneath the hem of her dress—we are nevertheless primarily treated to the Mammy who, as described by Mitchell, continuously chastens those she loves.[21] When Mammy ceases fussing and breaks down in tears, she reveals how well she knows *her* "white folks," understanding that Scarlett has the strength to bear Bonnie's death, that Rhett has been driven to the edge of sanity by the loss, and that Melanie is the only person capable of bringing him to his senses. This scene is essential because it makes manifest elements of the mythological mammy that blunt the potentially subversive and even insubordinate aspects of the character.

What McDaniel brought to the role was her own determination to "create in it something distinctive and unique."[22] The irony that she hoped to do so while playing Mammy, an icon of slavery so general that she did not even possess a given or family name, is difficult to miss. But what is more, McDaniel's performance, in its own unprecedented degree of visibility, given the momentous publicity and attention devoted to *GWTW* as both a book and a film, emerged as a coda to a historical battle about the representation of American history and African American womanhood, one over which the idea and image of mammy loomed extraordinarily large.

As white southern women, led by groups like the United Daughters of the Confederacy (UDC), strove to memorialize and legitimize the Confederate dead in the post-Civil War era, the figure of mammy became an essential support for their sanitized legend of the antebellum period. Through mammy and her love for, fidelity to, and trust of her white masters, white southerners could fully vindicate a slaveholding history and legacy as humane, affectionate, and even familial. Yet their attempts to have a national mammy monument built in Washington, D.C., as a public and civic certification of this narrative, were countered fiercely by African American women's organizations. These women's campaign *against* the mammy monument was part of a commitment to a very different ideological mission, the "uplift" of African American women's lives and opportunities. The charge was led by the clubwomen of groups like the National Association of Colored Women (NACW), and the Women's Convention (WC) of the National Baptist Convention, groups who saw what Evelyn Brooks Higginbotham has termed "the politics of respectability" as essential to the success of their efforts.[23] Joan Marie Johnson has described how "many African American clubwomen strongly believed that earning respectability through demonstrating Black women's morality was key to racial progress. Proponents of racial uplift contended that if African Americans could prove their respectability, they would show that they did not deserve to be oppressed."[24]

The women engaged on either side of this conflict recognized mammy as a central site of ideological struggle. The section that follows explores McDaniel's history-making role by placing both her onscreen performance in *GWTW* and her offscreen commentary about the film in the context of this charged contest. As *Gone with the Wind*'s Mammy, McDaniel was inextricably caught between these competing doctrines. She provides the focus for an explication of the way that this era's "show stealing" African American performers developed their own discursive and performative strategies for pulling themselves into the center of the cinematic frame and, once there, for managing the meanings of their images for a variety of audiences.

SUCH STUFF AS MAMMIES ARE MADE ON
Myths and Monuments

I hope that Mammy, when viewed by the masses will be the exact replica of what Miss Mitchell intended her to be.

—Hattie McDaniel, December 11, 1939 letter to David O. Selznick

My country needs me, and if I were not here, I would have to be invented.

—Hortense Spillers, "Mama's Baby, Papa's Maybe"

Writing in a *Los Angeles Times* review of *GWTW*, Edwin Schallert declared that "Miss McDaniel is worthy of academy supporting awards in that, through her work, she expresses the spirit of the Old South as if she were a commentary like ... a Greek chorus."[25] Schallert's assessment succinctly captures the interdependency of McDaniel's performance and the medium through which it would be expressed—mammy—in generating her "worthiness" for official recognition and acclaim by the motion picture industry, and indeed by white Americans more generally. As a Black woman expressing the spirit of the Old South, even "through her work" as Schallert claimed, McDaniel lent credibility to *GWTW*, and to the cultural and political agenda set by the conquered South soon after the end of the Civil War and the Emancipation of African American slaves. The need for monuments that would advocate for southern culture, to ensure that it gained greater legitimacy by declaiming its loss, was clearly pressing. Such testaments would ideally consolidate the nation's sympathy for the South as courageous and victimized, while simultaneously promoting southern ideals now more easily made romantic by the distance imposed by time. Ultimately since "the nobler side had lost the war . . . its case had to be advanced boldly in the public memory."[26] Mammy would become central among the ways in which this cause would be advanced in the late nineteenth and early twentieth century.

Mammy as an image is fairly well-known, and much has been written about "her" significance and origins. Made manifest through material culture and media advertisements as well as through film and television, from the early twentieth century up through the present, mammy is typically an overweight, dark-skinned, older African American woman often involved in the preparation of food. She may be happy, even jolly, though she also may fuss, scold, and/or be "sassy." In any case, mammy is associated with a kind of maternality that operates at a remove, perhaps as a result of her advanced age, her race, or some combination of the two. To put it another way, mammy is not a proper "mother," even as she performs most and sometimes all of the functions associated with motherhood. She is too old or too Black, differences that carefully distinguish her from the "real" mothers for whom she plays a supporting role.

Certainly one of the most significant media manifestations and uses of mammy iconography is Aunt Jemima, the long-running "spokeslave" for the Aunt Jemima brand of pancake mixes, syrup, frozen waffles, et cetera. Scholars like Kimberly Wallace-Sanders, M. M. Manring, and Micki McElya have commented upon the way that Aunt Jemima provided an ideological and cultural bridge between the South and the North in the late nineteenth and early twentieth century.[27] As a national commodity, Aunt Jemima products "created a world that invited the consumer to enter" the imaginary world of the gallant South that had been destroyed by the Civil War.[28] With Aunt Jemima at the center of that faded, sentimental landscape, the advertisements carried myths of white southern benevolence and Black contentedness under white rule across the country, while at the same time promoting a technologically modern comfort—premixed pancake batter—that would do "Aunt Jemima's" work for busy white wives and mothers.[29] Yet the mammy upon whom Aunt Jemima was modeled is historically elusive. Nancy Green, the woman who played Aunt Jemima at Chicago's 1893 World Columbian Exposition had "not come to Chicago at the behest of a milling concern, nor had she arrived with a secret recipe for terrific pancakes, and no one had ever called her 'Aunt Jemima' before."[30] Similarly, as a personage or even as a role played by Black women in slavery, mammy was not at all what she appeared to be.

Scholars like Deborah Gray White, Catherine Clinton, Cheryl Thurber, and David Blight have found that much of the evidence for the existence of mammies comes from sentimental memoir and fiction written by white southerners after the end of the Civil War. "Loyal slaves," Blight writes, "who never really wanted their freedom, were far more prominent in the Southern imagination in 1915 than they had ever been in 1865."[31] Likewise, Catherine Clinton has demonstrated that "in the primary records from before the Civil War, hard evidence for [the mammy's] existence simply does not appear."[32] And Cheryl Thurber notes that the

> Federal Writers' Project of the Works Progress Administration's interviews with former slaves reflect the variety of the slave experience but give very little indication of the widespread existence of mammies. Very few former slaves mentioned any older relatives who had the role of mammy in antebellum times. In fact, they more commonly mentioned former slaves as having been raised by the white mistress as opposed to the adult black women who took care of the white children."[33]

Thurber adds that slave women more frequently had the experience of caring for white children when they were children or teenagers themselves.[34] Herbert Gutman further undercuts this mythic character by demonstrating that in white southern households in the era just following the Civil War, more often than not "black domestic workers . . . were young single women," as opposed to the "aged mammy who remained in her antebellum place out of loyalty to a white family."[35] This distinction between the reality of *young* Black women as domestic workers and caretakers of white children, and the fantasy of the aged, Eurocentrically "ugly" (dark-skinned and heavyset), and largely asexual mammy archetype, illustrates what numerous scholars have acknowledged as one of the main function of the icon, both during and after slavery. Its erasure of the widespread illicit and exploitative sexual relationships between white male masters/bosses and Black female slaves/servants, is one of the primary concealments that the cipher of mammy was employed to perform in American culture.

And while some southerners saw fit in these years to praise, remember, and even build monuments to gender-neutral or even male "faithful slaves," the contemporary specter of the Black male as rapist rendered such nostalgia controversial.[36] In response to one such memorial, a

Daughter of the Confederacy from Memphis wrote an angry letter demanding to know if there would "be a black monument erected in every fair Southern city or State, when there is not a State in the South not in mourning for some beautiful woman whose life has been strangled out by some fiend?"[37] As the South pressed its sentimental tale of slavery alongside its demonization of emancipated Black men as dangerous brutes, mammy emerged as a safer and more palatable Black witness to the southern version of history.

Reflecting the national flourishing of the revisionist history of the Lost Cause and the ideal of the mammy in the post-Civil War and post-Reconstruction eras, was a twenty-year campaign waged by the UDC to erect mammy memorials in every state, and to create a national mammy monument in the nation's capital. Established in 1894, the UDC rose to become the most prominent of a number of ladies' memorial associations (LMAs) that emerged in the South following the Civil War. The group's special interests included inculcating the next generation of white southerners with formal education steeped in Lost Cause ideology. As such, UDC chapters frequently pursued initiatives having to do with school libraries and curricular materials, sponsored essay contests with topics based on confederate history, and lobbied for monuments that would represent and teach Lost Cause doctrine.[38] As their movement for the monument gained Congressional support in the 1920s, it did so "amid particularly high tension due to the return of black soldiers from World War I, African American migration North, race riots, the rise of the second Ku Klux Klan, and the 'New Negro,' a more outspoken manner adapted by many urban blacks."[39] Apropos of such tensions, the 1922–23 monument campaign was oriented around the notion of the use of "public sculpture as producing power relationships, rather than simply memorializing times past."[40] Put another way, the UDC intended that the mammy monument would serve as an example for contemporary Blacks, a teaching tool for the subservience, faithfulness, and commitment to white families that was the best attitude for them to adopt for the maintenance of "harmony" between the races. One white southern monument supporter summed up this position by asserting that "if negroes [sic] of the present generation and generations to follow, measure up [to mammy] in citizenship, character, intellect, dependability, industry and godly living . . . they, as well as the white people of this country, will have a right to feel that they are doing mighty well."[41] Led by the organization's Jefferson Davis Chapter No. 1650 of Washington, D.C., as the campaign came to a head in 1923, sketches and plans generated by the monument's would-be designers began to circulate around the nation's capital.

Many African Americans were outraged and disgusted by the "honor" that the UDC sought to bestow upon the South's chimerical mammy. Much of the Black press was vocal in its protest of the planned statue, especially once the bill sponsoring it began to make its way through the U.S. legislature. The Senate's Committee on the Library passed the monument bill unanimously in January 1923, and then sent it on to the Senate at large, where it also passed by a safe margin. The *St. Louis Argus* denounced the proposal and argued that for the majority of Blacks, "No subject has brought forth a more unanimous protest, except lynching, since the Civil War, than has the proposed Black Mammy statue."[42] The *Chicago Defender* and the *Baltimore Afro-American* published satirical cartoons featuring derisive versions of "faithful slave" monuments. The *Baltimore African American*'s cartoonist sketched a dark-skinned, heavyset Black woman clad in an apron and headtie, standing atop a washtub with a rub board bearing the wording "IN GRATEFUL MEMORY TO ONE WE NEVER PAID A CENT OF WAGES DURING A LIFE TIME OF SERVICE."[43] The caption below the illustration explained that "the right hand of the statue is extended for the back pay due."[44] The *Defender*'s editorial illustration was even more scathing, depicting a moonlit statue with two figures in a clinch, a white male grasping and leering lecherously at a tan-skinned young African American woman trying to escape his clutches. Behind them, the figure of a child in a nightgown rubs her eyes, apparently awakened by the sounds of struggle. The placard beneath the statue reads "A WHITE DADDY."[45] With such words and images, the African American press sought to expose and highlight the shameful texts that the cipher of mammy was meant to obscure and encode.

In addition to the Black press, African American women were emphatic dissenters against the mammy monument. Mrs. Ada R. Cotson from Snow Hill, Maryland, sent her original poem, "Dead Mammy Cries," to the editor of the *Baltimore Afro American:*

If the grass grown graves of our mammies dear
By chance should crack or creak
And their snowy white heads be raised once more,
And they permitted to speak
Their cries would be: "No marble statue can bury my thoughts
Of the brutal assault I bore

Or ease the memory of selling my babies
That made me groan till my heart was sore.
Now—if you want to give me honor
For the Good deeds I have done
Just take to heart that Dyer Bill
And please have mercy on my sons."[46]

Coston attempted to provide a voice for the slave women that she clearly saw white southerners as ventriloquizing for their own political and social ends. Her poem brings together the strands of many of the varied protests and criticisms lodged against mammy monument supporters by African American clubwomen's groups and their leadership. Her veiled reference to the brutal sexual exploitation of Black women in slavery as well as to the wholly inhuman cruelty they endured by having their children stolen and sold away from them were absolutely in line with the objections raised by her contemporaries in the NACW in particular. Likewise, she references the Dyer Anti-Lynching Bill ("that Dyer Bill"), which was working its way through the halls of the U.S. Congress at the same time as the bill for the mammy monument. The reference echoes Black clubwomen's scorn for the hypocrisy of southerners who claimed to love mammy, yet continued to terrorize and oppress "her" descendants through the vicious practice of lynching.

Three founding members of the National Association of Colored Women, Hallie Q. Brown, Mary Church Terrell, and Charlotte Hawkins Brown, were among the many to challenge and counter the plans for the monument in no uncertain terms.[47] As NACW's President in 1923, Hallie Q. Brown wrote a letter protesting the monument in the organization's newsletter, the *National Notes*. She castigated the UDC for the hollow and self-serving symbolism of the mammy monument, angrily declaring

all this in a land where a body of civilized, intelligent women would erect a STONE to a class of dead saints for faithfulness when the living descendants cry for succor, for a fair chance in life .... The proper inscription for that monument should be "They asked for bread and ye gave them a STONE."[48]

Mary Church Terrell also wrote a widely reprinted editorial criticizing the UDC's efforts. Originally appearing in Washington, D.C.'s mainstream paper of record, the *Washington Evening Star*, it was also published in the mainstream *Literary Digest* in a special section entitled "For and Against the 'Black Mammy's' Monument."[49] In it, Terrell asserted that the black mammy was often faithful in the service of her mistress's children while her heart bled over her own babies, who were thus deprived of their mother's ministrations and tender care, which the white children received. One cannot help but marvel at the desire to perpetuate in bronze or marble a figure which represents so much that really is and should be abhorrent to the womanhood of the whole civilized world.[50]

Charlotte Hawkins Brown was also at work attempting to stop the monument in 1923. She had previously criticized the popular sentimental notion of mammy in the short story *"Mammy": An Appeal to the Heart of the South,* which featured a faithful slave woman left to freeze to death by her neglectful, "loving" white family. Brown was the president of the Palmer Institute in Greensboro, North Carolina, and had significant experience with courting and cultivating white patrons in support of the school. She was an astute judge of white people's limitations with respect to their perceptions of Blacks, and when necessary, she emphasized aspects of her school's industrial education to donors, to get and keep their support.[51] However, under Brown's leadership, the Palmer Institute evolved into a solely academic institute, regarded as "one of the finest preparatory schools for African Americans in the United States."[52] Brown used similarly shrewd tactics in lobbying against the mammy monument, sending a telegram to Representative Charles Stedman, a congressman from Greensboro who championed the bill in the House. The missive gently suggested that the members of the UDC, while well-intentioned, were misguided: "If the fine spirited women, the Daughters of the Confederacy, are desirous of perpetuating their gratitude, we implore them to make the memorial in the form of a foundation for the education and advancement of the Negro children descendants of those faithful souls they seem anxious to honor."[53]

The planned UDC monument to mammy, though approved in the Senate, would ultimately die in committee in the House. Its demise was certainly due in part to the fierce public controversy that erupted following Senatorial approval of the bill. Yet as Micki McElya has observed, at its heart the rejection of mammy was substantially engaged with the concept of "monumentality itself, reflected in the common use of monumental language and imagery to frame protests to the commemoration drive."[54] And on the pro-monument side of the dispute, a one-time president of the UDC, Rassie Hoskins White, was quoted in a history of the organization as stating that the Daughters "knew monuments would speak more quickly, impressively, and lastingly to the eye than the written or printed word."[55] She also emphasized that monuments did

incalculably valuable "visible work . . . that has brought the organization publicity and acclaim . . . and will speak to a world indifferent to
that vast amount of work which is invisible."[56] Notwithstanding the
failure of their campaign to erect a national monument dedicated to
mammy alone, the successful UDC-sponsored confederate monument at
Arlington National Cemetery includes the life-size figure of a weeping
mammy, complete with apron, headtie, and hoop earrings. With one
child clinging to her skirts, she holds up another infant for his father—a
departing Confederate officer—to embrace. Local chapters of the UDC
were likewise responsible for a variety of monuments erected to the Lost
Cause throughout the cities and towns of the South. Yet none of these
would come close to the effectiveness of the novel and film *Gone with
the Wind* in terms of the dissemination of Lost Cause ideology and a
Lost Cause-inflected view of southern history. The Georgia chapters of
the UDC would do all they could to stamp the premiere of the film with
their imprimatur and official approval, surrounding the screening of the
film with state and military ceremony as well as antebellum-styled gaiety
and spectacle. By the same token, contained within *GWTW* was Hattie
McDaniel's singular performance of Mammy, one which, like the
mammy monument the women of the UDC so desired, conveyed African American assent to white benevolence, power and supremacy.

WHITE COLUMNS IN HOLLYWOOD
Mammy and Lost Cause Monumentality

The manifesto "Nine Points on Monumentality," written by historian
Siegfried Giedion, architect Josep Lluis Sert, and painter Fernand Leger
in 1943, sets out a number of basic principles about monuments that
dovetail with the South's mania for memorialization in the wake of the
war and the failure of Reconstruction. Defining monuments as "human
landmarks which men have created as symbols for their ideas, for their
aims, and for their actions," they also assert that monuments "are
intended to outlive the period which originated them, and constitute a
heritage for future generations. As such, they form a link between
the past and the future."[57] Yet it is Giedion's analysis in his essay "The
Need for a New Monumentality" that provides a deeper sense of the
kind of monument-making that is so fundamental to *GWTW* throughout its reception and exhibition history.[58]

The film's visual homage to the splendid southern plantation—again,
Melvin Tolson's "Big House"—treats viewers to prime examples of

the kind of monumental structure that Giedion derides as "pseudo-monumentality," a neoclassical style so routinely repeated in the architecture of public buildings as to "make even the Parthenon seem dead." To achieve this style, Giedion remarks, "the recipe is always the same: take some curtains of columns and put them in front of any building whatever its purpose and to whatever consequences it may lead."[59] GWTW's Tara and Twelve Oaks (figures 1 and 2) are simply smaller versions of the plans and buildings that Giedion singles out as exemplars of this style (figures 3 and 4).

Giedion was likely not imagining these edifices when he wrote in 1943—just four years after GWTW's premiere—that "this is the period of pseudo-monumentality," and that "the greater part of the nineteenth century" belonged to this fashion.[60] Yet in referencing the international phenomenon of the column-laden Greek Revival style, in which America, and particularly the American South, participated substantially in the 1800s, he implicitly includes the plantation homes that inspired Tara, and the resurgence of American interest in Greek Revival architecture taking place in the 1930s.[61] Just as Giedion attributes at least part of the impulse toward pseudo-monumentality to a kind of cultural insecurity that precludes the bold originality needed for the creation of truly new monuments, art historians have argued that the Greek Revival style in America likely owed much to an American concern about "the display of proper taste," as well as to an inordinate desire "to be considered tasteful by English standards."[62] What is more, there is much to suggest that such taste-consciousness was especially acute in the South. Even Margaret Mitchell's omnipresent GWTW narrator notes the conviction among southerners that during the Civil War "naturally the British aristocracy sympathized with the Confederacy, as one aristocrat with another."[63] Likewise, the southern appreciation of the "class" that the British Vivien Leigh brought to her performance of Scarlett O'Hara bespoke the way in which identifying with European sophistication itself became a mark of aristocratic southernness.[64]

Yet the pseudo-monumentality of Tara and Twelve Oaks is supported by another truly American monument in *Gone with the Wind:* the mammy monument created by postbellum nostalgia, articulated by Mitchell and brought to life by McDaniel. Even at the end of the novel, as Scarlett, coldly abandoned by Rhett, resolves to go to Tara, Mammy is the human presence in her reverie of home:

> She stood for a moment remembering small things, the avenue of dark cedars leading to Tara, the banks of cape jessamine bushes, vivid green against the

1. Tara, ancestral home to the O'Hara family, with its Greek-revival style columns, in a scene from *Gone with the Wind* (1939). Courtesy of Granger, NYC, all rights reserved.

white walls, the fluttering white curtains. And Mammy would be there. Suddenly she wanted Mammy desperately, as she had wanted her when she was a little girl, wanted the broad bosom on which to lay her head, the gnarled black hand on her hair. Mammy, the last link with the old days.[65]

Mitchell's closing homage to Mammy echoes Giedion's assertion that the monument functions to "form a link between the past and the future."[66] By glorifying mammy, white southern women hoped to forge this link into stone; by forging it on celluloid instead, McDaniel connected past and present in a profoundly complex and contradictory fashion, at once exceeding and complicating what the white southern women of the UDC tried and failed to achieve.

Hattie McDaniel's performance in *Gone with the Wind* itself constituted a cinematic mammy monument that was even more effective than an immobile statue located in one specific American city—or even fifty—could have possibly been. As McDaniel's performance in *GWTW* became fused with the potent iconography of mammy, it was consumed by American audiences who had been well primed by various cultural ambassadors for the Lost Cause, including D. W. Griffith's "not forgotten" *The Birth of a Nation* (1915), other Hollywood films like *Judge*

2. Concept painting, by Dorothea Holt, of *Gone with the Wind's* Twelve Oaks Plantation, home to the aristocratic Wilkes family, also complete with Greek-revival style columns. Courtesy of Harry Ransom Center, The University of Texas at Austin.

Priest (1934) and *The Little Colonel* (1935), Claude Bowers's widely read "Dunning School" history classic *The Tragic Era,* the Quaker Oats Company's Aunt Jemima pancake mix and its ubiquitously pro-Dixie advertising campaigns, and of course, Mitchell's Pulitzer Prize-winning novel itself.[67] As Kimberly Wallace-Sanders observes, the success of McDaniel's Mammy "was predicated upon [the mammy figure] being deeply embedded within the popular imagination long before."[68]

As a cultural phenomenon, *Gone with the Wind* served a virtually propagandistic function for the UDC and other heritage groups like it, to the extent that their members and leadership eagerly capitalized on the public relations opportunity the film represented. For instance, Mrs. Ira E. Farmer, a former UDC president and the editor of the Thomson, Georgia UDC newsletter wrote a lofty, imperious piece in the 1939 Christmas Eve *Atlanta Constitution,* reflecting on the spectacular Atlanta premiere of *Gone with the Wind.* Farmer called the film

a dramatic presentation of the work of the United Daughters of the Confederacy for many years to preserve the culture and the history of the old south in the hearts of the nation. Never excelled, rarely equaled, the gracious living, the culture and learning of the antebellum day, the high courage of men

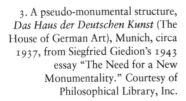

3. A pseudo-monumental structure, *Das Haus der Deutschen Kunst* (The House of German Art), Munich, circa 1937, from Siegfried Giedion's 1943 essay "The Need for a New Monumentality." Courtesy of Philosophical Library, Inc.

4. A pseudo-monumental structure, the Mellon Institute, Pittsburgh, circa 1937, from Siegfried Giedion's 1943 essay "The Need for a New Monumentality." Courtesy of Philosophical Library, Inc.

and women of the war period, the even greater courage of the Reconstruction period, should never be forgotten and this great contribution to the history of a unique civilization should mean the rapid growth and increased usefulness of the organization whose great purpose it is. It is a rare Christmas gift to the United Daughters of the Confederacy from a native daughter and an understanding producer.[69]

Along with the then-mayor of Atlanta, William B. Hartsfield, the UDC membership throughout and beyond the state of Georgia created extensive levels of ceremony around the Atlanta premiere of *GWTW*. Although he ultimately agreed to participate in many of these festivities, David O. Selznick—no stranger to showmanship and publicity—was exasperated and embarrassed by the level of pomp and circumstance that Atlanta's civic leaders were organizing. In a November 1939 letter to Selznick International Pictures' eastern representative, Katharine Brown, he complained that

> the parade, or anything else in connection with the opening festivities that smacks of the reception of a conquering hero, is going to be so ridiculous as to make [Clark] Gable, the picture, the entire trip, MGM, and ourselves laughingstocks of the whole country . . . the idea of a town receiving us as though we had just licked the Germans is something that I for one will not go through with.[70]

Still, in the end, nearly all of the *GWTW* principals and production team took part in the Atlanta premiere festivities. The notable exceptions were the film's African American principals, Hattie McDaniel, Butterfly McQueen (Prissy), and Oscar Polk (Pork). City officials instructed Selznick that their presence would constitute an unforgivable breach of southern etiquette.[71] Given that Jim Crow, second-class accommodations for Blacks were entrenched as both law and tradition in 1939, had Polk, McQueen, and especially McDaniel attended, Atlanta's city fathers would have been caught between the embarrassing Scylla of somehow publicly segregating them, or the wholly untenable Charybdis of treating them with the same "southern hospitality" offered to other supporting players like Evelyn Keyes (Suellen O'Hara) and Ann Rutherford (Carreen O'Hara). Had the Black cast members attended the party, they likely would have dressed like (white) movie stars, instead of in period maid and butler uniforms, as McDaniel was reported to have done for her audition with Selznick.[72] Making the *GWTW* party "whites only" simplified matters, screening out the dissonance of a visually spectacular, wealthy, aspiring-star-type Blackness. Such a presence would have thwarted the city's escape into a magnolia-scented past, by suggesting that Negroes could possibly desire—and acquire—something more for their lives than devoted servitude to whites. Their structured absence also consolidated the conjoining of the film's Black cast members with their roles as a subservient class of slaves and servants who might well have been tastefully below stairs and out of sight for such an event.

Ultimately, Selznick struck an appropriate chord in his observation that the city fathers (and Daughters) intended to receive them as conquering heroes. *Gone with the Wind* was an important symbol of the way that the Civil War begot a loss and a reversal in which "romance triumphed over reality, sentimental remembrance won over ideological memory."[73] Film scholars and historians generally agree that *GWTW* was "the single most powerful influence on American perceptions of the Civil War."[74] The immense popularity of both the book and the film were important victories, and Atlanta's civic leaders, prominently including the UDC, did not shy away from staging the premiere as such. Thus, the festivities of the three-day premiere celebration began on December 14 with a ceremonial raising of the Confederate battle flag at the center of Atlanta's downtown, on the corner of Peachtree and Ponce de Leon streets.[75] Another ceremony held later the same day was the rededication and relighting of a historic gas lamp that had been shot down by Union artillery. The lamp, located at the corner of Whitehall and Alabama streets, was lit anew "at a ceremony hallowing the lamp post as an 'eternal flame of the Confederacy.'"[76] Mrs. Thomas J. Ripley, the president of the Atlanta chapter of the UDC, presided over the ceremony, lighting the lamp while dressed in period costume.[77] Notably, Loew's Grand Theatre was made over in monumental fashion for the premiere; the theater, behind huge white plaster columns, appropriated the grand front porch of the southern plantation to spectacularly mark the film's moment of celebration and nostalgia (figure 5).

Restaging and re-placing Civil War artifacts at the same time that *Gone with the Wind* restaged, revised, and replayed events of southern history indicated that southerners, led by the women of the UDC and other memorial clubs, had effectively reimagined what "conquering" could look like for the South. And the widespread popularity of *Gone with the Wind* as both book and film indicated that much of the country as a whole accepted this revision, and were thus conquered in this battle of ideas.

McDaniel's monumentality as Mammy is not solely an aesthetic feature of her presentation in the film, though the visual idea of mammy is arguably captured and further concretized in her image (figure 6). Mammy's dark skin, her large, round body, and her costume—headtie, neck scarf, cameo, shirtwaist, and white apron—all would have been familiar elements communicated in household "ethnic notions" like salt shakers, cookie jars, and dolls. Thus, McDaniel's live, human presentation of these elements is charged by these inanimate replicas of the stereotype that precede her, including Mitchell's painstaking description of the character in the novel. Her acceptance as credible in her performance of Mammy undoubtedly relies upon the synchronization of this visual concordance with her channeling of the idea of mammy in other aspects of her performance. The staircase scene is also important in terms of the visual aesthetic of Mammy, in moments when McDaniel's

5. Loews's Grand Theatre in Atlanta, adorned with plaster columns in plantation/Greek-Revival/pseudo-monumental style for the premiere of *Gone with the Wind,* December 15, 1939. Courtesy of George Karger/The LIFE Images Collection/Getty Images.

black-clad silhouette appears like a dark carved sculpture, the planes of her shining face in high contrast (figure 7). This effect is enhanced by the visual contrast between McDaniel and de Havilland, with McDaniel's Mammy representing the earthy maternality associated with Black women and de Havilland's Melanie representing the essentially divine femininity of ideal white southern womanhood. It is especially pronounced at the top of the stairs where she and Melanie are the most in shadow, and where Mammy is exhausted, at the end of her tale and at her most vulnerable.

Mammy's cinematic monumentality inheres in a medium-specific ability to go beyond the static representationality of a statue, enacting

6. Hattie McDaniel as "Mammy," in a publicity photo from
Gone with the Wind. Courtesy of the Academy of Motion Picture
Arts and Sciences.

the relational meaning of mammy as a loving fixture of the white southern household in slavery and freedom. No statue could have reminded
a vivacious and careless southern belle "that you can always tell a lady
by the way she eats in front of folks like a bird . . . [she ought not] eat
like a field hand and gobble like a hog," as Mammy tells Scarlett early
in the film. And though the UDC's proposed mammy monument would
have certainly depicted mammy with white children, the statue would
have been unable to pridefully declare "this sho' is a happy day to me"
at the birth of a child who marked the third generation of the family
who once owned her, or to weep bitterly at the catastrophe of that
child's death. Likewise, the filmic medium also made it possible for this
walking and talking monument to have a profound national impact;
through MGM's distribution system, McDaniel's Mammy brought the

7. Hattie McDaniel as "Mammy" and Olivia de Havilland as "Melanie Wilkes," ascending the staircase in a scene from *Gone with the Wind*. Courtesy of the Academy of Motion Picture Arts and Sciences.

monument to Americans in their own cities and towns, making it unnecessary to travel to the nation's capital to learn her illusory lessons of "race relations founded on paternalistic benevolence and maternal fantasy."[78] Rather than the pseudo-monumentality of Tara and Twelve Oaks' derivative architectural style, McDaniel effectively carried her monumentalization of mammy into the dynamic realm of film, her performance reinforcing the mammy figure as memory, history, and reality.

Southerners were vocal in their appreciation of McDaniel's performance of Mammy as monumental in its function of paying tribute to what they "knew"—and wanted others to know—about African Americans and the South. The *Atlanta Constitution* published a short, smug editorial that appeared after McDaniel won her Best Supporting Actress Oscar, trumpeting this aspect of her performance. The author opined that though in general there would be no "southern disagreement with the awards given *Gone with the Wind*, by the Academy of Motion Picture Arts and Sciences, one award . . . will probably delight all genuine southern people more than any other. That was the choice, for best actress in a supporting role, of Hattie McDaniel, the Negro woman who portrayed Mammy. She is the first of her race to be included in the annual lists of "Oscar" winners and there can be no one who, having seen her performance, will cavil at the honor bestowed . . . . the award to Hattie McDaniel undoubtedly brings greater pleasure to the south, as a whole, than any other. For she was, in that picture, the southern mammy as southerners know her. She gave to the world a characterization that was true to fact and tradition. She was, in short, a grand mammy and the south, first to recognize this fact, will be the first to tell her how well she deserves the honor she has won.[79]

By playing "the southern mammy as southerners know her," this writer indicates, McDaniel is lucky enough to have, in one master stroke, won the Oscar for Best Supporting Actress, delighted and pleased all "genuine" southern people, and brought pride and credit to her race. Indeed, the article's thin veneer of pride in McDaniel herself (as opposed to feelings of satisfaction by and for southerners publically vindicated by her officially spotlighted performance) reinforces one reason given for white southern desire for the mammy monument—that it would "tell future generations that the white men of the South were the negro's [sic] best friend then and that we are the negro's [sic] best friend today."[80] The writer of the *Constitution*'s piece seems to hope that his praise for McDaniel will be taken in this spirit of unselfish "friendship" toward African Americans. Yet such pride inhered primarily in the national acclaim afforded to the southern mythic creation that was and is mammy. After all, as the writer states, the South was "first to recognize" and to spread the mammy legend and doctrine.

Another southern voice that praised the pitch of McDaniel's performance as in keeping with the "truth" of mammy was Susan Myrick, Margaret Mitchell's friend and confidante. Myrick, the daughter of a Confederate soldier, was born and raised in Macon, Georgia. On Mitchell's recommendation to Selznick's eastern representative Katherine Brown, Myrick was hired as a technical advisor on the set of *GWTW*. Mitchell called Myrick a "common sense, hard headed person with an awful lot of knowledge about Georgia people and Georgia ways, not only of this time but of times past."[81] But by way of properly credentializing Myrick for the post, Mitchell also made specific, extensive note of her friend's familiarity with Blacks:

And good grief, what she doesn't know about negroes [sic]! She was raised up with them. And she loves and understands them. Since going on the paper [Myrick was a reporter for the *Macon Telegraph*], she has been the paper's official representative at most of the negro affairs of her section. Mr. W. T. Anderson, owner of her paper . . . is strong for the colored folks and tries to get a square deal for them and the saying among the colored folks in the district is that "De Race is got two friends in dis County, sweet Jesus and de *Macon Telegraph*."[82]

Myrick served as *GWTW*'s technical advisor, essentially a consultant for all things southern, "the authenticity and rightness of this and that, the accents of the white actors, the dialect of the colored ones, the minor matters of dress and deportment, the small touches of local color, etc."[83] Initially she disagreed with Selznick's casting of McDaniel in the role of Mammy, and felt that the actress lacked "dignity, age, nobility and . . . . the right face" to play the role.[84] However, once filming was underway, Myrick became a convert. Turning her work on the set into an opportunity to write a regular column, "White Columns in Hollywood," for the *Macon Telegraph*, Myrick's effusive praise of McDaniel was a regular staple of the fifty-eight accounts she filed with the paper. In one installment, Myrick delightedly wrote that under her tutelage in authentic Black Georgia dialect, the film's Black cast members "fell easily into the Negro dialect as it was written by Margaret Mitchell and carefully preserved in the script."[85] McDaniel received special praise, for as Myrick sentimentally confessed to her readers, "she says Yassum and No'm to me in a way that makes me mighty homesick for my Mary Brown back in Macon." (One wonders whether Mary Brown missed Myrick quite as much.) Myrick's conflation of McDaniel with "her" Mary Brown certainly helped, as McDaniel biographer Jill Watts observes, "to blur the lines between what remained of the real Hattie McDaniel and Mitchell's fantasy Mammy."[86] Myrick served her own ego by obfuscating the meaning and intention of McDaniel's "yassum" and "no'm"; was McDaniel acting? Or was she serving as Myrick's maid on the set of *Wind?*[87] Ultimately, the admiration that Myrick professed for McDaniel's performance carried the whiff of the tautological inherent in mammy; having taught McDaniel how to talk like a proper mammy, Myrick praised her apt pupil for "authentically" rendering up precisely the figure that Myrick (and Mitchell) imagined.

The conundrum at the heart of this reportage from Myrick conjures up one of the many post-Civil War narratives that helped to shape the Lost Cause mythos around slavery, Edward J. Thomas's 1923 *Memoirs of a Southerner*. In this slim text, Thomas makes a similarly circular case for the need to monumentalize mammy and all such faithful slaves, declaring that the day must come when a noble monument will be erected to their memory; and this loyal conduct refutes in burning language the assertion that the master was cruel to his slave, and I believe this same good conduct would still prevail, if the infernal fanatics had not insisted on [Blacks] enjoying political preferences and social advantages, two privileges they were unfit for, and not prepared to receive.[88]

Thus such a monument does not and cannot serve only to honor the loyalty of slaves, but must also serve to reverence the master whose kindness merited their loyalty. Both Myrick and Thomas aspire to create an image that functions fundamentally as a reflection of their own glory and as an inversion of the Quaker injunction to "speak truth to power." The Pygmalionesque relation between white southerners and the mammy they created in their own preferred image is an essential part of the mammy monument that the UDC and other southerners campaigned for, and an equally crucial component of the way that McDaniel's Mammy took on a monumental proportion and function.

Perhaps the enduring legacy of McDaniel's filmic mammy monument is most evident in her continued association with both the role and the icon so many years after the movie's release, not to mention her own death. A May 2013 article in the *Atlantic Monthly* about the history of the UDC's mammy monument campaign featured a still photo from *GWTW* just below its headline. In the photo, Hattie McDaniel scowls angrily out of a top-floor Tara window, her headtie, scarf, and cameo neatly arranged above and below her feisty round face. Just below the image, the piece commences with the sentence, "If I say the word 'Mammy,' you're likely to conjure up the character from *Gone with the Wind*."[89] McDaniel is not mentioned by name until several paragraphs later. Here as elsewhere McDaniel's fusion with the character is nearly complete. Likewise, a contemporary Google image search of the word *mammy* pulls up image after image of McDaniel in *GWTW* stills and promotional images. Her image is easily the most prevalent among African American actresses of the period, outnumbering, for instance, Ethel Waters by fifteen to one. Yet in these search results, likenesses and photographs of McDaniel are intermingled with stock illustrations of indistinguishable round, dark, grinning, and head-tied Black women, reproductions of advertisements, photographs of unidentified African American slave and servant women with white babies in their laps or at their sides, the occasional image of a blackfaced Al Jolson, as well as photos of dolls and ceramic kitchenware figurines with shining black faces and rotund bosoms. McDaniel has become an indelible part of the cultural meaning of mammy, a referent that cannot be overlooked when defining and coming to grips with the icon. This is the long-term price she paid for her fame, yet she sought to complicate the role by establishing other historical and contemporary referents for Mammy and for herself.

REFRAMING MAMMY

"To Glorify Negro Womanhood"

As Black performers like McDaniel cultivated opportunities for greater visibility and recognition, they were in turn obliged to work harder to square their common performative aesthetic—the roles that actress Fredi Washington derisively called "yessum parts"—with the racial sensibilities of Black audiences.[90] I term this process *reframing,* and characterize it as these performers' attempt to reimagine and redefine themselves and/or their cinematic performances and characters, usually to Black audiences, and usually in an extra-cinematic context. McDaniel's performance of Mammy in *GWTW* carried exceptionally high stakes for this process. The film's excessive publicity and popularity, the runaway popularity of the novel, and the figure of mammy as a national icon that held power and meaning outside both texts, all worked together to amplify the significance of the role. McDaniel's Oscar win only raised the ante further, as African American audiences considered whether or not this "landmark of an era" was something to celebrate.[91] In an extra-cinematic act of show stealing, McDaniel attempted to reframe Mammy in this moment, drawing upon the history of African American women's dissent and revolt against slavery, and the discourse and ideology of racial uplift.

In the summer following *GWTW*'s release, Selznick International Pictures (SIP) received a variety of requests for appearances by McDaniel at African American institutions and events geared toward Black audiences. David O. Selznick made a concerted effort to have his SIP staffers accommodate such requests. His directive reflected his interest in having McDaniel's success draw a profit from African American audiences, a constituency which major motion picture studios typically ignored altogether.[92] Even before production began on *GWTW*, Selznick had been vocal about his concerns that Black audiences not be alienated or angered by the way that *GWTW* presented them (in contrast to the very public battles over *The Birth of a Nation* some twenty years earlier).[93] He may have therefore felt gratified that African American institutions like Bennett College, the sorority Sigma Gamma Rho, and the organizers of the 1940 American Negro Exposition in Chicago sought McDaniel out for accolades and appearances.[94] Likewise, in June 1940, CBS wrote to McDaniel's management on behalf of the popular radio program *Wings Over Jordan,* asking if it would be possible for the actress to appear on one of their weekly Sunday broadcasts. *Wings Over Jordan* was a national radio program that ran on CBS from 1939 until 1949, featuring the African American "Wings Over Jordan" choir. The Cleveland-based choir, founded by Gethsemane Church's Reverend Glenn T. Settle, first performed on the air in 1937, on a radio show called *The National Negro Hour.* The popularity of the choir's weekly Sunday morning broadcasts grew, especially among African American audiences, and in 1939, the show, now renamed *Wings Over Jordan,* was picked up for a regular broadcast on the CBS national network.[95]

Ultimately McDaniel appeared on the July 7, 1940 episode of *Wings.* In her remarks, she attempted to supply added significance to the attention and space her performance as Mammy had so effectively stolen. The mammy monument as imagined by the UDC would have inevitably counseled that "how the white and colored races can best get along together" would have much to do with African American submission and faithfulness to whites. Yet McDaniel was no talking statue, and offered a significantly different message to the *Wings* audience, asserting that she took the role as

> an opportunity to glorify Negro womanhood—not the modern, stream-lined type of Negro woman who attends teas and concerts in ermine and mink—but the type of Negro of the period which gave us Harriet Tubman, Sojourner Truth, and Charity Still. The brave, efficient, hard working type of womanhood which has built a race, mothered our Booker T. Washington, George W. Carver, Robert Moton, and Mary McLeod Bethune. So, you see, the mothers of that era must have had something in them to produce men and women of such caliber.[96]

In doing the largely unprecedented work of promoting a film produced and distributed in association with major Hollywood studios to a Black audience, McDaniel attempted a careful and direct act of reframing, tying her role as Mammy to a history and legacy that directly contradicted the notion of her character as the "faithful slave" immortalized in Mitchell's novel. McDaniel invoked historical figures in an attempt to reference an alternative and far more radical origin for her own characteristically sassy, independent performance style.

McDaniel named three African American women as Mammy's historical prototypes, women who likely would have been better known among Black audiences than white for their acts of resistance and defiance during slavery—Charity Still, Sojourner Truth, and Harriet Tubman. Tubman is likely the best known of this trio, for her work as an Underground Railroad operator and abolitionist. Dubbed "Moses" for the reputation she earned as a liberator of African American slaves, Tubman, having herself escaped from bondage at the age of twenty-nine, made some fourteen return trips into the slave states (primarily Maryland) between 1849 and 1860. She directly rescued seventy to eighty slaves, and indirectly freed about fifty others by providing them with valuable information about the Underground Railroad.[97] Less known, though no less significant, is her success as a spy during the Civil War. Tubman's information was frequently useful to the success of Union campaigns. Most notably, in the summer of 1863, Tubman led a successful reconnaissance expedition along South Carolina's Combahee River. Her mission ultimately disrupted Southern supply lines, and freed over 750 slaves as well.[98]

Historian Nell Irvin Painter has called Harriet Tubman and Sojourner Truth the "two most widely known nineteenth-century black women," asserting however, that "Truth is remembered more for a few memorable utterances than for her acts."[99] Like Tubman, Truth was born into slavery, and spent thirty years in bondage. Unlike Tubman, she did not escape slavery by running away, but was freed in 1827, when the state of New York, in which she was captive, freed all slaves within its boundaries. Nevertheless, Sojourner Truth—born Isabella Bomefree—became an ardent and outspoken abolitionist. She was also a tough-minded feminist, who advocated for women's rights, as well as a spiritual seeker, her chosen name reflecting the profound influence of evangelical and religious commitments upon her path. Her life was itself somewhat overshadowed by the phrase with which she was so closely associated, yet did not utter, "Ain't I a woman?"[100] As a former slave working for the abolition of slavery and the achievement of women's rights in the middle of the nineteenth century, Truth "became the emblematic nineteenth-century black woman and the symbol of the conjunction of sex and race."[101]

Finally, McDaniel references Charity Still. Still was better known as the mother of William Still, an admired steward of the Underground Railroad.[102] Charity Still escaped from her Maryland plantation twice to join her husband Peter in the free state of New Jersey; the first time she took all four of her young children with her, but was recaptured by bounty hunters. The second time, she was able to take only two of her children. Still never again saw the two children she left behind.[103] Reunited in freedom with her husband, she bore fifteen more children with him; her youngest, William Still, would become a lifelong agitator for the abolition of slavery, and an agent for the Philadelphia Underground Railroad. In 1872 he published a widely circulated collection of interviews, accounts of escapes, and information about the methods slaves used to emancipate themselves.[104]

Thus even as her performance was largely contained in the context of *Gone with the Wind* by the myth and script of mammy as an American icon, outside the frame of the film, McDaniel attempted to complicate the figure, by linking her to examples of Black women who disrupted and defied the laws that bound them under slavery. Through such connections McDaniel implied that Black women like Mammy who "answered back" were always potentially destabilizing to the slave system, always potential runaways, always potential liberators. In this way, McDaniel took aim at the notion of the "faithful slave" and suggested that such people hid their own minds and agendas to their own ends—while also implying that in addition to Mammy, she herself was such a person. By citing three slave women who were abolitionists in theory and in practice as Mammy's counterparts and sisters, McDaniel also subtly anticipated scholar and cultural critic Melvin Tolson's assertion that receiving the privilege of the master's "crumbs" preceded a demand for a full portion and a seat at the table besides.[105]

With this rhetoric, McDaniel also emphasized the way in which her body evoked and signified the bodies of Black women who had brazenly challenged the peculiar institution. In fact, the totalizing impact of the mammy image was such that all three of the historical figures McDaniel named—Tubman, Truth, and Still—would have been marked by their physical bodies as "mammies" in the popular imagination. Tubman's success as a spy during the Civil War, predicated upon her ability to move undetected and unsuspected through the South, likely owed something to such assumptions.[106] The historical facticity of Still, Truth, and Tubman's lives led in full revolt against the slave system stands in stark contrast to Mammy's apocryphal and chimerical life story, yet the visual language and cultural imagination of the 1930s was wholly insufficient to differentiate between them. McDaniel both played upon and revealed this slippage when she made this trio of heroic Black women Mammy's compatriots.

McDaniel also reframed Mammy as a Black slave mother, supplying her with a Black family who benefited from her labor and nurturing—a phantom family that never appeared onscreen with her in *Gone with the Wind*. In attempting to turn her readers' minds from "mammy" to "mother," McDaniel reproduced the tactics of African American middle class clubwomen, who constituted some of the most vocal opposition to the UDC's 1920s campaign for a mammy monument. In an interview with the African American newspaper the *New York Amsterdam News* during the shooting and production of *GWTW*, McDaniel used language nearly identical to that in her *Wings* speech, but elaborated at greater length upon the image of a generous, sacrificing mother:

> I saw in the Mammy of the O'Hara household the type of womanhood which has built our race, paid for our elaborate houses of worship, and sustained our business, charitable, and improvement organizations. This is the type that is responsible for the outstanding success of such children as Marian Anderson and Roland Hayes. I am proud that I am a Negro woman, because members of that class have given so much. Bending their backs over wash tubs, they have smiled encouragement to daughters who wanted an artistic career. Hobbling about kitchens, they have inspired their children to become doctors of philosophy and law.[107]

McDaniel draws parallels between herself and Mammy in both of the comments cited here, yet she does so in a way that actively seeks to reimagine the character and to undermine some of her most fundamental mythic qualities. Instead of being chiefly concerned with the welfare of her white family, McDaniel suggests that Mammy's hard work and loving sacrifice benefited her successful African American children. Overall, McDaniel redirects the fruits of Mammy's labors to various units of Black communities. The meaning of these revisions is amplified by the overdetermined nature of McDaniel's relationship to Mammy.

Victoria Sturtevant has asserted that "even under the glory days of the star system, rarely was a performer typecast with quite the iron-clad uniformity that was accorded Hattie McDaniel." Sturtevant argues that an essential element of this typecasting was the phenomenon that Darlene Clark Hine has called the "culture of dissemblance" among African American women. Hine describes dissemblance as a kind of "self-imposed invisibility" whereby Black women attempted to "protect the sanctity of inner aspects of their lives . . . . creating the appearance of disclosure, or openness about themselves and their feelings, while actually remaining an enigma."[108] The mammy as an idea and a set of behaviors that whites found familiar and expected was exceptionally well suited to strategies of dissemblance, especially for African American women engaged in the kind of domestic service that McDaniel so routinely enacted in film. For these women, dissemblance was a performative strategy meant to protect them from white employers, minimally from intrusion and prying into their private lives, and more seriously, from the sexual predation that was a routine occupational hazard of the domestic's job. For McDaniel, dissemblance became part of keeping her own glorified and complicated domestic's job in Hollywood movies. Her relationship with an influential figure like Susan Myrick is just one site of this kind of dissemblance. As McDaniel biographer Jill Watts notes, "playing to white expectations was a strategy of deception and self-preservation that black laborers had practiced dating back to the days of slavery, and McDaniel liberally used such a tactic to promote and protect her Hollywood aspirations."[109]

McDaniel's public appeal as Mammy in *GWTW*, and SIP's success at marketing her as a "real" mammy, were both facilitated by the way that white viewers who had Black maids at home would have been encouraged by those women's dissemblance "to believe that many black women are 'natural' domestics: contentedly self-effacing and maternal, enjoying the work in the white household."[110] On the reverse side of this coin, Sturtevant argues that McDaniel's live tour after *GWTW*'s release, a tour for which she wrote and performed her own material, was an extended moment in which she

> played upon and attempted to crack open the culture of dissemblance. The negative aspects of dissembling as outlined by Hine (the static invisibility, the cheerful sexlessness, and the self-effacement stereotype), were particularly debilitating to a performer who was attempting to use her position as a woman in the public eye . . . . to change the performance of black womanhood.[111]

Building upon Sturtevant's work with dissemblance, I turn to the concept of "respectability"—an organizing political ideal especially relevant for African American women—as a related and sometimes competing aspect of McDaniel's offscreen "selling" of Mammy, particularly to African American audiences. Evelyn Brooks Higginbotham has argued that for Black women, strategies of dissemblance were "part of a larger discourse that . . . explicitly deployed manners and morals to challenge charges of Black immorality. Such manners and morals as deployed by Black women were perceived as protection from sexual insult and assault. They were also perceived by some as tools for winning sympathetic white allies."[112] This larger discourse, which Higginbotham terms "the politics of respectability," exercised an equally significant influence upon the way that McDaniel attempted to reframe Mammy in her own public commentary about the character. Thus even with Margaret Mitchell's paradigmatic Mammy looming in the cultural foreground, McDaniel drew philosophically upon the politics of respectability to describe herself and Mammy in ways that might oblige those watching to reevaluate them both.

A through line of respectability cuts through McDaniel's descriptions of Mammy for the audiences of *Wings Over Jordan* and the *New York Amsterdam News*. McDaniel made materially equivalent statements to the *Chicago Defender* and the *Atlanta Constitution* as well. Her language in all of these instances can be connected to the rhetoric, ideology, and work of African American clubwomen of groups like the NACW and the WC (an auxiliary of the National Baptist Convention)—organizations that flourished in the late nineteenth and early twentieth century. Like the UDC's membership, these women's goals were significantly informed by the post-Civil War and post-Reconstruction era American landscape. They were also like them in understanding that "the images they promoted, the texts they wrote, and the monuments they erected legitimized collective memories."[113] But unlike their white southern sisters, these women had little use for nostalgic sentimentality about slavery. Instead they concerned themselves with the exigent challenges and political implications of Black women's domestic responsibilities within their own homes, as well as their paid domestic labor in the homes of whites. Their work was rooted in the hope and belief that "earning respectability through demonstrating black women's morality was key to racial progress."[114]

Founded in Washington, D.C., in 1896, the NACW was a leading organization in the Black clubwomen's movement that flourished at the beginning of the twentieth century. Noted for their work as social reformers who fought against lynching, they also advanced a broader program of racial uplift, stressing the public representation of African American women and mothers.[115] The NACW's membership attempted to assist Black women in their roles as homemakers, and to promote wholesome and decent images of African American domesticity. They were active participants in a variety of social welfare programs in support of Black communities, including running campaigns against tuberculosis.[116] Yet they focused significantly on women and children, opening kindergartens, organizing mothers' meetings to instruct and educate mothers on childcare, establishing homes for juvenile delinquents, and the like. They believed that "respectable" Black mothers were central to the progress of the race, and that through their leadership in establishing stable homes, educating their children in African American history and racial pride, serving as a grounding moral authority, as well as training children to be well mannered and neatly dressed (and exemplifying the same), such women contributed to Black social, political, and economic uplift.[117]

A centerpiece of the NACW's work was the purchase, restoration, and maintenance of Frederick Douglass's former home, Cedar Hill, in Washington, D.C. NACW President Mary B. Talbert envisioned the home as "a national shrine similar to Mt. Vernon," the memorial home of George Washington.[118] Cedar Hill also served as "a model for citizenship rooted in respectability." As Joan Marie Johnson observes:

> In addition to artifacts from Abraham Lincoln, Charles Sumner, and John Brown, the home contained 'long lace curtains, high walnut beds, marble-topped bureaus, Victorian sofas and arm chairs.' The home itself—and not just the man it honored—fit perfectly with the NACW agenda for racial uplift through an emphasis on the family, home life, and respectability that would demonstrate African American progress and ability.[119]

McDaniel's public characterizations of Mammy reflect the significance of Black women's clubs like the NACW, including such clubs' interest in motherhood as evidence of Black respectability and racial pride. The successful fundraising carried out by the NACW over decades for the civic and symbolic mission of purchasing, restoring, and maintaining Cedar Hill is an example of what she referenced as Black women's role in "building our race, paying for our elaborate houses of worship, and sustaining our business, charitable, and improvement organizations."[120] And when McDaniel attributed the success of Black performers like Marian Anderson and Roland Hayes (or leaders like Booker T. Washington, George W. Carver, Robert Moton, and Mary McLeod Bethune, in her *Wings* speech) to their *mothers,* she reinforced what the organization, as well as many other uplift-minded Blacks, saw as the great power that African American mothers had to mold and rear sons and daughters who would be a "credit to the race."

McDaniel's subsequent allusion to the importance of women as financial providers through their paid domestic work attempted to assign them respectability, not least of all in terms of the way that such work supported the race's higher aspirations, in the persons of the "daughters who wanted an artistic career" and the children who would "become doctors of philosophy and law."[121] She thus sought to legitimize Mammy's work "bent over wash tubs" and "hobbling about in kitchens."[122] As much as one might argue that she dissembled in mainstream media interviews when talking about her own cooking and cleaning, I conjecture that McDaniel frequently and somewhat obstinately insisted on space for the reality and worth of this kind of domestic work. Her plain-spoken assessment that there is "nothin' wrong with washin'. I do it," carries a class-specific note of prideful defense within it that is not unlike her assertion that Mammy had a kind of dignity to her womanhood, even if it was not "the modern, stream-lined type" that attires itself "in ermine and mink."[123]

In all of its classed complexity, McDaniel's rhetoric about the dignity of domestic work echoes the related work and philosophy of the influential WC. Established in 1900, as a separate auxiliary body to the National Baptist Convention, and active through the 1970s, the WC's membership shared many of the same household-centered objectives as the NACW, including a concern for motherhood and the domestic sphere.[124] They too placed significant authority and responsibility in the hands of Black mothers, in terms of what might be imagined as the mundane, everyday tasks of their households. For instance, housecleaning became a point of citizenship and racial pride, as instructors for the WC's Home Mission encouraged its membership to

> give more attention to civic improvement . . . . Clean out the rubbish; whitewash and put things in order. Clean out germ-breeding cellars and rubbish corners in our homes. This is the only practical way to show that education and Christianity are counting in the development of the race . . . . [The] woman who keeps a dirty home and tolerates trifling shiftless inmates . . . [is] as great an enemy to the race as the man who devotes his life to persecuting and maligning the race.[125]

The WC was possessed of a distinct collective ethos that reflected the class diversity of its membership, and that especially sought to "glorify" Black women who labored as domestic servants. Even as its leadership consisted of upper- and middle-class clubwomen, the organization drew the majority of its general members from the working poor.[126] In their literature and speeches, the WC's leaders characterized its constituency as "the 'persevering poor,' 'daily toilers,' 'common everyday women,' and the 'common people of whom God made more of than the other kind.'"[127] According to Higginbotham, the WC's annual reports also

> frequently counterposed images of domestic servants against images of elites. The washerwoman and cook, whose productive labor and sacrifice had

made possible needed institutions and services, stood arrayed against elite "parasites [who] make a social kingdom, and never consider the comfort of the humble who live on the rim of their realm."[128]

For the WC, the "daily toilers" best represented the lot of all African American women, especially in light of the urgent need for all Black women to offer their toil in service to the race. This transgression and conflation of class boundaries is relevant to the WC's ecclesiastical origins, especially because "in the church, more than any other institution . . . black women of all ages and classes found a site for 'signifying practice'—for coming into their own voice."[129] And the notion of gender trumping class for the able and ready hands of the women who served under the WC's aegis recalls McDaniel's statement that "I am proud that I am a Negro woman, because *members of that class* have given so much" (emphasis added).[130] Such rhetoric suggested that Black women's toil, on behalf of themselves, their individual families, or the race as a whole, combined with their shared oppression as women to bind them together as a distinct and indispensable "class."

The WC's intention to dignify and professionalize domestic work found its most concrete expression in the opening of the National Training School for Women and Girls in October 1909. The school was opened under the leadership of WC founding member Nannie Helen Burroughs. Burroughs served as the Training School's president until her death in 1961.[131] Again, for Burroughs and the leaders of the Training School, the respectability conferred by the legitimate and proper instruction it offered to its students was intended to engender respect for them in their working lives, and provide them with means of protection from the financial, social, and sexual exploitation that was the lot of so many Black women who did domestic work in the early twentieth century. Nannie Burroughs was acutely aware of the limited employment opportunities available to Black women of this era, just as McDaniel knew that her own options were largely limited to "playing" or "being" a maid. Given the disproportionate role that domestic service played in the economies of Black families and communities, Burroughs sought to place an equal or greater stress upon the sustainability and moral and economic viability of female domestic workers' labor to the progress of African Americans as a whole. She argued that "teachers, preachers and 'leaders' cannot solve the problems of the race alone. The race needs an army of skilled workers, and the properly educated Negro woman is the most essential factor."[132]

The WC's rhetoric carried a sense of pride and a tone of defiance analogous to McDaniel's carefully phrased defenses of Mammy and herself. And such a philosophical framework and praxis clearly made a potentially legitimizing space for a character like Mammy. Both Nannie Burroughs and McDaniel hoped that their words would prompt Black people to reconsider the semiotic meanings they ascribed to gender and class (not to mention color and size), as well as the stigma that attached to domestic labor itself. And both women brought a mixture of pragmatism and optimism to their efforts. For Burroughs, this was crystallized in the National Training School's simple maxim: "Until we realize our ideal, we are going to idealize our real . . . . we may have the poorest, but we are going to do the best that can be done with what we have."[133] McDaniel shared a similar pragmatic idealism. Determined to make the most of the role of Mammy, she likely felt vindicated by her Oscar, that she had indeed "idealized the real" of her situation. And her use of Mammy, a slave character, reinforced the notion that class status need not be a barrier (nor an automatic entry) to African Americans' carrying themselves with dignity and respectability. McDaniel's background undoubtedly contributed to her perspective on Mammy; the domestic work that she had seen her mother do, and that she herself had done from childhood, kept her family of origin afloat. And her family's racial pride, rooted in no small part in Henry McDaniel's record of military service, was not diminished by such work. Though McDaniel loved to entertain and perform, she was practical in ways born of long privation and necessity.

McDaniel's public commentaries were likely written with the assistance of McDaniel's "best friend, secretary, confidante, and 'right arm,'" Ruby Berkley Goodwin.[134] Goodwin was clearly a race woman in her own right, one with a vibrant and multifaceted life and career. An ambitious, versatile writer, she wrote two books of poetry and a memoir; beginning in the late 1920s she also covered the Hollywood beat for African American newspapers like the *Pittsburgh Courier* and the *Chicago Defender,* providing interviews and reportage on Black performers like Stepin Fetchit, Nina Mae McKinney, and child star Farina.[135] Indeed, Goodwin and McDaniel met on the set of James Whale's 1936 production of *Show Boat*—Goodwin was covering it, and McDaniel was cast in the film as "Queenie." They would be devoted friends for nearly two decades, until McDaniel's death in 1952.

Goodwin was also a member of the African American sorority Sigma Gamma Rho, and is credited with recruiting McDaniel into membership. Like other Black Greek letter organizations established during the early twentieth century, Sigma Gamma Rho was more than a club whose activities were bound to members' college years. Sigma Gamma Rho was, and is, a national women's organization rooted in the same spirit of racial uplift and respectability that motivated the memberships of the NACW and the WC.[136] McDaniel became a prominent member of the sorority, as a founding member of its Sigma Sigma chapter in Los Angeles.[137] McDaniel's involvement with Sigma Gamma Rho—especially as someone who had never attended college—suggests her interest in adopting a stance of political and social activity with respect to the broader African American community. The work that Sigma Gamma Rho undertook on behalf of the race was similar to that of the NACW and the WC; they established employment bureaus during the Depression, advising Black women entering the workforce on deportment and attire. Sigma Gamma Rho's members also created partnerships with the Red Cross and the USO during World War II.[138] The sorority's slogan, "Greater Service, Greater Progress," likewise resonates with the kind of personal humility and collective pride that McDaniel attempted to marshal behind her performance in *GWTW*. As McDaniel became more involved with the work and politics of racial uplift, with the support of a veteran activist and community leader like Goodwin, it is unsurprising that she began to mingle such ideas into her understanding of what Mammy could, and perhaps should mean. And McDaniel, like Burroughs and the WC before her, sought to undermine the associations between Black domestic labor and Black shame. Reframing her performance in *Gone with the Wind* through these discursive means, McDaniel sought to steal the show away from an uncomplicated notion of Mammy. By cloaking Mammy in ideological vestments that were respectable and carried the pride of a resistant Black history, McDaniel clearly hoped to make an argument for the validity of her own pride and respectability in portraying the character as well.

WHITE COLUMNS IN WASHINGTON

In her interview with the *New York Amsterdam News* in May 1939, McDaniel opined that a woman like Mammy was undoubtedly "responsible for the outstanding success of such children as Marian Anderson and Roland Hayes." Her reference to these two popular African American artists, who embodied an alternative, sophisticated and urbane version of Black manhood and womanhood in their classical concert performances, is perhaps the height of McDaniel's attempt to provide Mammy with a story that ennobled and dignified her life and her work. Her reference to Marian Anderson would have been especially timely, because at the beginning of 1939 Anderson had been denied access by the Daughters of the American Revolution (DAR) to sing a concert at Washington, D.C.'s Constitution Hall. Moreover, that same year Anderson had sung a triumphant open-air Easter Sunday concert on the National Mall instead.[139] By 1939, Anderson was an internationally acclaimed contralto singer, whose repertoire included Italian operas, German lieder, African American spirituals, and other arranged concert fare. She had toured Europe throughout the 1920s and 1930s, training with distinguished vocal instructors in Germany, performing throughout Scandinavia, and eventually in "virtually every major European city—in London, Paris, Amsterdam, and Brussels, in Geneva, Vienna, Budapest, and Prague."[140] When she returned to America for good in the latter half of the 1930s, she was much in demand, and routinely heard on nationally syndicated radio programs such as *The General Motors Hour* and *The Ford Hour.* In 1936, First Lady Eleanor Roosevelt invited Anderson to sing at the White House.[141] Such widespread crossover acclaim meant that in 1939, when she was invited to sing at historically Black Howard University, the university chapel was quickly oversold, with public demand for tickets still growing. In search of a larger venue, Howard's administrators applied to rent Constitution Hall, then the "largest and finest auditorium in Washington, D.C."[142]

Constitution Hall was built in 1929 as part of the national headquarters for the DAR, a lineage-based patriotic association whose membership consisted of women directly descended from those involved in the war for U.S. independence. As an elite white women's group concerned with monument building and preservation, and one that was conferred a particular legitimacy through its connection to a key national conflict in American history, the DAR had much in common with the UDC. And its conservatism in barring Anderson's performance likewise had the effect of obstructing a publicly performed version of African American womanhood that would have conflicted with the predominant, Lost Cause image of mammy.

Technically, the DAR's action was due to their enforcement of a "white artists only" clause of their standard hall rental contract. The prohibition nevertheless calls to mind the questions around race, womanhood, and the domains that Black and white women could inhabit that so pervaded the glorification and monumentalization of mammy. Micki McElya suggests that the

8. Celebrated soprano Marian Anderson performs in an open-air concert on Easter, 1939, before the majestic columns of the Lincoln Monument, after being refused the use of Constitution Hall because of her race. Photo from the Harris and Ewing Collection, Library of Congress.

> UDC's construction of loving, servile blackness 'emancipated' feminine whiteness from the domestic impediments to public activity. In this manner, the [Confederate] Daughters campaigned to recast the gendered dichotomy of public and private space—with public life traditionally reserved for men, and women confined to the domestic sphere—into a bifurcated, racial division. For them, black people's labors could enable a new white public, composed of both men and women unified through racial homogeneity.[143]

In barring the distinct and countercultural version of Black womanhood that Anderson proffered from the public and civic space of Constitution Hall that they controlled, the northern women of the DAR reinforced this bifurcation. Anderson herself asserted that she was "shocked beyond words to be barred from the capital of my own country after having appeared in almost every other capital in the world."[144] Yet ultimately her grand civic and democratic, public, and federally sanctioned performance on the National Mall before the Lincoln

Memorial was far more powerfully symbolic. Appropriately, she opened her performance with "America (My Country 'Tis of Thee)," before an assembled crowd of seventy-five thousand that covered the Mall from the base of the Lincoln Memorial all the way to the Washington Monument. Flanked by stately neoclassical columns and the massive figure of the Great Emancipator, Anderson claimed a monumental, national space for a species of Black womanhood not bound to prove faithfulness to white families or communities in order to demonstrate its worth (figure 8). Instead, powerful white people moved and stood behind Anderson, to make her performance possible.[145]

When McDaniel referenced Anderson, she was tying Mammy to the more radical politics of a Black woman engaged in an open struggle against blatant racial discrimination; she was also claiming and endorsing Anderson and the version of Black womanhood that she embodied as a distinct point on a vastly underrepresented spectrum of Black women's humanity. In claiming Anderson's historic performance and its monumental significance as both scion and counterpoint to her own, McDaniel marshaled the singer's image as perhaps the ultimate talismanic symbol available to her. Hortense Spillers writes that "if the 'black woman' can be seen as a particular figuration of the split subject that psychoanalytic theory posits, then [the twentieth] century marks the site of 'its' profoundest revelation."[146] McDaniel's performance of Mammy indisputably took place within a pivotal moment in this process as outlined by Spillers. What is more, McDaniel herself certainly grasped something of this import, attempting to splinter and fragment that figure in extra-cinematic discourse, even as she immortalized it on the screen.

TWO

Bill Robinson and Black Children's Spectatorship

"Every Kid in Colored America Is His Pal"

As one of the first movies to feature a Bill Robinson-Shirley Temple pairing in the 1930s, the Fox Film Corporation's 1935 film *The Little Colonel* stars Shirley Temple as "Lloyd Sherman," the daughter of a southern, confederate-descended mother, and a northern, unionist father. In this film in typical "Little Miss Fix-It" fashion, Temple's character charms and dimples her way into the heart of her curmudgeonly maternal grandfather, Colonel Lloyd (Lionel Barrymore), and ultimately repairs the familial rift between him and his daughter Elizabeth (Evelyn Venable), who has married a Yankee (provocatively named Jack Sherman, played by John Lodge) in spite of her father's strong objections and his overtly anti-northern bias. In the meantime, young Lloyd Sherman is looked after by Black servants, primarily her mother's maid, Mom Beck (Hattie McDaniel), and her grandfather's loyal butler, Walker, played by Bill Robinson. In one scene, Walker and Lloyd dance together in the stables as Lloyd's Black playmates May Lily (Avonne Jackson) and Henry Clay (Nyanza Potts) look on. A sequence featuring Walker and Lloyd talking and then dancing is intercut with shots of May Lily and Henry Clay happily looking on. May Lily even aids the dance by playing her harmonica as accompaniment, while Henry Clay is obviously delighted and laughs with genuine enjoyment.

The next shot pulls back to show Walker and Lloyd just right of the center of the frame, as May Lily and Henry Clay continue to

9. Bill "Bojangles" Robinson and Shirley Temple dance in a scene from *The Little Colonel* (1935), as African American child actors Avonne Jackson and Nyanza Potts look on. Copyright 1935, Fox Film Corporation.

look on from the left side (figure 9). The dance sequence lasts only for about two minutes; the narrative stipulates that Walker does not have time to dance with Lloyd, since he has work to do. Nevertheless, he begins teaching her simple steps, declaring in time to the harmonica music, "I ain't got time . . . to dance . . . with you . . . today." Somewhat predictably, the Black children never join the dance, but are apparently contented to look on and watch. This image is an invaluable symbol for the work mounted in this chapter, raising as it does myriad questions about the cinematic relationship between Bill Robinson and Shirley Temple, about the relationship between Robinson and Black children as both spectators and performers, and perhaps most provocatively, about the kinds of looking relationships that Black children forged when they went to the movies in the 1930s and 1940s. Beholding such racialized spectacles as Henry Clay and May Lily witness here, how did African American children receive and respond to what they saw?

BLACK CHILDREN WATCHING;
BLACK CHILDREN, WATCHING

To some extent this chapter follows a spatial schema inspired by this moment of *The Little Colonel,* moving from a focus upon the characters at its center, outward to the spectators at its margins, outward once more, to the spectators watching from beyond the frame, and then outward yet once more, to consider those spectators' engagements with cinematic subjects existing beyond this particular frame. The chapter commences with an exploration of Bill Robinson's star persona and its connections to notions of childhood. These connections include Robinson's famed onscreen partnership with child star Shirley Temple, but also encompass aspects of Robinson's stardom that significantly emphasized play, mentorship, and a philanthropic streak that particularly benefited African American children. Reversing angles, as it were, the chapter then moves to focus upon African American children's consumption and reception of Hollywood film in the 1930s and early 1940s. Using historically relevant memoir and autobiographical sources that provide examples of Black children's spectatorship of Bill Robinson as well as of such other 1930s performers as Bette Davis, Joan Crawford, Kay Francis, and Humphrey Bogart, I apply the work of scholars whose theorizing complicates the notion of the oppositional gaze as the default stance for Black spectators as a whole to African American child spectators in particular. I argue for a range of theoretical spectatorial possibilities for African American children as moviegoers, for a decentralization of Shirley Temple in conceiving of the locus of Robinson's appeal among these youngsters, as well as for the importance of "all-Black" locales of performance (casts) and exhibition (segregated theaters) in mediating their moviegoing experiences. These children mingled play, formal and informal instruction about race and other social mores, family struggles, and gendered notions about beauty, strength, and power in their trips to the movies.

BILL ROBINSON'S DANCING BLACK BODY
STEALS THE SHOW

Bill Robinson was born in Richmond, Virginia on May 25, 1878. The son of Maxwell and Maria Robinson, Robinson was named Luther by his parents, but in adolescence he grew to dislike the name, and bullied his younger brother Bill into switching names with him. Both boys were orphaned in 1885 when their parents died, and would be raised primarily by their paternal grandmother, Bedilia Robinson. But even as early as 1883, at age five, Robinson was already dancing for spare change in local beer gardens. He spent the majority of his childhood "scuffling," as he might have put it, watching out for himself, alternately dancing on the street for money and working various odd jobs as bootblack, racehorse stable attendant, and the like.[1] At age twelve, his break into show business was a role in the chorus of the successful traveling minstrel revue *The South before the War.*[2] By his early twenties, Robinson had gained more visibility by working in a series of duo acts. The most successful of these was "Cooper and Robinson," which featured Robinson opposite well-known vaudevillian George W. Cooper.[3] Robinson remained a popular staple of the Black vaudeville circuit for decades, well known to predominantly African American audiences throughout the country. It was not until his Broadway turn in Lew Leslie's *Blackbirds of 1928*—when Robinson had reached the venerable age of fifty—that he became an "instant" hit for New York City's urbane white crowds and a broader mainstream audience as well.[4]

Despite his stature as an exceptional entertainer, Bill Robinson's acting ability could in no way rival the performances of his counterparts in the movies. However, his dancing style was regularly deployed as a spectacular "show stopper" in Hollywood films. Given the centrality of dance to his renown as a performer, Robinson's status as a cinematic novelty act is perhaps the most explicit of all the African American performers surveyed in this book. As a *Variety* review of his appearance in the 1935 Fox film *In Old Kentucky* opined, "Robinson . . . commands attention by the artistry of his footwork."[5] The innovations that "Bojangles" brought to the American jazz dance style of tap dance are significant indeed. Robinson is generally credited with popularizing a more upright, erect style of tap dancing, executed on the toes or the balls of the feet, in contrast to "an earlier, earthier, more flat-footed shuffling style."[6] His footwork was also notable because of the clarity with which he made individual, percussive taps audible in sync with the music that accompanied him. Dance historian Constance Hill has described his style as a kind of "Afro-Irish" fusion, innovative in its blending of the upright technique common to English and Irish jig and clog dancing with the precisely executed syncopated rhythms so central to African and African American aesthetics.

Robinson's signature was the "stair dance," a routine that he perfected on the vaudeville stage in the 1920s. Robinson, who claimed that

10. Bill "Bojangles" Robinson with the portable staircase he had built for his signature "stair dance," circa 1928. Photo by Vandamm Studio©, Billy Rose Theatre Division, the New York Public Library for the Performing Arts.

he had initially improvised the dance while descending stage-steps into an audience, later developed a full routine from this spark of inspiration. As he incorporated it as a standard element of his vaudeville performances, he had a portable staircase built for the number (figure 10).[7] As the name of the dance suggests, the "stair dance" consisted of Robinson deftly dancing his way up and down a set of stairs, rhythmically tapping his way along each step, sometimes stopping on one step to execute a set of taps, other times quickly taking one step after another in quick succession, as if his feet were fingers rapidly playing a scale on a piano keyboard. The "stair dance" was the perfect vehicle for Robinson to showcase the unique elements of his style. His upright, Irish-inflected jigging put his vertical body at a visually striking perpendicular angle to the horizontal steps upon which he danced. Meanwhile, his movement from one step to the next emphasized the distinct clarity with which he sounded his complex rhythmic taps.

As he moved from the vaudeville and Broadway stages to film appearances, Robinson garnered approbation from other veteran showmen, including American humorist Will Rogers, who had made his own way up through medicine and Wild West shows to become a folksy, everyman-styled Hollywood star. Rogers was one of numerous prominent movie stars at a May 1935 birthday party for Robinson on the Fox lot, where he toasted "Bojangles," quipping,

> You know, for twenty years, I had to be bothered with this "Bojangles" stealing shows from me, and so I moved into pictures to get rid of him. And now, what do I see? Nothing less than the face and taps of this same Bill Robinson cropping up in pictures to steal the show from me again. Will this fellow ever leave me alone?[8]

At the time of the party, Rogers and Robinson were filming *In Old Kentucky,* with Robinson cast as "Wash Jackson," the stable boy and general manservant to "Steve Tapley," Rogers's horse trainer character. Whatever joking claims Rogers may have made about others' stealing, the plot of *In Old Kentucky* obliged him to effect a species of racialized theft that illuminates the symbolic and contingent nature of Robinson's cinematic status. As Tapley, Rogers dons blackface and a stable hand's cap, and pretending to be Jackson (Robinson), executes some extremely rudimentary tap dancing, made all the more humorous by its very lack of technical skill or stylistic flair. It is a scene that underscores Robinson's function in this and so many of his films—on one level, he is little more than an embodied trope of the dancing Black body. And Rogers's temporarily successful impersonation of Robinson—so that his character Steve Tapley can escape from jail—demonstrates a kind of freedom and access that reinforces the assumption that the filmic "show" is in fact Rogers's to be "stolen" in the first place. Ultimately Robinson's function is but one of the film's many effects that are at Rogers's disposal.

The novelty of Robinson's dancing is inextricably linked to race, given the historic centrality of music and dance to the way that African Americans were imagined and represented. As such, comments like Rogers's in which Robinson was accused of "stealing" attention and applause from their rightful (white) recipients are further amplified; it is both because he is a conditional and appropriately marginalized African American presence onscreen, and because he is a mere novelty dance act (and the two intertwined) that he has a less than legitimate claim to the "show."

Robinson's pairings with Shirley Temple make this dynamic even more pronounced and complex, with the toddler occupying as primary a presence as the adult Will Rogers with respect to Robinson. Fully one third of all of Bill Robinson's Hollywood films in the 1930s feature him alongside Temple, acting as her reliable servant, friend, and guardian, and of course, as her dance partner. As the preeminent child star of the 1930s, Temple received similar tongue-in-cheek accusations of "stealing," as she too was accepted as a conditional, novel performer, given the way that her age made her fundamentally different from the "real" actors and actresses of filmdom. Her novelty as a child star provided a singular magnetism and appeal of its own, one that it would have been decidedly difficult for an adult to "steal" attention from. By the same token, Temple's power required careful nurturing and protection. In her autobiography she recalls her mother's unwillingness to have her photographed with other children "because it could provide opportunity for comparison in which Shirley, potentially, could look 'less cute' than the other child."[9] Meanwhile, adult actors and dignitaries were eager to have their pictures taken with Shirley, for the guaranteed positive publicity of the "Shirley Temple photo op." Unlike Robinson, Temple was afforded film vehicles designed specifically to showcase her talent, films in which she was the protagonist and heroine. These are the sorts of films in which Robinson appears, beginning with *The Little Colonel* and *The Littlest Rebel,* both in 1935, followed by both *Rebecca of Sunnybrook Farm* and *Just around the Corner* in 1938. The onscreen relationship between Robinson and Temple in these films reflected a symbiosis in which each contributed something to the other's visual and cultural effect upon an audience. In her analysis of the Robinson-Temple duo, Karen Orr Vered argues that Robinson was carefully absented from the publicity surrounding Temple's films.[10] This structured absence is but one indication of the inequitable nature of this symbiosis. Temple's net cultural gain was achieved at the expense of Robinson's ability to be fully articulated onscreen, as he was denied even the conventional terms of masculinity and humanity that were routine and essential aspects of Temple's film narratives.

Robinson's serial screen pairings with Shirley Temple have a somewhat legendary origin. In her autobiography, Temple writes that venerated filmmaker D. W. Griffith suggested the team to Fox executive Winfield Sheehan. According to Temple, in his correspondence with Sheehan,

Griffith contended "there is nothing, absolutely nothing calculated to raise the goose-flesh on the back of [a white] audience more than that of a white girl in relation to Negroes."[11] This is an oddly sinister story of origin for the happy-go-lucky Robinson-Temple duo, especially given that Griffith's most significant experience with the effect he describes was likely the tempest of emotions stirred by the Black male would-be rapist characters Gus and Silas Lynch from his 1915 epic *The Birth of a Nation*.[12] Still, his comment calls attention to the way in which Robinson and Temple's pairing would ultimately create a dynamic that conscripted each of the two performers as distinct symbols of the interconnected politics of race and gender.

For her part of this dynamic, Temple rendered Robinson's Black male persona innocuous and nonthreatening. As an adult who had charge of a white child, Robinson's worrisome Black male sexuality was diminished (if not wholly effaced), and his presumptive respectability and good character firmly established. Robinson was in his late fifties when he made his films with Temple, though very much at the height of his powers as a dancer. Nevertheless, in many of his films with her, his hair is whitened with powder to give the impression of advanced age. This aging and attendant desexualizing of Robinson's "Uncle Billy" characters is akin to the way that the female stereotype of the Black mammy is imagined as elderly, and therefore sexually irrelevant. His physical proximity to Temple in their scenes together was scrupulously managed, and Robinson's characters could be relied upon to keep a "respectful" distance. Though he was much beloved by the youngster in real life, and though he appeared in more films with Temple than any other individual, Robinson was never depicted hugging or kissing Temple onscreen, as white male actors like Lionel Barrymore or Spencer Tracy routinely were (figure 11). On the contrary, Robinson and Temple's dance scenes were typically the sites of their closest physical contact, as in *The Little Colonel,* in which Robinson holds Temple's hand as he leads her in a version of his "stair dance" (figure 12). As scholar Ann duCille observes, "the same little girl who spent most of her film career in the arms and laps of white men never got closer to Robinson than a handshake."[13]

Robinson's interactions with Temple in their films together are cute exchanges in which he emerges as her playmate and protector. The viewer rarely sees Robinson without Temple; if he appears alone, he is usually talking about her or referencing her in some way. Such performances firmly established Robinson's role as her caretaker, but also as her

11. Spencer Tracy and Shirley Temple cuddle in a promotional image from *Now I'll Tell* (1934). Courtesy of the Academy of Motion Picture Arts and Sciences.

dependent, one who was largely without any personal interests of his own. In such roles, Robinson's virtuosic dancing is typically deployed as a function of his characters' relationships with Temple. Typically he is shown performing at her direction, teaching her steps, or dancing as a way to comfort and cheer her.

The flip side of this dynamic is the way in which Robinson's filmic presence was tailored to emphasize Temple's innocence, a particularly American brand of colorblind innocence typically bounded by the onset of adolescence. Robin Bernstein has used the evocative phrase "holy obliviousness" to describe this imagined phase of white American childhood, a moment which

> provided the perfect alibi: not only the ability to remember while appearing to forget, but even more powerfully, the production of racial memory through the performance of forgetting. What childhood innocence helped Americans to assert by forgetting, to think about by performing obliviousness, was not only whiteness but also racial difference constructed against whiteness.[14]

For adult white audiences, watching the guileless Temple be befriended and comforted by a Black servant activated the utility of white childhood innocence, and allowed them to partake of a culturally sanctioned, vicarious, erstwhile pleasure without having to engage with race meaningfully

12. Bill "Bojangles" Robinson and Shirley Temple share a dance at arm's length in a scene from *The Little Colonel*. Courtesy of the Academy of Motion Picture Arts and Sciences.

beyond the confines of a segregated movie theater. To some extent, Robinson was only the most consistently cast African American to enable this aspect of Temple's star persona. She appeared alongside various other Black performers of the era including Hattie McDaniel (mentioned before in *The Little Colonel*), Stepin Fetchit (*Stand Up and Cheer*, 1934, and *Dimples*, 1936), Willie Best (*Little Miss Marker*, 1934, and *The Littlest Rebel*, 1935), and Gertrude Howard (*Carolina*, 1934). Even Robinson's biographers make note of the "inside Hollywood joke that a Temple picture was incomplete without at least one darky."[15] Still, her "Uncle Billy" was clearly a special case. And the place that he held in her heart and in her pictures allowed Temple to capitalize on both aspects of Robinson's novelty—his race and his dancing body.

All the same, the very frequency with which Temple and Robinson were cast together sits in odd juxtaposition with the careful narrative and visual control that their act apparently necessitated. The wide popularity of the duo suggests that the very tensions raised by their physical proximity in dance, tensions being so consistently and aggressively managed by their film texts, were indeed a part of the cultural appetite for their performances together. Recalling once again Griffith's alleged comment about the cinematic power of "a white girl in relation to Negroes," perhaps his own overtly malevolent manipulation of this theme is not as distant from the superficial innocence of Bojangles and Temple as might first be imagined. Gaylyn Studlar has recently argued for the overdetermination of the theme of sexuality in contemporary feminist analyses of Temple's screen image. She mounts the alternative theory that Temple's serial relationships with adult men in her films have a domesticating function, aimed at gruff male characters who stand in for the American husbands and fathers potentially alienated from the nuclear family by the emasculating, demoralizing force of the Great Depression. Using the Victorian literary trope of "cosseting" as interpretive frame for the petting and cuddling that Temple routinely lavishes on her white male costars, Studlar argues persuasively that her films routinely stage "a spectacle of child-centered sentimentalism that narrativizes the emotional impact of the tiny girl on the grown man." The child's tenderness binds the man "to domesticity in a way that adult femininity cannot."[16] Following this logic, the chief cultural aim of Temple's films is the redemption of adult masculinity in crisis. Yet the wholesale absence of Robinson from this argument is pronounced, especially given his status as the adult male who appeared most frequently with Temple in her pictures.[17]

Indeed, Robinson's characters were never quite the full-fledged father figures to Temple's characters that those of her white male costars were. More often he was cast as a temporary caretaker who comforted and protected the child until a curmudgeonly white guardian, an Uncle, Papa, Grandfather (or occasionally an Aunt or Godmother) fell fully under Shirley's thrall. But that his Black, male, dancing body would have invariably altered the meaning of Temple's caresses is made manifest by the fact of their imposed distance. Even their handholding in *The Little Colonel* is prompted by a disagreement that Temple's character has with her irascible grandfather (Lionel Barrymore), after which she threatens to run away from his lavish home. As Robinson's character Walker takes her hand, he assures her that "the Colonel loves you too, Miss Lloyd. It's just because his rheumatism is botherin' him that he's so cranky."[18] As he dances her upstairs to bed, it is *Robinson* who uses the intimacy of dance itself to perform the work of cosseting *Temple* for the good of the white family. He calms and encourages the unhappy child who might have chosen to abandon her grandfather, his intervention keeping her within the fold. Robinson's body serves to bridge the chasm between the estranged grandpapa and granddaughter.

By the same token, their dancing, whether executed while holding hands or standing at a distance, provided the performative pretext for a choreographed interracial erotics between Robinson and Temple. Given Fox's repeated casting of the two as dance partners during the 1930s, these limited, safely executed physical exchanges were apparently pleasurable, commodifiable moments for white audiences. The taboo and repressed sexuality of their relationship as "the screen's first interracial couple" ultimately had less to do with Temple's body as sexualized white femininity than with Bill Robinson's body as freighted with the excess of imagined Black male sexuality.[19]

Thus the Robinson-Temple duo disrupts Studlar's argument in two intersecting ways. The first is that in *The Little Colonel,* as in their other films together, Robinson routinely used dance to perform the cosseting function for Temple, enabling her to enact her role of reuniting the white family unit. The second is that Robinson's repressed sexuality always already threatened to disrupt an asexual and innocent reading of Temple, if only with respect to Robinson himself (though given the frequency with which Robinson appeared in her pictures, this was not an insubstantial threat). To the extent that "Temple's films were the kind of family fare that needed to appeal first to women and children," the tandem pleasure in and policing of Robinson and Temple's onscreen intimacies provided a politically charged dynamic in which white women and children were allowed to consume Robinson as simultaneously close and distant, safe and unsafe, comforting and threatening.[20]

In films like *Stormy Weather, One Mile from Heaven,* and *Hooray for Love,* in which Robinson appeared alongside African American children, his presence apparently required far less careful regulation. Robinson hugged these children, picked them up, held them on his lap, and generally acted *in loco parentis* with little restraint. In the following section, I assess the importance of African American children for Robinson's stardom. Beyond Shirley Temple, whose image often seems to dominate contemporary considerations of Robinson, his 1930s stardom included a recurrent exchange and intimacy with children—less formal and differently racialized in their implications than with Temple, and yet with significant overlap in the way that Robinson embodied and performed these connections.

ROBINSON PERFORMING CHILDHOOD
Play, Mentorship, and Philanthropy

The straitened conditions of Robinson's childhood—his young life as an orphan eking out a meager living on the streets of Richmond—undoubtedly contributed to his reputation as a tough, somewhat hardened man, whose temper was known to flare easily, and who gambled away much of the money that he did not give away during his career. But the difficulty of Robinson's childhood years also appeared to shape a concern for children and their welfare that would persist throughout his lifetime. Likewise, his onscreen and offscreen personae and performances evoked the theme of childhood in unique ways.

The motif of childhood typically surfaced in Robinson's stardom in one (or more) of three aspects. The first of these is the notion of play, an element of Robinson's stardom that was strongly apparent both onscreen and offscreen. In his films, a sense of playfulness is suggested primarily in his dancing and performance; off the screen, it comes through in Robinson's somewhat eccentric public persona. I want to suggest that Robinson's "play" is part of what made him appealing to Black moviegoing children, especially as it was seen in both Black and white diegetic contexts, onscreen in the company of Black children as well as white children. A second way that childhood recurs as a motif in Robinson's star text is through the idea of mentorship. Both on and off the screen, Robinson was frequently credited as a role model, mentor, or teacher to children and young people. A third and final way that childhood emerges in Robinson's stardom is through the copious acts of philanthropy that he performed in his offscreen life. While Robinson was known as a philanthropist whose acts of charity benefited African Americans of all ages, many and perhaps even the majority of his donations and benefit performances were directed at Black children in particular.

The notion of play may be the most racially loaded of the three elements I identify here. Essentially I mean to suggest that aspects of Robinson's performance and persona emphasized innocence and joy, childlike characteristics stereotypically associated with African Americans in early twentieth-century America. That being said, throughout his entertainment career Robinson clearly worked to cultivate an aspect of his image that was whimsical and wholesome. His storied penchant for ice cream is one example; newspaper articles as early as 1927 reported that Robinson ate anywhere between two and four quarts of vanilla ice

CHAMPION RUNNER TO STAGE BENEFIT RACE

13. A newspaper clipping showing Bill "Bojangles" Robinson demonstrating his famous backwards-running prowess, in an exhibition race against champion one-legged runner Charles Benning in Buffalo, New York. Image published with permission of ProQuest, LLC. Further reproduction is prohibited without permission.

cream a day. Another salient example is his regularly demonstrated speed and prowess as "the world's fastest backwards runner," a talent that he often displayed in charity benefit races (figure 13). Such idiosyncrasies lent an air of innocence to Robinson's image; they were played up in publicity by his manager, Marty Forkins, perhaps in the hope that they might balance out Robinson's more adult, worldly tendencies—his well-known "sporting" of various kinds, his legendary fiery temper, and his gun-toting.[21] The duality of his persona was perhaps summed up ironically in his billing (dating from his vaudeville days) as "The Dark Cloud of Joy."[22]

The 1935 backstage musical/comedy/romance *Hooray for Love* provides an extended example of play as an important function of Robinson's onscreen persona. Robinson appears as himself in a musical production number, alongside celebrated "stride" jazz pianist Fats Waller and up-and-coming tap dancer Jeni LeGon, who was a tender nineteen years old at the time. The musical number featuring this trio is a Harlem set piece, with LeGon playing an unhappy young woman who has been evicted from her apartment; we find her sitting "outdoors" surrounded by her furniture and other possessions. Robinson's role draws upon his well-known status as the honorary "Mayor of Harlem," and it is in this guise that he appears to LeGon in her hour of need. At the start of the sequence, he emerges from a door marked with a placard that reads "MAYOR." Smartly dressed in a light-colored three-piece suit and black bowler hat, with a sparkling lucky horseshoe-shaped tiepin at his throat and a hooked cane in his hand, Robinson quickly spies the disconsolate LeGon. "What's the matter, honey? What are you crying about?" he asks. Then indicating himself with his thumb, he firmly and kindly encourages her to "tell the mayor." When she explains her predicament, he advises her not in legal or municipal terms, but instead engages her whimsically and playfully, by singing the Dorothy Fields and Jimmy McHugh song "I'm Living in a Great Big Way."[23] The song proclaims:

I got a snap in my fingers, got a rhythm in my walk
As the elephant say, "I'm livin' in a great big way."

Got a handful of nothin', and I watch it like a hawk
Well I'm doin' OK, I'm livin' in a great big way.

I'm the salt in the ocean, I'm the sun in the sky,
I'm a Franklin D. Roosevelt, I'm a million dollars, long as I've got a

Snap in my fingers, got a rhythm in my walk
Got the devil to pay, I'm livin' in a great big way.

Robinson encourages her to "tell *that* to the landlord!" The two sing the song together, their duet intercut with shots of a trio of African American children who take turns singing a handful of lines.[24] Though the children's solos are brief, their presence is emphasized by a shot of the show's producers reacting to their cute singing, and by an establishing shot of them together earlier in the sequence (figure 14). Their appearance seems less coincidental given the idea of play and children as recurrent motifs of Robinson's screen persona. Robinson and LeGon follow by dancing a tap duet together (figure 15), and LeGon exits to negotiate with the landlord. Robinson and Waller (who plays one of the movers evicting LeGon) duet and scat the same tune together, accompanied by Waller playing on LeGon's piano, which he has carried from her apartment (figure 16). At the end of their duet, LeGon emerges from the apartment building, apparently having come to terms with the landlord—she is allowed to move back in.

14. The Cabin Kids cutting up as they watch Bill "Bojangles" Robinson and Jeni LeGon singing "I'm Livin' in a Great Big Way," in a scene from *Hooray for Love* (1935). Copyright 1935, RKO Radio Pictures, Inc.

15. Bill "Bojangles" Robinson and up-and-coming tap dancer Jeni LeGon perform together, in a scene from *Hooray for Love*. Copyright 1935, RKO Radio Pictures, Inc.

16. Bill "Bojangles" Robinson and "stride" jazz pianist Fats Waller trade verses of "I'm Livin' in a Great Big Way," in a scene from *Hooray for Love*. Copyright 1935, RKO Radio Pictures, Inc.

Play is central in multiple, layered ways in this sequence; *Hooray for Love* is a backstage musical, and this scene is a dress rehearsal of "the Bill 'Bojangles' Robinson number," part of the musical that is being staged by the film's protagonists. As such, it is a spectacular performance that has little to do with the advancement of the plot. And at nearly ten minutes long, it constitutes a substantial diversion. Its idealized and fanciful corner of Harlem is twice removed from reality, as a site of escape and projection both for the profilmic theater audience and for the actual viewers of *Hooray for Love*. In addition, the nature of play in this scene certainly underscores the multiple ways in which African Americans as a group were infantilized in the white imagination; Robinson's position as the fantasy "Mayor" of a two-dimensional set-piece Harlem; Robinson and LeGon's easy, jiving approach to what in real life would be a personal catastrophe; Robinson's near-constant smile; the sincere pleasure and enjoyment that the assumed white audience is expected to experience as conscientiously modeled by the two white producers, who are shown watching the rehearsal. All of these elements point to the rosy, picturesque, childlike simplicity that functioned as one of several controlling narratives about

African American life. LeGon's eviction dilemma is magically resolved in a way that draws as much upon racial stereotype as it does upon a truncated version of Hollywood's "happy ending"-oriented narrative logic.[25]

Moreover, Robinson's playful persona is on full display, from his very first appearance emerging from the door of his "Mayor's" office. He walks out smiling hugely, spinning his cane in a high, slow circle, easily balancing it on one finger. The musical scoring reflects Robinson's joyful swagger; while a semiclassical horn fanfare and one-two marching theme accompanies the close-up shot of the "MAYOR" placard on his door, this soundtracking gives way to an ostentatious blues trumpet solo that makes a less straightlaced announcement of Robinson's arrival on the scene. Robinson strides a short pace out his door, then leans upon his cane and easily runs off a short patter of taps as he proudly looks about, surveying his dominion. His smile fades to a worried grimace when he notices the unhappy LeGon sitting on the sidewalk. Sensing his duty, he rapidly taps down the stairs towards her, stopping momentarily to tip his hat and smile upward at a female admirer who waves at him from an apartment window above. Back on task, Robinson effects short, sharp, and businesslike taps over to LeGon's heap of belongings, and theatrically knocks at the tall mirror that serves as the "door" to her "home." When LeGon relates her plight, Robinson attempts to lighten the mood, describing her predicament in the same joshing terms that their song will take up. Pointing at her things, he exclaims, "Here you got an apartment right smack on the corner." Gesturing upward to the sky, he continues "with the highest ceilings in Harlem." He points out her "electric lights!" and "running water!" as the camera shows us streetlamps and neon signs, then a fire hydrant with a steady stream of water issuing from one side. "Ahh!" he scoffs, then says admiringly, "Child, with that smile you got everything," and we are treated to a reverse shot of LeGon smiling happily at Robinson. "You the richest gal in Harlem!" Robinson proclaims. "What you care about being outdoors?" As Robinson and LeGon perform the number together, Robinson's smiling face is further illuminated by his dancing eyes, which he opens as wide as possible and swivels about from side to side in an expression of apparent delight. As LeGon sings each line, he responds with an ad libbed rejoinder, to express mock surprise or disbelief; when LeGon sings, "Got a handful of nothin'" Robinson quickly responds, "Why, you a rich millionaire!" When she sings, "But I watch it like a hawk," Robinson smiles, closes his eyes and looks away from her with a gratified expression, quietly murmuring, "Well hush my mouth."

The exchange with Robinson and Fats Waller that follows extends the scene's play, both in terms of the comical nature of their duet, and the jazzy, improvisational spirit that animates their repartee. Indeed if Robinson can be said to have incorporated a spirit of play as part of his star persona, one may as easily claim that Fats Waller was the very personification of play in his own performance style. His virtuosic stride piano playing was inevitably accompanied by a host of facial expressions exaggerated enough to be called tics. Added to this, his multitude of priceless one-liners, delivered with expert timing in sardonic tones ("Suffer, excess baggage, suffer!" "Ain't that a killer?" or the now famous, "One never knows, do one?"), confirmed Waller as a performer who reveled in a madcap humor that was simultaneously urbane and earthy. By the mid 1930s, Waller was well known enough for witty songs like "Ain't Misbehavin'," "Honeysuckle Rose," and "Viper's Drag," that Robinson may have been rightfully concerned that his corner of *Hooray for Love* might be "stolen" by Waller.[26]

Yet in their sequence together, these two virtuosic performers are spellbinding, with each delivering his own brand of jazz in ways that enhanced and amplified the other. Their exchange begins when Jeni LeGon leaves the stage to talk with the landlord, and Robinson, delighted with her performance, happily asks Waller, "Did you hear what the lady said?" Waller, looking uncharacteristically low key, takes the bait and responds, "Not exactly ... what did she say?" As Robinson begins "Living in a Great Big Way" anew in a key ½ step higher in pitch, Waller ad libs, initially watching him archly beneath raised eyebrows. When Robinson sings the line, "As the elephant say, I'm livin' in a great big way," Waller grumbles in mock disbelief, "Oh get away from here, that's too much." Robinson takes one whole verse to buzz the song with his lips, achieving the effect he perfected in his days on the vaudeville stage, of creating the sound of "an automobile or a mosquito having a fit."[27] He points and gestures at Waller to amplify the effect, sometimes frowning from apparent effort, other times grimacing as if to emphasize the cryptic meaning of his buzzed utterances. Waller sometimes ad libs irritated responses like, "Aw, I don't play that," and other times throws in scatting of his own, all while playing piano and making eyes, alternately lifting and molding his well-arched eyebrows. When Robinson holds one note, buzzing madly like a dentist's drill, widening his eyes and pointing one index finger intently at Waller, Waller turns towards the play's audience and demands incredulously, "What's the matter wid 'im?" Robinson completes the duet by asking Waller, "Do

DANS

FLETS   CE

RE   MI

LES   ROIR

SONT   JE

ME   SUIS

CON   EN

NON   **Guillaume**   CLOS

ET   **Apollinaire**   VI

CES   VANT

AN   ET

LES   VRAI

NE   COM

GI   ME

MA   ON

I

G. Apollinaire
Mirror
from "Coeur Couronne et Miroir"
Les Soirées de Paris, July/August 1914

you understand me?" Waller responds with a hearty, "Well, all right," smiling, and offers his hand to Robinson to shake.

Taken together, this scene's key elements are evocative of the aspects of Depression-era popular culture that effected "a displacement of the social uses and the efficacy of money."[28] We have the spectacular scene of LeGon's eviction and dispossession, added to the song that she, Robinson, and Waller sing, which simultaneously names and negates the importance of money, and finally, Robinson's function as a catalyst for LeGon's restoration to her household—without any apparent exchange of funds. Yet the performance of the song also makes a kind of argument for the inherent worth and value of these three African American performers as persons—"I'm the salt in the ocean, I'm the sun in the sky/I'm a Franklin D. Roosevelt, I'm a million dollars"—in a way that should not be underestimated in our readings of Black presences in film at this time. Perhaps what is most remarkable about the sequence as a whole is the way that it resists easy codification as a performance of Black buffoonery. The trappings of stereotype are inescapable throughout the routine, and yet there is a nuanced sense of incipient African American humanity, "smuggled like contraband" to use James Baldwin's phrase, that radiates through the very creativity and joy that the three performers evince. LeGon adopts Robinson's loose and swinging yet upright tap style perfectly, and as the two dance together, they effect a kind of insouciance that renders the moments of clear-cut mugging (Robinson's saucer-wide eyes, LeGon's wagging head and campy "trucking") so obvious as to seem silly, and self-consciously intentional. LeGon's understated costuming only adds to this sense of casualness; she is hardly "costumed" at all, but wears a simple, modern outfit consisting of a light-colored turtleneck and loosely fitting dark-colored pants. The "rehearsal" frame of the sequence likely contributes to this sensibility as well.

Likewise, Robinson and Waller's musical conversation attains a miraculous balance between performance and intimacy. The practiced nonchalance with which Waller especially responds to Robinson's lines, and even with which he delivers his own, reinforces the viewer's sense of the two men as seasoned professionals in their craft. By the same token, because Robinson and Waller are "talking" to each other, playing with each other, upstaging and seeking to outdo each other in this sequence, they seem less outwardly focused on an audience's response to their shenanigans, and more interested in finding inventive ways of making one another laugh, smile, or respond. And because many of the playful ways in which they engage with one another are so individualized—Waller's suave smart aleckry, Robinson's zany and expressive buzzing—it is difficult to place their performances within a recognizable lexicon of Black stereotypical behavior.

Still, these charming, funny, and lighthearted exchanges must be considered in terms of the notion of play in Bill Robinson's star persona and in the popular conception of African American identity more broadly. Whereas acts of play by definition contain within them the understanding that "these actions in which we now engage do not denote what those actions *for which they stand* would denote," these particular acts of play certainly correspond to a popular understanding of Black life as carefree, as innately more joyful and easygoing than the norm of white life.[29] As such, in the 1930s (as now), representations of Black life in general often functioned as a kind of visible cipher for play in the white imagination. For Robinson, a presentation style couched in playfulness sweetened his virtuosic performances, making them all the more palatable for mainstream audiences, and softening their potential meaning as African American talent and ability given only a marginal place in mainstream culture. Registering his dance as "only playing" meant that white audiences could enjoy it without wondering about whether someone so enormously gifted, who worked hard so at his craft, shouldn't have had a different level of fame or a greater place in Hollywood's spotlight. Dance as playfulness (as opposed to exertion, discipline, or even as seriously executed elegance and stylishness) carried notions of the dominant ideology around careless, joyful Blacks, and also communicated Robinson's own volition in ways that would generally put white audiences at their ease. This reading also potentially dilutes or erases the significant work of his dancing, in terms of dominant stereotypes that constructed African Americans as having "natural" talents in music and dance. This erasure is even more pointed given Robinson's frequent partnership with a "child" who was necessarily less experienced than he was, and who he had to be careful not to upstage or outshine.

The work that it takes to produce the star is regularly elided or erased, and this was especially so in this era of Hollywood stardom.[30] Yet the difference that race makes for an African American star is in the very tenuousness and conditional nature of his or her stardom in the first place. The erasure of the work that it takes to produce fame works in this case against the star, further undermining a legitimate claim to fame, and helping to support the kinds of assumptions that whites made in joking (or serious) reference to African American performers "stealing the show."

Bojangles's playful mien provides a natural foundation for the idea of teaching and mentorship as another key facet of his stardom. His significance as a mentor, teacher, and icon, especially to a younger generation of dancers and performers, was poignantly revealed in the months following his death in 1949. Reverend Adam Clayton Powell Sr. presided over his nationally broadcast funeral on November 27. Harlem schools closed at noon that day to mark the occasion.[31] In his remarks, Powell observed that the legendary dancer "never missed an opportunity, whether seeing a little boy on the corner, or Shirley Temple in Hollywood, of teaching part of his artistry to someone on the way up."[32] Less than a week after Robinson's passing, the Copasetics, a "friendly, benevolent" organization for Black tap dancers, was founded in his honor, named for Robinson's favorite upbeat expression, "Everything is copasetic." Founding members of the Copasetics included composer Billy Strayhorn as well as young dancers Charles "Honi" Coles, Charles "Cholly" Atkins, Clayton "Peg-Leg" Bates, Ernest Brown, and Eddie West, many of whom had been informal pupils of Robinson's in years past.[33]

Robinson had a special affinity for encouraging young up-and-coming performers. An article from the July 6, 1935 issue of the *New York Amsterdam News* suggests that numerous African Americans saw Robinson as an ad hoc talent scout who could help Black children "break into" Hollywood films. Robinson was cited as being "very successful in helping to place youngsters in the motion pictures." The article further quoted Robinson as saying that "my fan mail includes any number of requests from colored people all over the country, asking my aid to get their children into the screen business. In many attempts," Robinson continued, "I have been successful in placing talented boys and girls in the good graces of studio casting directors."[34] Robinson certainly enjoyed being linked with the success of "talented boys and girls," and is credited with having been a mentor to many. For instance, tap dancer Fayard Nicholas, the elder of the Nicholas Brothers duo, was about seventeen years old when he first met Robinson; his younger brother Harold would have been ten or eleven. "It's a funny thing," Fayard recalled,

> when he first met us, he fell in love with us right away. We were very young at that time. And we said to him, "Let's do something together." We called him "Uncle Bo," and we were his "nephews." He taught us one of his soft shoe numbers. Whenever we played a benefit with him, say, at the Madison Square Garden in New York, he'd call us up on the stage and we'd do this Soft Shoe with him.[35]

Robinson's biographers assert that in his later years, he enjoyed performing at the Apollo Theater because the place was "a forum for new talent," and he liked to hang around backstage, meeting the up-and comers. Haskins and Mitgang speculate that Robinson's childlessness only heightened his interest in young people as he grew older.

Again this is a part of Robinson's stardom that emerged on the screen as well as off. Robinson appears in this teacherly mode with Shirley Temple in movies like *The Little Colonel* and *Rebecca of Sunnybrook Farm.* His teaching role is explicit in the 1937 Fox film *One Mile from Heaven,* in which he plays tap-dancing New York policeman Joe Dudley. Dudley works the beat of the film's Harlem-esque Black district, "Maple Heights," looking in particular after the neighborhood's children. We meet him for the first time in a scene that begins with a close-up of his dancing feet; their audible, rhythmic tapping has a pied piper effect upon children who pop their heads out the windows of an assortment of apartments and houses to listen delightedly, then rush excitedly into the street. Robinson's tapping is performed a cappella and takes absolute center stage; his lone, clear taps sound a kind of percussive reveille that alerts the children to come down and see "Officer Joe." His upright, "feet-centric" tapping style is equally important to the sequence's staging; there is no need for a wide shot to capture acrobatics or full-body movements; Robinson's feet—first alone, and then with the throngs of children's feet that join him—carry these compelling shots and simultaneously convey his character's strong influence and leadership. Dudley taps the crowd of children up to an ice cream stand, treating the entire group to cones. When one young girl stands apart from the group to ask, "Uncle Joe, how do you do that 'Chicago'?" he offers an extended breakdown of the step, then challenges a smaller group of children to demonstrate "those taps I taught you a couple of months ago." As the children dance, Dudley enthusiastically coaches them from the sidelines, calling out various combinations: "Now gimme that 'Boston'! Now the 'Cincinnati'!" and exclaiming "Hit it, children! Make it perfect!" In this performance as in many others, Robinson's playful register transitions seamlessly into a proverbial "teachable moment."

The recurring trope of Robinson as nurturing teacher arguably takes on culturally specific dimensions in moments like this, when his exchanges with Black children evoke a perennial trope of African American narrative traditions: the ancestor or elder, who is often responsible for the preservation and transmission of Black culture to a new generation.[36] Given this context, the teacherly aspect of Robinson's stardom had the potential to resonate in deep-seated ways for African American audiences.

Throughout the 1930s, Robinson was also known as a philanthropist, giving generously of his time and money to a number of charitable causes and organizations, many directly benefitting African American children. For example, in 1937, he persuaded John D. Rockefeller Jr. to lend, and later donate outright, a plot of land in Harlem to be used as a park for the neighborhood's Black children.[37] The playground was immediately dubbed the "Bill Robinson Playground," and still exists in Harlem, on 150th Street near 7th Avenue, directly across the street from the Dunbar Apartments, where Robinson lived for most of the 1930s.[38] Robinson performed another charitable act in his hometown of Richmond, Virginia, when he paid for stoplights to be erected in a major intersection on the African American side of town. His motivation, according to his biographers, was his concern that the heavily trafficked intersection was located near a Black school, making the corner dangerous for schoolchildren who had to cross the street there.[39] By the same token, many historical accounts of Robinson suggest that his magnanimity did not come without a price. While his altruism might have been motivated by compassion and race pride, it also evidenced an imperious streak in his disposition and the "darker, less engaging side to his personality."[40] Dancer and Copasetics founding member Charles "Honi" Coles, called his mentor "a very complex person . . . proud, the soul of generosity, but a card player . . . a poolroom man. He'd give you anything, anything under the sun, but he'd have to tell everybody . . . . He had that kind of ego."[41]

Still, Robinson's prominence did give heightened visibility to the various charitable causes he championed. Throughout the 1930s and 40s, he donated his time, money, and talent to numerous children's charities, including the Utopia Children's Home, the St. Benedict Day Nursery, the Harlem Children's Aid Society, the Urban League, and the Harlem Children's Center. Between his benefits, films, and paid shows, Robinson gleefully raced Harlem's Black children backwards, got them access to segregated swimming pools during summer heat waves, and hosted elaborate kids' parties for them at "his" playground, inviting not only their families, but "Mayor and Mrs. Laguardia and other city officials" as well.[42] And though Robinson's inflated ego earned him some criticism in the African American press, his efforts on behalf of Black children were also a source of public praise. In his write-up of a 1935 interview with the performer, a reporter for the Associated Negro Press enthused that "every kid in Colored America is his pal. Watching the fifty-seven-year-old tap dancer rehearse . . . one gets a close-up of Bojangles's endurance that is as uncanny as are so many of his good deeds for the colored children throughout the land."[43]

The perceptions of African American adults notwithstanding, did Robinson's dancing, his playful mien, his acts of mentorship on and off the screen, and his generous giving of his money and time actually make "pals" for him of the Black children in his audiences? These varied aspects of his stardom do emerge in the recollections of Black people who watched him as children in the 1930s and 1940s. Robinson's stardom and its reception also provide a provocative starting point for imagining and theorizing the experiences and perspectives of Black children at the movies in the 1930s and 1940s.

BLACK CHILDREN AS MOVIEGOERS
Shading the Oppositional Gaze

Toni Morrison's 1970 novel *The Bluest Eye* indicates in a fictional register some of the exasperation that real African American children may have felt at the Robinson-Temple pairings, but which his onscreen association elsewhere with Black children may have ameliorated. Set in Morrison's own hometown of Lorain, Ohio, *The Bluest Eye* is told primarily from the perspectives of three Black children; eleven-year-old Claudia MacTeer, her thirteen-year-old sister Frieda, and their friend, eleven-year-old Pecola Breedlove. Abused in her family and nearly invisible to her community, Pecola longs for blue eyes, feeling sure that they will make her loved and valued. *The Bluest Eye* advances a blistering critique of American popular culture, with Hollywood films from the classic era of the late 1930s and early 1940s central to Morrison's analysis. At one point in the novel, we learn that Claudia does not share her sister's or Pecola's enthusiasms for Shirley Temple. On the contrary, she acknowledges,

> I hated Shirley. Not because she was cute, but because she danced with Bojangles, who was my friend, my uncle, my daddy, and who ought to have been soft-shoeing it and chuckling with me. Instead he was enjoying, sharing, giving a lovely dance thing with one of those little white girls whose socks never slid down under their heels.[44]

Claudia articulates a perspective that evokes film scholar Manthia Diawara's discussion of "problems of identification and resistance" for Black spectators, and a gendered, raced spectatorial position which

Black feminist scholar bell hooks theorizes as the "oppositional gaze." Diawara writes, "whenever blacks are represented in Hollywood, and sometimes when Hollywood omits blacks from its films altogether, there are spectators who denounce the result and refuse to suspend their disbelief."[45] bell hooks takes this idea several steps further, arguing that both the white supremacist representations of race and the heteronormatively male-centered gaze inherent in most mainstream entertainment (and even in early "race films") potentially negate Black women's (and girls') viewing experiences, noting that critical Black female spectators "looked from a location that disrupted."[46] Claudia's view of Bill Robinson and Shirley Temple is explicitly concerned with both race *and* gender, and it disrupts her playmates' seemingly uncritical adoration. Shirley's "cuteness" is plainly a function of her glorified white femininity, and Robinson's role as her playful and loving father or uncle is clearly mobilized in the films as a further function, or buttressing, of her idealization. Though Morrison represents other Black children's perspectives, as personified by Frieda's adoring of Temple and by Pecola's self-destructive identification with her, Claudia's critical dissent is centered by her position as a primary narrator of *The Bluest Eye*. Yet she also articulates a poignant ambivalence that anticipates the shifting "notions of fluidity, negotiation, heterogeneity, and polyphony" inherent in theories of African American spectatorship like Anna Everett's framework of the "recalcitrant gaze" and Jacqueline Stewart's conception of "reconstructive" African American spectatorship.[47] Even as Claudia rejects Shirley, she nonetheless evidences love and affection for Bojangles by laying claim to him as not only "friend" but also "uncle" and "daddy." Using terms both community-familiar and collective-familial, while at the same time criticizing Hollywood's attempt to erase or obscure these intimate bonds, Claudia interpellates Robinson in ways that imply a reading of him informed by aspects of his stardom like play, mentorship, and philanthropy, which signified—especially for Black children—more strongly than his cinematic relationship to Shirley Temple.

The resistant, oppositional perspective of the African American spectator is perhaps the easiest to imagine, understand, or validate politically. From an adult perspective, especially one already critical of the white supremacist assumptions of Hollywood films, it is easy to assume that this was the way that Black children experienced films, even when presented with evidence to the contrary. For instance, beginning in 1937, Herb Jeffries, a popular 1930s jazz musician who was a contemporary of Robinson's, appeared in a series of Black-cast westerns produced by Poverty Row movie concerns like Associated Features and Hollywood Productions. These "B" movies, including *Harlem on the Prairie* (1937), *Two Gun Man from Harlem* (1938), and *The Bronze Buckaroo* (1939), made Jeffries a beloved singing cowboy tailor-made for Black audiences—and especially Black children—in segregated theaters, a racialized analogue to popular white singing cowboys like Gene Autry and Hopalong Cassidy. In latter-day interviews about the origins of his singing cowboy persona, Jeffries has offered the story of an encounter he had while on tour with Earl "Fatha" Hines's jazz band. Ultimately, according to Jeffries, a Black child's thwarted play helped inspire his decision:

> It was in Cincinnati, Ohio . . . there were a bunch of children running up the alleyway, a group of little white children and one little black child running along behind, and he was crying . . . . We called him over and says, "Hey, what's the matter, those guys hit you?" And he said "No, they're my friends . . . we're playing cowboy and I want to be Tom Mix and they won't let me be Tom Mix because Tom Mix ain't black." And ah, boy, the guys in the band were really set back by that and we talked about it and said, "Gee, you know, little black children cannot relate in a cowboy picture because who can they be, you see?" . . . . So, I came back to Hollywood, decided I was going to come out here and somehow instigate a black cowboy picture that could play in thousands and thousands of segregated black theaters through-out the south. I said, "I gotta make that cowboy picture somehow."[48]

It is certainly not my intention to detract from Jeffries's wildly popu-lar Black singing cowboy, or to disparage the many compelling cultural imperatives and political implications that existed to justify the creation of race movies. Yet Jeffries's response and his interpretation of the situ-ation are so telling in what he assumes and glosses about the perspective of the child he encountered. The youngster's statement, as Jeffries him-self recounts it, suggests that the child did indeed "relate to" Tom Mix despite race. Tom Mix's whiteness was no obstacle to this Black child's imagined identification, despite the objections of his white playmates. This distinction gets lost in Jeffries's (and his band mates') reaction. Moreover, Jeffries's comment and its attendant assumptions were and are quite commonplace. His account suggests both the temptation and the pitfalls of assuming the resistant or oppositional spectator in think-ing about Black children or adults—and how doing so can potentially flatten out the nuances and contradictions of reception.

The movies was certainly one of the places in which African Ameri-can children were both implicitly and explicitly instructed about the existence and limitations of the racially exclusionary social order that organized and circumscribed their lives. Both the segregation that regulated their viewing habits and the racially exclusive and discriminatory nature of the content that they saw at the movies would have contributed to their discovery of the social implications of race. I want to suggest that some Black children would have nevertheless come to the movies with a far more flexible and transitory sense of the meaning of what they saw than did their parents. In addition, the importance of play to Bill Robinson's performance style and star persona reinforces the way that a sense of play, for younger children especially, had the potential to make the content of movies accessible and enjoyable in ways that exceeded the expectations and experiences of older viewers. Such fluid spectatorial perspectives also complicate the uniform, uncomplicated pleasure modeled by onscreen Black children like *The Little Colonel*'s Henry Clay and May Lily.

A dearth of pertinent primary source materials essentially means that a concrete, composite picture of the moviegoing practices of African American children remains elusive. Despite attention paid to children's viewership by reformers, particularly via the Payne Fund studies of movies' effects on children conducted in the early 1930s, African American children were not generally included as the subjects of such sustained inquiry. To the extent that these studies considered race at all, it was with respect to the way that movies could influence white children's perception of people of "other races."[49] And while film historians like Stewart, Charlene Regester, Matthew Bernstein, Arthur Knight, and Gregory Waller have done much to trace something of the kinds of experiences Black moviegoers would have had in segregated accommodations in white theaters and in segregated Black-only theaters, even this important work has not posed explicit questions about African American children's viewership, or considered the import of matinees, serials, cartoons, or other "child-friendly" fare.[50] Given such limitations upon the sources for research and the available literature, I turn to first-person accounts of childhood moviegoing taken from autobiography and memoir, explicit instances of the phenomenon that Patricia White terms *retrospectatorship*.[51] White argues that *all* film viewership takes place in a retrospective frame, drawing upon previously encountered cultural texts, collective experiences, and internal fantasies, all of which contribute to the viewer's structuring of the cinema's meaning for herself. These instances of remembered viewing participate in this process from a doubled distance, with memories of these already structured experiences of classical Hollywood cinema themselves recalled from the vantage point of "a present that affords . . . new ways of seeing."[52]

Although my analysis of these accounts is necessarily impressionistic and incomplete, it nevertheless begins to outline the intriguing picture of Black children as moviegoers in the classical movie era.[53] The variety expressed by and even within individual recollections recalls Stewart's carefully customized application of the Benjaminian notion of *flânerie* to Black migrants in the North, emphasizing the dynamic blend of unprecedented choice, visual distraction, and racialized self-consciousness that must have governed their moviegoing experiences. So too, the African American children whose remembrances are collected and shared here reveal the extent to which they, though not explicitly courted, or even acknowledged, by Hollywood, nevertheless sought out their own distinctive and personal connections to what they saw, sometimes negotiating identity across the boundaries of race, gender, and class, sometimes ignoring such limitations altogether. These instances demonstrate the ways in which Black spectators engaged at the level of fantasy, and illustrate the complexity of these engagements, of their "translation of social representations into subjectivity and self-representation, and thus the adaptation or reworking of public fantasies in private fantasies."[54]

In all but one of the accounts that follow, the writers remember instances of moviegoing from their preadolescent years. The memories that they share indicate what a lasting impression their inaugural experiences with movies made on them. Some of these accounts are memories evoked in reference to the Robinson-Temple duo; the rest are concerned with other stars and films of the 1930s and 1940s. Nevertheless, all of these accounts complicate the notion of the oppositional spectator in a variety of interconnected ways. They demonstrate that Robinson's star text was definitely not limited to Shirley Temple as a point of reference for Black children spectators, and that his appearance in the all-Black-cast film *Stormy Weather* was an equally if not more important cultural touchstone for these young audiences. Relatedly, these accounts suggest the significance of the "public dimension of reception" in terms of the impact of all-Black segregated theaters upon the way that Black children viewed Robinson.[55] These children's memories also provide examples of concepts that I am calling *racially transcendent play* and *racial transposition* as significant processes of identification, fantasy, and desire for Black children's spectatorship. The two concepts underscore specific and individualized uses to which Black children put their cinematic experiences, illuminating a richly textured personal and even psychoanalytically relevant engagement with Bill Robinson and classical Hollywood film.

BILL ROBINSON, ALL-BLACK THEATERS, AND *STORMY WEATHER*

In her autobiography, *Miss Rhythm,* blues singer Ruth Brown remembers her own level of insight about the roles offered African Americans as nuanced by the lived realities of class. As a child, "seeing blacks in movies playing domestics didn't strike a sensitive chord" with Brown, "for that was what my mama did."[56] The pervasiveness of domestic work as one of the few consistent employment options for Black women who sought to make a living in the 1930s and 1940s provides important context for the reception of these roles with African American viewers more broadly. Still, Brown adds, "what did come over as demeaning was that slow-walkin', slow-talkin' shuffle that Stepin Fetchit and a few others made their specialty . . . . their dialect was completely alien to my ears."[57]

Born and raised in Portsmouth, Virginia, Brown grew up with weekly trips to one of Portsmouth's Black theaters, the Capitol, as a regular ritual. "Apart from any other consideration," she recalls,

> the Capitol had something the [white] Colonial [theater] could never offer: all-black movies! Yep, all through the Depression years, right through wartime, we enjoyed our own black heroes in westerns, dramas, musicals, and gangster movies . . . . We got a kick out of those movies and maybe they did raise our aspirations somewhat. If Bill "Bojangles" Robinson could land on the silver screen, so might we![58]

Despite Robinson's own onscreen relationship to subservient behavior, Brown notes that as a child she associated Robinson with the racial pride of all-Black-cast movies. And in that context, the mentorship aspect of Robinson's stardom clearly took on even greater significance, through Robinson's presence as a sign of what Black children like Brown "might" achieve, and providing an alternative and even a corrective to "demeaning" representations of cinematic Blackness. Robinson's playful vigorousness onscreen is a marked visual and tonal contrast to Stepin Fetchit's sluggish, weakened bearing; both were virtuosic performances, to be sure, but while Robinson's phenomenal dancing potentially existed both within and without the boundaries of race, as

Fetchit, Lincoln Perry's comedic performance was a wholesale reinforcement of racial limitations.

Like Ruth Brown, poet and essayist Calvin Hernton, as a child, read Robinson as a kind of contrast to degrading "servant" images, and did so by placing him in the context of Black-cast movies. In his autobiographical essay "Chattanooga Black Boy," Hernton recalled the gradual process through which his own nascent racial consciousness evolved; from "about five or six years old" when he first comprehended "somehow . . . that black people and white people did not associate . . . . I was aware that even though colored people and white people might be in the same spaces or places together, they were nevertheless somehow apart from each other."[59] Hernton's essay takes us from this moment of early childhood, when he was "without comprehension" of the significance of such realities, to a later time when "in the eighth grade," he recalls, "I began to hurt inside and feel a bitter resentment toward the white superintendent who strolled into our classroom and sat in judgment over us and the teacher. The void would open up in me." In this same passage, Hernton acknowledges that "without knowing it, a sense of race inspired by racism was becoming an integral factor in the way I identified myself."

Hernton describes his interactions with Hollywood images in the context of this emergent sense of the social meanings of race. As a youngster, he noted the contrast between the stories told to him by his grandmother, "that we had all been brought originally from . . . Africa, where we were a proud people" and "the black men and women I saw in the movies . . . maids, mammies, servants, clowns, and buffoons who said 'yessum' and 'nawsum' to white folks and who rolled their eyes and ran from ghosts—Butterfly McQueen, Hattie McDaniel, Mantan Moreland, Rochester, Stepin Fetchit."[60] For young Hernton, the *screen* images that countered these troubling figures were those that he saw in segregated Black theaters, especially "the entertainers who entertained us (me) the most—Bojangles, Cab Calloway, the tap dancing Nicholas Brothers, Billy Eckstine, the absolutely white-looking Lena Horne, and the sensuous, seductive, 'naughty' performer, Eartha Kitt, whose voice was like sandpaper marinated in maple syrup." The attention to Horne and Kitt's looks in this recollection points up the raced, gendered, and sexualized aspects of Hernton's seeing (and hearing) as a young, heterosexual Black male. As importantly, here Hernton names nearly every major player in the 1943 film *Stormy Weather*.[61] Bill Robinson appeared in Twentieth Century Fox's production of this all-Black-cast film alongside Cab Calloway, Lena Horne, the Nicholas Brothers, and Billy Eckstine, as well as Fats Waller, Katherine Dunham, and Ben Carter. Robinson appeared in two other Black-cast films in his career: the independently produced *Harlem Is Heaven* in 1932 (Sack Amusements), and the Vitaphone's musical short *King for a Day* in 1934.

Brown and Hernton's accounts suggest the way that appearances with all-Black casts allowed Robinson to be enjoyed and consumed as one of "our own black heroes" by African American children in the early twentieth century. It is likewise significant that in his account, Hernton apparently associates Robinson primarily with *Stormy Weather,* suggesting that this film, and not those in which he appeared with Shirley Temple, was his archetypal memory and image of Robinson. In *Stormy Weather,* he is cast as "Bill Williamson," a talented tap dancer who seeks out both fame and romance by pursuing the lovely and well-connected Selina Rogers (Lena Horne). The film's narrative, about the ups and downs of Williamson and Rogers's on-again, off-again relationship, and the ups and downs of Williamson's meandering career in "show business," provides only the sheerest pretense: the real reason for watching *Stormy Weather* is the series of talented African American musicians, singers, dancers, comedians, and general entertainers that troop across the screen. Though Robinson and Horne share top billing, Robinson is unquestionably the lead. While the film's plot definitely strays from its intended purpose as a Robinson biopic, it nevertheless evokes his life and times as a well-traveled, highly accomplished dancer.

Moreover, African American children play an important role in the framing of *Stormy Weather*'s meandering tale. The film opens with Bill Williamson happily dancing amidst a circle of Black children on the front porch of his home. Williamson is rhythmically chanting "Oh, the rang-tang-tang," as he and the children tap out an combination of steps, a cappella.[62] The session is interrupted by a small Black girl, who calls out "Uncle Bill!" and brings Williamson an item from his mailbox—a large magazine bearing his photograph. As the children crowd around him, Williamson explains that he is being honored for his life's work as an entertainer. The magazine provides the pretext for Williamson's life story to be told in a series of flashbacks, with explanations to the assembled children punctuating these long sequences (figure 17). Later in the film, the same little girl who brought the magazine does a simple time-step duet with Williamson; she beams happily as he holds her hand and leads her through the tapping.[63] Afterward he smiles and praises her, saying, "Why you haven't forgotten it—you did that fine!" as he lifts

17. Bill "Bojangles" Robinson in affectionate, teacherly mode with African American children in a scene from *Stormy Weather* (1943). Copyright 1943, Twentieth Century-Fox Film Corporation.

her onto his lap and embraces her. As his alter ego Bill Williamson, Robinson intermittently soft-shoes and chuckles with these African American boys and girls, hugging them and calling them "honey." The plot device of their interactions lasts well into an hour of *Stormy Weather*'s seventy-eight minute running time. Thus in *Stormy Weather* we find Robinson in the company of African American children whose comfort and intimacy with him onscreen could potentially have satisfied *The Bluest Eye*'s Claudia's longing for a Robinson who could be "*her* uncle, *her* daddy." Indeed, all of the children call Robinson "Uncle Bill" repeatedly in their sequences with him, as they ask questions—"What happened after that, Uncle Bill?" "Did you keep dancing, Uncle Bill?"— that allow exposition of the plot. The intentional slippage that the film creates between "Bill Robinson" the star and "Bill Williamson" the character coincidentally facilitates a more personal reading of Robinson's affectionate exchanges with these youngsters. And Robinson's physical closeness with these children far exceeds the semi-distant intimacy he performed with Shirley Temple, providing an opportunity for young Black viewers' more express claim upon his persona.

Stormy Weather's plot also models the interconnected and communally linked path to and from African American stardom theorized by Arthur Knight in his essay "Star Dances." Knight's "star dance" framework uses the notion of a migration from the margins of celebrity, in which stars are primarily appreciated by Black audiences, to the center of broader fame and stardom, in which they win recognition by mainstream audiences. He uses the culturally specific symbol of a circle of audience members/performers from which stars emerge, move to the center ("cross over"), and then return.[64] Knight's formulation of the star dance also acknowledges the ways in which individual Black stars can function to facilitate others' stardom. In this particular aspect, the star dance concept inherently carries within it ideas about mentorship, and possibly philanthropy as well, given the importance of the relationships that make any individual Black star's journey into the center of the circle possible. In the case of *Stormy Weather,* it is Robinson's legendary status as a tapper, linked with Horne's rising stardom, that facilitates the appearances of the many other Black performers that populate the film.

Brown and Hernton's accounts of childhood moviegoing also begin to suggest the ways in which Black children's remembered experiences in segregated Black theaters constitute the kinds of memories that Jackie Stacey calls "personal utopias," or "utopian fantasies" of the past. In keeping with other British cultural historians' interest in "popular memory," Stacey's work posits that the pleasures in these memories derive from their function as "an escape from the constraints of daily life," and that the kinds of personal utopias produced "will partly depend upon present feelings about past events." For many African Americans, a nostalgic view of the spaces of segregation is tied to a sense of opportunity lost, and to the notion that the politics of integration did not yield the kinds of widespread economic, political, and social access or enfranchisement hoped for by the architects of the modern Civil Rights movement.[65] Like Ruth Brown's triumphant assertion that the Capitol had something that the white movie theaters could never offer, these memories also claim a kind of power and collective pleasure at the implicit or explicit expense of white moviegoers, in a way that turns the meaning and intention of segregation on its head.

These memories also suggest the potential impact of the public dimension of cinematic reception as addressed in Jacqueline Stewart's theorizing, in terms of the way in which a segregated venue could affect the meaning of what Black viewers saw there. Stewart makes a case that the space of the segregated cinema helped to facilitate a range of spectatorial possibilities and responses for Black viewers during the pre-classical cinema era. What is more, this function was not wholly dependent on films with all-Black casts for its efficacy. For example, Fayard Nicholas remembered seeing Robinson for the first time on film in the 1930 Wheeler and Woolsey musical comedy *Dixiana.* Fayard would have been sixteen years old at the time, and his brother Harold, nine. The two saw the film at the Standard Theatre in Philadelphia, one of the city's foremost African American-owned and patronized entertainment venues.[66] Fayard recalls that seeing Robinson perform his "stair dance" in *Dixiana* was the moment "that did it for me, that's when I fell in love with him."[67] *Dixiana* was Robinson's first film; his performance is barely two minutes long. He dances not in his signature top hat and tails, but in a tattered bumpkin outfit, complete with straw hat and a feather duster he uses to enter the scene as something akin to a whimsical janitor. That Nicholas, who grew to adulthood emulating the smooth, sophisticated chic of Duke Ellington, was unfazed by the servile conceit required of Robinson in this appearance also suggests Robinson's ability to use his talents as a dancer as a wedge between himself and the abject disguises he was obliged to wear in his pursuit of a show business career.

Yet it is likely that an African American theater like the Standard carried the film in large part because of Robinson's fleeting cameo. African American theaters routinely carried mainstream films featuring Blacks in small parts, then advertised to their audiences on the strength of these appearances, often giving the Black players more prominent billing than their white "costars." Baltimore's segregated Royal theater also ran *Dixiana,* advertising it in the *Baltimore-Afro American* newspaper as "'DIXIANA' with Bill 'Bojangles' Robinson," and "World's Greatest Tap Dancer Bill Robinson in DIXIANA."[68] The advertisement included a photograph of Robinson with an attractive African American woman directly under the official promotional photo of Bebe Daniels and Everett Marshall, the film's (white) lead couple. Robinson does not appear with his own ingénue in *Dixiana;* the image has nothing to do with Robinson's brief specialty dance in the film, and is completely gratuitous on the part of the Royal's advertisers. As odd and even fatuous as such practices might seem, Fayard Nicholas's vivid memory of Robinson in *Dixiana* (to the exclusion of any other episode of the film) testifies to the kind of cultural longing that Black segregated viewing spaces successfully catered to, even in such a piecemeal fashion.

Experiences like those recalled by Brown, Hernton, and Fayard Nicholas have the potential to draw Stewart's theorizing about the significance of Black theaters from the preclassical into the classical cinema era of the 1930s and 1940s, supporting the notion that Black theaters, like other segregated venues, continued to function "as an important corollary (or alternative) to other spaces in which modern black life was experienced."[69] These memories of moviegoing and Bill Robinson imply that for Black children, Robinson's screen image was not necessarily dominated by his association with Shirley Temple, given that Black audiences in particular had the opportunity to see Bojangles in a range of other contexts. The impact of all-Black-cast films like *Stormy Weather, Harlem Is Heaven,* and *King for a Day,* compounded by the communal experience engendered by the space of the segregated movie theater, provided a frame of reference in which some Black children indeed read Robinson as part of the discourse of racially resistant or oppositional viewing.

FROM OPPOSITIONAL VIEWING TO RACIALLY TRANSCENDENT PLAY

Mel Watkins and Ann duCille

My Son Joe:
  Reading him stories . . . and watching him play games in his cowboy suit, or his Mouseketeer hat, or sitting in his Indian tent engaged my imagination and provided a constant example of how real the unreal is. It was all a moving example of how people (from early childhood) naturally take on other identities.
—Adrienne Kennedy, *People Who Led to My Plays*[70]

I offer this quotation from Adrienne Kennedy (from her own unconventional memoir, *People Who Led to My Plays*) as a way to introduce the concept of racially transcendent play among African American children. We might consider Herb Jeffries's aspiring Tom Mix as an example of this concept in action. Racially transcendent play was a potentially risky way for Black children to assert an engagement with Hollywood movies; as suggested by Jeffries's account, the successful performance of such play was heavily dependent on audience, the circle in which children deployed their acts of transcendence. In the two reminiscences that follow, children attempt to enact racially transcendent play through their spectatorial identification with Bill Robinson and Shirley Temple as a pair. The first narrative is taken from the autobiography of cultural historian Mel Waktins, *Dancing with Strangers,* and the second, from an autobiographical accounting of literary scholar Ann duCille's viewership in her personal essay "The Shirley Temple of My Familiar."

Mel Watkins recalls an afternoon in the early 1940s when he was walking home from baseball practice through an all-white neighborhood. At the time, Watkins had just begun attending elementary school, and as a result, had entered a point in his young life when racial distinctions began to play a more prominent part.[71] Born and raised in Youngstown, Ohio, he and his family had recently moved from Shehy Avenue on Youngstown's working-class east side to "the more fashionable south side." As such, their new neighborhood was in the process of blockbusting out to Black families, or "countrifying," as Watkins terms it. Many of the neighborhoods adjoining his family's were still predominantly white at this time.[72] Watkins's stroll home was interrupted

> when a three- or four-year-old, curly-haired blond child skipped out onto her lawn flashing a cherubic smile and looking like Shirley Temple. I responded with my best Bill Robinson grin. After all, I'd seen the movie *The Little Colonel* along with *Lucky Ghosts* [sic] with Mantan Moreland and *Harlem Rides the Range* with Herb Jeffries on a triple bill at the Regent Theater, an East Federal picture show that offered its almost exclusively Negro clientele a steady diet of 1940s race films. And on that day I felt as cheerful and nearly as light on my feet as I imagined Bojangles had been in the movie.

Yet Watkins's sense of well being would be short-lived. "My grin disappeared," he writes, "when she began shouting, 'Nigger! Nigger! Nigger!' as if excitedly confirming the sighting of an alien."[73]

Watkins's fascinating anecdote is rich in what it suggests about his own boyish, innocently hopeful reading of Bill Robinson and Shirley Temple. It points up the appeal of the explicitly playful mien that Robinson affected in his films, given that young Watkins adopted Robinson's style and manner in attempting to play with another child. Though his exchange with this unnamed white girl-child would teach him that race and gender in 1940s America were not the stuff of fun and games, Watkins walked into the experience with an expectation shaped by Robinson's infectious onscreen sense of joyful play. By the same token, his recall of the exchange was surely influenced by the discord of this would-be Shirley Temple's response to him. As bell hooks points out, Temple's cinematic interactions with African Americans like Bill Robinson were designed primarily to show "just what a special little old white girl Shirley really was," that Temple's tolerance of and even love for Black characters proved her pure and unaffected innocence.[74] Watkins's youthful reaction to the white child he encountered suggests that Shirley Temple's visual embodiment and representation of this species of "specialness" had been effective.

Watkins names this moment as a kind of turning point in his racial education, remembering that it was the first time he learned to "identify with the word [nigger] on a personal level." Before, Watkins had heard "nigger" used intraracially among his family and understood it to denote specific undesirable actions or manners, noting that "it was nearly always used to point out some individual's rowdy or inappropriate behavior . . . . I grew up thinking of it as defining the kind of loud, unruly behavior that my parents disapproved of." As such, this incident initially left Watkins surprised and confused. "Since I'd been on my best behavior," he recalls in his biography, "definitely not acing rowdy or unruly . . . I couldn't believe that she had actually mistaken me for a nigger!"[75]

Significantly, Watkins also mentions having seen Robinson at the Regent, a Black theater in Youngstown. Here, as with Ruth Brown, Fayard Nicholas, and Calvin Hernton's remembrances, the public dimension of reception is relevant, as Bojangles's cinematic presence can be imagined as having special signification for a segregated Black audience, and was likely capitalized on by the Regent's promotion in some of the ways described above. Watkins saw Robinson's performance in *The Little Colonel* in the context of the Regent's "steady diet of 1940s race films." And though *The Little Colonel* was neither a 1940s film nor a race film, Robinson's presence in it could connect it to such films for Watkins, could carry a luster apparently tinged with race pride, or at least racial familiarity and shared community, when seen by a "race" audience and set in the company of comedian Mantan Moreland and Black cowboy Herb Jeffries. Young Watkins's response to Bojangles, his admiration and imitation of Robinson's "light-footed" moves and mannerisms, implies that the communication of the dancer's virtuosity and joy was facilitated in the communal, segregated space of the all-Black Regent Theatre.

Another instance of racially transcendent play occasioned by the cultural meaning of Robinson and Temple as a duo, Ann duCille's personal essay "The Shirley Temple of My Familiar" provides an equally provocative instance of spectatorial identification. Part cultural analysis and part memoir, duCille's essay opens with the voice of Toni Morrison's aggrieved girl-child from *The Bluest Eye*, including her envy of "Shirley's" relationship with Bojangles. DuCille's account focuses much more specifically upon the impact of Shirley Temple as cinematic icon, exploring the visual power of her bouncing blonde curls. She concedes that

> my own relationship to Shirley Temple is a vexed one. I didn't worship the child star like the ill-fated Pecola, but I didn't have the good sense to hate her either. The truth is most of the time I wanted to be Shirley Temple. That is, I wanted that trademark Shirley Temple A-you're-adorable-B-you're-so-beautiful-C-you're-a-cutey-pie cuteness: the ability to charm the pants off old codgers—or, better still, virile young men, whose mottoes always seemed to be, "Oh, come let us adore you."[76]

DuCille recalls being eight or nine years old and asking to have her hair fixed like Shirley Temple's by a local beautician, who pressed her hair straight and then curled it into ringlets. At the end of "what seemed like hours of pulling, twisting, and frying," she gazed into the mirror to see a "gap-toothed, black face that looked back at me from beneath a rat's nest of tight, greased coils [that] was anything but cute." Yet the young duCille was philosophical about her blunder, recognizing that "however hideous, silly, and absurd I found myself at that moment, I also understood, as only a child can, that mine was a self-inflicted homeliness, begot of my own betrayal: in attempting to look like the white wunderkind, I succeeded only in making my black difference ridiculous."[77]

DuCille's account reinforces the significance of gender and sexuality to the way that Black children saw Temple *and* Robinson; though the sampling of children's accounts shared here is evenly balanced between "boys" and "girls," it is likely that many African American boys of this era would have been less interested in a "Shirley Temple movie" with or without Bill Robinson, than would girls, coded as these films were as "girl stuff." Moreover, duCille, like many girls, was eager to comprehend and reproduce Temple's powerfully gendered effect. As such, Robinson is simply one of the various men that the perfect Shirley is always able to charm. Thus as a child watching this duo, duCille does not solely identify with Robinson's significance as Black, but also aspires to Temple's significance as female. Both duCille and Watkins are attentive as children to the interplay between the two characters, but each child is looking at something different: duCille sees in terms of the dynamic of attraction that Temple's looks command upon Robinson and others, while Watkins sees Robinson's fancy footwork and the seeming camaraderie that it engenders with Temple and others. Just as Morrison's doomed Pecola fantasizes that blue eyes alone can transform her, duCille hopes that by borrowing one aspect of Temple's iconic look—her hair—she can graft onto her own Black body the full Shirley Temple effect. For his part, Watkins's imitation of Bojangles's grin and stance is elicited only by the appearance of a Shirley Temple look-alike. In related ways that are facilitated by the filmic image and distinguished by gender and sexuality, both duCille and Watkins initially imagine Robinson, Temple, and the relationship between the two as having the potential for racial transcendence, rather than existing as a sign of racial difference itself. This is partially a result of the social myths that the Robinson-Temple dyad promoted so powerfully. The differences between Watkins and duCille responses are marked by gender and sexuality, but also speak to a heterogeneity of African American subject positions that might be accounted for by any number of other differences between individual spectators.

Neither duCille nor Watkins complete the transformations they envision in imitating and copying Shirley Temple and Bill Robinson, yet the potency and staying power of their memories are clearly tied to the significance of these events as "transformative moments." Stacey writes that transformative moments are memories "of Hollywood stars which concern their role in the transformation of spectators' own identities." For both children, the ways in which their public acts of identification are frustrated provide them with important, even fundamental instruction and socialization about how difficult or hazardous it can be for African Americans to attempt to transcend the social and visual boundaries of racial difference. These moments underscore the distance between stars and spectators, between the cinematic world and the real world, and between Black and white. Watkins and duCille do experience transformation through these experiences, though in significantly different ways than they had imagined for themselves. Nevertheless, thwarted transformations, or even a sense of the boundaries of the escape offered by the movies did not necessarily signal an end to Black children's imagining and playing with the possibility of racial transcendence. The accounts that follow provide us with a sense of the potential for such practices. Though these accounts do not focus upon Bill Robinson, they are nonetheless useful and relevant to the theorizing of Black childhood spectatorship that this chapter initiates with Bojangles's screen image.

FROM TRANSCENDING TO TRANSPOSING RACE
Moviegoing with Dick Gregory, James Baldwin,
and Maya Angelou

The potential for complexity and diversity in Black children's viewership of early twentieth-century Hollywood films itself compels our attention.

"Every kid in colored America" who went to the movies in the 1930s and 1940s was largely overlooked by mainstream filmmakers, yet these children potentially brought in much of motion pictures' African American revenue. Studios found that white children of the era attended the movies more often than their parents, and arguably catered to these young spectators through the marketing of child ensembles like the Little Rascals and the Dead End Kids; child stars like Mickey Rooney, Freddie Bartholomew, Jane Withers, Jackie Cooper, and of course, Shirley Temple; popular adventure serials like *Tarzan the Fearless* (1933), *The Miracle Rider* (1935), *Robinson Crusoe of Clipper Island* (1936), and *Undersea Kingdom* (1936); as well as cartoon characters like Mickey Mouse, the Three Little Pigs, and Donald Duck, whose popularity with children was exploited by lines of merchandising in toys and games.[78] Yet in keeping with the heterogeneous perspectives represented in the previous pages, Black children's viewership as represented in the following accounts is not at all confined to "children's" fare. These children enact moments of racially transcendent play in which they imagine themselves to be the white stars they see on the screen; they also reverse that process, engaging with Hollywood stars through a process I call racial transposition, in which they "recognize" or "claim" white performers—even briefly—as Black. The three accounts that follow center Black children's spectatorship, providing a sense of the ways that their interest in and adaptation of white stars served a variety of complex purposes, which often had nothing at all to do with the kind of racial self-hatred symbolized by a character like Pecola Breedlove. They instead underscore "the irreducibility of each viewer's experience," and provide concrete examples that make it possible to refuse the temptation of proceeding from a monolithic conception of historical Black movie-going experiences.[79]

In his book *Nigger*, the 1963 autobiography of African American comedian and activist Dick Gregory, the author recalls his childhood in St. Louis. Gregory uses his autobiography to take the reader through years of poverty in the segregated slums of St. Louis. Gregory, born in 1932, and his two younger brothers were raised primarily by their mother; their father was largely absent, and when present was abusive to both his wife and his sons. For Gregory, movies were one kind of escape from the injuries of life as the "skinniest kid on the block, the poorest, the one without a Daddy."[80] In the autobiography, his memories of moviegoing directly follow his recollection of childhood experiences of church, and in some ways they parallel his explanation of why he so loved church as a child: it was "a place to get all wrapped up in a God who was stronger than any teacher, or social worker, or man who owned a second-story window." Gregory's accounts of moviegoing in the late 1930s and early 1940s straddle the line between a certain kind of spectatorial identification that seems to ignore race, and the kind of resistant or oppositional spectatorship that is often theoretically identified with the African American audience.

Gregory's memories of childhood movies shared with his best friend Charles "Boo" Simmons stress the escape provided by both the cinema and its stars. Part of their love of movies was imitating the "so cool" coolness of Alan Ladd and Humphrey Bogart. "We used to walk like they did and talk out of the sides of our mouths like they did, and smoke like they did, sucking that last puff right down to our toes," Gregory writes.[81] In addition, like many young boys of their generation, Gregory and Boo loved serials, like *Spy Smasher* and the *Tarzan* movies. Tarzan raised the specter of race uncomfortably—as Gregory recalls, "[We] used to sit there and laugh at those dumb Hollywood Africans grunting and jumping around and trying to fight the white men, spears against high-powered rifles."[82] Yet their smirking at the "dumb Hollywood Africans" had a limit, he recalls:

> Once we had a riot in the movies when Tarzan jumped down from a tree and grabbed about a hundred Africans. We didn't mind when Tarzan beat up five or ten, but this was just too many, a whole tribe, and we took that movie house apart, ran up on the stage and kicked the screen and fought the guys who still dug Tarzan.[83]

Remembering that Gregory was a comedian before becoming an activist is instructive given the hyperbole of the "about a hundred Africans" of this memory. Exaggerated though the account may be, it still points toward Gregory's (and Boo's) growing consciousness of the inequities of power accompanying racial difference in representation, of the way that Tarzan could only be strong if Africans were made correspondingly weak. That they would rebel because Tarzan was able to best "too many" Africans is a provocative indicator of the way that Gregory and Boo recognized the inflated value placed upon Tarzan's life as opposed to the lives of the "dumb" Africans, and connected those slanted ratios to their own experiences.

At this point in Gregory's narrative, he also recounts more resistant reactions to and engagements with Hollywood films. "We used to root for Frankenstein, sat there and yelled, 'Get him, Frankie baby,'" he recalls.

"We used to root for the Indians against the cavalry, because we didn't think it was fair in the history books that when the cavalry won it was a great victory, when the Indians won it was a massacre."[84] Gregory and Boo seem to be embracing the resistant spectatorial perspective described by Manthia Diawara, of "spectators who denounce the result [of Hollywood films] and refuse to suspend their disbelief."[85] In this instance in particular, the politicized language of "victory versus massacre" suggests that Gregory's adult Civil Rights activism likely exerted some retroactive pressure upon the shape of these memories. Yet a position of resisting spectatorship is neither total nor continual for Boo and Gregory, however factual or fictitious these "memories" may be. The Indians and Frankenstein notwithstanding, in addition to loving and emulating the "cool" white masculinity exuded by Alan Ladd and Humphrey Bogart, or admiring the strong and sure white masculinity of Tarzan (to a point), the boys also embrace an unquestioningly patriotic view, "always" cheering for American soldiers onscreen and booing Japanese and German soldiers. "We never noticed," Gregory adds, "that there weren't any Negro soldiers on the screen, even though we saw them on the street."[86]

Memories like these also highlight the significant presence of other Black children, of sisters, brothers, or friends who might, like Boo, support racially transcendent play and fantasy, encouraging their playmates to be Tom Mix or Humphrey Bogart. Other children served as audiences for these performances, witnesses providing a kind of legitimacy and sanction through the permission that their gazes granted, in spite of the apparent disjuncture threatened by race. Theories of resistant and oppositional spectatorship do not necessarily stipulate constancy in the spectator. All the same, it is useful to see so explicitly the vacillation between these varied points of view in one person's memory as a way of further complicating the way we imagine Black children as viewers during the early twentieth century. Dick Gregory's oscillating child's-eye view is an apt bridge to recollections that exemplify Black children's engagement in racial transposition, a highly personal mode of identification in which white stars are "read" as Black, sometimes in the service of addressing the viewer's specific psychological needs or traumas. Given the implicit and explicit value and importance of the whiteness of classic Hollywood stars, there is also a subversive element in their being put to uses that undermine that aspect of their star personae.

In *The Devil Finds Work* (1976), James Baldwin uses film as a lens to describe his coming of age in 1930s and 1940s Harlem. While he recalls films he saw as a child in order to bring a decidedly adult analysis to his meditation on history and cinema, Baldwin also provides a sense of his child's eye, of what the movies meant to his evolving sense of family, identity, race, gender, and power. Several of Baldwin's memories exemplify processes of racial transposition. Jane Gaines sums up this current in Baldwin's memoir when she observes that "it is clear to the boy [Baldwin] that he does not see himself when he looks at the white screen. And yet the cinema mirrors back images that he claims."[87] Indeed, one of the more striking aspects of Baldwin's memory of Hollywood and "B" films like *Dance, Fools, Dance* (MGM, 1931), *20,000 Years in Sing Sing* (Warner Brothers, 1932), *A Tale of Two Cities* (MGM, 1935), *The Last of the Mohicans* (Edward Small, 1936), or *You Only Live Once* (Walter Wanger, 1937) is his youthful capacity to identify himself and his community with the white people on the screen, across the ostensibly rigid boundary of race.

For instance, in *The Devil Finds Work*, Baldwin reimagines his childhood propensity for comparing individual stars like Joan Crawford and Bette Davis to Black women he knows, and even to himself. The complexity of his identification is clear, even for him as a young boy. "I was aware that Joan Crawford was a white lady," he recalls,

> yet I remember being sent to the store sometime later and a colored woman, who, to me, looked exactly like Joan Crawford was buying something. She was so incredibly beautiful . . . that when she paid the man and started out of the store, I started out behind her. The storekeeper who knew me, and others in the store who knew my mother's little boy (and who also knew my Miss Crawford!) laughed and called me back. Miss Crawford also laughed and looked down at me with so beautiful a smile that I was not even embarrassed. Which was rare for me.[88]

Later, Baldwin enters further into the intricacies of this process of identification as he remembers his own fascination with Bette Davis, whose "pop-eyes" reminded him of his own—for which, he believed, his stepfather condemned him as "ugly." That his eyes closely resembled his mother's rendered this insult doubly painful for Baldwin. Davis's eyes, her stardom, meant that Baldwin "had caught my father, not in a lie, but in an infirmity."[89] For the same pop-eyes in the face of Bette Davis, "a *movie star: white*," meant the possibility of reprieve for Baldwin and his mother. Watching Davis, he recalls, "I was held . . . by the tense intelligence of the forehead, the disaster of the lips: and when she moved, she moved just like a nigger."[90]

Davis's whiteness is paradoxical for Baldwin as a young viewer. How, he wonders, can she be visually idealized ("a *movie star: white*") and wield attendant cultural significance and power, while at the same time, looking so like him in ways both distinct and individual (her pop-eyes) and general and racial (her movements, which are "just like a nigger"). Moreover, in laying his racially-inflected claim to Davis, he also revels in his recognition of her as "ugly." While Davis's ugliness disarms her whiteness, Baldwin just as readily claims Joan Crawford, whom he deems "beautiful," identifying *her* with a Black woman as well. For Baldwin, his claim upon Davis is immediately related to issues of power and humanity. The cruelty and abuse that he and his mother both suffer at the hands of his stepfather have been justified to his child's mind by the "fact" of their shared ugliness. Yet, he reasons, Davis's ugliness does not subject her to such inhuman treatment.

From the young Baldwin's perspective, her whiteness does not change the "fact" of *her* ugliness. Baldwin seems mainly to be struck by the notion that it is possible to be ugly and yet still powerful, to be (or at least be *like*) a nigger and not only escape abuse but be celebrated. He muses that "if she was white and a movie star, she was *rich*: and she was *ugly*." Bette Davis is proof of a set of fresh possibilities for Baldwin: that white people can be just as ugly as "niggers," that ugliness need not condemn one for all time, and that humanity and subjectivity—"the tense intelligence of the forehead"—still exist within a person who is seen as ugly. Young Baldwin's claim upon Crawford seems to carry the opposite significance: to assert that Black people are just as beautiful as whites, and that the kind of beauty that Hollywood films routinely glorify and venerate also exists within Black communities. Finally, Baldwin's claiming of Crawford, like that of Davis, suggests a kind of shared humanity that renders the concept of race less absolute. Baldwin's spectatorship was surely influenced by his emerging identity as a queer person of color, as well as by the framing afforded his spectatorship by his frequently being accompanied to the movies by his (also queer?) grade school teacher, Miss Orilla "Bill" Miller, whose whiteness he recognized as "different" from that of other, powerful whites. "The cops who had already beaten me up, the landlords who called me nigger, she was not like the storekeepers who laughed at me . . . . She too, anyway, was treated like a nigger, especially by the cops, and she had no love for landlords."[91] Likewise, both Crawford and Davis, iconic though they were, nevertheless stood as schismatic representations of "conventional" white womanhood for the young Baldwin to have latched onto. Crawford's distinctively "mannish" dress and stance, and the strongwilled nature of many of her characters complicated the dimensions of beauty that Baldwin perceived and claimed for her Harlem doppelganger. And Davis's star persona was primarily built around her reputation as an exceptionally fine actress, while simultaneously resisting or even actively contesting discourses of beauty.[92] The idiosyncrasy of these two female icons of Baldwin's imagination does not render his racial transposition of them any less legitimate, but it does speak to the ways in which the process of racial transposition potentially relies upon chinks in the façade of stardom that serve as openings into which young Black viewers might enter.

I do not mean to limit the potentialities of this kind of process to either children or African Americans, especially since similar arguments have been made with respect to the viewing habits of, for instance, white gay and lesbian viewers of Hollywood cinema.[93] Baldwin's attention to these two "white female stars in the canon of camp" evokes and arguably signifies his own queer identity.[94] However, as suggested by the foregoing accounts, the general susceptibility of children to such readings would seem to be even greater than that of their adult counterparts, given their nascent sensibilities about the world around them, and about such constructs as race, gender, beauty, ugliness, sexuality, and so on. Their relative psychological fluidity increases the multiplicity of readings already possible and available for cinema audiences. Children are generally less psychologically inhibited, more able to imagine relationships or comparisons that adults have already learned to see as untenable or taboo. And they may venture into such areas in an attempt to resolve personal anxieties and tensions, as Baldwin uses both Davis and Crawford in the interest of addressing the dilemma of the abuse his stepfather allowed him to believe was the natural consequence of his "ugliness."

In her autobiography *I Know Why the Caged Bird Sings,* Maya Angelou recalls a similar experience of racial transposition, one relevant to psychological stress that she shared with her older brother, Bailey. Born Marguerite Johnson in St. Louis in 1928, Angelou offers memories of her childhood perceptions of the movies and its paragons that are at times so poignant as to be painful. The specter of Shirley Temple lurks unnamed in her remembrance of a childhood of being teased for being Black, female, and ugly, "a too-big Negro girl, with nappy black hair, broad feet, and a space between her teeth that would hold a number-two pencil." Young Maya imagines that the made-over hand-me-down dress her grandmother prepares for her to wear for a church Easter pageant will transform her into "a movie star .... I was going to look like one of the sweet little white girls who were everybody's dream of what was right with the world."[95] As might be expected, Angelou's desire for transformation is ultimately frustrated. Like Ann duCille (or indeed, Pecola Breedlove), this young Angelou hopes for an impossible, racial transfiguration, and in the end,

> Easter's early morning sun had shown the dress to be a plain ugly cut-down from a white woman's once-was-purple throwaway . . . . it didn't hide my skinny legs, which had been greased with Blue Seal Vaseline and powdered with the Arkansas red clay. The age-faded color made my skin look dirty like mud, and everyone in church was looking at my skinny legs.[96]

Angelou's account poignantly casts her as an impostor of idealized white femininity before a Black audience. While it is likely that Angelou's self-consciousness amplified her sense of these spectators' scrutiny, here as in other accounts, the presence of onlookers plays an important role in a child's sense of the failure or success of her performance of racially transcendent play and fantasy.

This experience as informed by ideal movie images might have led Angelou as a young viewer to harbor a fundamental distrust of the medium's pleasures. However, another significant cinematic encounter and identification further complicates her viewership. Angelou and her brother Bailey were raised by their maternal grandmother in Stamps, Arkansas, after their parents divorced. With both parents living in different states and away from their children, Maya and Bailey routinely struggled with feelings of estrangement and rejection, especially with respect to their "Mother Dear," Vivian Baxter. Angelou recalls a Saturday when Bailey returned home from a trip to the movies alarmingly late, and without explanation to their worried (and then angry) grandmother. She recounts his subsequent confession, that he had seen their Mother Dear in the movies. He explained, "It wasn't really her. It was a woman named Kay Francis. She's a white movie star who looks just like Mother Dear."[97] Made late because he stayed to see the film twice, Bailey confides his discovery only to his sister. "I understood," Angelou recalls, "and understood too why he couldn't tell Momma [their grandmother] or Uncle Willie. She was our mother and belonged to us . . . we simply didn't have enough of her to share."[98] The children waited nearly two months to go together to see another film featuring Francis, "a gay light comedy." Angelou recalls that "her maid, who was Black, went around saying 'Lawsy, missy' all the time. There was a Negro chauffeur too, who rolled his eyes and scratched his head, and I wondered how on earth an idiot like that could be trusted with her beautiful cars." While

Angelou remembers that she enjoyed the film, and even laughed, she adds,

> but not at the hateful jokes made on my people. I laughed because, except that she was white, the big movie star looked just like my mother. Except that she lived in a big mansion with a thousand servants, she lived just like my mother. And it was funny to think of the whitefolks' not knowing that the woman they were adoring could be my mother's twin, except that she was white and my mother was prettier. Much prettier.[99]

Angelou's mother's prettiness is given particularly powerful emphasis in *I Know Why the Caged Bird Sings,* in terms of Maya's sense of the literal and figurative distance that it creates. She recalls the realization, as she perceives her mother's beauty anew in a moment of reunion: "I knew immediately why she had sent me away. She was too beautiful to have children. I had never seen a woman as pretty as she who was called 'Mother.'"[100] Young Maya is not far wrong—it is largely her mother's personal and romantic life that keeps her from taking responsibility for her children in their early years. Physically, she sees her mother and her brother "as more alike than she and I or even he and I" because they share a beauty that she lacks—this too, creates distance.[101]

Angelou and her brother Bailey's process of racial transposition in their spectatorship of Kay Francis is at once personal and general, having on the one hand to do with her appearance, by which both children are arrested, given Francis's perceived resemblance to their own glamorous mother. Their pleasure in perceiving this similarity, given their individual and collective longing, is so strong that it cannot easily be shaken, even by the presence of stereotypically brainless Black servants alongside Francis onscreen. On the other hand, Maya embraces the subversiveness of their claiming of her, in the way that their enjoyment complicates any straightforwardly negative impact of racist portrayals on their moviegoing experiences. Both the racialized aspect of Hollywood films themselves, as well as the public dimension of moviegoing are invoked in Angelou's memory of watching Francis's film alongside her brother, from the segregated balcony of a white theater. "The whitefolks downstairs laughed every few minutes," she writes, "throwing the discarded snicker up to the Negroes in the buzzards' roost. The sound would jag around in our air for an indecisive second before the balcony's occupants accepted it and sent their own guffaws to riot with it against the walls of the theater." Angelou's perception of this manifest tension and anxiety among Black moviegoers about whether or not it was acceptable to laugh at the same things that the white audience found amusing underscores the anomalous conditions under which she found herself reunited with her "Mother Dear." Her description of this racialized contest of laughter also suggests the way that segregated space within movie theaters underscored sociopolitical tensions and the fundamental power differential between Blacks and whites. Even in the midst of the moviegoing experience, Black and white audiences enacted forms of everyday surveillance, policing themselves and each other, reflexively and collectively contemplating the unequal terms upon which the movies' spectatorial pleasure and escape were extended to them.

Still, Angelou remembers herself as overwhelmingly buoyed by the experience of seeing Francis and remarks that "the movie star made me happy. It was extraordinary good fortune to be able to save up one's money and go see one's mother whenever one wanted to. I bounced out of the theater as if I'd been given an unexpected present."[102] This extraordinary recollection quite exceeds any expectation that Black children rejected all that they saw in mainstream Hollywood films, or that their acceptance of such representations occurred primarily on Hollywood or mainstream terms. And the particularly personal and intimate connection Angelou makes between a "pretty" white movie star and her own "much prettier" mother recalls Baldwin's transpositions of Bette Davis, Joan Crawford, and his own pondering about Black and white ugliness and beauty. Such accounts suggest that cinema could provide Black children with the imaginative space to both invoke and defy the restrictions of race. For Angelou and Bailey, the cinema supplies their absent mother, in a psychoanalytically rich exchange that on the one hand invokes a standard Freudian reading of the "maternality" of the cinematic space, and on the other, recalls critiques of the flattening "universality" of psychoanalytic theories, and gestures toward the substantial gaps left by their lack of racialized and gendered specificity. The wholly unintended "present" that Kay Francis's performances supplied essentially allowed Maya and Bailey to envision their absent mother in a happy and munificent alternate universe. The "gay light comedy" in which they see Francis is a reassuring environment for their simulated visit with "Mother Dear," especially because it is one in which they could imagine that the diversions that took her away from them—primarily her relationships with men—were blithely romantic encounters which might end happily. They used Francis to mediate the anxiety of their estranged relationship with a mother whom they idolized as glamorous and spectacular even in her very distance and inapproachability.[103]

Like Baldwin, Angelou and her brother chose a somewhat vexed Hollywood star as the screen for their maternal projections. One of the highest paid female performers in Hollywood in the early 1930s Francis had, by the decade's end, been largely relegated to roles in B-movies. The film that young Maya and Bailey saw together may have been one of her earlier pictures, rerun in their local Stamps, Arkansas theater. Still, Francis's glamorous brunette looks, and her specific status as a movie fashion plate with a "sleek, model-like figure," made her a workable stand-in for the stylish, good-looking mother that Bailey and Maya so idealized.[104] Like Angelou's mother, Francis was an independent and unconventional woman by 1930s standards. She was a divorcee twice over, and a "bad girl" who bedded a variety of men during her Hollywood career. Her notorious speech impediment—Francis could not pronounce the letter "r" correctly—may have contributed to her slide from stardom, though the culprit was just as likely her outsized salary, and Warner Brothers' decision to banish her to low-budget B-movies one year before her contract ended, in a ugly and public attempt to force her out.[105] The likelihood that Francis was a falling, if not fallen, star when Angelou and Bailey encountered her renders their identification with her even more poignant and complex. Their "retrospectatorship" of Francis took her stardom largely for granted in spite or in ignorance of her industrial difficulties, perhaps even engaging with a version of her stardom that was no longer in circulation, and amplifying that stardom by dint of its connection to their own shared fantasy of "Mother Dear."

Maya Angelou and her brother Bailey, Baldwin, Dick Gregory and Boo, Mel Watkins, Ann duCille, Fayard and Harold Nicholas, Calvin Hernton, and Ruth Brown all behaved as spectators who had the agency to appropriate and utilize the images they saw in the movies in ways that fit their individual needs. Remembering his childhood spectatorship of Joan Crawford in *Dance, Fools, Dance,* Baldwin notes, "I don't remember the film. A child is far too self-centered to relate to any dilemma which does not, somehow, relate to him—to his own evolving dilemma. The child escapes into what he would like his situation to be."[106] These accounts point to the various ways in which actual Black children put Hollywood movies to their individual, "self-centered" imaginative uses, whether they watched a white star like Bette Davis, Humphrey Bogart, Tom Mix, or Kay Francis, or a Black star like Bill Robinson. They complicate and enhance our sense of what identification or resistant and oppositional approaches could look like for Black children of this era. They press our understanding of the impact of the segregated theater space on African American experiences of film and perhaps other cultural forms as well. They suggest how organically African American children engaged in racially transcendent play in their encounters with Hollywood cinema. And they offer us a sense of how these same children might have claimed white movie stars as their own, while simultaneously putting a conscious, layered sense of racial identity into play.

A HOOFER'S CODA

Bill Robinson, with his affinity for children and his public, politically complicated associations with the spirit and innocence of childhood, provides an apt starting and ending point for meditations on children as moviegoing spectators. In the end we are left to wonder what the youthful James Baldwin, Maya Angelou and Bailey, or Gregory and Boo would have made of the varied films of Robinson's corpus; his films with Shirley Temple in which he danced and served, his jazzy scatting and playful contesting with Cab Calloway, Jeni LeGon, and Fats Waller in mainstream films like *Stormy Weather* and *Hooray for Love,* or his neat hoofing with the chorus girls in independent all-Black-cast films like *Harlem Is Heaven* and *King for a Day.* Despite his limited access to film vehicles, Robinson's film corpus was relatively diverse, and given the variable reception these Black children gave to mainstream Hollywood films, they may just have easily decided to cheer Bojangles on and imitate his cool stepping, as to boo the house down whenever he appeared.

The final public appearance of the performer's life adds a poignant postscript to this chapter's consideration of African American children moviegoers. On an evening in October 1949, a seventeen-year-old African American lad who styled himself "Wee" Willie Smith performed on the Dumont Network's national talent competition, *The Ted Mack Original Amateur Hour.* Smith won Mack's amateur competition, tap dancing in an upright, bouncing style that Robinson's second wife, Elaine, remembered as influenced by Robinson's own.[107] Emcee Ted Mack congratulated Smith, then startled the young man by informing him that Bill Robinson was in the show's audience that day. Pulling away from Mack in disbelief, Smith excitedly scanned the audience. The camera cut to a smiling Robinson, who rose from his seat in the studio audience and joined Mack and Smith on stage. Breathing hard from the exertion of his performance, Smith was thunderstruck and stammered that he'd always waited for this moment and "now, I don't know how to take it." But even more surprising was Robinson himself, who briefly lost his trademark cool and "copasetic" mien, and broke down in tears. Haltingly, he struggled to explain himself to Smith and to Mack's viewing audience:

> I started on the stage from Richmond, Virginia when I was four years old . . . and I'm now seventy-one . . . and I want to tell you, this is the first time that I ever been broke up on stage. Ladies and gentlemen, I'm going to ask you to forgive me, but the kid really . . . I started in Richmond when I was a kid . . . and you're wonderful and it just . . . I been sick and it just broke me down. You're wonderful, and the only thing I'd like to say to you . . . it's not what you do on the stage, it's what you do after you leave the stage.[108]

Still speechless, Smith continued to clutch Robinson's hand in amazement. After the audience's applause for Robinson died down, Smith fumbled with his suit coat buttons, apologizing for his own tongue-tiedness, and hesitatingly offering that he was "not very good at making speeches." Whatever Smith may have thought at that moment, he was clearly overwhelmed by the presence of a celebrity of stage and screen, as well as an idol of the tap dancing world. Despite being overcome with emotion, Robinson stayed true to form, encouraging and dutifully advising a young up-and-comer. He would pass away just over a month later.

This final public appearance with a young fan brings Robinson's star connection to Black children full circle. Even in this instance, his repeated invocation of his own childhood recalls his affinity with children throughout his career. The motifs of play, mentorship, and philanthropy that dominated the manifestation of this relationship on and off the screen are thus indicative of how important the moment of childhood was for Robinson personally. Ironically, in this moment so close to the end of his life, Robinson found himself in the role of the spectator who identified strongly with the performer he watched. Judging from his emotional response, the implications of this reversal were profoundly affecting. His vulnerability in this moment, as he associated himself with his own childhood and with Smith, also pointed up the symbolic import of Black children as reminders of the impact of American racism and Jim Crow upon African American potential and promise. Even as Robinson's life stood as an individual testament to the possibility of surmounting the challenges posed by the forces of institutional racism, it was simultaneously the site of the question: What rewards might such dazzling talent and fortitude have borne without the obstacles that Robinson's race placed in his way? Even as his conservative advice to Smith about the importance of his offstage "character" stressed personal responsibility, it simultaneously implied that Smith's talent could be overshadowed by any mishandling of the personal burden of representation imposed by the meanings ascribed to African American identity in 1949. The seventeen-year-old Willie Smith would have been born in 1932, the year that Robinson starred in a low-budget, all-Black-cast film called *Harlem Is Heaven*. Smith's obvious admiration gestures once more toward the question of how African American children of this era saw a star like Robinson. It is my hope, in this work, to have begun to pose some answers.

THREE

Louise Beavers and Fredi Washington

Delilah, Peola, and the Perfect Double Act

The 2002 musical film *Chicago* features jazz-era "murderesses" Roxie Hart (Renee Zellweger) and Velma Kelly (Catherine Zeta-Jones), who find that they must be shrewd self-promoters if they wish to escape life— or death—in prison. As the movie's tagline reminds us, "With the right song and dance, you can get away with murder." The film makes a wink-ing critique of the appealing mix of sex and violence that female criminals embody for news outlets, via the cynical lengths to which Roxie and Velma will each go to make the most of her currency. In an "act of des-peration," just as Roxie begins to receive the lion's share of all-too-precious media attention, Velma approaches her, proposing that the two team up to reprise the vaudeville act she once shared with her sister, claim-ing that together they would make the "perfect double act." Velma uses the vaudeville act as a metaphor for her vulnerability, her need for some sort of partnership or at least rapprochement with Roxie, admitting, "I simply cannot do it alone!"[1] Though Roxie declines, she and Velma do finally join forces in *Chicago*'s lush fantasy dance finale, and the results are dazzling visuals that revel in their duality. One woman is light, one is dark; one is curly-haired, one straight-haired; one is gamine, the other statuesque. Dressed exactly alike, they dance, sing, and move in perfect sync. As Velma predicted, together the two women magnify and reinforce one another in ways that are both direct and oppositional.

The phrases highlighted above, "the perfect double act" and "I sim-ply cannot do it alone," resonate for my purposes in terms of their reference to the dynamics that obtain between *Chicago*'s two female protagonists. Admittedly, *Chicago* is a very different film from John Stahl's 1934 *Imitation of Life,* the film that constitutes the center of this chapter's analysis of Louise Beavers and Fredi Washington. Likewise, *Chicago*'s stars, Catherine Zeta-Jones and Renee Zellweger, are two white actresses whose centrality to the film is undeniable and need not be "stolen." Yet there are fertile points of intersection between the films that make *Chicago* a useful contemporary point of reference. After all, the topic of discussion for the characters Roxie and Velma in these pivotal scenes, and arguably in *Chicago* as a whole, is the question of upstaging, of attention-seeking and visibility. More specifically, the very intentional visual contrast between Roxie and Velma underscores their opposition and competition in *Chicago*. In these ways, Roxie and Velma's dynamic recalls the show-stealing, mythic pairing of Louise Beavers and Fredi Washington in the 1934 film *Imitation of Life.*

As the film's Black mother and daughter, "Delilah Johnson" and "Peola Johnson" respectively, Beavers and Washington effect a unique structural dynamic that likewise cannot be achieved "alone," but relies on their relationship to and comparison with one another. For both Delilah and Peola as characters, as for Beavers and Washington as performers, seemingly superficial elements like skin color, hair texture, and body shape are extremely important to what these women come to mean, on and off the screen. Such elements are markers for race, class, and gender that signified with *Imitation*'s Black audiences in ways that I explore here. Notably, both Beavers and Washington achieved their greatest visibility as a result of their performances in *Imitation of Life.* Their performances and their reception among African American audiences are at the center of this chapter.

Produced by Universal Pictures, and directed by John Stahl, *Imitation of Life*'s top-billed stars were Claudette Colbert, Warren William, Rochelle Hudson, and Ned Sparks. Yet if stars get to be stars when "what they act out matters to enough people," then Louise Beavers and Fredi Washington's performances in *Imitation of Life* surely qualify.[2] Though there was not enough general acceptance of African American performers in leading roles to sustain their stardom in the movies, the celebrity derived from what they acted out in John Stahl's melodrama would follow them for years to come. Having played Peola, a species of tragic mulatto who passed for white, Fredi Washington endured many interviews answering questions about her own experiences of racial passing. Louise Beavers was criticized for decades for the subservience and resignation of her mother character, Delilah, despite her constant requests that audiences differentiate her from the fictional role. And each woman would subsequently star in a low-budget film that pulled on the same generic and thematic threads of race, melodrama, and motherhood so central to *Imitation of Life*.[3]

To the extent that this book is focused upon the phenomenon of Black performers who "stole the show" from their white counterparts, *Imitation of Life* is an excellent case study. The film, based on Fannie Hurst's bestselling 1933 novel of the same name, follows the interconnected fortunes of two small families, one white, one Black, both headed by widowed women. With her daughter Peola (played in adulthood by Fredi Washington), Delilah Johnson (Louise Beavers) comes to work as a maid for Bea Pullman (Claudette Colbert), and helps to raise Bea's daughter, Jessie (played in adulthood by Rochelle Hudson). As the families grow together, Delilah gives Bea her family's recipe for pancakes, which Bea markets and parleys into a profitable restaurant, then a money-making business. But both women struggle with their growing daughters. Peola's light skin raises painful, awkward questions about her identity; though she is Black, she is often mistaken for a white girl and longs to leave Delilah behind in order to "pass." Meanwhile, Bea sends Jessie to boarding school, and when Jessie returns as a young lady, she falls in love with her mother's suitor. When Peola finally leaves her mother in order to pass into the white world, Delilah falls ill and dies—almost immediately—ostensibly of a broken heart. Peola initially joins the crowds of onlookers at her mother's lavish funeral, then, overcome by grief, throws herself onto Deliliah's casket, guiltily assuming responsibility for having "killed [her] own mother." Bea draws understanding of the importance and fragility of the mother-daughter bond from Delilah and Peola's tragedy. She sacrifices her relationship with her beau and and presses instead to reconcile and reconnect with Jessie.[4]

In 1934 and 1935, Black and white press reviews alike praised Fredi Washington and especially Louise Beavers for their performances in the film, even though their narrative was clearly subordinate to *Imitation of Life*'s other plots. Andre Sennwald, reviewing the film for the *New York Times*, called it

> a gripping and powerful if slightly diffuse drama which discussed the mother love question, the race question, the business woman question, the mother and daughter question, and the love renunciation question . . . . the race

question promised to be the most interesting, but the photoplay was content to suggest that the sensitive daughter of a Negro woman is bound to be unhappy if she happens to be able to pass for white.[5]

Similarly, in his review for the *Los Angeles Times*, Norbert Lusk says that the film, "while missing critical raves, has what it takes to please the paying public." Lusk goes on to assert that

right here and now is the proper time to credit Miss Louise Beavers with projecting those heart throbs to which the picture undoubtedly owes the majority of its success. Virtually unknown except in a succession of servant roles, the colored actress proves herself an artist in achieving disarming naturalness and comforting warmth in a leading role . . . . Fredi Washington also garners praise for her vivid and emotional performance. In fact, it is the drama furnished by Miss Beavers and Miss Washington as mother and daughter which exceeds in interest and intensity the problems of the other characters.[6]

The Boston Globe's reviewer is equally direct in crediting the film's significance to its Black plot, declaring that

although Claudette Colbert is the nominal star of *Imitation of Life*, at the Keith Memorial Theatre, the most powerful and affecting sequences in the film deal with the tragedy of a Negro girl, who despises her own race and yearns to be white. Her mother [is] admirably and sympathetically portrayed by Louise Beavers . . . . Fredi Washington . . . plays the role of the pathetic Peola. She gives a moving performance and there is tremendous sincerity in her work.[7]

Many Black newspapers also gave *Imitation of Life* positive press, largely on the strength of its two key African American roles and its sympathetic focus on the issue of racial passing. In a syndicated article for the Associated Negro Press, Byron "Speed" Reilly wrote that director John Stahl "has been recommended in all walks of life for his great directing of *Imitations of Life* [sic] . . . . Miss Beavers has her greatest role and one of the most important ever held in a picture by a sepia artist." Likewise, the *Atlanta Daily World*'s Ric Roberts called the film "by far the best portrayal of Negro life and hope and problems ever to reach any screen," and assured readers that "you have my word for it that the Picture out there is the best thing you will see in many years." In his column in the *Chicago Defender*, Harry Levette argued that *Imitation of Life* wrote a new "page in motion picture history . . . in the fact that in all the annals of the cinema world there has never been a picture made similar to it. It shows life just as it is and everything flashed on the screen is absolutely possible." A later *Defender* review by Hilda See concurred, calling *Imitation* "a great picture with two Race performers doing more than just a little to make it so."[8] And the *California Eagle*'s radical editor, Charlotta Bass, pronounced *Imitation of Life* "the best picture of the year," and "a presentation of the social problem that is on trial in this Nation today."[9]

Imitation of Life was incredibly popular wherever it played. New York City's Roxy theater, which catered to a white clientele, announced that the film's run had shattered a five-year attendance record for the weekend of its opening in November 1934.[10] In early 1935, when the film's run reached Harlem's Black theaters, it was held over for a week; the same situation ensued in Chicago's segregated Metropolitan Theatre, with hundreds of eager African American moviegoers paying for standing room tickets.[11] Black Atlantans also gave *Imitation of Life* a particularly successful run in their segregated theaters, placing *Imitation* among these venues' most frequently screened films in 1935.[12] Surprisingly, given the constant specter of "southern objections" to movie fare that featured African American players and plots, *Imitation of Life* also did reasonably well in the white south. It outgrossed comparable melodramas like John Stahl's *Only Yesterday* and Frank Borzage's *Little Man, What Now?* in numerous southern cities including Charleston, Charlotte, Little Rock, Louisville, Memphis, Norfolk, Richmond, Baltimore, San Antonio, Dallas, Houston, and New Orleans.[13] In addition to its strong box office, *Imitation of Life* was nominated for "Best Picture" at the 1935 Academy Awards.

Even at Universal, a small but significant industrial concession was made to *Imitation*'s compelling African American storyline, and its decided appeal for Black audiences. Despite the effective decentralization of the film's "white plot," most of the publicity emerging from Universal focused on its "nominal" star, Claudette Colbert, and to a lesser extent, her leading man, Warren William. Posters for *Imitation* often pictured them exclusively, and the film's original trailer included sentimental shots of Bea and baby Jessie, and sensational images of Bea, richly dressed and throwing lavish parties, dancing, and being embraced by her beau Steven Archer. However,

for the first time, owing to insistent demand on the part of theatres in African-American neighborhoods for special accessories on the picture, the exploitation department at Universal made up a special trailer, which was to be screened together with the regular production trailer .... The special promo consisted of "flashes of newspaper criticism which highly praise

Louise Beavers and Fredi Washington," and was expected to increase the box office of "colored houses" substantially.[14]

There was a nine-month lag between *Imitation*'s release and the production of the "colored" trailer, a delay consistent with the typical wait for first-run films to appear in Black movie houses. The prevailing run-zone-clearance exhibition system privileged white movie palaces first and white neighborhood theaters next, with "colored" theaters served long after. Such delay notwithstanding, Universal's decision to create a trailer aimed at a Black viewership was unprecedented in the context of Hollywood's otherwise wholesale disregard of and ignorance about African American audiences. Their efforts indicate the impact of African American audiences' active reception of *Imitation of Life* across the country.

Clearly, Beavers and Washington displaced the white characters and plot of *Imitation of Life* to become the center of attention for both Black and white audiences. Moreover, that Beavers and Washington were the center of *Imitation of Life*'s diegetic interest is as evident at the present as it was in the 1930s. Critical essays find little to examine in the dramas of *Imitation*'s white characters Bea and Jessie in the absence of their relationships to Delilah and Peola. In conversations with contemporary viewers, my anecdotal experience is that without fail, the mother-daughter tragedy and "passing" subplot are what audiences identify with *Imitation of Life*. As Beavers and Washington's Delilah and Peola Johnson stole the show from Colbert and Hudson in *Imitation of Life,* their displacement of the film's white focus facilitated discourse among African American audiences. Black moviegoers watched, claimed, and interpreted these African American characters in ways that made the most of *Imitation*'s resonance with critical currents and tensions circulating within Black communities of the time. Black communities, both in the wake of the Great Migration from South to North and those still in its midst, were urbanizing, modernizing, and wrestling with issues of class, color, racial "passing" both as a form of protest against discrimination and a means toward social mobility, gender roles, and the emergence of the first post-slavery generations into positions of power and influence. *Imitation of Life*'s Black characters provided an unprecedented opportunity for African American audiences to use a mainstream Hollywood film as fodder for their public contemplation of such sensitive, culturally specific issues. Ultimately Louise Beavers and Fredi Washington functioned as the sites of these viewers' engagement, both on the screen and off.

SETTING THE STAGE

Life before Imitation

Louise Beavers and Fredi Washington had each appeared in other films before working together in *Imitation of Life,* and the nature of those appearances is suggestive in terms of how they ultimately functioned as a pair. So much of how they signified for Black audiences was tied to skin color, hair texture, and what each symbolized socially, culturally, politically, and historically. At the same time, their respective physical appearances were also central in determining the kinds of opportunities and roles they were offered in the entertainment business, from stages small and large, to the silver screen.

Beavers was born in Cincinnati in 1902. As a child she moved with her family to California, where in 1918 she attended Pasadena High School. After graduation, Beavers performed with a local ensemble called "The Ladies' Minstrel Troupe" for a year before being recognized by talent scouts. Beavers began her Hollywood career playing a maid to leading lady Hope Hampton in the 1923 Warner Brothers film *The Gold Diggers.* Indeed, early in her career, Beavers was a real maid offscreen, as an alternative way of earning an income and staying close to the Los Angeles film colony. From 1920 to 1926 she worked in Hollywood as a dressing room attendant, and later, as the personal maid of silent film actress Leatrice Joy. In 1927 Beavers landed a role as a cook in *Uncle Tom's Cabin,* followed in 1929 by roles in *Coquette* and *Nix on Dames.* She earned positive notices from the white press in the early 1930s for performances in films like *Ladies of the Big House* (1932), *What Price Hollywood?* (1932), and *Bombshell* (1933).[15] By 1934, Beavers had already been in over sixty Hollywood films, including *True to the Navy* (1930) with Clara Bow, *Annabelle's Affairs* (1931) with Jeanette MacDonald, and *She Done Him Wrong* (1933) with Mae West. In each, Beavers plays a maid, mammy, cook, or some variation on the theme.

Even as Beavers could "get work" in Hollywood, it was work of a specific and one-dimensional kind, given her race, her gender, and her color. She began playing aged cinematic "mammies" while still in her twenties. Indeed, Beavers was only one year older than Fredi Washington, even as she played mother to Washington's character in *Imitation of Life.* Louise Beavers was one of a handful of brown-skinned Black actresses like Hattie McDaniel, Gertrude Howard, Theresa Harris, Libby Taylor, Hattie Noel, and Lillian Randolph, all seemingly fated to populate early Hollywood filmdom with any manner of maids, mammies, cooks, and washerwomen. These were the primary Hollywood roles available for Black women during the 1930s—indeed, throughout the early twentieth century—and studios' casting methods adhered fairly rigorously to the physical type—dark skin, heavy build, classic West African facial features—established by decades of stereotyping in minstrelsy, literature, vaudeville, print ads, and other cultural forms. Notably, these Black women were often deployed onscreen as visual foils to conventionally and Eurocentrically beautiful white female stars.[16] Beavers was not the only African American actress of the era who reportedly ate heartily in order to remain overweight enough to fit this casting type's girthy dimensions.[17]

Fredi Washington was born in 1903 in Savannah, Georgia. While Washington's young life is not well documented, her mother's death was a pivotal event of her childhood; it resulted in Fredi and her sister Isabel being sent from Georgia to a suburb of Philadelphia, to be educated at St. Elizabeth's Convent. Some years later, the two moved to New York City to live with their grandmother and to attend Julia Richman, an integrated girls' high school in Manhattan. Washington soon dropped out of high school and began working as a typist and bookkeeper for W. C. Handy's Black Swan Record Company. There, in 1921, she was "discovered" and induced by the promise of a significant pay hike to join the chorus of the Broadway musical *Shuffle Along*. The first Broadway musical entirely written, produced, and performed by African Americans, *Shuffle Along* also inaugurated the tradition of the light-skinned chorus girl as a staple of Black "jazz age" stage productions; Washington, lithe and fair, fit the bill.[18] She had not previously trained as a dancer, but quickly learned on the job with the show's company. Washington spent the next decade primarily working as a dancer, first as a chorus girl at the New York night spot Club Alabam' and then on the road with friend and dance partner Al Moore as the ballroom dance act "Moiret et Fredi." The pair performed together at Club Alabam', and toured both Europe and America as well. They also appeared in Fats Waller's wildly popular Broadway musical *Hot Chocolates* in late 1929. As early as 1927, African American newspapers were touting Moore and Washington's appearances on Broadway and at Harlem's Lafayette Theater, as well as overseas.[19]

Between dance engagements, Washington appeared in her first dramatic role, opposite Paul Robeson in the 1926 Broadway play *Black Boy*. As the 1930s began, she appeared in other Broadway stage productions, including *Sweet Chariot* (1930), *Singin' the Blues* (1931) with her sister Isabel, and the Hall Johnson folk drama *Run, Little Chillun* (1933).[20] By the 1930s, she was well known as a dancer and an actress on the "legitimate" stage. In 1933, when Washington married Lawrence Brown, trombonist for Duke Ellington's band, African American newspapers covered the nuptials based more on Washington's fame than Brown's. *The Chicago Defender* ran a story with a New York byline titled "Fredi Washington Weds Duke's Trombonist: Stage's Prettiest Star Signs a Mate." Written by *Defender* staffer Bessye Bearden, the article referred to Washington as the "adagio dancer and dramatic star."[21] Though Washington's resume in motion pictures would never be as full as Beavers's, by 1934 she had appeared in two other films; Dudley Murphy's jazz short *Black and Tan* (1929) with Duke Ellington, and opposite Paul Robeson in *The Emperor Jones* (1933).

The importance of color for Washington's career is as clear as for Beavers's, even as it operated in distinctly opposed terms. Washington's opportunities were largely predicated on her light skin representing more "genteel" and "refined" notions of Black identity. Given long-standing American and African American investments in a European standard of beauty, her light skin also functioned as a marker of a more beautiful and desirable Black womanhood in particular.[22] It certainly added a literally "high-toned" credibility to the affectation of her ballroom dancing act as "Moiret et Fredi." The stage name had a sophisticated, continental ring and made the most of both Washington and Moore's light-skinned, "exotic" looks; the act would have lacked a certain *je ne sais quoi* as "Washington and Moore." At the same time, the racial indeterminacy of Washington's body made her a difficult commodity for the medium of film. In a form that visually overdetermined Black identity and its accepted social connotations, Washington's light skin, straight hair, and blue/green eyes made her a visually destabilizing force. Her appearance as a version of herself, "Fredi," a beautiful Harlem dancer, in the RKO musical short *Black and Tan,* alongside renowned jazz pianist Duke Ellington, drew upon the 1920s and 1930s icon of the light-skinned club chorine for Washington's racial legibility (figure 18).[23] The film's all-Black casting, in addition to its costuming and dialogue, effectively framed her image and designated her racial identity. Yet her image required further management in a movie like 1933's *The Emperor Jones,* in which Washington played "Undine," a love interest of Paul Robeson's titular character. For this role, Washington's skin was darkened with pancake makeup, in order to make her

18. Fredi Washington as a "tragic" light-skinned chorus girl in the 1929 jazz short *Black and Tan*. Copyright 1929, RKO Radio Pictures, Inc.

character's Blackness unambiguous to viewers (figure 19). The manipulation is evident in contemporary viewings of the film, and was effected in response to early dailies; seeing Robeson and Washington together, white studio executives feared that audiences would think Robeson was being allowed to romance a white woman onscreen.[24] In the medium of film, Washington's skin could not always be relied upon to mark itself properly, and sometimes had to be altered in order to be read "correctly." It is worth noting the comparison with Beavers's experience: by "dieting" to stay overweight, Louise Beavers worked to mark herself for a specific, raced reading as well, for even as her brown skin signified Blackness unambiguously, her body nonetheless had to be altered to produce the brand of Blackness current with mainstream American culture and Hollywood studios in the thirties.

The color dynamics so evident in Beavers and Washington's individual careers emerged even more forcefully when the two women joined forces to form a potent Janus-faced figure in *Imitation of Life*. *Imitation*'s popularity, and Beavers and Washington's heightened visibility as a result of their stealing the show, would assure their roles in a wide and complex set of discourses that took their characters as primary subjects.

19. Fredi Washington, her face darkened with pancake makeup for her role as "Undine," love interest to Paul Robeson's titular character in *The Emperor Jones*. Courtesy of the Academy of Motion Picture Arts and Sciences.

"I SIMPLY CANNOT DO IT ALONE!"
Playing Delilah, Playing Peola

Many film scholars have emphasized Washington's role in drawing Black audiences, implicitly suggesting that Beavers's Delilah was a role so "old hat" that it could not possibly offer much of interest to African American viewers. Anna Everett, for example, connects Black audiences' overwhelming response to the film to the phenomenon she calls "the Peola discourse." "Far beyond the limits of the tragic mulatta icon," Everett writes, "Washington's Peola generated a signifying chain of highly complex social, historical, economical, racial, and psychical meanings for black spectators."[25] Washington's "degree zero of representational whiteness" imbued Peola's longing to pass for white with the realities of Black people's experiences of oppression in Jim Crow America.[26] Karen Bowdre makes the related argument that from the perspective of representation alone—"how many other black men and women look like this?"—Fredi Washington had the potential to fundamentally unsettle white audiences' assumptions about the fixity or mutability of race.[27]

These are undoubtedly important points; indeed, part of what sets the 1934 film version of *Imitation of Life* apart from the 1959 Douglas Sirk version of the film, and from other mainstream films that deal with a "passing" plot, is its casting of Fredi Washington as the Black "passing" character. Washington's appearance in Stahl's *Imitation* stands as the lone example of such a casting choice in a Hollywood film for some fifty years after its release—such roles were otherwise, without exception, played by white actors.[28] Yet I want to suggest that Peola did not "do it alone," that both Peola *and* Delilah, their onscreen relationship to one another, as well as the intraracial politics of color and gender specific to urbanizing Black communities in the 1930s, all played a part in motivating Black audiences' responses to *Imitation of Life*. Susan Courtney has argued persuasively for the ways in which the two characters are scrupulously interconnected for the purposes of mitigating (white) viewers' anxiety over the racial indeterminacy associated with Peola. She identifies consistent visual patterns in *Imitation* that mobilize Louise Beavers's Delilah "to counterbalance and overcome Peola's potentially troubling image."[29] I identify a different, though related, set of readings of the dynamics between Delilah and Peola, and suggest that their interactions inadvertently furnished Black audiences (most of whom would be familiar with the legacies of the American legal and cultural traditions of hypodescent and race mixing) with opportunities to understand the two women in terms of tensions around meanings of African American identity relevant to the era. Delilah and Peola's respective visual and ideological conformity to the opposed and contending images of the "Old Negro" and the "New Negro," sets the stage for a culturally charged battle that would have flown above the heads of many of the film's white viewers, even as it hit home on various levels with Black audiences.

Their appearances in the film bear out this interrelation, with spatial and performative oppositions characterizing their interactions with one another. An emblematic sequence takes place ten years after Miss Bea's boxed pancake mix company—based on Delilah's recipe and labor—has been incorporated and become a success. In this time, Bea and Delilah have moved their families from the nicely furnished back rooms of the pancake restaurant to a lavish mansion; Bea and Jessie live in the house's sumptuous upstairs, while Delilah and Peola occupy its lower quarters, themselves comfortable and tasteful, if not quite as grand. We see Bea at a party in honor of the tenth anniversary of the business,

20. "Pancake queen" Bea Pullman (Claudette Colbert), flush with success from her colored maid's pancake recipe, is toasted by male admirers at a party celebrating the tenth anniversary of "Aunt Delilah's Pancake Mix," in a scene from *Imitation of Life* (1934). Copyright 1934, Universal Pictures Corporation.

effortlessly hosting a throng of elegantly attired, champagne-sipping guests. We hear the strains of "hot" jazz as she is heartily toasted by a collection of male admirers (figure 20). The camera quickly cuts from this lively shot of Bea and her friends at the bar to the comparatively restrained and static image of Peola and Delilah, who are experiencing the party only vicariously, from the house's downstairs balcony (figure 21).[30] Their presence in the night air, as opposed to within the house, reinforces their status as outsiders to all that is going on at the party above. And they appear hedged in by structures that further enclose and separate them. Peola stands with her face and body in profile, her back literally against a wall, with her arms clasped across her chest, a pose that is reminiscent of the archetypal crossing of the arms of a corpse prepared for viewing. Her bland expression might be read as melancholy, or as simply reflective. This is the first appearance that Fredi Washington makes as the adult Peola in the film, and her costuming makes the most of her light skin; her dark hair is cut short and marcelled in waves close to her head (similar to both Delilah and Bea's hairstyles). She also wears a very

21. Peola (Fredi Washington) and her mother Delilah (Louise Beavers) enjoy Miss Bea's party vicariously from their downstairs balcony, in a scene from *Imitation of Life.* Copyright 1934, Universal Pictures Corporation.

dark, perhaps black, form-fitting peplum dress with a contrasting white scarf at the neck. The color of Peola's skin—her face, her arms, and her manicured hands—is far closer to the white of the scarf at her throat than it is to the dark color of the dress, making the very dilemma she faces in the film fully manifest in her costuming. Because hers is the only face that is visible for the first few seconds of the sequence, the viewer's focus is inevitably drawn to it. The first few moments of silence between the two characters provide an opportunity for viewers to realize that this young woman is the Peola we last saw crying, as a child, over having been called "black" by Jessie, or raging "I hate you!" at her mother, who had inadvertently "outed" her to white schoolmates.

Though Delilah stands next to Peola in this shot, initially she is seen only from behind, as she looks out into the night at the George Washington Bridge in the distance. Her right hand rests on a black, spear-topped wrought iron fence before her, a structure which, like the wall against which Peola rests, can be read as both barrier and enclosure. Her light floral-print dress flutters behind her in the breeze, and her head above it, capped by soft, black, waved hair, turns up to listen to the jazz horns blaring out of the "Miss Bea's" french doors. The reverse shot of Bea's guests dancing is shown from Peola and Delilah's perspective, with more than half of the image partly obscured by another wrought iron fence, this one adorned on one side with flowered iron scrollwork. Delilah smiles admiringly, remarking, "Them boys sure play good for white boys." With just the hint of a wry smile on her own face, Peola replies, "They ought to play well. They get paid enough for it." Delilah responds to her with a puzzled, "What's that got to do with it, Peola?" With a wearied air, Peola replies, "Oh, nothing," then turns and walks away from her mother, and toward the camera, leaving Delilah looking perplexed and worried in the background. We learn much about the characters from this minimal dialogue and careful mise-en-scène; Peola knows that she and her mother are trapped, even as simple, sweet Delilah is too busy enjoying the view—that promising bridge, those enchanting dancers—to realize it. The customary roles of mother and daughter are reversed, with daughter Peola's cognizance and wordly-wiseness in the ways of race contrasted with mother Delilah's unsophisticated innocence.

Louse Beavers invariably plays Delilah with a kind of wide-eyed gentleness and sincerity; she uses the character's southern dialect as a device to soften and round her speech, such that even her rare scolding word comes out sounding like teasing. Her baffled and distressed responses to Peola's unhappiness threaten to indict any viewer brave or honest enough to see how fully powerless Delilah is rendered via *Imitation*'s diegetic frame. Simultaneously, Fredi Washington performs Peola's desperate melancholy from the very first time we see her, through her crossed, coffin-ready arms and her stoic, vacant expression. Through these and other acts of gestural and facial withholding—pressing her lips together, swinging her head away from Delilah as if to keep from wounding her with angry words, crossing her arms, pressing her hands down, clipping her speech and breaking off her sentences—Washington indicates how much more Peola would like to say, and even needs to say, were she not constrained from doing so, both by her mother, a listener who can never fully comprehend her, and even more, by the frame of the film in which we encounter her.

It is the contrast between Delilah and Peola that renders their circumstances so compelling and poignant. We are led to believe that Delilah is wholly unable to conceive of the reasons for Peola's unhappiness; this scene and everything we know of Delilah up until this moment contributes to such an assessment. As Sterling Brown and other African

American critics of the time noted, such an extreme level of unaware-ness about race would have been nearly impossible for a woman of Delilah's place and time.[31] Historian Darlene Clark Hine's notion of "dissemblance," referring to the mask of apolitical deference and jollity that Black female domestics like Delilah donned in the presence of their white employers, seems an extremely apt point of reference for Delilah's character, even as it raises nagging questions about where Delilah's mask ends and she herself begins.[32]

The distance between Delilah's simplicity and Peola's sophistication is effectively enlarged by the way Beavers and Washington speak. Bea-vers's Delilah consistently uses the Black dialect typical for African Americans appearing in mainstream Hollywood films. Thus, her line to Peola about the "white boys" playing jazz at the party sounds like "Dem boys sho play good fo' white boys."[33] By contrast, Peola's response is spoken in straight, unaccented English. She even corrects her mother's grammar indirectly, replying to Delilah's assertion that the musicians "play good," that they "ought to play *well*." As she walks away, her "Oh, nothing" over her shoulder to Delilah is not "nothin'" or "nuthin'" or "nuttin'"—but "nothing," with all consonants present and accounted for. Beavers's dialect speech and Washington's careful diction, as elements of each woman's performance, heighten our sense of the oppositional dynamic between Delilah and Peola. Left to their own devices, both actresses would likely have sounded more like the film's construction of Peola than its conception of Delilah. A 1935 inter-view with Beavers in the *New York Amsterdam News* pointed out that the actor, as a Cincinnati native who grew up in Los Angeles, "had to learn the Negro dialect just as one learns a foreign language." Else-where in the interview, Beavers comments that she "couldn't even understand the language of the southern colored people when I started . . . but I kept studying, reading books, and poems and finally mastered the dialect sufficiently to use in screen roles."[34] However ersatz or authentic, Beavers's performance of Black dialect speech effectively sets off Washington's "new" articulation of a Black voice.

Peola walks away from Delilah and toward the camera, moving through a lower hallway of the house just below the party. This walking sequence is one of the few in which the camera rests on Fredi Washing-ton alone, and she makes the most of it, moving gracefully, her arms swinging gently at her sides, her flowing movements recalling her back-ground in dance and investing Peola, her frustrations notwithstanding, with an air of nonchalant poise. The camera cuts from its view of Peola to Bea, who has two short conversations as she walks toward the camera through a seemingly parallel upper hallway just above Peola. She greets a couple passing by, then chats with an older male friend who compliments her and notes that that Jessie, who is away at boarding school, "will come home a young lady." Bea agrees, "Yes, I'm afraid so," and laughs. The camera returns to Peola at the end of these exchanges; she is looking up the staircase, evidently listening in on Bea's small talk. She turns, sighs, and walks away. This moment invites provocative comparisons between both Peola and Bea *and* Peola and Jessie. Peola's dark hair and pale skin, her slender figure and her graceful walk down the hallway are all reminiscent of Bea's own looks and carriage, even as Peola walks alone and Bea is surrounded by friends.[35] And the camera's transition back to its focus on Peola over the sound of Bea's amused acknowledgement that Jessie is growing into "a young lady" instigates a comparison of Jessie and Peola and their very different lives.

As Peola overhearing this conversation, Washington initially puts on an expressionless face worthy of Kuleshov, which in its very blankness invites the audience's projections, but is nevertheless decidedly out of step with the gaiety of Bea, her guests, the light, jovial dance music playing in the background, and the innocently happy spirit of Delilah, who seems satisfied with enjoying the party by proxy. Of course, one could argue that any African American character of this era who failed to grin or smile approvingly in reaction to a film's major white character might be interpreted as lodging a species of protest. Nevertheless, our sense of Peola's melancholy is certainly informed by what we have seen of her in the film's previous exposition of her childhood, spent "battling" dilemmas of race, color, and identity. Walking away from the staircase, Washington makes certain that her whole body conveys Peola's state of mind. She breathes a soft sigh of resigned frustration; her face is not openly sad, but blank and somewhat listless; her set mouth and dull eyes communicate withdrawn moodiness. Her limbs droop at her sides, and her gait is unhurried. As she walks into a beautifully furnished living room, she spots a book, picks it up, and immediately begins to read intently, bending low over the open pages, as if willing herself to disappear into its leaves, to effect a fantastical escape from the party and her own dissatisfaction. She first sits, then lies down on a couch in the room, making herself comfortable, her head on a pillow, her legs crossed at the ankles, with the book, from which she has never taken her eyes, resting open in her hands.

Yet when Delilah enters the frame to join her daughter, the opposition and tension between the two characters is immediately reestablished.

In spite of Peola's studied attempt to tune out the party and its associations, Delilah's first words upon entering the room, "Come on honey, I'll
dance with you," bring Peola back to reality, thwarting her bid for escape.
And where Peola is intensely cerebral, brooding, Delilah is light, even
silly, in her attempts to distract her and cheer her up. Beavers has Delilah
use cloying "baby talk" in this exchange, asking in a low, mock-pouting
tone "What's the matter with my baby?" and then, "What's my baby
want?" Peola answers the second of these questions provocatively, saying
in her carefully articulated speech, "I want to be white . . . like I look!"
When Delilah exclaims a low, horrified "Peola!" her daughter responds in
near-poetic terms, gesturing to the mirror and saying, "Look at me. Am I
not white? Isn't that a white girl there?" Once again Delilah's innocence is
trumped by Peola's seriousness, her simple happiness confounded by Peola's demands. To some extent, Delilah symbolizes *Imitation of Life*'s persistent oversimplification of matters of race, gender roles, business,
romance, and family. As Ruth Feldstein notes, *Imitation* makes a concerted attempt to turn the political wholly personal, coding socially significant conflicts as "maternal and private," and displacing "overlapping
political anxieties . . . onto the two mothers."[36]

Delilah's attempts to "baby" Peola through her real and adult concerns about race remind us of their shared past, when Delilah attempted
to cradle and rock a preadolescent Peola through her distress, but they
also gesture toward their future, when, in response to Peola's decision to
abandon her in order to pass, Delilah proclaims, "You can't ask your
mammy to do this. I ain't no white mother. It's too much to ask. I ain't
got the spiritual strength to beat it. I can't hang on no cross. You can't
ask me to unborn my own child!"[37] Even as Louise Beavers took credit
in the African American press for ridding the script of *Imitation of Life*
of the word "nigger," the word "mammy" clearly remained, and was
linguistically significant in its own right.[38] Delilah uses it to distinguish
herself from "white mothers" who can, evidently, stand to lose their
children.[39] It comes up again in the sequence directly following the party/
confrontation. Delilah pleads with Peola to go to a "colored" school in
the South by saying "Do this for your mammy," and Peola, evidently
repulsed by the term, lodges her own quiet entreaty: "Don't say
mammy." The term is a subtle yet powerful emblem of the ideological
and identificatory distance between Delilah and Peola as African American female characters. Delilah is allowed to be little more than a two-
dimensional "mammy," who cuddles and coos at her child no matter
the situation, and who is ultimately undone by the threatening implica-

tions of American racism. Peola's rejection of "mammy" in word and in person is clear throughout the film. Yet even as the problems she poses cannot be solved by "mammy's" inexhaustible loving-kindness, Peola is ultimately as bound by *Imitation*'s narrative and ideological limitations as is Delilah. While the film positions her as conventionally beautiful, she is allowed scant diegetic room to be anything more than "not-mammy." The inchoate nature of her grievances require Delilah for their explication, both as audience and as the embodiment of all that Peola wishes to repudiate.[40]

MYTHIFICATION
The Antithetical Figures of the Black

As two sides of the same coin, Delilah and Peola manifest a unique and pointed instance of the concept James Snead has called *mythification*. Mythification is "a process of glorification or magnification by contrast."[41] More to the point, it is a description of the way that raced, usually Black and white, characters in film relate in ways that communicate commonly accepted myths about race. These mythified relationships both draw from and contribute to racial myths. As such, interracial Hollywood duos are especially rich exemplars of the potential implications of mythification. Snead gestures toward the mythic significance of quasi-serialized interracial pairings from 1930s film, using as examples Bill "Bojangles" Robinson and Shirley Temple, and Mae West and actresses like Gertrude Howard and Libby Taylor who played her Black maids.[42] The relationships between these Black and white characters draw upon and reinforce white supremacist myths about who and what Black and white people are, how they should and do behave toward one another, and how they feel about one another.

Though mythification as a concept is usually applied to interracial screen duos, I apply it here to a raced intraracial duo as a way of exploring the difference these characters embody, and the power of their conjoined and combined images. The power of Peola and Delilah's pairing in *Imitation of Life* is further amplified by a persistent tension in African American intellectual history, a struggle between "two antithetical figures of the Black: the curious heritage of the 'New Negro'; and the white figure of the Black as Sambo, as well as the complex relation that obtains between them."[43] Scholars like Henry Louis Gates have identified the trope of the New Negro as part of a tradition of "black intellectual Reconstruction" that "commenced in the antebellum slave narratives, published mainly between 1831 and 1861." This long tradition of reconstruction was aimed at countering mainstream, white supremacist conceptions of Black people and their culture. The presence and potency of the concept of a "New Negro" was manifest as early as the 1890s, as response to the totality of "Old Negro" representations, determined by white supremacist and pro-slavery ideologies. Of particular significance were

> the *features* of the race—its collective mouth shape and lip size, the shape of its head . . . its black skin color, its kinky hair—[which] had been caricatured and stereotyped so severely in popular American art that black intellectuals seemed to feel that nothing less than a full facelift and a complete break with the enslaved past could ameliorate the social conditions of the modern black person.[44]

In *Portraits of the New Negro Woman,* literary historian Cherene Sherrard-Johnson takes Gates's analysis to its next logical step, identifying and explicating the figure of the mulatto woman, or "mulatta," as a visual anodyne, offered in "attempts to counter stereotypes of black women as subhuman, immoral, and hypersexual."[45]

Perhaps the most compelling aspect of *Imitation of Life* for contemporary Black audiences, and especially Black urban audiences, was the explicit opportunity it offered, through Beavers/Delilah and Washington/Peola, to wrestle with these very tensions. The film's positioning of Beavers and Washington fit nearly seamlessly with other contemporaneous Black–authored visual signifiers of New Negro womanhood, particularly print representations in Black newspapers and uplift-oriented journals. The way that African American uplift organizations like the NAACP and the Urban League depicted the New Negro woman in the 1930s corresponds with the notion that the ultimate function of the New Negro was in "revising" the image of the "modern black person."

The journals *The Crisis* and *Opportunity,* as the organs of the NAACP and the Urban League, respectively, were key voices in articulating the aims and concerns of the race through a middle-class, Northern, urban perspective. Both published up-and-coming artists' essays, poems, stories, photographs, and drawings, ran special literary editions, and sponsored contests, thereby playing an instrumental role in establishing many of the foremost artists and writers of the New Negro Movement. In the 1920s and 1930s, the covers of *Opportunity,* and particularly of *The Crisis* reflected, visually, a gendered "full facelift" of the race through their regular presentation of photographs and drawings of light-skinned

OPPORTUNITY
A JOURNAL OF NEGRO LIFE

ly, 1929   Price, 15c.

22. "Thelma," by Elmer Simms Campbell, on the cover of the
National Urban League's *Opportunity: A Journal of Negro Life,*
July 1929. Copyright 1929, National Urban League.

Black women on their covers. The practice reinforces Noliwe Rooks's
observation, that "racial ideologies [were] written primarily onto the
bodies (skin and hair) of African American women."[46] Through them,
the hierarchy that Maxine Craig calls the *pigmentocracy* was made
manifest—a system that valued lighter skin as more beautiful, and as a
symbol of modernity, education, class status, and refinement. This system, as reflected on the covers of these journals, was an essential element
of Black filmgoers' reception of Louise Beavers and Fredi Washington.[47]
During the late 1920s and early 1930s, the covers of *Opportunity* tended

MARCH, 1930   FIFTEEN CENTS THE COPY

THE CRISIS
Reg. U. S. Pat. Off.

23. Nina Mae McKinney on the cover of the NAACP's
The Crisis, March 1930. Courtesy of The Crisis Publishing
Corporation, Inc.

to focus less on human faces than did those of *The Crisis*. In fact, *Opportunity*'s covers more often featured artwork that might be abstract or static in conception, from various visual artists. However, the use of light-skinned women in cover shots as emblems of "black beauty" was quite commonplace by this time and *Opportunity* regularly ran covers like the one adorning its July 1929 issue (figure 22).

The covers of *The Crisis* and *Opportunity* suggest that one part of the way that the New Negro sought to be known was by "his" women. Through such images, the concept of the New Negro woman as mulatta became a key cultural referent for urbanizing African Americans. Sherrard-Johnson calls the mulatta "an iconic figure at the cusp of the Harlem Renaissance, a period in which narratives of passing preoccu-

24. Fredi Washington on the cover of the National Urban League's *Opportunity*, April 1933. Copyright 1933, National Urban League.

pied Black and white modernists, just as the legal designation of mulatto/a was disappearing."[48] Beavers and Washington's roles would have resonated within this culturally specific discourse about gender, class, uplift, and color. The coverage that the African American press gave these two women in the wake of *Imitation of Life* demonstrates the salience of these very connections.

The *Crisis* cover frequently featured images of African Americans, either in candid ("taken from life") or posed photographs, or in sketches or painting. The great bulk of these are representations of Black women, the overwhelming majority of whom are light-skinned and have straight

25. Advertisement from the *Kansas City Call* for March 1935 screenings of *Imitation of Life* at the segregated Avenue Theater. Image sourced from Tuskegee Clippings File, available from ProQuest, LLC.

hair. For instance, eight of the twelve issues of the 1930 run of *The Crisis* featured a portrait or photograph of a light-skinned woman. One of these, the March 1930 cover, was a photograph of actress Nina Mae McKinney (figure 23). Likewise, Fredi Washington was one of the "pretty race girls" that appeared on the cover of the April 1933 issue of *Opportunity* (figure 24).[49] The credit in the magazine's table of contents promoted Washington's appearance in the popular play *Runnin' Wild*. Even as *The Crisis* altered its cover format toward the end of 1932, using the space for headlines and story titles, the journal continued to use light-skinned women as primary symbols and representatives of its stated and express concern with racial uplift and "race pride."[50]

DELILAH (BEFORE) / PEOLA (AFTER)

Advertisements for *Imitation of Life* in the African American press often displayed side-by-side photographs of Beavers and Washington,

26. Advertisement from the *Philadelphia Tribune* for February 1935 screenings of *Imitation of Life* at the segregated Lincoln Theatre. Copyright 1935, Philadelphia Tribune.

their names given large print and top billing, with the film's other players relegated to small print, sans images. This was certainly not unusual in advertisements placed by segregated theaters; touting any relatively well-known Black player who appeared in a film, in order to draw Black audiences, was a standard practice.[51] Yet the visual pairing of Beavers and Washington connoted an opposition that constituted the very basis of their mythified relation to one another.[52]

Kansas City's Avenue Theatre promoted a midnight showing of *Imitation of Life* to its colored clientele in the February 1935 *Kansas City Call* with an advertisement that helps to illustrate this idea (figure 25). On the left side of the ad, a smiling image of Washington is enclosed within a circle iris. Washington's photo is set at an angle; she is posed with her head facing the camera, but looking slightly over her shoulder in a way that suggests movement and a carefree, youthful attitude. Meanwhile, in the adjacent photo, Beavers faces the camera head on, her image set in a more static, square shape. She smiles broadly, though somewhat less naturally, recalling the artificial smile Delilah assumes for Bea's benefit in the film. Beavers's head is topped with the puffy white chef's hat that reinforces her character Delilah's association with cooking and serving; even as an element of costume, the hat makes Beavers/Delilah specific in ways that limit the possible readings attributable to her image—she is ideologically marked here in ways that Washington as Peola is not. The segregated Lincoln Theater's ad for *Imitation* from the February 1935 *Philadelphia Tribune* also features side-by-side images of the two actresses, though they are more similar in their staging and composition. In the two equal-sized head shots, each woman sports a wavy crown of neat dark hair; Beavers's eyes glance to the left and Washington's to the right (figure 26). What is most obviously opposite between the two images is Beavers's dark complexion on the left and Washington's light complexion on the right.

The visual difference between Beavers and Washington, especially as effected through black-and-white photography and print, is curiously reminiscent of advertising images that African American studies scholar Noliwe Rooks uses to theorize the long history of gendered discourses of African American beauty in her seminal text *Hair Raising*. Rooks explicates nineteenth- and early twentieth-century mail-order and newspaper advertisements for "beauty" preparations aimed at Black female consumers. She argues that these texts draw upon and advance the commonly held belief "that only through changing physical features will persons of African descent be afforded class mobility within African American communities and social acceptance by the dominant culture."[53] The "before and after" style images that Rooks analyzes consistently locate Black women as the sites of intersecting discourses on race, gender, beauty, class, and social acceptance.

One need not go back to turn of the century to find comparable images and advertisements in the African American press. On the contrary, numerous cosmetic preparations, including Black and White Soap, Marlé Bleaching Lotion, Palmer's Skin Whitener Ointment, Nadinola Bleaching Cream, Elsner's Pearl Cream, and Wavine Skin Whitener frequently appeared in analogous advertisements during the 1930s. One such advertisement from 1930 featured photographs of the stars of MGM's all-Black-cast musical *Hallelujah;* Daniel Haynes and Nina Mae McKinney were pictured and quoted offering their endorsements for Palmer's so-called "Skin Success" soap and ointment. Meanwhile, the ad proclaimed:

> No matter what kind of success you want—social, business, or a place among the movie stars, a light, bright, smooth and healthy skin is going to help you get there. Look at Daniel Haynes, that hearty handsome boy, Nina Mae McKinney, that beautiful bit of femininity—see what skin perfection

did for them. Get the Palmer "Skin Success" Treatment, find what it can do for you. Unknown but a short time ago, they gained over-night fame—now they're getting the good things in life.[54]

A banner across the center of the ad declaring "Screen King and Movie Queen GAIN FAME OVERNIGHT" further advanced the suggestion that Palmer's preparations were wholly responsible for Haynes and McKinney's acquisition of "the good things in life."

The presence of relatively brown-skinned actor Daniel Haynes (he is significantly darker than McKinney, for instance) in this advertisement only reinforces the notion that light skin disproportionately signified upon the bodies of Black women as an indicator of African American beauty, femininity, refinement, social and economic mobility, and, to use Palmer's all-purpose term, "success."[55] By depicting Haynes, the ad could imply more general benefits of the Palmer's treatment, even as it did not feature a darker brown-skinned young actress like blues singer Victoria Spivey, who also appeared in *Hallelujah*. The product claims always describe the improved skin that use of Palmer's will bring about by associating "light" with other positive terms, in phrases like "light, bright, smooth and healthy;" "a light, lovely, silken smooth complexion," and "light and bright, petal-soft and satiny-smooth." Thus, the text simultaneously conjoins "light" and generically "beautiful." Haynes and McKinney's association with the modernity and celebrity of motion pictures is also connected to "the *value* of a perfect complexion"; for a man like Haynes, this need not necessarily include light skin, though for a woman like McKinney, evidently it must.[56]

This was just one of many advertisements for skin lighteners (and hair straighteners) that featured African American stage and screen celebrities. Many such ads included photographs or drawings of light-skinned actresses and chorus girls: Lena Horne, Beulah Marsh, Ida Anderson, and numerous others.[57] The manufacturers of such potions capitalized upon the circulation of a star discourse that would resonate specifically with an African American readership at the same time that they commodified the pigmentocratic idealization of light-skinned Black women's' beauty.

Contemporaneous ads for these sorts of products sometimes featured side-by-side drawings or photographs that invited comparison between the proffered images, implying that the superficial transformation from dark to light was more than "skin deep." Print promotions from the 1930s for Jarodene and Elsner's bleaching creams all used some version of the "before and after" format, alongside advertising copy that fully

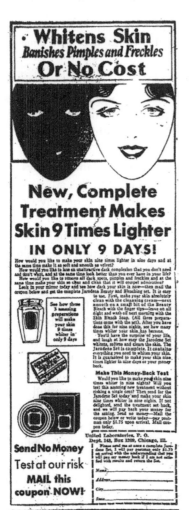

27. Advertisement for "Jarodene Beauty and Bleaching set," from the *Pittsburgh Courier,* April 19, 1930. Image published with permission of ProQuest, LLC. Further reproduction is prohibited without permission.

28. Advertisement for "Elsner's Pearl Cream" skin lightening lotion, from the *Topeka Plain Dealer,* March 21, 1931. Image courtesy of ReadEx, a division of Newsbank.

associated dark skin with taint, imperfection, and disease (figures 27 and 28). These preparations varyingly promised to "loosen blackheads," "soften roughness," remove "blotches and skin eruptions," and fade "blemishes and freckles" alongside uniform claims for delivering "a lovely fair white skin that everyone envies and admires."[58] Such rhetoric categorized a dark skin tone as one of a number of curable dermatological maladies, an unnecessary burden and obstacle that Black women could overcome. Just as the manufacturers of Palmer's whitening ointment represented lightened skin as the pathway to success, "no matter what kind of success you want—social, business, or a place among the movie stars," United Laboratories' offered their Jarodene preparation to Black women who wanted "to lose an unattractive dark complexion that you don't need and don't want," and the makers of Marlé ("pronounced Mar-Lay") Bleaching Lotion asked potential customers "Why envy Society Beauties and Revue Actresses their complexions? Use Marlé if you would be an immediate 'success!'"[59]

Ironically then, Black press advertisements for *Imitation of Life* that featured side-by-side images of Louise Beavers and Fredi Washington visually invoked these "before and after" advertisements, while simultaneously referencing the African American "star" discourse that constituted another typical strain of ads for skin bleaching products. All of these advertising texts are united by an implied or explicitly stated ideological association of dark-skinned African American women with a historicized notion of Blackness as symbolic of the immobility and servility of slavery, versus light-skinned African American women's association with youth, modernity, beauty, and a mobility that presupposes greater access to the benefits of American citizenship. These associations only further reinforced the conjoined star text through which Beavers and Washington were read and understood by African American moviegoers who saw them in *Imitation of Life*. Even as Fredi Washington's performance as Peola became the ostensible focus of much of these audiences' attention, the inevitable commentary about Beavers's Delilah character is equally revealing, however sidelong or inadvertent it may appear.

FOILING PEOLA
The New Negro versus the "Fat, Black, and Ugly"

Numerous reviews in the African American press emphasize the importance of the Peola character. The *New York Age*'s first mention of the release of *Imitation of Life* is merely a small advertisement for the film in the *Age*'s "Screen and Stage Theatricals" section, for a screening at the Loews Victoria Theater. The ad lists only the film's white leading lady, Claudette Colbert, as the star of note. However, the following week, *Age* reporter Vere Johns penned a review of *Imitation of Life* for his "Screen and Stage Theatricals" column, "In the Name of Art." Johns first praises the film according to his own criteria that "propaganda plays" on behalf of African Americans are at their most effective when and if they are "put on by the majority group, namely the white group." He commends the film's political implications, which he suggests are explicated through the parallel and unequal lives of daughters Peola and Jessie. Johns writes that though the writers and producers do not attempt to provide solutions to the racial problem *Imitation* explicates, nevertheless, "they have shown up a situation where two girls can have the same education and cultural training and yet one is denied all the social and business opportunities that the other enjoys because of her race." Johns is quick to add, "I do not make out a case for Peola because of her light complexion—it is a case that any boy or girl, no matter of what color should have equal opportunities, if they have the requisite qualifications."[60]

Pittsburgh Courier film critic Fay Jackson reviewed *Imitation of Life* one month earlier in an article titled "Fredi Washington Strikes New Note in Hollywood Film." Like Johns, Jackson praises *Imitation of Life,* calling the film a sign that "slowly but surely, Hollywood films are growing up." She also names Fredi Washington's performance as Peola as central to her positive assessment. Peola, Jackson declares,

> utters a cry, "I want the same things other people enjoy," that found an echo in the hearts of 12 million smoldering Negroes throughout the United States .... Actress though she be, Fredi Washington expresses the desire for freedom and equal justice in this picture that is more convincing than any mere performer could have voiced.[61]

Commentaries like Jackson's and Johns's are central to the notion of the "Peola discourse." As Miriam Thaggert observes in her 1998 essay on *Imitation of Life,* "we identify with the divided Peola precisely because she herself perceives contradictions; we identify because this character personifies cinematic double-consciousness."[62] Yet in these and other 1930s Black press assessments that drew upon the "Peola discourse," Delilah was often the foil against which Peola's appeal was measured. For example, early in Fay Jackson's positive review of *Imitation of Life* in the *Pittsburgh Courier,* Jackson muses upon how "a comparatively short time ago, motion pictures seemed to have restricted Negro performers to jungle types . . . [and] only the 'fat, black, and ugly' of the race were able to crash filmdom's gates."[63] It is thus Washington's function as a contrast to these unacceptable types that makes her a valuable representative of the race. Though Jackson's reproach is at least in part pointed at Hollywood's stereotyped casting, she nonetheless seems satisfied to throw thinly veiled shade at Louise Beavers in the bargain. The slur seems especially pointed given that Jackson's review does not mention Beavers or acknowledge her presence in *Imitation* in any (other) way, even as it heaps garlands for the film at Washington's feet.

Likewise, Vere Johns's *New York Age* review of the film offers up Beavers's Delilah to increase the sense of Washington's Peola as particularly compelling and admirable. Though Johns claims that the tragedy of *Imitation of Life*'s situation is not necessarily more acute because of Peola's light skin, he does exclusively champion Fredi Washington's career as a performer, declaring that with her "ability there is no reason in the world why she could not be permitted to play roles that have nothing to do with racial problems." By contrast, Johns notes that Beavers "does a swell job as she always does, but her part is what they always refer to as 'typically Negro.'"[64] Beavers's *ability*, or even her desire to act beyond this scope, receives none of Johns's attention.

Thus one part of the "perfect double act" of Delilah and Peola is the way that Delilah's "Old Negro" act amplified Black audiences' sense of what was so different, so "new" about Peola as a Black screen character. Both of these reviewers use Beavers's Delilah as counterpoint to Washington's Peola, whether explicitly or by implication, rehearsing the comparison of "before and after" in their analyses. There is substantial slippage between praise and criticism of the actresses, and praise and criticism of the characters they play. Neither reviewer seems inclined to question whether Beavers's "typically Negro" or "fat, black, and ugly" roles are all she would have aspired to play, given a choice. Meanwhile, both attribute political implications to Washington in ways that may have been more properly attributable to Peola. Delilah was typically the Black character that drew white audiences' interest and sympathies most comfortably, and this response was clearly tinged with a racist approval of her subservient nature. Yet in this vein, some Blacks approved of the film because of its potential as sympathetic and pro-Black "propaganda . . . put on by the majority group, namely the white group."[65]

E. Washington Rhodes's review for the *Philadelphia Tribune* calls the film Hollywood's "Greatest Condemnation of Prejudice in America." In his lengthy discussion of *Imitation,* Rhodes meticulously reads the film against the grain to illustrate its value as antiracist cinematic propaganda. He notes, for instance, that once the palatial home was built with the proceeds from Delilah's pancake recipe, "'Miss' Bea lived upstairs and Delilah down. 'Never the twain shall meet.'" He identifies the source of Peola's unhappiness, arguing persuasively that Peola

> had grown into young womanhood bitter and disillusioned because, even though her mother had wealth and had made a white woman rich, the color line prevented her from enjoying the full fruits of her labor. Because of these things she wanted to 'pass' as white. This angle is in the picture. But one must find it.[66]

Rhodes also discusses the significance of Delilah's elaborate funeral as indicative of the repression of the color line, musing that perhaps "Delilah realized that the only way for her struggling soul to find solace was in death .... that might be the reason that colored people have big funerals. In death they have the opportunity to approach equality and they take it." Like "colored people" whose lavish funerals make the most of a paltry opportunity, Rhodes's review is obliged to make whatever it can out of the scanty "bit of meat" offered by *Imitation of Life.* He himself acknowledges that these are but "glimpses" offered by the film, "of the stupid situations created because of their [whites'] system of segregation," and that whites will only see these glimpses "if they are wise."[67]

Well-known Black film critic Bernice Patton wrote a December 1934 review for the *Pittsburgh Courier* entitled "Critics Weep at the Premiere of *Imitation of Life*" that took the notion of *Imitation* as an effective piece of pro-Negro propaganda several steps further.[68] Like many other Black critics, Patton argues that the film is a sign of better things to come from Hollywood. Her review also makes much of the significance of Louise Beavers's role in *Imitation of Life.* Like Rhodes, she counsels Black audiences to be patient with the film's shortcomings. She writes that

> naturally, there are sequences in the film that will grieve my people .... I beg of them to be tolerant; use discretion in their thinking and grow into the industry that ... aims to erase the color line. Don't destroy possibilities in the movies by intolerant criticism. You must remember that this picture gives you your first real star, Louise Beavers, fabulous financial gains to the race, and opens the way for other Negro artists in the films.[69]

Patton is careful to omit any specific discussion of the scenes that she fears "will grieve my people." And while she touts *Imitation*'s "fabulous financial gains to the race," it is not at all evident what she would have meant by this. It is likely that Fredi Washington and Louise Beavers were paid as much about five hundred dollars a week for their work, salaries that were exponentially less than those of Claudette Colbert, Warren William, or even supporting character actor Ned Sparks.[70] Their income could hardly be counted toward the enrichment of the race as a whole. Patton argues diplomatically that *Imitation* "really serves its purpose, inasmuch as it proves to white people that they have been more than unkind and unjust to their American brothers of African descent." Significantly, Patton suggests that whites' newfound understanding of the injustice of race relations was manifest in white viewers' behavior at the preview, where she "saw some of the nations [sic] most prominent critics in tears .... Louella Parsons ... cried openly as I did, and others." Seeing white moviegoers' apparent compassion for Delilah and Peola seems to be proof enough for Patton of their remorse for their "unkind and unjust" history toward Black people as a race. She furnishes further proof of the sympathetic stripe of the white audience at the premiere through this description of an exchange with Louella Parsons, which apparently occurred after the screening. Patton writes:

> Her [Parsons's] hearty greeting was most cordial as she clasped my hand, and said, "O, Miss Patton; I admire your paper, *The Pittsburgh Courier,* and your work is good." In reply I said, "Thank you; I am so happy to know you and I want to thank you for the generosity you give the Negro artist in your column." With still a firm handshake, she replied, "I am glad to do it because I think they are fine."[71]

Patton conjures the image of a theaterful of weeping white patrons to signal *Imitation*'s power to move and transform white perceptions and behavior, one screening at a time. And the interaction with Parsons that follows it, complete with stiltedly respectful dialogue and an extended "firm handshake" across racial lines, is meant to serve as confirmation of the film's success, even as an example of what post-*Imitation* race relations might look like.

The realpolitik of Patton's presence as what she characterizes as "the only sepia invited" to this advance screening has some bearing on the tenor of her review.[72] During this time, the *Courier* and Patton were both granted greater access to Hollywood studio previews and interviews than other African American newspapers. Patton's "singular presence as the black press representative allowed at the screening suggests a powerful motive" for her conciliatory tone toward *Imitation of Life*.[73] If Patton intended to protect The *Courier*'s (and her own) professional interests, she may not have thought it wise to jeopardize her entree through offering or fostering "intolerant criticism."

Their motivations notwithstanding, Patton and Rhodes's reviews suggest a thread of analysis in Black viewership of *Imitation of Life* that sought to claim the picture in terms that reflected Black audiences' pragmatism in the face of racial restrictions and limitations. Both reviewers implicitly acknowledge *Imitation of Life*'s limitations, and yet attempt some alchemical sleight of hand, in the hopes of turning the film's leaden racial ideology into gold. Their reviews are instructive instances of the way that stealing the shoat—taking advantage of expedient, immediate solutions—was as much an aspect of African American viewership and criticism as African American performance during the 1930s.

SHIFTING SHAPES
Beavers, Washington, and the "Recalcitrant Gaze"

Just as African American interpretations of Beavers were not limited to her role as a lightning rod for critiques of *Imitation of Life*, Black viewers' readings of Fredi Washington did not uniformly hold her up as an idealized Black female. Black moviegoers received both actresses in complex ways, reflecting what Everett has called "the recalcitrant gaze," a perspective "rendered unruly by a historically racialized subjectivity always impossibly multiple, always shapeshifting, and always in constant self-redefinition that is the negotiation of what W. E. B. DuBois calls 'double consciousness.'"[74]

In a fitting example of this "shapeshifting" gaze, shortly after Fay Jackson's article in the *Courier,* another brief article touching on the film appeared in the *Defender*. The piece, "Louise Beavers in Pittsburgh," was penned by William Lee, and covered a promotional appearance that Beavers made at that city's Granada Theater. Lee states that "the show proved to the audience that Louise was not bad looking or dark as the screen shows her to be, but she is light skinned, straight hair, about five and one half feet and well shaped. Miss Beavers speaks very good English."[75] Lee's clumsy attempt to salvage Beavers from the "fat, black, and ugly" camp of African American performers invokes the "lovely race girls" of *The Crisis* and *Opportunity* and reinscribes the political significance of color and appearance for African American women. Lee's reference to Beavers's "very good English" ties together his melding of beauty and light skin with other key elements of New Negro status: standards of education and respectability. His need to physically reimagine Beavers speaks volumes; apparently claims for her good English alone would not have been sufficient to establish her respectability, or to justify his defense of her, because an unreconstructed Beavers did not *look* the part. It is as if Lee attempts to prosaically represent Beavers as an "after" image, from a "before and after"-style advertisement for Palmer's or Nadinola. With her skin lightened, hair straightened, and body "well shaped," she is now a fitting racial ambassador.

Lee's shifting of Beavers's shape also testifies to the way that Beavers's Delilah represented a modest step forward in representation, toward what Donald Bogle has called "the humanization of the Negro servant."[76] At times Beavers's character in the film appears as little more than a stock mammy, reflecting the idiosyncrasies and contradictions so often inherent in racial stereotype. In his scathing 1935 review of the film in *Opportunity* magazine, "Once a Pancake," Sterling Brown remarks upon Delilah's patently illogical and inconsistent behavior, noting that she "is canny about the ways of men and women where Miss Bea is concerned; but when her daughter is yearning for music and parties, she says, 'Come on, honey, I'll dance with you.'"[77]

Yet the Delilah who is a submissive mammy in life, in death arguably manifests elements of a character that could be recognized as a "modern black woman . . . imbued with dignity and character."[78] When Delilah refuses to take even a paltry 20 percent of the pancake fortune that rightly belongs to her, she defers the fortune with the request that Bea set aside the money for her funeral. Ironically, her extensive funeral provides a sense of the life she leads offscreen, beyond the walls of Bea's mansion. Its solemnity and grandeur is a site for the expression of Black self-respect, through uplift-oriented institutions like churches and benevolent clubs and organizations. *Imitation of Life*'s funeral scene would become a source of pride for Black moviegoers who might otherwise have had an easier time identifying with Washington's Peola than Beavers's Delilah. The *Chicago Defender*'s Harry Levette reviewed the film in an article entitled "*Imitation of Life* Is Possible Best Seller." Levette calls the funeral "the picture's greatest sequence . . . . over 500 local citizens were drafted to re-live the roles they enact in everyday life, rather than attempting to train actors to do it." Ultimately the funeral would feature

some seven Negro lodges, including the Knights Templars, Elks, Calanthi-
ans, Daughters of Elks, and Households of Ruth, all dressed in their customary uniforms and presiding with the dignity they usually show at the ceremo-
nies over a late "brother" or "sister." . . . it would have taken more than a
week of rehearsal to have trained them [Hollywood extras] to act with the
dignity and solemnity desired for this impressive scene. The least lack of
tenseness by a member of the marching orders would have brought laughs
instead of sad feelings and turned the whole spectacle into an "Amos and
Andy" burlesque. Instead all over the world will be seen some of the best of
our local citizens, representatives of the business and professional world as
well as the clergy.[79]

Even though there is no sign of the Black community that turns out in
full for Delilah's funeral during the character's life onscreen, viewers
could still point with pride to the "solemnity," "dignity," and *authenticity* of her funeral. Posthumously, she is celebrated and represented in a
style befitting one of the "best of our local citizens." Articles and reviews
of *Imitation of Life* in other African American newspapers, including the
California Eagle, the *Atlanta Daily World,* and the *Los Angeles Sentinel*
all note Delilah's spectacular funeral and the genuine African American
extras appearing in it.[80] The significance of fraternal organizations to the
life of the urban, modern, "new" Negro helps to pull Delilah further
from the legacy of "Amos and Andy burlesque." Ultimately her paltry
20 percent wins her some attention and pride from Black audiences.[81]

Despite her death at the film's end, Delilah is definitely more prominent than Peola, with significantly more screen time.[82] As such, Louise
Beavers became an integral part of Universal's promotion of *Imitation
of Life,* and she toured a number of U.S. cities, making personal appearances at both Black and white movie houses. Her Delilah character is
unquestionably tied to the American myth and icon of mammy/Aunt
Jemima. Obviously, these ties would have been part of her appeal to
white audiences. Yet her reception by Black audiences suggests the way
that Beavers's fame could in fact be mobilized and understood in the
name of race pride and middle-class respectability.

For example, between February 23 and March 14, 1935, the *Baltimore Afro-American* covered Beavers's appearances in New York and
Washington, D.C. Over the course of that time, the newspaper ran some
ten interviews and articles relating to her.[83] Two of the *Afro-American*'s
articles make reference to Beavers's role in having the word "nigger"
stricken from *Imitation of Life*'s script. The first appeared in the February 23, 1935 edition, and referred somewhat obliquely to the film's
intended use of the "n-word":

She revealed that she had flatly refused to deliver certain lines in the original script of *Imitation of Life*. Upon her insistence, the lines were deleted. "I knew I didn't want to say them," she stated, "and I knew that the public would not want to hear them. I have always tried to protect my people and to show directors that they are just as sensitive and particular about their race as whites are about theirs. I wouldn't sell my race for a dollar.[84]

A week later, on March 2, the newspaper published Beavers's interview with freelance journalist Louis Lautier. Beavers explained that Delilah's dialogue in the original script called for her to use the word "nigger" frequently. She told Lautier that she took her concerns to William Hurlbut, a writer at Universal who had adapted the film's screenplay from Fannie Hurst's novel. Apparently Beavers or someone else also alerted the NAACP to the situation, because according to Lautier's article, "the next day after her conversation with Mr. Hulbert [sic], the NAACP sent the studio a letter of protest." In the end, the word "black" was substituted for "nigger" in the script, specifically in a sequence when, in childhood, Jessie insults Peola.[85]

Similar claims for Beavers's advocacy in changing the script can be found in the *Chicago Defender* and the *New York Age*.[86] Yet in letters from the MPAA's Joseph Breen to Universal, Breen is also direct in arguing that the word "nigger" should be stricken from the script.[87] Perhaps the combined objections of Breen, Beavers, and the NAACP convinced those in charge at Universal. Whatever the case, Beavers's emergence as a champion for this particular cause after *Imitation of Life*'s release was important to facilitating a reading of her as a "race woman," who cared what other African Americans thought and felt, and who, in short "wouldn't sell [her] race for a dollar."[88]

The following week found Beavers in Washington, D.C., lecturing to the students of two African American schools as well as being honored at a luncheon given by the Washington Repertory players. To the students of the District's Dunbar High and Francis Junior High, Beavers preached hard work and good grades, while maintaining a distinctly modest and respectable bearing. The *Baltimore Afro-American* article covering the event depicts Beavers "talking informally in a soft, low-pitched mellow voice," delivering "a message of hope and courage in the field of professional dramatics." She cautioned students that "a child could not act in the movies in Hollywood unless his average in his studies was high" and advised children interested in such a career that "there is no better time to start trying than now." The article closes by describing Beavers's attire:

> She was simply dressed in a black dress with a black-and-white collar and cuffs, a small black tam, a Hudson seal coat, trimmed with Fitch collar. She always wears dark clothes, the actress told the AFRO reporter later, because she is sensitive of her size, and believes that she should be inconspicuously dressed.

After her speech, students and teachers alike reportedly "rushed to the platform and requested autographs and handshakes of the star."[89]

Beavers's position as star and respectable role model is further extended by coverage of her lunch with the Washington Repertory Players, D.C.'s local Black theatrical troupe. William Smallwood, one of the repertory's members, wrote up the luncheon for the *Afro-American*; his account does some measured shape-shifting of Beavers from *Imitation*'s Delilah. He writes that upon meeting Beavers, he was "agreeably surprised, as I had pictured Miss Beavers as a much older woman. Instead, she's young, buoyant, and filled with quips and puns." Smallwood enthuses about the actress's visit, describing it as "brilliant hours of intense interest, some eighteen of us listening raptly to her intimate and thoroughly charmingly personable bits of her career." One notable presence among this group was then-Howard professor Ralph Bunche. Smallwood's article indicates that Bunche was an active contributor to the luncheon conversation with Beavers because he "knew Miss Beavers years ago when they were both appearing in church playlets together."[90] In addition to Smallwood's article, the *Afro-American* ran a photo of the festivities, which featured Beavers seated and smiling among some of Washington's "best local citizens."

The letters about *Imitation of Life* to the *Afro-American*'s editor which *preceded* Beavers's appearances in New York and Washington, D.C., were largely critical of *Imitation of Life*. One writer, signing off only as "A Constant Reader," called the film "a most disgraceful screen example," given that it suggested that African Americans' "only visible desire . . . is to reach for, obtain, and hold, all that pertains to being white?" Another writer, Mr. Rothall Gardner of Baltimore, was less specific in naming what he disliked about *Imitation of Life*, but nonetheless blamed the *Afro-American* for recommending the film, and canceled his subscription to the newspaper altogether.[91] By contrast, letters appearing in the "*Afro* Readers Say" section after Beavers's promotional tour more uniformly praised the film, and even singled the actress out for particular kudos. Ms. Dorothy Doleman of White Plains, New York, submitted the following letter, which appeared in the March 16 issue:

To the Editor of the AFRO:

I wish to extend the credit that is due to Louise Beavers. In *Imitation of Life* she shows loyalty and love for her race. If not convincing in the picture, when appearing in person she leaves no doubt in mind or heart as to her sweet, kind, and loving personality. I wish for her continued success and happiness. She is not only helping herself, but earnestly raising the standard of her rapidly rising race.

Similarly, a letter that appeared on March 23 complained about a theater program that made no mention of *Imitation*'s Black "stars." Calling the omission "evidence of real slimy-guttered American race prejudice," the writer, Ms. Marie Alexander (of Washington, D.C.) argues "there is no denying . . . the fact that Miss Louise Beavers plays the stellar role of that production."[92]

Beavers received similar treatment by the *Philadelphia Tribune* during her promotional tour through that city just weeks later. For instance, she appears on the front page of the March 14, 1935 issue of the newspaper, photographed sipping tea with dignified local matrons, sisters-in-law Mrs. S. Willie Layten and Mrs. M. Layten Tillman, who hosted her during her visit to Philadelphia. The *Tribune*'s caption of the photo reads "OUT OF THE FILM 'KITCHEN'—A Gentlewoman."[93] Below the photo, the *Tribune* capitalizes on the sensational to some extent, running an interview with Beavers entitled "The Inside" directly next to an article discussing Sterling Brown's scathing attack on *Imitation of Life* in *Opportunity* magazine. Yet the characterization of Beavers as a "gentlewoman" with "insider" status in Hollywood mirrors the *Afro-American*'s view of the actress as a respectable Black woman who had "made good" in a difficult field. Like the *Afro*, the *Tribune* ran several intimate, complimentary articles about Beavers's visit to the city, including "The A. Drews Entertain for Miss Beavers," "Louise Beavers Gives Exclusive Interview," and "Philadelphia Welcomes Lovely Louise Beavers."[94]

In such publicity Beavers emerges as a star and as a genteel woman of whom other Blacks could be proud. In the film, as half of the double act of Delilah and Peola, Delilah's docility and accommodation clearly serve as a foil for Peola's assertive and discontented disposition. Yet in reception by Black audiences, the double act's dynamics become less straightforward. Just as Beavers/Delilah can be celebrated as the film's symbol of "loyalty and love for her race," Washington/Peola can easily be vilified as a symbol of racial disloyalty and conflict.

TENSION IN THE DISCOURSE

Washington/Peola as Racially Disloyal

The less celebratory aspect of the "Peola discourse" is the way that Washington's light skin also made her vulnerable to negative readings by African American audiences. Chief among these was the charge that Washington, like Peola, wanted to "pass" for white. Washington's star image may well have invoked the progressive and assertive spirit of the New Negro, but the New Negro ideal itself provoked questions of racial loyalty and identity, not only of those fair enough to "pass" for white and slip the bounds of the veil in anonymous northern cities, but also of upwardly mobile African Americans whose lives put the instability and hardship of both northern migration and Jim Crow living into relief. Members of the Black economic and intellectual elite that W. E. B. Du Bois termed the "talented tenth" represented another species of "passing," beside or in addition to the kind based on light skin color, one which entailed exclusivity, "classing off" from the masses of African Americans who were less affluent or educated than they. Both movements were potentially about passing *away from* the broader African American community.

Even before *Imitation of Life*'s release, Fredi Washington's looks, her work as a popular stage dancer, as well as her entertainment work abroad on the legitimate stage and onscreen, associated her with these sorts of passing, as they made her part of a class of African Americans distinguished by celebrity, talent, access, and pigmentocratic privilege. As cultural historian Jayna Brown observes, the bodies of light-skinned African American chorus girls were particularly potent sites for the displacement of a multitude of intraracial class hopes and anxieties. The majority of Washington's opportunities before *Imitation* functioned to establish and reinforce her association with the dancing chorus girl; her stint as a chorine at Club Alabam', her part in the choruses of *Shuffle Along* and *Runnin' Wild*, her dancing in Europe as half of "Moiret et Fredi," her appearance as "Fredi, the dancer" in *Black and Tan*, and her role as Undine, a dime-a-dance speakeasy girl in *The Emperor Jones*, all reference this figure. As part of African Americans' collective cultural iconography of the early twentieth century, "the sleek-haired girls of the chorus lines remained public figures of black mobility . . . . [they] provided the black world with a language of the resilient, mobile modern body constituted betwixt and between nation-states and their colonial outposts."[95] Washington's ability to make good on a Harlem chorus line, better in London, Paris, and on the Broadway stage, and then best in Hollywood films is emblematic of the very geographical and cultural mobility that Brown describes.

Washington may have anticipated the kinds of anxieties her performance as Peola would conjure for African American audiences. In the spring of 1934, only a little over a month before notices began appearing in Black and mainstream press outlets about her casting, she gave an interview to Associated Negro Press (ANP) reporter Fay Jackson in which she blasted whites in the movie industry for their suggestions that she "pass" to get better film roles. Washington asserted that

> managers, producers, and film executives have tried to get me to "pass for white" in order to get the break they claim I deserve . . . . Why should I have to pass for anything . . . but an artist? . . . I don't want to "pass" because I can't stand insincerities and shams. I am just as much Negro as any of the others identified with the race.[96]

The article ran in Black newspapers in mid-April; by the end of May, announcements of her casting in *Imitation* began to appear.[97] The timing of the interview could have been sheer coincidence, or Washington may have been aware that she was being considered for Peola (or even that she had already been cast). It is possible that she was attempting to do some preemptive damage control for her own star persona, to establish her bona fides as a loyal race woman before her association with Peola became the dominant note of her celebrity.

Whatever the case, after *Imitation of Life*'s release, Washington was asked direct questions about whether she herself wished to pass for white far more frequently in her interviews with the Black press. For instance, in early March 1935, the *Pittsburgh Courier* ran an article titled "Fredi Washington Has Problem Not Bared in *Imitation*."[98] The item covered Washington's promotional appearances in African American theaters in Chicago, and noted that often in question-and-answer sessions with audiences after the film, Washington was asked "if in real life, being a light-colored girl she felt as Peola did in the picture." Washington responded that "she did not, but the part was one she was employed to play and she thought she had done that successfully because most people did not like Peola." In one appearance, Washington "related having overheard children in Kansas calling her a 'hussy.'"[99] The reporter declared that the "problem of color for Miss Washington is exactly the opposite of that of Peola. Fredi wishes she were brown," then quoted Washington as saying "Oh, for the color of Nina Mae McKinney," and explained the dilemma that her color poses:

> Miss Washington is a colored girl and must work as a colored actress. But as a matter of fact, she is not colored. Her skin is white. For that reason, she does not fit into many colored productions. She is too colored for white pictures, and too white for colored. Thus her work opportunities depend upon the chance of something like Fanny Hurst's story coming along . . . . her success upon the legitimate stage and her experience would enable her to open doors if she only had the right color. She doesn't want to be white, as Peola did. She would have greater opportunities if she were dark.[100]

"Dark" and "brown" are, of course, relative states of being. That is to say, it is notable that Washington ostensibly yearned for the "brown" color of Nina Mae McKinney (cover girl for *The Crisis* and Palmer's Skin Whitening Ointment) and not the considerably darker brown hue of her *Imitation of Life* costar, Louise Beavers. McKinney's own relative racial indeterminacy made her nearly as likely to be cast in the "tragic mulatto" role as Washington, and in the end, McKinney enjoyed only marginally greater success and visibility in Hollywood films.[101] But the general climate of discrimination and exclusion that African American performers faced in the entertainment industry arguably led to this kind of hair-splitting, even as the opportunities enjoyed by ostensibly "successful" actors and actresses were drastically limited in number and scope.

News media, in the attention they paid to the possibility of Washington's passing, often accepted *Imitation*'s construction of passing as an act that in and of itself bespoke disloyalty to "the race." Of course *Imitation of Life* was only one of numerous contemporaneous texts, both Black- and white-authored, that posited passing in such terms.[102] Jessie Redmond Fauset's *Plum Bun* (1928) and Nella Larsen's *Passing* (1929) also largely characterized passing in terms of betrayal, even as these texts also provided examples of "harmless passing," enacted inadvertently, temporarily, or for convenience (examples that *Imitation of Life* wholly omitted). Fauset and Larsen's doomed heroines possessed "depth and complexity that Peola never attains in either Hurst's novel or John Stahl's film adaptation."[103] Still, this dominant, negative reading of passing undoubtedly influenced Black audiences' reception of Washington when she appeared in person to promote *Imitation*. The January 19, 1935 *Chicago Defender* carried two pieces which spoke to this interpretation. The first, a short item in Clifford MacKay's weekly gossip column, "Going Backstage with the Scribe," announced that

> Fredi Washington, Harlem actress who plays the daughter to Louise Beavers in *Imitation of Life*, wants the news broadcast that she does in no way wish

to deny her race. The little star feels that the part she played in pictures may influence patrons to dislike her whenever she appears in legitimate houses.[104]

The newspaper's facing page carried an interview with Washington under the headline "Part in *Imitation* Is Not Real Me," Says Fredi." To her interviewer, Washington "smilingly disclaims" any interest in passing.

> "I have never tried to pass for white," she says, "and never had any desire to do so. On the stage in New York I have appeared in such colored revues as *Shuffle Along* and *Singing the Blues,* and opposite Paul Robeson in *Black Boy.* On the screen I have been in *Emperor Jones* and other pictures—but always as a colored girl. Perhaps I have been able to show in the new picture how a girl MIGHT feel under the circumstances, but I am not showing how I feel myself."[105]

As news items like these indicate, Washington seems to have concluded that the wisest option was to flatly deny any interest in passing. In the *Pittsburgh Courier* piece, she takes this strategy a step further, holding out Nina Mae McKinney as her "brown" ideal, to counter the notion that her own light skin provided her with any advantage over African Americans of a darker hue.

In the climate directly following *Imitation of Life*'s release, Washington publicly distanced herself from the idea of passing as thoroughly as possible, yet in interviews years later, she acknowledged that she accepted some privileges of passing, though not in the manner of full renunciation of the Black race sought by *Imitation*'s Peola. In a 1945 interview with the *Chicago Defender*'s Earl Conrad, Washington admitted, "I just go in, if it's a [white] hotel, and get a room; or if a [white] restaurant, I eat." When asked if this was not "passing," Washington replied, "Well I suppose you might call it that, but I don't think about it one way or the other. If a place is open to the public that means anyone who can pay the tariff."[106] In the same interview, she disclosed that she sometimes "passed" long enough to make whites who insulted Blacks in her presence aware that she was "Negro" as well.[107] Such admissions would have been more difficult for Washington to justify right after *Imitation*'s release, because the film generally polarized and oversimplified passing, treating the practice only as a complete rejection of African American life, family, and community. As importantly, by 1945, a full decade later, Washington had long given up on pursuing a film career, and had far less to lose with respect to protecting an emerging star persona.[108]

Washington's later comments embody the spirit of a kind of subversive and defiant "passing" that no Hollywood film of the early twentieth century dared portray. The experiences she describes, of surreptitiously eating in segregated white restaurants, or sleeping in hotel beds reserved by law for white bodies, underscore the reason that Hollywood productions that did tackle the topic were always careful to depict such acts as racially duplicitous—because of their potential to be enacted in ways that were at least symbolically destabilizing for whites. What Washington suggests here is that at least one species of passing in Jim Crow America had far less to do with racial disloyalty than with questions of access, equality, and even convenience. Nevertheless, in these later comments, Washington also skirts the uncomfortable issue of her own privilege. She is helped in this by interviewer Earl Conrad, who attempts to ease any tension by trivializing the issue of color, referring to Washington's dilemma as "the whole silly mess," and "these simple color irritations."[109] Yet Washington had the means to evade the degrading system of Jim Crow segregation at will, a privilege that brown-skinned Blacks did not enjoy. Moreover, within African American communities, Washington's looks gave her privilege based on the workings of the pigmentocracy, which linked her skin color with positive associations regarding her pedigree, class status, and femininity. By the same token, her color was of unquestionably little help with respect to giving Washington a long and varied career in motion pictures—so long as she insisted on self-identifying as Black.

Fredi Washington was obliged to tend to the tense nature of some Black audience discourses about her and her character Peola. Her negative reception was one indication that Peola's "New Negro"-inflected protest was not uncomplicatedly read by Black viewers as a plea lodged on behalf of all African Americans. Washington was also somewhat constrained by the way that *Imitation of Life* designated and determined the parameters of the conversation it initiated about passing, wholly emptying it of any political or historical context with respect to American racial discrimination.

"SEE THESE TWO GREAT ACTRESSES!"

Ironically, the seventy-second "special" trailer that features Beavers and Washington as *Imitation*'s putative "stars," made in 1935 for exclusive consumption in segregated Black theaters, is now the trailer that turns up most frequently to represent the film in Internet searches, lending a particularly skewed, presentist idea of its reception and promotion in the 1930s.[110] The special trailer's survival, over and above that of Universal's regular preview film, speaks to the reimagining of *Imitation of Life* over time as a film that was intentional in being primarily about race, gender, and the politics of passing. The trailer opens on a dark screen with stock silhouette drawings of a movie camera and a star; at the center of the screen is a large medal. The words "Special Announcement" appear across the entirety of the screen, followed by the words "See These Two Great Actresses!" An iris opens out of the center of the medallion, revealing Louise Beavers's smiling face; her name appears in large print below the image. Beavers is wearing a straw hat and the dress that she wears in the film when Delilah first meets Bea. Beavers's name and image are followed by Fredi Washington's. Washington's face is neutral, with only the hint of a smile at the corners of her mouth. A bland nonsynchronous musical score, consisting primarily of woodwinds and strings set to a brisk, waltzing tempo, accompanies the entire clip. From a purely contemporary standpoint, the entire trailer is little more than a Powerpoint presentation. There are no moving images, only a series of stills of Beavers and Washington from the film, plus publicity shots, film titles, and accompanying text.

The preview is most attentive to foregrounding the mainstream press's critical response to Beavers and Washington. After these introductory credits, we see an intertitle that boasts tantalizingly "READ . . . what the critics wrote about them!" The next image is a still from the film, a medium shot of Louise Beavers who seems in the midst of conversation. Her mouth is agape, and her expression is one of mild confusion. The odd image is accompanied by a quote from the *Minneapolis Tribune* declaring that "Miss Beavers reveals herself as the finest colored actress in films!" Next, we see Fredi Washington in medium close-up, her upper body in semi-profile, her face turned directly toward the camera. The image is more like one of Washington's professional head shots than a situational image from *Imitation,* with Washington wearing a serious and determined expression. The quote that appears from the *Los Angeles Examiner* reinforces the image's "professional" tone: "Fredi Washington is a splendid young actress!" These first images of the trailer reinforce the "marked" and "unmarked," "mobile" and "immobile," even "before" and "after" dichotomy of the Beavers/Delilah–Washington/Peola dyad. Beavers is frozen in a diegetic world that frames her as mammy; Washington is potentially freer, yet landless and liminal. Whereas Beavers is "the finest *colored* actress in films," Washington is "a splendid young actress," who may never find a place in which to act.

The next image, a publicity shot, frames Louise Beavers and Claudette Colbert next to one another, looking off to the left and smiling. A quote from the *New York Daily News* calling Beavers's performance "perfectly corking!" appears beneath. The quotes continue to alternate between praise for Beavers and Washington, presented over images of them, mostly from the film. From the *Hollywood Reporter,* "Fredi Washington is superb!"; from the *Minneapolis Shopping News,* "Miss Beavers is excellent in the greatest screen role ever played by a colored actress!"; from *Liberty Magazine,* "The outstanding role, played by Fredi Washington, is unforgettable!" Finally, over a now-iconic shot of Delilah pleading with Peola from a scene near the end of *Imitation of Life,* appear the words, "The whole world applauds their supreme artistry *in,*" just before the last title sequence proclaims "*Imitation of Life*—A Universal Picture," credits that then have the words "Coming to this Theatre!" superimposed over them. At this, the light musical theme closes out its waltz with a gentle and dignified finale.

Universal's creation of the special trailer for *Imitation of Life* is arguably little more than an industrial footnote. After all, there is no evidence to indicate that the studio wanted to make more movies that interested Black viewers, though it did want to sell an existing product to any audience who cared to see it. Yet even such perfunctory acknowledgement of Black audiences had the side effect of implying the studio's recognition of Louise Beavers and Fredi Washington, even temporarily, in terms of the discourse of stardom through which so many Black viewers actually engaged them. The language of the trailer scrupulously avoids the word "star," preferring the noun "actress" coupled with respectful, decorous phrases like "perfectly corking," "splendid," and "supreme artistry." Yet it is impossible to miss that Beavers and Washington are being promoted by the studio as key attractions of *Imitation of Life,* especially because this promotional gambit is more borne out in the film than not; their performances, their characters, and their actions are in fact the most interesting part of the movie. And the fact of their pairing in the film—their "perfect double act" recalling once more *Chicago*'s Roxie and Velma, with whom the chapter begins—provides the basis for the trailer to make a greater appeal to race pride among Black audiences than could a Hollywood film featuring only one performer of "the race." This brief agreement between Hollywood's conditional use of them and African American audiences' engagement with them and all they stood for, is rendered particularly powerful in Universal's "special" trailer.

As Delilah and Peola, Louise Beavers and Fredi Washington were subject to varied, interconnected readings by African American audiences. As stars and characters, they embodied key aspects of what it meant to be Black, female, urban, modern, dark- or light-skinned, politically progressive, racially loyal, and respectable in early twentieth-century America. Their performances in *Imitation of Life* invited Black moviegoers to engage with these ideas, using these two women to mediate the discourse. Their show stealing enabled and facilitated this dialogue in unique ways. Though Delilah and Peola made *Imitation of Life* diegetically compelling for most white audiences as well, the culturally specific response of Black audiences pushed the significance of their act of stealing beyond its benefit to the Hollywood studio that produced it.

FOUR

Lincoln Perry's "Problematic Stardom"

Stepin Fetchit Steals the Shoat

Elsewhere in this work I have called "stealing the shoat" the shadow figuration for the potentially affirming notion of stealing the show. In the African American folktale from which the notion of stealing the shoat is drawn, a Black slave confronted with his crime of stealing a young pig, or "shoat," which he has roasted and eaten, defends himself on the basis that he has not stolen his master's property, but only used his discretion to redistribute it. The joke is on the master, with the slave's explanation that he is merely "improving [the owner's] property." But the joke is also on the slave, who by his own admission is still "property." His ruse has not altered the prevailing power dynamic between the master and himself. As a concept based in African American folklore, this idea explicitly races and theoretically complicates the individualist assumption that "stealing the show" is in and of itself a kind of triumph for the screen actor, while at the same time acknowledging that Black performers possessed agency and play in the creation of their filmic personae. Its associations with slavery, with survival, with a certain kind of performance, and with deception and dissemblance suggest the kinds of power relations that African American performers were required to negotiate in 1930s Hollywood. It is therefore a useful way of framing what Arthur Knight terms the "problematic stardom" of Black Hollywood regulars in the 1930s.[1]

In his essay "Star Dances," Knight responds to the pioneering stardom scholarship of Richard Dyer with cogent questions about the place of race in an understanding of the construction of Hollywood stars. Knight also calls up the subject of this chapter, actor and comedian Lincoln "Stepin Fetchit" Perry, naming him as a poster boy for the type of "problematic " African American star that emerged out of Hollywood's experiment with all-Black musicals and musical shorts during the rise of sound film technology in the late 1920 and early 1930s.[2] What is problematic about this kind of Black star for Knight, is that s/he occupies a liminal space of near-stardom. From the perspective of Knight's circular "star dance" construct—in which African American stars move from peripheral celebrity in the midst of Black community/ies, to "cross over" into the center of mainstream stardom, and then to periodically "return" and maintain their connections with Black audiences—1930s stars like Stepin Fetchit were stagnant. "The problem," Knight writes,

> which came to crisis in the mid-1930s and early 1940s around figures like Louise Beavers and Stepin Fetchit and gained focus with Hattie McDaniel's Oscar for *Gone with the Wind,* was this: the Hollywood Black supernumeraries were stable enough onscreen figures that they verged on being minor Hollywood stars—certainly regular, recognizable, credit line-worthy character actors. The Hollywood Blacks, however, were not moving. They were neither true "motion picture stars" nor, more importantly, circulating Black stars who kept in touch with their Black audience through live performance and touring. They had not quite crossed over—passed into white culture—*and* they would not come back, and this made an increasing number of Black viewers feel vulnerable.[3]

This final chapter uses Lincoln Perry/Stepin Fetchit to theorize some of the shape and dynamics of this problematic stardom.[4] Perry's unique Hollywood career as Stepin Fetchit provides a specific opportunity to examine the mechanics of the highly raced and mediated nature of stardom for "Black supernumeraries" like himself. As importantly, the details of his career place him squarely at the intersection between the semiotic/sociological notions of stardom, as articulated by Richard Dyer in *Stars,* and Knight's culturally specific "star dance." These elements coalesce in a unique position for the career, cultural visibility, and ideological meanings of Stepin Fetchit in American culture more broadly.

Much extant popular and scholarly analysis of Lincoln Perry as Stepin Fetchit has either adjudged him guilty of cultural crimes against African Americans, or sought to recuperate and redeem him by emphasizing the trickster aspect of his persona.[5] The second of these two stances is eloquently summed up by Ossie Davis in a 1981 tribute to the actor:

> Consider a slave like old Stepin Fetchit: so dumb that if the master sent him to get a hoe, he would come back with a plow; if he told him to go and kill a chicken, he would go out and kill a cow, or if he said go to the fields and go to work, Old Step would misunderstand and go back to his shack and sit down .... And anyway, nobody ever got lynched when Stepin Fetchit pictures were in town. He made everybody feel so comfortable and so superior that they didn't need to go out and hurt anybody .... our hero: a one-man strike against the system, but they didn't know it. Old Stepin Fetchit—the man who invented the coffee break in the cotton patch.[6]

Davis's rhetoric evokes the mocking tone of the stolen shoat story, yet like many fables that tip their scales in favor of the oppressed, his subversive reading of Stepin Fetchit glosses the specific power dynamics that make the trickster both necessary and appealing. This chapter mines the archival record of Stepin Fetchit's Hollywood trajectory in order to examine his career beyond these two poles, and as exemplary of a kind of limited and closely racially mediated mainstream stardom. I place particular emphasis upon his emergence as a "talkies" star, his promotion by the Fox studio in the mid 1930s, and the proliferation of his image in animated cartoons of the late 1930s. Perry's problematic stardom inheres in the Stepin Fetchit character's evolution as a new and specifically sonic, cinematic stereotype of Blackness, infused with freshness and contemporary appeal because of Perry's own performance and because of the authenticating power of his Black body. However the popularity and visibility of Stepin Fetchit gradually endowed the character with a life of its own, in ways that exceeded Perry's control or influence. Perry's limited and limiting stardom illuminates a flickering between stealing the show and stealing the shoat for Black actors, in that even as his performance of Stepin Fetchit gained visibility and cultural appeal, the type's growing rigidity also made Perry himself redundant; over time he grew less essential to the reproduction of the racial fantasy Stepin Fetchit represented.

STEPIN FETCHIT

"The First Actor Who Has Caused Me to Thank God for the Talkies"

One of the foremost aspects of Stepin Fetchit's stardom was his cinematic emergence in the midst of the advent of synchronized sound-on-film technology, a coincidence that gained him a significant following among white as well as Black audiences. As has been extensively documented by film historians and scholars like Knight (in *Disintegrating the Musical*), as well as Alice Maurice and Ryan Jay Friedman, the coming of sound technology to Hollywood film ushered in an extended industrial interest in "Black sound," and in representations of African American culture as a vehicle for bringing this sonic phenomenon to movies.[7] Every one of the major film studios produced at least one Black-cast film, whether a short or a feature, in an attempt to compensate for the fact that a medium previously driven by action was now being driven by dialogue. Sound's evident deceleration of film plots and narratives was exacerbated by the fact that the filmmaking apparatus also changed in ways that often made motion pictures look less dynamic. With the addition of sound synchronizing equipment, onscreen action typically slowed, and as MGM director King Vidor observed, "the nailed-down tripod of [film's] early days" returned.[8] Using African American actors, themes, and settings was one way in which the industry sought to offset the slowness of the talkies. The commonly held ideas about African Americans and about Black culture—that Blacks were naturally rhythmic, musical, comic, energetic, and *authentic*—made this solution an obvious one that most studios were willing to try. Hollywood's experiment in "colored sound" was also fueled by widespread mythmaking and assumptions about the superior technological fidelity of "Negro voices," what Alice Maurice insightfully describes as a kind of "pseudotechnical wisdom that had begun to creep into discussions of talking pictures."[9] Finally, the coincidence of sound technology's advent with the emergence of the New Negro Movement and the "Jazz Age" meant that there was potential public interest in African American culture to be engaged, especially among northern, urban audiences. *Chicago Tribune* entertainment writer Rosalind Shaffer confirms this connection in her 1928 article "All-Colored Casts Invade Hollywood," asserting that the "popularity of the Negro plays and dancers and musicians that originated in New York some few seasons ago is finding an echo in film production".[10]

Hallelujah and *Hearts in Dixie* are the two major Black-cast musicals of this period, produced by MGM and Fox, respectively. Both center upon rural African American families, and of course, feature copious amounts of Black musical performance, including singing and dance, and both sacred and secular music. I focus here upon *Hearts in Dixie,* which featured Stepin Fetchit in his breakout talkies role as "Gummy." In the film, Gummy is the lazy and shiftless husband of the long-suffering Chloe (Bernice Pilot), and son-in-law to the old and kindly Nappus (Clarence Muse). Gummy and Chloe have two children, Chincapin (Eugene Jackson) and True Love (Richard Brooks). When Chloe and True Love fall ill, Nappus tries to procure a doctor, but others in the community, including the Deacon (Zack Williams) insist that only the Hoodoo Woman (A. C. H. Bilibrew) can effectively treat Black patients, and both mother and daughter die. Gummy quickly moves on after Chloe's death, leaving his surviving son Chincapin in Nappus's care. Gummy woos and weds Violet (Vivian Smith) in short order, and attempts to return to his easy-living ways in spite of her frequent and frustrated demands that he work and help her keep house. Meanwhile, Nappus sells all of his possessions and, as the film concludes, tearfully sends his grandson Chincapin north for an education in medicine, in hopes that the boy will escape the "superstition" that claimed Chloe and True Love's lives.

As the foregoing suggests, "Gummy" is central to the narrative and action of *Hearts in Dixie*. Though his negligence and foolhardiness are generally played for laughs, they nevertheless contribute to the tragedy that propels the film's plot. In this moment when "black became the fad" in moviedom, Stepin Fetchit emerged as the "Black" par excellence of the talkies in mainstream media discourses, with his performance in *Hearts in Dixie* central to this assessment.[11] Indeed, amid an all-Black cast, Stepin Fetchit was often singled out for individual praise in mainstream press reviews, as the best *Hearts* had to offer. For instance, a reviewer writing for the *Baltimore Sun* claimed that "the photoplay has an undercurrent of artificiality," yet was pleased to conclude that "Stepin Fetchit as Gummy, is the notable exception. He is real and is a character long to be remembered as about the laziest Negro one has ever known."[12] In a notable article published in the Urban League's *Opportunity* magazine, *Vanity Fair* and *New Yorker* columnist Robert Benchley wrote, "I see no reason in even hesitating in saying that he is the best actor that the talking movies have produced. His voice, his manner, his timing, everything that he does, is as near to perfection as one could hope to get in an essentially phony medium such as this."[13] In a published interview with Stepin Fetchit for *Motion Picture* magazine, reporter Elizabeth Goldbeck gushed that Fetchit is "the first actor who has caused me to thank God for the talkies," and described him as

> Nothing fancy. Nothing educated or emancipated. He typifies his race. All the traits and talents that legend gives to colored people are embodied in him. He has their joyous, childlike charm, their gaudy tastes, their

superstitions. And as for singing, dancing, and strumming a mean banjo—he does them all. And would probably steal chickens if he hadn't promised the Lord never to do anything illegal again.[14]

Goldbeck's effusive description was prompted by an anecdote that she related of *Hearts in Dixie's* premiere, when, evidently, Stepin Fetchit could not be found in the theater's audience. The next day, when asked by a Fox employee where he had been, he explained, "I was there, suh. I was upstairs in the gallery where I belong."[15] Mainstream reviewers' depictions of Stepin Fetchit as the ultimate, essential representative of Hollywood's "legend" of Blackness underscore the bond between his stardom, his sound, and the way that both were vehicles for American racial commodification. Ultimately, Fetchit's stardom derived primarily from his function as a potential tool and symbol of the kind of racialization that Frantz Fanon describes in *Black Skin, White Masks,* in which Black people become the objectified thing that whites imagine them to be, in order to be seen at all. Fanon writes that his own body was

> given back to me sprawled out, distorted, recolored, clad in mourning . . . . A man was expected to behave like a man. I was expected to behave like a black man—or at least like a nigger. I shouted a greeting to the world and the world slashed away my joy. I was told to stay within bounds, to go back *where I belonged* [emphasis mine].[16]

Stepin Fetchit was often read as the "most genuine" representation of Blackness as crafted by a white supremacist imagination, even as such Blackness was already fetishized as more genuine and authentic in the context of the talkies' emergence. These mainstream reviews also recall Richard Dyer's discussion of "star versus character," in which he argues that stars

> unlike characters in stories . . . are also real people . . . . This means that they serve to disguise the fact that they are just as much produced images, constructed personalities as "characters" are. Thus the value embodied by a star's existence guarantees the existence of the values s/he embodies.[17]

In this same sense, Lincoln Perry's public existence as Stepin Fetchit was aptly described by the *Baltimore Sun* reviewer who explained, "he is [both] *real and a character."* As such, Stepin Fetchit was routinely marshaled to demonstrate that a limited range of stereotypical values and characteristics did indeed "typify his race," as *Motion Picture* reporter Elizabeth Goldbeck declared. By providing a guarantee of such characteristics' circulation in popular culture, Stepin Fetchit was in turn guaranteed an unprecedented level of cultural significance and visibility. Beyond reference to *Hearts in Dixie,* Fetchit was frequently the sole African American performer featured in media discussion and representation of the talkies craze in general. He is the only Black performer featured on *The Voice of Hollywood,* a celebrity newsreel series, which ran from 1929 until 1931, capitalizing entirely upon "the essential novelty of sound," by holding out to the audiences of early talkies, the appeal, promise, and possibility of "sync" between film stars and their voices.[18] This series of theatrical shorts often featured behind-the-scenes footage of celebrities filmed red carpet-style at movie premieres or other social events. Stepin Fetchit was also the only Black performer identified in the industry newspaper *Film Weekly*'s "Who's Who of Talkie Stars," alongside notable white stars like John Barrymore, Gary Cooper, Maurice Chevalier, and Joan Crawford.[19] This critical commentary, promotion, and publicity around Stepin Fetchit in the first half of his film career suggests the ways in which his sonic performance of a particular brand of Black identity bought him a limited kind of mainstream stardom. After all, during Hollywood's "classic" era, "a black performer could never hope to be a Hollywood star without appealing to a vast, white-dominated audience."[20] Perry's consciousness of this dynamic was made manifest by the contours of the Stepin Fetchit character itself, and by his own ideas about how he might best position himself in the movies.

Being a film's "only" African American, or at most one of a very few, was a recurring theme in the shape of Stepin Fetchit's stardom. At the end of 1928, he was criticized in a *Chicago Defender* article titled "Actor Too Proud to Work in Films with Own Race."[21] The article emerged amidst advance publicity about Stepin Fetchit's casting in *Hearts in Dixie.* The unnamed writer of the piece cited industry allegations that "Stepin Fetchit . . . . does not like to be surrounded by black actors," but "prefers to be an actor in a white cast," and also asserted that his "preference" was a source of consternation at Fox, that "this week all was not so well between [William] Fox and his new protégé." According to the *Defender* report, "the trouble began when Fetchit decided that he did not belong in a picture made wholly by members of his Race."[22] Perry's written rebuttal appeared in another African American paper, the *Pittsburgh Courier,* two months later. He defended himself on the grounds that his preference was not a matter of having a penchant for whites, as the *Defender* article implied, but an entirely professional matter. Signing himself "Stepin Fetchit," Perry wrote that the article was defamatory, that it

> makes it appear that I am trying to high-hat my own race, which is untrue. I know my place and that story has made me do a lot of explaining among friends, besides the harm it will do me among people of the race around the country that happen to read it .... I really said ... that I much preferred to work as comedy relief in a company of white people rather than in an all-colored picture, because in the former company I have no competition as to dialect and character, and, therefore, have a much better chance for recognition.[23]

Perry tendered an oblique compliment to African American actors here, suggesting that they were tougher competition than white players. Nevertheless, neither the largely self-interested tone of the response, nor Perry's suggestion that it was among whites that Stepin Fetchit could truly "shine" improved upon the unflattering implications of the original *Defender* article. His unabashed prioritizing of his own "chance for recognition" underscores the way that Perry largely defied and disregarded the implicit ethical and communal notions of the star dance ideal. The "return" from the center of mainstream stardom to the circumference of Black community has as much to do with remaining connected to African American audiences as it does with the possibility of facilitating the rise of new Black stars, an enterprise for which "race" films seemed a likely vehicle.[24] Perry's stated cognizance of the increased visibility and potential value borne by his character in the context of an all-white cast is, on the one hand, a shrewd attempt to make the individualism of mainstream stardom work disproportionately in his favor, given what otherwise would be the handicap of his racial difference. This instance of public self-interest, especially in the context of major studios' seeming interest in Black-cast projects like *Hearts in Dixie* and *Hallelujah,* demonstrates part of what is theoretically problematic about Stepin Fetchit's stardom from the perspective of the star dance. The notions of stealing the show/shoat and of the star dance are in this way fundamentally opposed, given their respective ethical imperatives to the individual versus the community. In the 1930s, Stepin Fetchit was probably the most extreme exemplar of this tension between the two paths available to African Americans in show business.

To appeal to Hollywood's "vast, white-dominated audience," Perry served old wine in new bottles; his minstrel-inflected performance of Black masculinity as bizarre, languorous, and indigent was stylized enough to seem novel and unique. But the character's singularity could be undermined in an all-Black context; Perry shrewdly viewed racial contrast as central to Stepin Fetchit's impact. His cynical perspective rendered any collective of Black performers as an undifferentiated, "colored" mass—"All Coons Look Alike to Me"—to quote Ernest Hogan's popular turn-of-the-century ditty. At the same time, his concern for decreasing his "competition as to dialect and character" anticipated the way that his performance of Stepin Fetchit would be shadowed constantly by imitations. To some extent, these imitations were called forth by the Stepin Fetchit character's roots in the American cultural form known as minstrelsy.

"SOUNDS WHAT YOU CAN'T UNDERSTAN'"
Stepin Fetchit and Audible Pantomime

In the decade and a half preceding the talkies, Lincoln Perry built a career in show business in the humblest of ways. In his teens, Perry left the Florida home where he was raised by Bahamian parents, to go on the road as an entertainer.[25] Perry toured in medicine tent shows, as well as in carnivals that traveled through small-town venues in the South and Midwest. According to biographer Mel Watkins, "by the mid-1920s, Lincoln Perry had moved up the ladder . . . to engagements at larger, urban Theater Owners' Booking Association (TOBA) and black-circuit theaters."[26] He was regularly working as one half of a Black vaudeville duo called "Step 'n' Fetch It," sometimes with a performer named Buck Abel, and in other engagements with Ed Lee.[27] Step 'n' Fetch, like a multitude of other vaudeville comedy duos, was a team whose cachet drew upon the interaction of distinct, mismatched personalities. The act "relied heavily on a variation of the contrasting comic figures—scheming city slicker and slow gullible rube—that prevailed at the time . . . [with the] role of the slick, conniving city boy . . . filled by Perry's various partners."[28] Meanwhile, Perry regularly assumed the role of the "slow gullible rube," adapting that role in ways that would make it unique and memorable. Ultimately Perry took the whole name of the act for himself, affixing it to the Stepin Fetchit persona that he fashioned on stage and later, onscreen.

There is a certain irony in an African American performer who rose to popularity during cinema's sound era ultimately becoming known for a voice that was often wholly unintelligible. The idiosyncratic voice of Stepin Fetchit went beyond a simple "Southern drawl," often taking on a whiny, even sobbing quality; at other times he would murmur in a glum and barely audible tone. He often spoke in rapid, unintelligible mutterings, with unpredictable dips and turns in pitch and cadence. His use of malaprop was simply a further impediment to the listener's comprehension of what he was saying. This was a consistent and well-known element of the Stepin Fetchit persona, reflected in many of the reviews of his films. Bosley Crother complained in the *New York Times* that "Stepin Fetchit . . . is getting as stylized as James Joyce; it is now almost impossible to form any idea of what he is trying to say." And a 1935 profile of Stepin Fetchit for the *New Movie Magazine,* discussed at length below, referenced him as "the actor who makes sounds you can't understand."[29] The irony of this coincidence is only heightened by the mainstream approbation of Stepin Fetchit as the genuine Black article, as "authentically" and "essentially" Black.

Michel Chion writes that "particularly in the cinema, the voice enjoys a certain proximity to the soul, the shadow, the double."[30] Fetchit's garbled sonic representation of the essential "soul" of Blackness potently reinforced notions of African Americans as both senseless and indecipherable. The voice of Stepin Fetchit was also an aural emblem of Constance Rourke's 1931 observation in *American Humor* that to "the primitive comic sense, to be black is to be funny, and many minstrels made the most of this simple circumstance."[31] That is, Stepin Fetchit's voice captured the idea, largely inaugurated by minstrelsy, that being Black is essentially and naturally funny, in that what Fetchit said was far less important than how (Black and funny) he said it. Perry's own self-consciousness about this aspect of the Stepin Fetchit character emerges in a 1929 interview in which he encouraged the reporter to "make it light, make it funny, 'cause that's what folks want from me. A colored man's greatest gift is his humor. When he tries to camoflag [sic] an' be a white man he's no good." Moreover, the reporter himself suggested that this was a moment in which Perry was "shrewd beneath his happy negro humor."[32]

The implications of Stepin Fetchit's unintelligible voice are amplified by Perry's assertion of an original aesthetic philosophy behind this aspect of his performance, and one with specifically cinematic significance. He claimed this philosophy in a number of mainstream media interviews in the 1930s. In his 1935 profile in *New Movie Magazine,* Perry claimed that "in transferring his art from silent pictures to sound he was confronted with the same problem as [Charlie] Chaplin," but proudly declared that he "solved the problem whereas Chaplin couldn't.

Ah solved it like dis. Ah make sounds, but Ah make sounds what you can't understan'. Dat way, see, Ah don't destroy de illusion. Ah calls it audible pantomime."[33] Perry elaborated further on the notion of "audible pantomime" in a 1940 interview with a Philadelphia newspaper, crediting himself with the creation of

> a new art, born with talking pictures. I made my start in Hollywood on the silent screen, when pantomime was all important. When speech came along, film comics were up against a new program—to fit their funny gestures to words, or fit the words to gestures, however you like to look at it. I decided to go ahead pantomiming just as I had always done. I picked out the important words in the lines I had, the ones important for laughs, or that gave cues to other actors; I consciously stress them—the rest of the speech doesn't matter. I mumble through the rest, gestures helping to point the situation.[34]

The startling difference between the ways that Stepin Fetchit's voice is rendered in print here—first in 1935 when he was under contract with Fox, and subsequently in 1940, after he had been fired from the studio—is itself truly revealing.[35] The ample distance that his speech evinces between the theory and practice of "audible pantomime" in the second interview indicates the increased latitude for self-representation that Lincoln Perry enjoyed once he was free from the studio's contractual restrictions. Here as elsewhere, the Lincoln Perry/Stepin Fetchit dyad suggests a near-literal performance of DuBoisian "double consciousness," in its shifting between an autonomous Black self and an objectified product of the white supremacist imagination.

That said, Perry's dubbing of his particular performance style "audible pantomime" is incredibly provocative, in its succinct distillation of the overdetermined cultural relationship between African Americans and notions of physicality and embodiedness. Perry's claim was that in his performance style, he attempted to make *sounds* that sounded like a Black body's gestures (his own). Stepin Fetchit's bodily movements onscreen were certainly distinctive, characterized by a languorous, shambling gait and a sloping pose, sometimes augmented by one arm flung over his head allowing his hand to scratch or tug at the ear on the opposite side. Perry's height and angular figure further emphasized the impact of his bodily performance. In close-up shots in films like *36 Hours to Kill* (1936), he can sometimes be seen executing an analogously exaggerated facial pantomime, raising and lowering his eyebrows in a way that conveys confusion and disorientation. That said, the notion of audible pantomime explicitly depended on the racialized sound-image synchronicity that made African Americans the captivating new test subjects of the talkies boom. As Alice Maurice points out,

> one thing white producers and moviegoers were looking for in these new cinema voices was race. The very term *black voices* would of course make no sense in the absence of race; even if sounds can be said to evoke the visualization of color, the black of *black voices* signifies much more than color. And in the case of *black voices,* the action is reciprocal: color/race promises a particular kind of sound, and that sound, once heard, is supposed to refer back to the color/race that produced it.[36]

Perry's audible pantomime concept was implicitly about the creation of a "black voice" of the sort described here, one that would simultaneously connote a Black body and a Black sound.

In addition, Perry makes apt reference to Charlie Chaplin, a performer well known to have "held out against the talking film longer than most, and who defended the silent cinema as an art of 'pantomime.'"[37] Relevant to both Chaplin and Stepin Fetchit is the way that the *idea* of vocalized gesture also conjures Michel Chion's notion of "the Debureau effect." Named for nineteenth-century pantomime Jean-Gaspard Debureau, the concept refers to the allure created for a silent performer by an audience's curiosity about his or her *voice.* Chion explains that the questions at the heart of the Debureau effect in film are "what precisely do we expect in hearing someone's *voice,* and how can we even imagine for a moment . . . constructing an entire story on a hidden object . . . which cannot even circulate through the narrative, and which once revealed turns out to be no longer desirable?"[38] Chion claims that once revealed, the voice is inevitably disappointing, since it cannot possibly live up to the audience's expectations of it. Their curiosity makes a fetish of the absent voice, charging it with meaning that can be neither met nor matched by the real thing. Arguably, this aspect of the Debureau effect is the conundrum that Perry claims to have resolved, even in the face of Charlie Chaplin's evident failure to do so. When Perry asserts that by making "sounds what you can't understand," he thus manages not to "destroy the illusion," he invokes several elements and intended effects of his vocal performance style: first, his maintaining of the illusion of silence itself, even as he creates a voiced performance in a talking picture; second, his maintaining of the socioculturally acceptable illusion of Black voicelessness, unintelligibility, ignorance, and passivity, even as he as an African American performer appeared on the screen with an opportunity to speak and be heard; and third, his maintaining of the audience's curiosity about his voice by performing and speaking in a way that continued to construct him as having *not yet been fully heard*. These aspects of Stepin Fetchit's cinematic voice—especially the last—were essential to his initial novelty and appeal in film. Through them, Perry attempted to protract the energy and interest of the moment of sound technology's "appearance" in the movies and to emphasize and maintain Stepin Fetchit's association with that powerful moment.

Perry's enigmatic reference to his use of audible pantomime as a means of maintaining "the illusion" also brings to mind Chion's theorizing about the place of mute characters in sound films. He writes that in "the modern cinema they can represent, by a sort of proxy, the memory of a great Lost Secret the silent movies kept."[39] Perry certainly cast Stepin Fetchit in this mold, in his reference to Chaplin and in his characterization of his performance as one rooted in the spirit and style of silent film acting. Stepin Fetchit's ability to "steal" an audience's attention was tied to this tension between silents and talkies, playing upon the audience's curiosity about what he was in fact saying at any given moment.

Besides its connection to an historical pantomime like Debureau and an iconic silent film pantomime like Chaplin, the *pantomime* in "audible pantomime" is also connected to the Black vaudeville and minstrel tradition. At this point in popular cultural history, such a reference inevitably invoked the image of famed Black minstrel performer Bert Williams. Though Williams died in 1922, his poker player pantomime was a signature piece of his stage and screen persona, one undoubtedly well known to Perry, whose father Joseph had been an aspiring minstrel performer of Williams's generation.[40] Stepin Fetchit would often be compared to Bert Williams in the 1930s; references to him as "the Bert Williams of the screen" could be found in both African American and mainstream newspapers.[41] Given Bert Williams's widespread fame and credibility, it is not difficult to imagine the savvy, self-promoting Perry capitalizing on this ostensible lineage, in an attempt to bolster his own legitimacy. By the same token, given Perry's roots in the medicine show and minstrel troupe idiom, it is no surprise that Stepin Fetchit would bear traces of Williams's imprint, though any public comparison between the two was made to the consternation of some of Fetchit's African American critics.[42]

Stylistically, there is some overlap in their performances; both men included broad slapstick elements of bodily gesture to attract and entertain their audiences. In a scene from the 1916 silent film *A Natural Born Gambler*, Williams bolts from a graveyard in terror, having seen two

29. Stepin Fetchit, in his signature slumping pose, with Will Rogers in a promotional image for *The County Chairman* (1935). Image courtesy of Photofest Digital.

"devils" who are scheming to capture his soul.[43] He employs various kinds of bodily slapstick as he flees. For instance, at the gate of the cemetery, we are treated to a shot of Williams futilely running in place, producing the impression that he is building up speed in order to sprint away. Towards the end of the sequence, there is a long shot of him running on the sides of his feet/shoes in a performance of exhaustion. This is the kind of pantomime that audiences frequently saw from Stepin Fetchit (albeit radically slowed down)—moving his body in ways that were comic in and of themselves, that were about the humor of the physicality itself, he invited viewers to laugh at his bodily awkwardness, gyrations, oddity of movements, and so on. The bodily posture that might well be called Stepin Fetchit's signature pose, in which he stood or walked in a deep slump, sometimes with one arm slung over his head, is a strong example of the kind of humorous pantomime that both Williams and Stepin Fetchit employed (figure 29). Such pantomime made the body into a comic object, though its humor also rested on broad, received notions about Black inferiority.

Yet Williams's pantomime routinely went further, with gestures and expressions that communicated more nuanced specifics of his character's

30. Bert Williams's facially expressive pantomiming from the silent film *A Natural Born Gambler* (1916). Copyright 1916, Biograph Company.

personality and a variety of emotions. Returning to *A Natural Born Gambler,* we find strong examples of this tendency. Williams's character is portrayed as something of a miser, and when he is called up to pay his back dues at a meeting of his fraternal organization, he slowly counts out the money, and drags out the process of paying it to the club's treasurer, his eyes fluttering, his hands shaking as he counts and recounts his last three dollars and painstakingly hands each bill over, one at a time. Later in the film, Williams's character is brought before a judge, having been arrested for gambling. The judge tells Williams's defense lawyer that "the spoils of the game belong to you as lawyer's fee," and Williams's face registers his disgust with a series of puffings, blowings, eye-rollings, and grimacings (figure 30). Finally, the film closes upon Williams rendering his famed solo poker player pantomime, in which he conveys scheming, hope, frustration, and finally resignation. The daggers that he looks at one imaginary player who apparently has the better hand, contrast with his futile examining and reexamining of his own poor cards.

The level of complexity that Williams exhibits through pantomime in *A Natural Born Gambler* makes Stepin Fetchit's perennial lazybones performance appear as a relative one-trick pony. Clearly, the two men had different kinds of onscreen performance, due in large part to Williams's emergence during the silent era and Stepin Fetchit's emergence as a colored darling of sound technology. How Williams might have "solved" the problem of the transition from silent film to sound is a matter of speculation, given the man's death nearly a decade before the advent of film-sound technology. In the end, Perry's theory and practice of audible pantomime can be read in part as an announcement of the comedian's sense of his own descent from Williams's tradition.

Perry's allusion to audible pantomime ties his vocal stylings to another element of his Black vaudeville and minstrel roots. The actual unintelligibility of Stepin Fetchit's speech, the way that it hides meaning (or the potential for it) from the audience by design, suggests its connection to the African American minstrel performance form known as "indefinite talk."[44] Also known as "incomplete sentence," indefinite talk was a traditional comedy act in African American minstrel performances that some cultural historians have referenced as akin to a "Black version" of the Abbott and Costello routine "Who's On First?" In routines using indefinite talk, two performers carry on a lively, chatty, and familiar discussion about past experiences, mutual friends, enemies, family members, and the like, while continually interrupting one another's sentences with knowing interjections about the people, places, and things being referenced. Mantan Moreland and Ben Carter, veterans of the Black vaudeville stage, performed versions of this routine in a number of the "Charlie Chan" franchise films in the 1940s.[45] Moreland appeared regularly in these films as Chan's chauffeur, "Birmingham Brown." Carter essentially appeared as himself opposite Moreland, turning up onscreen specifically for moments of indefinite talk. For instance, in *The Scarlet Clue* (1945), Moreland and Carter encounter one another as old friends, and begin to reminisce, talking indefinitely:

MM: Oh I haven't seen you in a long time! It's been . . .

BC: Longer than that! The last time I saw you, you was living—

MM: Oh, I moved from there.

BC: Yeah?

MM: Sure! I moved over to, uh—

BC: How can you live in that neighborhood?

MM: I don't know.

BC: Now where I'm living, I only pay—

MM: It ain't that cheap, is it?

BC: Sure it is.

MM: Look here, is you still married to—

BC: No, I divorced her.

MM: Yeah? (Laughs) I know you have a lots of—

BC: You got me wrong, you got me wrong—I got married again! . . . Say, not changin' the subject, but have you got any, uh—

MM: Naw, I don't smoke. Say, looky here, wasn't you in the—

BC: Yeah, but I got an honorable discharge.

MM: You did? . . . What was the matter?

BC: Well I developed a kind of—

MM: Oh, that's a terrible pain! [Gestures to his abdomen.] It starts right along—

BC: No, more in the back.[46]

Moreland and Carter continue for a full minute and a half before concluding in cheerful agreement and bid one another farewell. Meanwhile, Tommy Chan (Benson Fong) looks on in confusion and ultimately in impatient exasperation with their exchange. As Arthur Knight observes, "what most makes indefinite talk unique (and funny) is that the indefinite talkers always understand one another. While the audience struggles to figure out what the indefinite talkers are (not) talking about, the indefinite talkers themselves never require clarification and continue as if their conversation were ordinary and comprehensible."[47] Indeed, the audience position in the performance of indefinite talk in *The Scarlet Clue* is represented by Charlie Chan's "Number Three Son" Tommy Chan, whose utterly confused reactions model and reflect the audience's perplexity.[48]

Stepin Fetchit's was a different but no less literal species of "indefinite talk," in which the mystery and obscurity of the content was also the source of the performance's humor and interest. The convention typically demanded that indefinite talkers be duos (at least), to facilitate the comic device of interruption that created the conversation's "indefinite" aspect. As noted above, "Step and Fetchit" began as a vaudeville duo, a stage act in which Perry perfected the slow drag patter that would become his stock-in-trade. Yet in so doing, Perry also created a new kind of "indefinite talk" that he would ultimately customize to the contours of his solo act. Where the pair form of indefinite talk created an inherent sense of community and intimacy between the talkers, implicitly suggesting such intimacy between African Americans more generally, Perry's version emphasized his formal mastery alone, making his indecipherable monologue into a fetish for the audience. In the pair form, indefinite talk routines frequently concluded with one of the speakers happily declaring that "that's why you and me get along—'cause we 'most naturally agree on things!" Yet when Perry collapsed "Step and Fetchit" the duo into the single persona Stepin Fetchit, he evinced his own interest in moving away from the kind of community that the Black vaudeville stage, and even Black-cast movies potentially represented at this moment of popular cultural history. Even as Perry's "indefinite talk" linked him to the forms of Black vaudeville and Black blackface minstrelsy, it also implied the departure from those forms that his career would symbolize, in its aspiration to something more like the supreme individuality of conventional stardom.

The hybrid genealogy of audible pantomime placed Stepin Fetchit squarely at the intersection between essential and evolving American popular cultural genres. His performance planted one foot in Hollywood film at its moment of technological transition, and therefore in the rift between the silents and the talkies, and the other in the blackface minstrel tradition inaugurated by whites but adopted and thoroughly adapted by Blacks like Bert Williams and George Walker, Salem Tutt Whitney and J. Homer Tutt, Billy Kersands, and Perry's own father, Joseph.[49] The persona that emerged with Stepin Fetchit was as informed by one as the other.

The wild card of the equation was Lincoln Perry himself, whose assertive, mercurial, and highly visible self-destructive tendencies made working with him a tricky proposition. Perry signed two long-term option contracts at Fox. His first tenure with the studio lasted from the summer of 1928 until December 1929, when the studio terminated his contract. However, he was re-signed in 1933 and worked for Fox until 1937, when he was dropped for the second and last time. In both instances, his firings were ostensibly attributed to Perry's unpredictability on the set, in addition to his high-profile, high-living antics off it. His excessive drinking, driving accidents, disputes with other Black performers, and criminal and civil lawsuits made welcome fodder for mainstream and African American newspapers, and ultimately became part of the way that the Fox studio decided to market him when they hired him for the second and last time in 1933.[50]

SELLING "PRODIGAL PERRY"
Stepin Fetchit and the Fox Publicity Reports

Although he had brief contractual affiliations with other Hollywood studios, including Columbia and "Our Gang's" Hal Roach Studios, over the course of his career, Lincoln Perry's connection with Fox would be the most consistent and significant. It was at Fox that Stepin Fetchit would appear as Gummy in *Hearts in Dixie,* and in a series of movies that paired him with the incredibly popular American humorist and actor Will Rogers. Perry's affiliation with Fox also occasioned some of the most sustained studio-authored promotion that any African American performer of this era would receive, through the publicity reports authored for Stepin Fetchit in the mid-1930s.[51]

These publicity reports can be found in the Stepin Fetchit biographical file at the Academy of Motion Picture Arts and Sciences Margaret Herrick Library. Various studio publicity writers were responsible for writing them, including Fox's director of publicity, Harry Brand, as well as Robert Burkhardt, Joe Cunningham, and Lincoln Quarberg. The reports span the whole of Perry's second period of employment at the studio, and were widely disseminated in industry magazines, the mainstream media, and the African American press.

As a whole, the Fox publicity reports are surprisingly absent from discussions in the extant scholarship on Stepin Fetchit. Yet they are central to an evaluation that considers the possibility and limits of Stepin Fetchit as a star. Numerous works, including Richard Dyer's *Stars* and others, have assessed the historical influence of studio-authored publicity materials upon the phenomenon of stardom.[52] From an industrial perspective, publicity reports like these were part and parcel of a studio's promotion and investment. As such, they signaled the economic return studios generally expected from their stars. In the 1930s, such reports were rarely penned by major Hollywood studios for African American actors, especially if the reports were not being created to publicize a specific film appearance. Socially and culturally, stars were (and are) constructed in important ways by the promotional materials provided by studios. And studio promotion is engaged importantly and sometimes unpredictably by audiences, the moviegoers who determine stars not only as a "phenomenon of production," but as a "phenomenon of consumption."[53] For a Black actor like Perry, these reports were incredibly valuable opportunities to be part of the buzz of the motion picture industry. They increased his visibility as Stepin Fetchit, supplementing the minor roles routinely allotted to him in the 1930s. They could signify or induce greater public interest in his offscreen lifestyle, and essentially help to make him a star.

Given the significance of Stepin Fetchit's voice, it is no surprise that publicity writers regularly incorporated ostensible quotations by Fetchit into their reports, with his voice consistently rendered in dialect speech. Clearly, the studio sought to reinforce and reproduce his raced comic characterization in their promotions. Perry himself engineered this strategy in some part, telling a newspaper reporter in one interview, "If you put anything I say in the papah . . . it might be wise to kind of transpose it into my dialeck," though this was likely done in agreement with the studio's dictates.[54] All the same, the consistent use of dialect speech in these publicity reports, even after the fad of "Black sound" had faded in Hollywood, reinforces the potency of Stepin Fetchit's particular conjoining of sight and sound, and reaffirms the voice of Stepin Fetchit as a crucial part of the character's mainstream appeal. Fully aware of the distinct appeal of this aspect of his performance, Fox studio's writers very naturally attempted to capture or evoke something of the unique quality of Stepin Fetchit's voice.

Perry's emerging career in film in the late 1920s was marked by a series of high-profile scandals that found the actor involved in brawls, love triangles, lawsuits, and car accidents, all within a general climate of "high living" that also included tales of multiple chauffeured Cadillacs, liveried household servants, wild parties, and swell's clothing. Perry's offscreen antics combined with a variety of conflicts with Fox managers and executives in this early period to bring about a premature end to his contract.[55] Some scholars have argued that Perry's "bad boy" actions offscreen constituted his own species of resistance against the unequal treatment he received as an African American actor. For this chapter's purposes, of considering the shape and meaning of Perry's stardom, of equal or greater interest is the way that the studio's publicity department actively chose to narrativize this aspect of his history when Fox signed him for the second time in 1933. Publicity writers offered up Stepin Fetchit's "high-colored" past in a series of morality tales that I call the "Prodigal Perry discourse."[56] Reports employing this discourse presented the (formerly) wayward Stepin Fetchit for scrutiny and touted the "newly reformed" actor, with the implication that his reform was in large part the studio's doing. For instance, a 1934 biography written by Robert Burkhardt opens this way:

> Things looked very dark for Stepin Fetchit a few years ago when, after setting a new altitude record in going Hollywood, he awakened with a hangover one morning to find himself a penniless ex-star.

Now the colored comedian is staging a comeback and has reformed so completely that erstwhile fair-weather pals rather scornfully refer to him as "the black angel of Central Avenue."

But Step doesn't mind their jeers.

"Pitchers is de parlor end of de show business, and Ah craves to remain in de parlor," he says, giving *gin* parlors a wide berth.[57]

Here and in other "Prodigal Perry" stories, the designation "star" is applied only to Stepin Fetchit as he was in the past, and even then, only in reference to the time in which he was between signings with Fox and financially strapped, or an "ex-star." In the present tense, the biographies and reports call him a comedian, "featured player," or "character." This approach recalls Richard Dyer's discussion of failed performers whose stories are used as examples of "the [American] dream soured," though given Dyer's description, we would not expect this particular characterization to be used about someone who had just signed a new long-term contract with a major studio. The report is only one useful example of the ways in which, as an exceptionally popular Black performer, Stepin Fetchit occupied a kind of stardom that required mediating and bracketing; studio publicity like this did the work of announcing his renewed affiliation with Fox while at the same time containing his potential "stardom" in ways made necessary by his race, and conveniently facilitated by the "bad boy" behavior that had contributed to the termination of his first Fox contract. Stepin Fetchit paradoxically embodied aspects of the "classic" stardom articulated by Dyer, in that his personal (though very public) situation individualized and depoliticized his fall, making it unnecessary for viewers/readers to conceive of it as meaningful in ways informed by institutional and cultural forces. Instead, it could be understood solely as a mess of Fetchit's own making, caused by his individual choices and character.

Appropriately then, the Prodigal Perry stories carried the tinge of a particular Depression-era psychology that was both fascinated with and terrified of "coming down in the world," the overriding "fascination with success and failure that ran deep in the culture of the thirties" and manifests itself in gangster films like *Little Caesar, The Public Enemy,* and *Scarface,* as well as in backstage musicals like *Gold Diggers of 1933* and *42nd Street.*[58] Fox's tale of Stepin Fetchit as a rising star who had fallen, only to rise again ostensibly wiser for the experience, provided its audiences with the vicarious thrill of seeing someone else's failure, along with the edifying "lessons" of their experiences. The stories also implicitly capitalized upon the expectation that Fetchit would "fall" again. Aspects of Fox's stories written to sell Stepin Fetchit also moved from scoffing and mockery at his expense towards more pronounced notes of hostility against him. For instance, the imagined violence in a series of reports that jokingly referred to "the Hollywood ax" falling on Stepin Fetchit's "black and unsuspecting neck" suggest the need to manage the blatant contradiction of Fox selling its assumed white audiences a spectacularly lazy Depression-era Black man who made his living from, as one report put it, "the power in the art of doin' nuthin'."[59] Drawing upon the repressed and denied specter of lynching as an imagined punishment for Stepin Fetchit's (stolen) stardom was one way to do this. Such moments of antagonism in the reports highlight the tension that Perry's body conjured, given his perceived real-life wealth and fame in conjunction with his onscreen persona as a stereotypically lazy Black man. The paradox recalls a useful passage from Dyer's essay on Paul Robeson, in which he asserts that

> through slavery and imperialism, black people have been the social group most clearly identified by and exploited for their bodily labour. Blacks thus became the most vivid reminders of the human body as labour in a society busily denying it. Representations of blacks then function as the site of *remembering and denying* the inescapability of the body in the economy.[60]

Perry's Black body, already loaded by the historical and cultural associations that Dyer explicates above, took on far greater complexities of signification as issues of labor and work became paramount during the Depression. Fox's double-edged treatment of Stepin Fetchit in the publicity reports are a manifest example of active and motivated "*remembering and denying* the inescapability of the body in the economy." The reports alternately and/or simultaneously suppress the reality of Perry's own labor as a working actor on the Fox lot, spectacularize his ease in the supposed "parlor end" of show business, and represent punitive measures that had been or could be taken against him in the event of his failure to enact his "art of doin' nuthin'" to the studio's specifications.

Another important story element of the Prodigal Perry discourse is the claim made in several of the write-ups that Perry's new contract had essentially been designed to protect him from himself. Some stories asserted that the studio took the sensible step of establishing a trust fund to curb the notoriously out-of-control spending that had characterized the actor's earlier period of employment at Fox. One such report states that "as a guarantee that the dark-skinned funster doesn't relapse into his old ways . . . Fox Film Studio, which has him under contract, is putting most of his weekly salary in a trust fund for him."[61] Yet in consulting Fox's record of contracts and other legal dealings with Lincoln Perry, it becomes clear that no such fund ever existed. Actually, Perry declared bankruptcy in the amount of thirty-five thousand dollars in 1933 when he re-signed with Fox, and by the summer of 1934, a little less than one year into his new contract, documents in the company's records attest to the fact that Perry was already over eleven thousand dollars in debt to the Fox studio itself, for expenses paid on his behalf for an extensive variety and number of charges. Far from establishing a "trust fund," Fox was obliged to craft a complicated arrangement with Perry over the course of 1934 to repay his debts to the studio through garnishment of the wages that they paid him.[62] This fabrication provides a sense of the license that Fox's publicists took, license that was clearly not limited to a problematic African American star like Stepin Fetchit. As industry historians like Ronald Davis have noted, publicists from all of the major studios loved "puffery."[63] Over the course of Perry's term of contract, the stories they wrote about Stepin Fetchit became more and more fantastically racist, in ways that Perry himself was sometimes complicit with.[64] Yet ultimately these publicity reports were a significant public aspect of the Fetchit character that Perry had less and less control over. The next and final section of this chapter explores the consequences of the Stepin Fetchit character's growing popularity and concomitant potential for disconnection from the irascible Perry.

In Stepin Fetchit's onscreen life and persona, the "Fox trust fund" story finds its cinematic correlate in his cinematic relationship with Will Rogers, in a series of films in which Rogers exercises a paternalistic caretaking role for Stepin Fetchit's hapless and sometimes reckless characters. In all of their films together in 1934 and 1935—*The County Chairman* (dir. John Blystone), *David Harum* (dir. James Cruze), *Steamboat Round the Bend,* and especially *Judge Priest* (both directed by John Ford)—Stepin Fetchit's characters are would-be idlers who find themselves placed in white "protective custody," in the charge of Rogers's folksy, benevolent protagonists.[65] An ideal foil to Rogers's wildly popular everyman star persona, Stepin Fetchit's limited, problematic stardom is at its most coherent in its function as a coexpression of Rogers's idealized and sentimental portrayal of white American masculinity. For instance, in *Judge Priest,* we meet Stepin Fetchit's character Jeff Poindexter in the film's opening scene, at the same time that we are introduced to Rogers's eponymous character. In this scene, Jeff Poindexter is on trial for (what else?) stealing chickens. Jeff sleeps as the

31. Judge Priest (Will Rogers) and Jeff Poindexter (Stepin Fetchit) amble off fishing in a scene from *Judge Priest* (1934). Copyright 1934, Fox Film Corporation.

prosecutor outlines the case against him, while Priest, "presiding" at the bench, reads the funny pages. When it comes time for Priest to render an opinion, he orders the bailiff to wake Jeff up, remarking that "if anybody's gonna sleep in this court it'll be me."[66]

A number of the characters introduced in this opening scene are foils of one kind or another to Priest's unpretentious kindness and humanity, most notably the haughty Senator Horace Maydew (Berton Churchill), a prosecuting attorney who is after Priest's job. Yet the film is at pains to quickly establish the kinship between Priest and Jeff Poindexter in particular. In a written prologue to *Judge Priest* that appears just after the opening credits, Priest is described as "typical of the tolerance of that day and the wisdom of that almost vanished generation."[67] An unequivocal signifier of Priest's tolerance and wisdom is his immediate connection with Jeff. Peter Stowell calls Jeff and the judge "kindred spirits" in his analysis of *Judge Priest*.[68] Indeed, the courtroom scene closes with a long two-shot of Judge Priest and Jeff ambling off to go fishing together, chatting amiably (figure 31). Priest never even bothers to find Jeff innocent or guilty of the charges brought against him, although Jeff essentially spends the balance of the film in the judge's informal guardianship. Will Rogers's performance of Judge Priest, with his engaging, sensible, good-humored, and sentimental nature, provides the human, filmic analogue for the kindly beneficence with which Fox was ostensibly treating the wayward Stepin Fetchit, putting the "trust" in "trust fund," so to speak.

One particularly insightful reviewer from the *New York Sun* observed that "Will Rogers ... has a curious national quality. He gives the impression somehow that this country is filled with such sages, wise with years, young in humor and in love of life, shrewd yet gentle. He is what Americans think other Americans are like."[69] Of course, the relationships between Rogers's beneficent, paternalistic characters and Fetchit's subservient, shiftless characters demonstrated that what white Americans thought Rogers's characters were like in these idyllic films had something to do with what *white* Americans thought *Black* Americans "were like." Together, Stepin Fetchit and Will Rogers plainly effected what the late James Snead called "mythification," and Richard Dyer calls a "displacement of values." Namely, their relationship's cultural work obtained in concealing the contradictions and problems of American ideology around race, class, gender, and region. In *Judge Priest* alone, their relationship hid and/or suppressed the predatory southern legal system that worked hand in hand with southern industry to reenslave "indigent" African American men like Jeff Poindexter, for instance, as well as the everyday reality of the Ku Klux Klan and white-on-Black terrorism as staples of southern life in the turn-of-the-century South that the film sentimentalizes.[70] As Rogers's regular ideological costar, Stepin Fetchit steals the show and the shoat, making an unprecedented cinematic space for himself, gaining significant visibility for the character, and yet finding both circumscribed by their enrichment of the financial and ideological property of the Fox Studio as well as the American screen legends of Will Rogers and John Ford. The symbiosis between Judge Priest and Jeff Poindexter (who even share initials) reinforces the way that Fox's selling of Stepin Fetchit was one and the same with the studio's selling of itself.

Fox's publicity reports had an extremely significant effect upon the public perception and reception of Stepin Fetchit during the 1930s, with the Prodigal Perry discourse central to the way he was represented in the media. Both the Black and mainstream press picked up the reports, and circulated stories of Fetchit's reform and Fox's fiscally responsible, paternal relationship with the actor. Perry biographer Mel Watkins notes that during this period, "Stories hinting at [Perry's] 'childish' extravagance and the need for a paternalistic studio overseer abounded."[71] He cites a March 1934 *New York Post* article that repeated the prodigal line as well as the substance of Fox's trumped-up "trust fund" story. The *Post* reporter praised the new-and-improved performer who "drives his own flivver, lives in a modest home, is saving his money, or, rather, the studio is saving it for him."[72] The idea surfaced even earlier than this in a short October 1933 piece from Grace Kingsley's column "Hobnobbing in Hollywood" in the *Los Angeles Times*. In the column, which appeared directly after Fox had re-signed Perry, Kingsley noted that "a little bird whispers something to me . . . . [that] Fox persuaded him to sign an agreement that he would allow a manager to look out for him and his affairs, including his financial doings, to be appointed by the Fox Film Corporation."[73] With mainstream newspapers from both coasts reporting that Fox was assisting Perry in managing his money, Stepin Fetchit's return to movies was framed as proceeding from a sober, careful, and all but philanthropic action on the part of the studio. And the timing of Fox's public self-characterization as responsible fiscal and fiduciary corporate citizen on Stepin Fetchit's behalf (and at Lincoln Perry's expense), coincided with film industry executives' grander moves of self-preservation, executed in tandem with the discursive sacrificing of their stars. Tino Balio writes that as the brass of Hollywood's major studios collaborated on the governmentally mandated Code of Fair Competition in late 1933, these same "moguls took temporary cuts in pay, so that during the turbulence of preparing the Code, they capitalized on the situation by blaming stars for the financial difficulties of their businesses."[74] Balio notes that "in the minds of the public, Hollywood's chief industrial imbalance was . . . the overpayment of executives and talent." Deflecting their own culpability by pointing to their conspicuously consumptive "talent" as the public scapegoats, studio executives crafted a Code that succeeded in creating "government sanction for the trade practices that they'd spent ten years developing through informal collusion and that enabled them to make the highest possible profits. In short, the Code legalized the monopolistic structure of the industry."[75] As an African American performer, Perry's level of consumption and salary paled in comparison to that of white stars of the era. Fox's contract star Will Rogers's hefty annual income of $324,314 in 1934 easily dwarfed Perry's wages at their highest.[76] Nevertheless, Perry's flamboyant lifestyle in the late 1920s provided a convenient assist to the perception engineering that major studios like Fox were performing during the Depression.

For instance, a 1933 piece entitled "Fetchit Returns" in the *New York Times* propagated the narrative of Stepin Fetchit's extravagant past, elaborating upon Fox's publicity reports and capitalizing upon the image of excessiveness that they chronicled:

> Some say success went to his head. In any case he did accept his fame in a gaudy African style which makes the antics of Brutus Jones pale into reticence by comparison . . . . Stepin had thirty-six suits and so many shirts that his neighbors just stepped in and borrowed one whenever they felt like it. Once he held a seventy-five dollar telephone conversation with his mother in the East trying to come to a decision on the purchase of a thirty-six dollar dress by his sister.[77]

Around the same time, the *Washington Post* published a longer piece about Fetchit that likewise advanced the themes of the discourse. The article, "Stepin Fetchet [*sic*] Reinstated by Former Bosses," announced the "new chapter" being written for Fetchit, "that languorous Senegambian who surely must have been the living model for 'Lazy Bones,' the anthem of the lethargic." The reporter gleefully declaimed:

> From all report [sic] it is a subdued and chastened Stepin Fetchit who has returned to the Fox Movietone Studio, a son of midnight whose badge of humility is a broken down automobile he wouldn't have permitted his valet to drive in the days of his fleeting greatness . . . . At one time he owned four automobiles of the biggest and costliest models and had a different chauffeur in a different uniform for each car. The uniforms were a cross between those worn by a Swiss admiral and the Emperor Jones . . . . The kid was strutting his stuff in the grand, or Octavus Roy Cohen, manner![78]

This copy marshals potent, popular, white-authored icons of Black pathology for the *Post*'s readership. The reporter invokes both Eugene O'Neill's eponymous brutish, arrogant, and dangerous buck, the Emperor Jones (who himself is brought low and destroyed by his own crazed imagination by the play and film's end), and white author Octavus Roy Cohen, whose minstrel-inflected stories appeared regularly in the *Saturday Evening Post*. Foolishly arrogant Black characters who gave themselves airs, attempting to live beyond their limited means, were staples of Cohen's writing.[79] The "subdued and chastened" Stepin Fetchit who is this piece's subject could easily be a punchline from one of Cohen's stories; his past fame is rehearsed only to put his current situation into relief and perspective.

Watkins rightly notes that "in some mainstream press stories the overzealous crowing at the actor's return to the fold had as much to do with seeing an uppity Negro put back in his place as with true concern

Marcel DUCHAMP

Marcel Duchamp has not yet painted enough pictures and his work is too varied for us to assess his true talent from the available evidence. For Marcel Duchamp, as for most of the new painters, appearances are no longer sacred. (It seems that Gauguin was the first to abandon what was for so long the painters' religion.)

In his early days, Marcel Duchamp was influenced by Braque (the pictures he exhibited in 1911 at the Salon d'automne and the rue Tronchet gallery) and by Delaunay's *Tower* (*Sad Young Man in a Train*).

*
* *

In order to preserve his art from any perceptions which could become abstract ideas, Duchamp writes the title he has chosen onto the picture itself. In this way literature, which so few painters have been able to dispense with, disappears from his art —

but not poetry. He then uses forms and colours not to capture appearances, but to penetrate the very nature of these forms and formal colours, which cause such despair in painters that they would like to dispense with them and indeed try to do so whenever possible.

Marcel Duchamp creates a contrast between the actual composition of his paintings and their highly intellectual titles. He takes this technique as far as possible, unconcerned that he might be criticised for painting esoteric or frankly abstruse works.

*
* *

All men, all beings with whom we have passing contact have left traces in our memory, and these traces of life have a reality whose details can be examined and copied. Together, these traces thus acquire personalities with individual characteristics that can be captured in art through a purely intellectual process.

*
* *

Such traces are to be found in Marcel Duchamp's paintings.

Allow me to make an important observation here. Duchamp is the only painter of the modern school who today (autumn 1912) shows any interest in the nude (*The King and the Queen Surrounded by Swift Nudes; The King and the Queen Crossed by Swift Nudes; Nude Descending a Staircase*).

over his well-being or success."[80] But interestingly, these narratives were not confined to the mainstream press. The African American press also reported on Stepin Fetchit's return to Hollywood films, rehearsing some of the same ideas about his past excess and newfound stability, in similar language. An exemplary *Chicago Defender* article included a slightly grammatically improved version of a Fox publicity report in which the comedian declared the movies his preferred way of making a living. Fetchit is quoted as saying, "I'm a new boy . . . . [the] motion picture business is the parlor end of the show business and I'm gonna stay."[81] African American newspapers carried stories that repeated the "prodigal" line, derided Stepin Fetchit for his initially foolhardy and impulsive behavior, and made much of his ostensible "transformation" upon his return to filmmaking.[82] Yet in the Black press, these accounts often carried contextualization wholly absent in the mainstream press. Harry Levette, a Black syndicated entertainment columnist whose writing appeared in many African American newspapers, wrote an article for the *Philadelphia Tribune* that clearly articulates this position. Levette opined that

> Step has learned a lot of lessons since being out [of work] . . . small vaudeville engagements, barnstorming in the South and odd-jobbing around did not nearly measure up to that old hot $1500 a week he used to get. Although we're friends Step used to feel mistreated when this writer condemned his misbehavior back in 1928 and made "hot copy" of his frequent escapades.

Levette concluded by arguing that Stepin Fetchit's "return will help Negro screen players no little for you can look for a cycle of pictures using numbers of Negroes as before if his first to be started on his arrival, October 11, makes good."[83] Levette literally refers to Fetchit as Fox's "prodigal" in this piece, appraising the potential benefit of his return for other African American performers in terms that invoke the communal circle, center, and circumference structure of the star dance. Levette is unapologetic about exposing and critiquing Fetchit's past actions, implying that he will continue to hold the comedian to a "professional" standard of conduct in the present as well. His claiming of Perry as his friend, in spite of such criticisms, likewise places the actor within a community ethic, implying that Levette holds him accountable in the name of their shared communal and cultural ties, rather than to make him an easy object of ridicule. This assertion of friendship likely stemmed from Perry's brief tenure as an entertainment columnist for the

Chicago Defender between 1927 and 1929. Levette, a seasoned journalist, had long covered the entertainment beat for a variety of newspapers, including the *Defender*. His "Coast Codgings" and "Gossip of the
Movie Lots" columns had appeared in various newspapers since the
1920s, so it is likely that the West Coast-based Levette encountered
Perry through one or another intersections of show business and jour-
nalism. Levette's article adds a racially specific dimensionality and complexity to the mockery of Fox's Prodigal Perry stories, demonstrating
that this discourse took on a distinctive flavor and meaning in an African American cultural context.

The *Baltimore Afro-American* newspaper appears to have had its
own ideological and editorial axe to grind when it came to Stepin Fetchit,
and did a fair amount of "crowing" at the performer's expense.[84] The
Afro-American was the only major African American newspaper to
republish one of the more scathing articles from the white press about
Stepin Fetchit's return to Fox. Appearing in the February 3, 1934 *Afro-
American* largely unchanged, and without equivocation, as "Can Lazy
Bones Stepin Fetchit Come Back?" the article was a reprinting of the
Washington Post report from December 1933 that commented upon the
"subdued and chastened" Stepin Fetchit's return, and that mocked his
previous high living in the "grand, or Octavus Roy Cohen, manner."[85]
African American newspapers routinely used news services that provided
clippings or reports, or "borrowed" articles in part or whole to fill out
column inches. Yet the pointedness of this reprinted article's gibe at
Stepin Fetchit was made more explicit by a later piece by columnist Louis
Lautier, ironically entitled "Stepin Fetchit Reforms." Lautier opened
with language from the same 1933 *Washington Post* article, which
pointed out that after his first big break, Fetchit "'went Hollywood' so
wide, high and handsome that thumbs were turned down on him."[86]
Lautier also lifted parts of the *Post* article that specifically mocked Fetchit's love of automobiles and gaudily dressed chauffeurs, whose uniforms
in this case became "a cross between those worn by a Bolivian admiral
and Emperor Jones."[87] But in the second half of the piece, Lautier
revealed the sarcasm intended by his assertion of the actor's "reform."
Lautier recounted Stepin Fetchit's embarrassing appearance at a New
York City NAACP benefit, at which he evinced anything but a reformed
state of mind. Only four months after his re-signing with Fox and his
putative redemption, at the benefit a drunken Stepin Fetchit, Lautier
reported, proceeded to make a nuisance of himself, refusing to leave the
stage even when it was time for other entertainers to go on:

He went on plastered . . . did his number, then had Bill (Bojangles) Robinson, the ace tap dancer, to bring him a chair. Stepin sat down . . . . Other actors came on and tried to lead Stepin off the stage, but he would not go. Finally, Lucky Millinder, leader of the Mills Blue Rhythm Band came on, introduced another act—and then said: "All of us are here in this benefit, and even the queen of the stage, Ethel Waters, has come her to do what she can and does not try to hog the show." Stepin went to the front of the stage and asked who wanted to hear him say something about Greta Garbo. Some drunks in a box said they would. The rest of the audience hissed. "You don't want to hear me," said Stepin. "I didn't come here to put on a show: I came here to have a good time. He then laid down on the stage and said: "This is something you have never seen before: you have never seen an international actor go to sleep before."[88]

Lautier's stinging, sardonic critique of Stepin Fetchit was designed to undermine the narrative of his reform advanced through the Prodigal Perry discourse. The specificity of the critique's recourse to in-group notions of responsibility and African American self-help is subtly sounded by Lautier's implicit praise of other Black performers at the event, especially his reference to "Bill (Bojangles) Robinson, the ace tap dancer." Robinson's personal philosophy of hard work, reputation as a self-made man, and philanthropic giving in Black communities, would have been well known among the *Afro-American*'s readership, and clashed with the image of a drunken Stepin Fetchit egotistically hogging the stage. The implicit and negative comparison that Lautier raises between Robinson and Fetchit only underscores the article's discrediting of Stepin Fetchit as less than a model, less than a "credit" to the race.[89]

Ironically, as a Black newspaper like the *Afro-American* used the NAACP benefit to hold Perry accountable to other African Americans, and even to refute the meaning of the Prodigal Perry discourse for its readership, Fox issued a pair of publicity reports referencing his participation in this same event. These reports touted Stepin Fetchit's contemporaneous appearance in the Shirley Temple vehicle *Stand Up and Cheer* (1934), but tellingly made no mention of his actual performance in the benefit, nor of his drunkenness or objectionable behavior. Instead, Fox's writers simply portrayed Stepin Fetchit as an overdressed Negro clown who attended the event despite his bone-jangling fear of flying in an airplane from Los Angeles to New York. Among other things, the first report claimed that Stepin Fetchit had grown religious by dint of his fear of flying and that his "parish priest reported that Stepin got him out of bed at 5:30 A.M., to say a special mass for him, and insisted that the padre accompany him to the airport." The writer of the second report claimed that his character's gaudy costume from *Stand Up and Cheer,* which Stepin Fetchit wore to the event, had been copied as high style by the Black folk of Harlem, such that at the benefit, "Step counted 15 other coats exactly like his."[90] This latter quotation makes explicit the way that Fox's mockery of Stepin Fetchit by its very nature also implicated other African Americans as garish buffoons like those he represented in film. Such a notion is diametrically opposed by the kind of critique that the *Afro-American* advances, which singles Fetchit out as an object lesson to be avoided at all costs.

Fox's Prodigal Perry rhetoric in the 1930s resonated for Black audiences because of the way that Stepin Fetchit's image potentially rebounded upon African Americans as a collectivity. Given his speedy rise to fame in Hollywood films, the actor "was considered a role model of sorts for black success in motion pictures."[91] As such, many African American newspapers adapted Fox's Prodigal Perry stories, using Fox's rhetoric from the perspective of racial "insiders" with an intimate understanding of the actor's potential harm or benefit to the mainstream perception of African Americans and to Black individual and collective aspirations.

At least superficially, Lincoln Perry's second period of employment with Fox came to an end for many of the same reasons that doomed his first contract there in the late 1920s. A few short years of "good behavior" and a low profile were eventually succeeded by new, embarrassing lawsuits, semi-public rivalries with other Black performers, and erratic and vexatious behavior on the set.[92] Perry's artistic temperament helped to undermine major studios' interest in him, but the Stepin Fetchit persona was already so popular and firmly entrenched with the American viewing public that many studios resorted to casting actors who could provide some Stepin Fetchit *flavor* without the bother occasioned by Stepin Fetchit himself. The concluding section of this chapter examines the implications of Stepin Fetchit's onscreen imitators, both the human pretenders to his throne, and the animated shadows that impersonated him within the filmic realm that Donald Crafton has dubbed the Tooniverse.[93]

THE ART OF DOIN' NOTHIN' IN THE AGE OF MECHANICAL REPRODUCTION

Various scholars have observed the way that Perry's "stylized coon" performance, which relied so heavily upon the fact and fantasy of racial difference, was readily and promptly imitated by other 1930s Black

32. Willie Best (right) simulates Stepin Fetchit's signature pose in a scene from the 1935 film *The Littlest Rebel*, with Bill "Bojangles" Robinson and Shirley Temple. Copyright 1935, Fox Film Corporation.

movie actors. These performers recognized both the cultural appetite for the Stepin Fetchit character and Perry's unprecedented success in selling it to studios and audiences. Donald Bogle devotes a whole section of his popular survey history, *Toms, Coons, Mulattoes, Mammies, and Bucks,* to the actors he calls "Step's Step-Chillun."[94] Likewise, Yuval Taylor and Jake Austen observe that in the 1930s Stepin Fetchit "instantly became the new prototype . . . for modern audiences. [Other] black actors . . . had lengthy careers doing xerographic impersonations of Perry's heavy-lidded, molasses-witted rube in hundreds of film and television appearances from the 1930s through the 1960s."[95] The imitators were especially successful when it became common knowledge that Perry was "difficult" to work with. Both during the hiatus of 1930 (Fox terminated Perry's first contract at the end of 1929) until 1933, when Perry had no major studio contract, and in the mid- to late 1930s, when he had again begun to alienate Fox studio executives and appeared in fewer and fewer films, there were various would-be Stepin Fetchit-types who turned up to borrow the character's hapless, lazy demeanor and occasionally, to literally take Perry's place in a film. Among the clearest pretenders to the Stepin Fetchit throne were Willie "Sleep 'n' Eat" Best (figure 32), Nick "Nick O'Demus" Stewart (figure 33), and

33. Stepin Fetchit pretender Nick "O Demus" Stewart as "Lightnin'" in a scene from the *Amos 'n' Andy* television show, circa 1951. Copyright 1951, CBS Television Network.

apparently, one African American actor who styled himself "Stompen 'n' Sellit."[96]

For instance, although Stepin Fetchit was the first Black manservant to appear in one of Fox's "Charlie Chan" movies (*Charlie Chan in Egypt,* 1936), he was succeeded the next year, in *Charlie Chan at the Race Track,* by a little-known actor named John Henry Allen. Allen played a familiarly slothful and indigent Black stableboy appropriately named "Streamline" Jones. In an obvious allusion to Stepin Fetchit's appearances in movies like *Judge Priest,* when Streamline first appears onscreen he is inappropriately asleep—on the job in the rear of the stables he is supposed to be tending.[97]

Another imitator, Willie Best, was called upon to replace Stepin Fetchit in the 1935 Shirley Temple vehicle *The Littlest Rebel,* primarily because of Perry's poor management of the "tension and rivalry" between himself and the film's other featured African American player, Bill Robinson.[98] Best's performance as "James Henry," a slow, feckless slave, was only the most thinly veiled replication of the Stepin Fetchit style. Perry resented Fox's substitution of Best for him in this film for the rest of his life, contemptuously characterizing Best as his "understudy" in interviews in the 1960s and 1970s.[99] Best not only stole blatantly from the Stepin Fetchit character for his performance style onscreen, but also used the professional name "Sleep 'n' Eat," appropriating the pattern and rhythm of Perry's once unique sobriquet. A reporter writing for the African American newspaper *The Philadelphia Tribune* asserted that Best was often referred to as "Little Stepin Fetchit."[100] Mel Watkins describes Best quite aptly, noting that "with his lean, gangling, underfed appearance, from a distance he was a dead ringer for Fetchit. Moreover, he frequently appeared confused and drowsy, displaying a languor that bordered on the comatose. It was unvarnished mimicry, a near mirror image of the character that Fetchit had brought to the screen."[101]

Despite the obvious poaching by Allen, Best, and others, it is worth noting that these were Stepin Fetchit–"type" performances in a broad, yet immediately recognizable kind of way. The pretenders are lethargic, they fall asleep, they complain about work, they move with a sluggish gait and a weary, slack-jawed expression. Laziness is the key idea for their performances to communicate, given Stepin Fetchit's frequent billing as "the laziest man in the world." But for all of this, they also tend to *speak* relatively intelligibly, rarely even attempting to bring off Perry's trademark audible pantomime. This is a provocative and tellingly consistent alteration; instead of making unintelligible sounds to approximate the objectified Black body (as Perry claimed to), his imitators made sounds that could be understood, but which approximated the specific stereotyped meanings that accumulated around the Stepin Fetchit character. The aspects of the Stepin Fetchit performance that such actors stressed evoked the elements of the character that were most important to the audience that consumed his image. This process calls to mind Perry's own description of the audible pantomime technique, in which he emphasized the most important words and mumbled the rest. What is more, the flattening and distillation of the Stepin Fetchit character through such imitations and the proliferation of these imitative performances recalls Walter Benjamin's assertion that "the technique of reproduction detaches the reproduced object from the domain of tradition. By making many reproductions it substitutes a plurality of copies for a unique existence."[102]

Successful imitators made Perry's presence less and less relevant, even as they transformed the Stepin Fetchit character, paring it down to its bare bones. To be sure, Perry's act functioned in the same way in a larger cultural and historical sense, given that its performance of Black laziness and refusal was, in the context of slavery from whence it arguably sprang, a kind of resistance that contravened the peculiar institution's theft of Black bodies and labor. Yet Perry's "restored behavior" was wholly detached from this tradition and ultimately served the status quo far more effectively than it defied it.[103]

Some thirty years after his Hollywood heyday, Stepin Fetchit was excoriated for his perceived cultural crimes against African American identity in a 1968 television documentary made for CBS called *Black History: Lost, Stolen or Strayed*. Even before the documentary aired, Lincoln Perry found himself the object of criticism, especially from young African Americans taking part in the burgeoning Civil Rights Movement. He responded by publicly defending himself and his legacy. In a 1961 interview he opined that "I guess my worst enemies have been the imitators of my movie character . . . . I changed and they didn't, but they're still judging me on the carbon copies."[104] Some of the truth in Perry's assertion is evident in the CBS documentary, given that Stepin Fetchit is the sole Black actor singled out for attack by name, though Best, Stewart, Mantan Moreland, and others are all prominently featured in the vintage film clips illustrating the history of Hollywood's demeaning images of African Americans. Some images of Moreland and Best even accompany the narration pillorying Fetchit. Perry was one of the few visible performers of the 1930s to survive into the 1960s and 1970s. And for many among the Civil Rights and Black Power generations of African Americans, he became the shameful part of Black Hollywood cinema history that stood for the inglorious whole. And indeed, this synecdochal relationship ironically also acknowledges Perry's role as the original screen coon, the aesthetic father of the "step-chillun" who followed him and contributed to the dissipation of the Stepin Fetchit character's aura.

Perhaps the most literal and abject example of the life that Stepin Fetchit led beyond the reach of his creator is the way in which the character was widely represented in animated cartoons. These appearances are important both as a marker of the level of stardom and "household name" recognition that Stepin Fetchit had achieved, as well as a signifier of the limits of that stardom. Stepin Fetchit was unquestionably one of the African American performers most frequently represented in animation from the 1930s until the 1950s.[105] Lincoln Perry's vaudeville roots provide a provocative tie to animation, given that "cartoons became a symbolic repository of past culture and the accrued knowledge of vaudeville. Especially when cartoon acting was primarily in the figurative mode, up until the mid-1930s, the approach resembled and extended vaudeville's performativity."[106] The vaudevillesque performative style of Lincoln Perry as Stepin Fetchit is consanguineous with what Donald Crafton calls the "figurative" mode of cartoon performance, an extroverted mode in which "characters behave as recognizable types, marshaling a small range of instantly identifiable facial and body expressions."[107] It is no surprise that the Fetchit character would be taken up with such enthusiasm by animators whose primary point of cultural reference for the world they sought to create was the vaudeville stage.

Stepin Fetchit-type figures began appearing in animated cartoons as early as 1935, and continued to appear in some wise as late as 1950, though after this point, the more distinct and literal iterations of the character were far less common.[108] These figures appear in three main contexts:

(1) Stepin Fetchit or a Stepin Fetchit-"type" character puts in a random appearance among other (known or unknown) characters from the cartoon world.

(2) A Stepin Fetchit figure appears as part of an ensemble of other animated characters who represent other African American performers.

(3) A Stepin Fetchit character appears alongside animated versions of other white Hollywood stars.

In any and all of these contexts, the Stepin Fetchit character may be rendered as a human or humanoid form, or as an animal version of the character, like a frog or a bird. Many other African American performers were also depicted in cartoons during this time, with Fats Waller, Louis Armstrong, and Cab Calloway as particular favorites. Yet Fetchit's equally, if not more, frequent appearances precisely reinforce Arthur Knight's assertion about the gradual ossification of African American movie roles over the course of the 1930s.[109] The Stepin Fetchit character in so many of these cartoons even assumes the exact slumping, arm-slung-over-head pose, in a powerful visual testament to this idea. At the same time, the varied use to which Stepin Fetchit's likeness was put in cartoons is revealing in terms of the extent to which the character permeated popular culture both in and of itself and as an emblem of African American identity.

In the early twentieth century, motion picture exhibitors generally preferred to book cartoons that featured popular characters or caricatures of well-known stars. As one of the era's best known and most

34. An animated replica of Stepin Fetchit from the Silly Symphony cartoon *Mother Goose Goes Hollywood* (1938). Copyright 1938, Walt Disney Productions.

widely recognized comic Black figures, Stepin Fetchit was a valuable animated commodity.[110] The character was rendered most faithfully when appearing alongside those of other, white stars. Cartoons like *Hollywood Picnic* (1937), *Mother Goose Goes Hollywood* (1938), and *The Autograph Hound* (1939) featured a distinctly recognizable, non-anthropomorphic Stepin Fetchit character (figures 34 and 35). Like the other stars featured in such cartoons, Stepin Fetchit usually appears briefly and says or does something in his trademark style. But Stepin Fetchit's Blackness still routinely overdetermines the way that he is depicted in ways that are not necessarily consistent with the Stepin Fetchit character, but are decidedly consistent with other stereotypes of Black people.

The 1935 Walt Disney animated cartoon *Broken Toys* helps to illustrate the ways in which the Stepin Fetchit character occupied a cultural position located somewhere between a particular and problematic stardom and the proliferation of "Stepin Fetchit" as a new racial stereotype. The cartoon takes place in a dump, where a motley collection of broken dolls, led by a plucky little sailor boy figurine, decide to fix themselves

35. An animated version of Stepin Fetchit from the Disney cartoon *The Autograph Hound* (1939). Copyright 1939, Walt Disney Productions.

up, and especially to help a blonde, curly-haired girl doll to find a needed new pair of eyes. In terms of identifiable figures, there are dolls who represent a handful of Hollywood stars: a grumpy Ned Sparks jack-in-the-box, a worried, red-headed Zasu Pitts rag doll, and a crotchety W. C. Fields roly-poly toy.[111] The Stepin Fetchit character in this film is a worn-out marionette slumped down inside a battered bowler hat, who explains lethargically that "I just needs to fix my feet," just before flopping back down in a jumble of exhausted limbs. Right after this introduction to the Stepin Fetchit doll, we are shown a Black mammy rag doll who rejoins "—and I just need a brand new seat," pointing emphatically to her tattered rear end. The mammy ragdoll carries none of the specificity of the white star toys, or even of the Stepin Fetchit puppet. Nor can she be identified with any one African American actor who serially played mammy figures, like Louise Beavers or Hattie McDaniel. Instead she is reminiscent of racial novelties and knickknacks, the housewares, games, toys, and decorative items that constituted the material culture of the American Jim Crow era.[112] Beavers and McDaniel stepped into a well-worn stereotype of Black female maternalism, girth, jollity, asexuality, and nurturance that absorbed them and their individuality almost immediately, making them, like the dolls, mere variations on the theme of mammy.

As his visual juxtaposition in this cartoon between the white "star" toys and the generic Black mammy doll suggests, part of the very utility of the Stepin Fetchit figure in cartoons is that the image was both recognizable as a specific and marketable Hollywood star, and at the same time, instantly communicated "ethnic notions" of Black male indigence and sloth.[113] As Christopher Lehman observes in his history *The Colored Cartoon*, the Stepin Fetchit character was "ripe for caricature—as himself or as the personification of the generic black male 'Jim Crow.'"[114] While stars in general are carriers of ideology cloaked within a humanized and individual persona, Stepin Fetchit would evolve into a figure which functioned much more like the mammy, a figure in which the equilibrium between ideology and persona was profoundly slanted toward the former. The copious imitations and reproductions of the character became variations on the Stepin Fetchit theme. They reinforced the character's ideological function and further marginalized Lincoln Perry's individuality and personhood. They also marked the border of Stepin Fetchit's problematic star persona; the limits placed upon his stardom corresponded directly to the limits of the white imagination in its conception of what it meant to be Black. *Broken Toys'* Stepin Fetchit character is therefore caught betwixt and between very different kinds of visibility and cultural signification. One could group him with the kind of distinctive and recognizable (though decidedly B-grade) Hollywood star represented by the Sparks, Pitts, and Fields dolls, or instead pair him with the nondescript mammy doll as a ubiquitous, popular, and even beloved African American racial stereotype.

Here I am reminded of Donald Crafton's assertion that in the fantastical zone of performance he terms the Tooniverse, the animated residents appropriate stardom in ways that go far beyond imitation. Crafton writes that

> although drag acts and race masquerades were commonplace in vaudeville, cartoons trump the stage because the characters are not simply imitating others .... Instead, toons perform a figuration, extracting the celebrities' looks, idiosyncrasies, ethnicity, sex, charisma, and personhood—in short, their stardom.[115]

This point is illustrated and elaborated by the way that cartoon figurations of Stepin Fetchit appropriated his stardom by reperforming his specific star persona as a sluggish, carping lazybones, as well as various of the concatenation of other stereotypical notions of Blackness that his character summoned and interpolated. The literal animation of the Stepin Fetchit figure had an ideologically and psychologically animating effect upon the white American spectator (not to mention the cartoonists who shaped this figure), in the sense of Roland Barthes's theorizing of the "it animates me and I animate it" dynamic between seer and seen.[116] The genealogy of diverse racial stereotypes that the figure invoked reinforces this reciprocal process, suggesting that his image merely whetted the cultural appetite for more performances of racial otherness.

The Columbia cartoon *Hollywood Picnic* provides another excellent example of these dynamics. *Hollywood Picnic* is a "star cavalcade" cartoon typical of the 1930s. It consists of a series of short vignettes featuring Hollywood stars like Katharine Hepburn, Laurel and Hardy, Mae West, Cary Grant, George Raft, Joe E. Brown, Marlene Dietrich, and Martha Raye. During the picnic's baseball game, Stepin Fetchit is shown lurching slowly around the bases, complaining loudly about exerting himself. When the call of "Come and get it!" for lunch is sounded off-screen, he breaks character for an awesome show of speed, legs pinwheeling him across the park. At the table, he tears into an enormous slice of watermelon, spitting out the seeds through puckered lips, like a rapid-fire machine gun.[117] Once he has finished eating, his face resumes its typical dumbfounded, dolorous look. These performances manifest the concept that Crafton calls *re-performance,* the ways in which cartoon performances transform and translate one kind of performance into another. But they also evoke the way that cartoons of this era relished what David Graver calls the "group representative" performance, indicated by the each actor's external characteristics such as skin color, sex, posture, accent, dialect and so on. Graver notes that "the interior of this body is an amalgam of ideological stereotypes and group narratives that establish the historical and social identity of the group, defining what values, talents, and behavior it has demonstrated and is capable of or expected to perpetuate."[118]

The intersection of these two notions, re-performance and group representative performance, in the animated Stepin Fetchit emerges from the way that the character routinely reperforms not only the well-known verbal and gestural spiel that Lincoln Perry popularized, but also any of a variety of the "ideological stereotypes and group narratives" relevant to Blacks more broadly (greed, speed, devouring watermelons, etc.). It recalls Homi Bhabha's assertion that "as a form of splitting and multiple belief, the 'stereotype' requires, for its successful signification, a continual and repetitive chain of other stereotypes."[119]

The cartoon appearances bring us full circle to Perry's splash as a talkies star, when the voice of Stepin Fetchit was what "real" Blackness sounded like. Animation provided the opportunity for audiences to consume physically exaggerated images that better matched that ostensibly racially authentic sound's fantastical quality. Lincoln Perry purposely distorted the sounds he made to extend and enhance Stepin Fetchit's mystique as a "talkies" star. Cartoon versions of Stepin Fetchit depended upon that trademark sound to organize a variety of animated forms— toys, animals, humans—around a rubric that initially associated them with a specific star, and gradually dissipated that star's specificity into the generality of African American stereotype. So while appearances like the ones I've described in *Broken Toys* and *Hollywood Picnic* were extended and relatively specific, the figure's appearances in films like *Porky the Fireman* (1938) or *The Goose Goes South* (1941) used the Stepin Fetchit figure far more briefly, as example of a Black "type" who bore either aural or visual resemblance to the character as a whole. In *Porky the Fireman*, we observe a white character falling from the burning building at the center of the cartoon's action. As he falls, clutching a suitcase, he excitedly shouts, "Help! Help! Catch me! Get the net ready!" He falls into a large cloud of smoke; when he emerges on the other side, his skin and hair blackened by the ash, he is falling much more slowly. He is also sitting back in repose on top of the suitcase, arms behind his head, eyes closed, carelessly drawling, "Catch me . . . I sho hope y'all catch me . . . " Transformations like this one, featuring characters who become blackened by smoke, fire, explosions, mud, ink, et cetera, and then take on stereotypically "Black" characteristics, were extremely common in cartoons from the 1930s through the 1950s. In 1940s and 1950s cartoons especially, Stepin Fetchit's set of aural and physical characteristics became one of a set of possible choices for this routine gag, gesturing both toward Stepin Fetchit's early, particular popularity as a classic cartoon figure, and toward the blackface traditions of the vaudeville and minstrel stages, in which audiences were treated to the spectacle of the blackface figure as well as the spectacle and fantasy of racial transfiguration itself, through staged glimpses of white performers blacking up, or via traditional minstrel publicity portraiture that posed white performers as mirror opposites to their "blackened" alternate visages.

Perhaps the cartoon is the most suggestive emblem of the kind of problematic stardom that Lincoln Perry inhabited as Stepin Fetchit. The role that Perry created became part of a vocabulary that outlived and outlasted him, and the different, evolving registers of borrowing and appropriation of his stardom-through-cartoons demonstrate how his limited stardom became the vehicle for a kind of politically and ideologically charged performative style.

A VULNERABLE AND TEMPORARY ARMISTICE

Losing control of Stepin Fetchit was undoubtedly a bitter pill for the ambitious Lincoln Perry to swallow. Having moved through gimcrack medicine shows and the vaudeville stage, finally making it to the putative "parlor end" of show business in the movies, and even benefitting from film's transition to sound technology, Perry clearly thought of Stepin Fetchit as "a thing I had built my own," a well-timed, well-deployed invention that he could manage as he saw fit.[120] More than once he talked publicly about the aspirational intentions he harbored for the character, that he hoped to gradually change Stepin Fetchit over time, making him less stereotypical and more fully dimensional.[121] In the fateful 1935 *New Movie Magazine* interview, Herbert Howe mentioned Perry's plans, noting that "he intended to become intelligible little by little until, I gathered, he would be enunciating with the clarity of Mr. George Arliss."[122] Arliss, a high-toned, monocled, British actor, was the star of the 1929 historical biopic *Disraeli*. His continental sound and sophisticated cultural signification could not have been more different from Stepin Fetchit. Howe's wisecrack attested to the absurdity of Perry's ambition, given how little the "vast white-dominated audience" of the 1930s cared to apprehend the cultural and ideological space that existed between Lincoln Perry the man and Stepin Fetchit the phantasm.[123]

Lincoln Perry's career as Stepin Fetchit is perhaps the most lucid example of the way that race limited the opportunities for Black performers to occupy a conventional Hollywood model of stardom in the early twentieth century, and to some extent, in the contemporary moment as well. Even as he excelled at the performance of the African American persona that the U.S. popular cultural moment demanded, and theorized a Black sound that comingled the rapidly disappearing arts of silent film and the vaudeville stage, Lincoln Perry would remain trapped by the long shadow and the lingering echoes of Stepin Fetchit.

The cleverness of stealing the shoat notwithstanding, within the context of continued slavery the joke ultimately ends with only a pyrrhic victory for the slave. The same can be said for Lincoln Perry's show/shoat stealing in the thirties. Perry's creation Stepin Fetchit lifted his individual star, brought him some wealth, some celebrity, some cachet with major Hollywood studios and some of the fascination of American moviegoers. And yet to extend the antebellum metaphor of the stolen shoat, Stepin Fetchit's stardom is likewise illuminated by Audre Lorde's damning declaration that the master's tools will never dismantle the master's house. The use of these tools guarantees that "only the most narrow perimeters of change are possible and allowable."[124] Using the tools at hand in the ways that he did, especially in eschewing collaboration with other Blacks while at the same time imagining his own role in African American advancement as essential and central, Perry's stardom effected what Lorde called "only the most vulnerable and temporary armistice between [himself and his] oppression."[125]

Ultimately, the many acts of imitation that recurred throughout Perry's career function as an important symbol of the way that the history and dynamics of American blackface minstrelsy fundamentally undermined Black actors' relationship to stardom. Scholars like Eric Lott, Jason Richards, and David Roediger have all argued that whites' historical performances of blackface minstrelsy had a deeply ambivalent cultural function, articulating "a simultaneous drawing up and crossing of racial boundaries."[126] In this sense, the imitation effected by white blackface minstrelsy offers a distinctly complicated version of Homi Bhabha's notion of colonial mimicry as a subversive act against the colonizer.[127] Nevertheless, Lincoln Perry's use of a minstrel aesthetic of Blackness in his production of Stepin Fetchit carried the potential for—even the *necessity* of—imitation within it from its beginning. His celebrity and appeal rested in part upon his negotiation of the tension between imitation and authenticity inherent in the spectacle of minstrelsy; as Perry reproduced broad, well-known, minstrelized versions of Black identity, he was immediately hailed in mainstream discourse as a highly authentic representation of "real" Blackness. Yet the varied ways in which he was imitated throughout his career—print reproductions of his speech, publicity reports which recreated his antics, live performers and animated figures who borrowed his mannerisms—all bespoke the American cultural habituation toward play with such Black "authenticity" that the minstrel show had made a national tradition. Before the pretenders to his throne proliferated onscreen, Will Rogers performed a Stepin Fetchit impersonation as a plot point of *Judge Priest,* mimicking "Jeff Poindexter's" voice in order to trick and manipulate another character. As imitators stripped away aspects of the Stepin Fetchit persona that were innovated by Perry, eroding Perry's individualized association with the character, they reinforced the centrality of the blackface minstrel persona, which was ubiquitous, unspecific, universally known, unchanging, and widely accessible, with none of the specificity or individuality inherent in the concept of the movie star. The dominance of this notion of Blackness in representation, indeed its virtual interchangeability with any meaningful concept of "real" Blackness, was the central ideological challenge to the possibility of Black stardom in the early twentieth century.

Conclusion

"Time Now to Stop, Actors"

The imperfect high of Hattie McDaniel's Academy Award for Best Supporting Actress in 1939's *Gone with the Wind* seems almost too apropos for the closing of the 1930s. As the decade waned, signs of the wear, duress, and decline of the problematic star were everywhere. Three cases in point from the early 1940s help to illustrate the growing tensions around these icons. Perhaps the most eloquent is an instance from the spring of 1943, when Langston Hughes wrote an earnest entry for his weekly *Chicago Defender* column, "Here to Yonder." The piece ran under the heading "Time Now to Stop, Actors," and Hughes began by acknowledging that the subject he attempted to broach was a touchy one:

> I know a great many [Negro actors] personally and like them, and like some of them much better as people than I do as actors—so I hope they don't get mad at me for what I am about to say. But the time has come for them to do better, particularly in Hollywood.[1]

Hughes went on to lament that degrading, comic, menial roles, "Yes sir, yes ma'am, come seven, come eleven, praise-de-Lawd, whaw-whaw-whaw, boss, roles . . . speaking by and large, are ALL [Hollywood studios] give us to do on the screen." While he threw some blame at white executives and producers, he nonetheless assigned Black actors and actresses an equal or greater share of responsibility, asserting that it is time now for the Negro actor to stop degrading the Negro people on the screen. With defense work running full blast, they can all get jobs elsewhere, if it is still a matter of bread and meat. Poverty used to be the old excuse. They used to say "But we have to make a living."[2]

Barely sufficient until now, by the 1940s the stolen shares of "meat" available in Hollywood roles seemed more or less rancid. Like a number of other visible and vocal African Americans, Hughes was asserting that the choice Black actors had long made between stealing the show and stealing the shoat was really no choice at all—especially for Black audiences.

Hughes's plea was largely in sync with a second example of strained patience with "the era of the servants": the campaign of NAACP Executive Secretary Walter White, who was pressing for Hollywood films to take "a more enlightened attitude in the picturing of so-called colored people."[3] Indeed, in 1940, with barely enough time for Hattie McDaniel to remove her Oscar ceremony gardenias from her hair, White made the first of a series of trips to Hollywood from New York, with the object of meeting with the movie industry's top directors, producers, and studio heads on this very subject. Hughes and White were by this time old comrades; they had first connected in the cultural flourishing of the Harlem Renaissance of the 1920s. While White had more definite commitments to the ideology of art as propaganda espoused by Renaissance architects W. E. B. DuBois and Alain Locke, Hughes was certainly faithful to a general ideology of Negro uplift through a fuller and more truthful explication of African American history.

Between 1940 and 1943, White traveled west several times, often in the company of Wall Street businessman and one-time U.S. presidential candidate Wendell Wilkie. Wilkie was an apt companion, since he had one foot in each of the worlds most relevant to White's operation; in 1940 he had been named special counsel to the NAACP *and* chairman of the board of Twentieth Century Fox.[4] White aimed to impress upon Hollywood studio brass the gravity of the situation. As the United States entered World War II, he explicitly emphasized the global implications of the movie industry's representations of Black Americans. In a 1942 letter to Will Hays, president of the Motion Picture Producers and Distributors of America (MPPDA), White wrote to ask if Hays would be willing to meet with him during an upcoming trip to Hollywood. "I would like very much . . . to have an opportunity to talk with you," White wrote, "regarding . . . the limitation of the Negro in the moving pictures to comic or menial roles. This has resulted . . . in fixing and extending the stereotype, not only in the minds of Americans, but of persons all over the world."[5]

During his visits, White met with white stars like Jimmy Cagney, Melvyn Douglass, and Jean Muir, as well as major producers like David O. Selznick, Walter Wanger, and Darryl Zanuck. Though many established members of the African American Hollywood film colony were in accord with the spirit of White's campaign, nonetheless many of them felt that his methods left much to be desired.[6] White explicitly ignored the problematic stars in the interest of engaging with white producers and studio executives. More grievously, he frequently held Black actors personally responsible for their limited roles, declaring that "for those actors in Hollywood who can play only comic servant roles, I trust they will not let their own interests spoil the opportunity we now have to correct a lot of things from which Negroes have suffered in the past in movies."[7] Such statements from White conveniently minimized the meager yet hard-won points of access attained by this cadre of established actors. The neat separation of "their" interests from the opportunity "*we* now have" makes his sense of their culpability, and their irrelevance to Black progress, unambiguous. White's own exceptional looks as an African American man who could have easily passed for white only made the Jim Crow treatment he afforded Hollywood's Black players more galling and suspicious to them. He made a lifelong enemy of Hattie McDaniel, who came to believe that White's campaigning during World War II had turned Black people against her personally. She was especially hurt by "insulting" and "ungentlemanly" letters she received from African American servicemen whom White encountered on his USO trips to support the war effort.[8]

White was also making the insulting assertion that the limits of Hollywood's familiar servant and slave roles were due to a lack of Black performative talent and range, rather than a result of America's racist cultural appetites and Hollywood's similarly racist industrial practices. He paired his pronouncements with his introduction of Lena Horne "as a new and improved representative of African American identity on screen."[9] Yet Horne had traveled many of the same routes—singing and dancing on vaudeville and small club circuits—as the generation of Black performers that White alternately vilified and ignored. White need only have looked to Fredi Washington's brief 1930s Hollywood career to recognize that Horne's middle-class pedigree, her talent, youth, beauty, and light skin guaranteed nothing in terms of her acceptance by major movie studios.

The outcome of White's campaign was decidedly mixed; his conferences were often little more than a perfunctory show of Hollywood's racial "tolerance" for the actors and studio heads with whom he met. And his alienation of local Blacks involved in show business did not end with old-guard actors like Hattie McDaniel, Clarence Muse, and Louise Beavers. Some California-based Black newspapers made light of his campaign, while others essentially ignored it. Almena Davis, editor of the *Los Angeles Tribune,* sent White a clipping of her own column suggesting that he was wasting his time, and would be more effective in his area of expertise, that is, in "his fight to integrate Negroes into industry; continue his legal battles against jim crow."[10] Even as East Coast Black newspapers like the *New York Amsterdam News,* the *Baltimore Afro-American,* and the *Pittsburgh Courier* gave substantial coverage of White's dinners, meetings, lunches, and speeches to Hollywood studio brass, Charlotta Bass's Los Angeles-based paper, the *California Eagle,* carried only two items mentioning White or his efforts between 1940 and 1945.[11]

Still, the entrance of the United States into World War II at the end of 1941 created an increased need for national solidarity, and government agencies like the Office of War Information (OWI) put pressure on Hollywood to portray African Americans more progressively, recognizing that they "were more likely to support the war effort if the national culture portrayed the race in humane terms."[12] White's activities in Hollywood serendipitously overlapped with OWI's propagandistic initiatives. As Thomas Cripps observes, "the trick would be for White or another to find some play in the government's propaganda and Hollywood's movies into which blacks might insinuate bargains for promised incremental social gains."[13] At the very least, White's campaign served as a bellwether of small shifts in portrayals of African Americans in Hollywood, most often in films depicting the nation's war effort. Key Hollywood war pictures in this vein included Tay Garnett's *Bataan,* Archie Mayo's *Crash Dive,* and Zoltan Korda's *Sahara*—all from 1943—and Alfred Hitchcock's *Lifeboat,* from 1944. All four were set during WWII, and spotlighted the role that African American men played in the U.S. military effort, casting Black actors like Kenneth Spencer and Ben Carter as heroic demolitions experts, courageous messmen, and patriotic soldiers who fought, and sometimes died, alongside their white compatriots.[14]

The pinnacle of such "positive" military-based portrayals was *The Negro Soldier,* a 1944 short propaganda film produced by the U.S. War

Department and distributed by the motion picture industry's joint War Activities Committee. Produced by Frank Capra, and written by African American actor/screenwriter Carlton Moss, *The Negro Soldier* formally and narratively exceeded Hollywood's individual, marginal approach to Black subjects by devoting its entire forty-four minutes to African Americans. Set in a church whose congregation includes a number of servicemen and servicewomen, the film is largely guided by the church's pastor (played by Moss), who departs from his planned sermon to express his gratitude and pride in Black participation in American military service, from the Revolutionary War through World War II. He cites specific African American heroes of the Revolutionary War, the War of 1812, the Spanish American War, and World War I, as well as enumerating a varied list of Black scholars, artists, and institutions and their contributions to American life. Moss exudes a firm, reverential, and ultimately dignified demeanor from his ministerial pulpit, and the film's close-up shots of the various quiet, sincere, proud, engaged, and intelligent faces of his male and female parishioners present a decidedly human and poignant contrast to dominant Hollywood representations of African Americans, even while treading the familiar territory of Black religiosity.

Walter White's clarion call for an end to comic servants was important as a site of African American engagement with Hollywood, and as a kind of barometric indicator of widespread fatigue with the stale rigidity of Hollywood's casting of Black actors. Yet the small victories of the early 1940s did not add up to much in terms of substantial change, in part because White's campaign "relied on influence-peddling, lobbying, and goodwill of the studio heads whose first allegiance was to the profitability of their companies .... White mistook his access to powerful persons for access to power itself."[15] With his efforts to persuade Hollywood studios to "do right" by African Americans rooted in only an ethical imperative, or in the temporary pressure exerted by the government as a result of the war, White failed to present white filmmakers with concrete terms of how Hollywood movies *should* present African Americans, ultimately requiring them to do relatively little besides stop casting Blacks in general to cut down on stereotypical representations.

Perhaps nothing more provocatively signaled the twilight of the servants than the great Paul Robeson's appearance in *Tales of Manhattan*. The 1942 Julien Duvivier film marked the end of Robeson's ventures (and misadventures) in Hollywood films. A light, slightly philosophical anthology film depicting the "life" of a silk tailcoat passing through the hands of six very different owners, the final vignette of *Tales of Manhat-*

tan featured Robeson, alongside fellow stage and screen veterans Ethel Waters and Eddie "Rochester" Anderson. The elegant tailcoat, whose tailor sheepishly admits that the garment may bear the curse of a disgruntled fabric cutter, begins its sojourn as the attire of a haughty, wealthy stage actor Paul Orman (Charles Boyer), and fulfills its cursed reputation by getting him shot (though not fatally) by the jealous husband (Thomas Mitchell) of his glamorous paramour Ethel (Rita Hayworth).

The coat passes to the possession of philandering playboy Harry (Cesar Romero), and again its curse is fulfilled in that Harry's infidelity to his fiancée (Ginger Rogers) is discovered on the day they are to be wed. She ultimately leaves him for his mild-mannered pal George (Henry Fonda). The coat goes next to Charles (Charles Laughton), a meek, talented composer who wears the coat on the night of his symphonic debut. Though the coat causes a sartorial disaster by being too small for the robust composer, whose strenuous conducting fully rips it at the seams, the beauty of Charles's composition is allowed to shine through in the end. We then follow the coat into the hands of a once-successful lawyer (Edward G. Robinson) who has hit the skids, and has the coat donated to him to wear to a class reunion. The coat then falls into the hands of a pair of mobsters (J. Carroll Naish and John Kelly) who rob an after-hours gambling club. On their way to Mexico, sparks from the cockpit of their aircraft set the coat afire, and one mobster hastily tosses it out of the plane, remembering too late that it contains their stolen fortune.

After this veritable cavalcade of white Hollywood stars, and their many Manhattan-centered tales, enters Paul Robeson, cast as Luke, a humble sharecropper who, with his wife Esther (Waters), finds the discarded coat, laden with cash. Deciding that it is nothing less than manna from heaven, they enlist the help of the Reverend Lazarus (Rochester) in sharing the money among all the colored sharecroppers of their segregated shantytown community. When nearly all the money has been doled out, pious Esther remembers "poor old Christopher" (George Reed), who, she insists, must receive his share. When asked what he has prayed for, the aged Christopher remarks that he asked the Lord for a scarecrow. The tattered tailcoat comes to the end of its journey mounted in his field to this very purpose, as Robeson's character Luke observes, "So that's what they mean when they says, 'The Lord moves in mysterious ways.'" The sharecroppers punctuate their collective good fortune by singing a thankful refrain, led by Robeson and assisted on the film's soundtrack by the Hall Johnson Choir.

Throughout 1941, both the mainstream press and African American newspapers alike ran optimistic coverage of *Tales of Manhattan*'s casting and preproduction, noting Paul Robeson's return to Hollywood films after a five-year absence.[16] Yet even before *Tales*' official New York premiere in September 1942, Robeson's expressions of disgust and frustration began to appear in the African American press, and in mainstream papers.[17] Black newspapers like the *New York Amsterdam News*, the *Atlanta Daily World*, the *Chicago Defender*, and the *Baltimore Afro-American*, as well as the *New York Times* and the *Boston Globe*, all carried stories quoting Robeson's strident criticisms.[18] Although Robeson explains that he

> thought I could change the picture as we went along . . . in the end it turned out to be the same old thing—the Negro solving his problem by singing his way to glory . . . . It makes the Negro child-like and innocent and is in the old plantation tradition. But Hollywood says you can't make the Negro in any other role because it won't be box office in the South.[19]

Robeson also asserted that although he'd wanted to buy himself out of his contract with Twentieth Century Fox, he could not afford to do so. Perhaps most stunning was Robeson's declaration that if protesters picketed the film's New York premiere, "I'll join the picket line myself."[20] Robeson stated in most of these accounts that he was (once again) finished with Hollywood films until the major studios could figure out how to portray Black people as something other than "plantation hallelujah shouters."[21]

Black perspectives on *Tales of Manhattan* were mixed; some viewers seemed to conclude that if the film wasn't much better than the usual Hollywood portrayal of African Americans, it certainly wasn't much worse. Newspapers like the *Pittsburgh Courier* and the *Chicago Defender* debated *Tales*' merits and deficits, coming to relatively positive conclusions about its impact and relevance for "the race." Though the *Courier* had run Robeson's critical interview with the ANP, calling his perspective on the film "interesting angles," the paper's editors also reprinted a review from the *Washington Times Herald* that criticized Robeson himself and attributed his comments to his Communist affiliations.[22] The *Courier* also published an interview with Henry Blankfort, the Fox screenwriter who wrote *Tales of Manhattan*'s final vignette, under the headline: "Writer of Colored Sequence In *Tales* Interviewed By [*Courier* Theatrical Editor Billy] Rowe: Blankfort Meant No Offense to Race—Is Staunch Advocate of 'Double V.'" Blankfort is quoted as explaining that "I tried to show the depth to which the unscrupulous landlords have pushed the Negro, the shambles in which they have been forced to live because of economic injustices. I tried my best to take a subtle slam at those things."[23] He also undoubtedly earned the *Courier*'s approval by showing solidarity with the newspaper's World War II "Double V" campaign for victory at home and abroad.[24]

The *Chicago Defender* also published an anticommunist, critical reading of Robeson's complaints about *Tales;* in addition, the *Defender*'s entertainment editor, Lawrence Lamar, penned an article defending the film. In "Here's *Tales Of Manhattan:* See If You Think It Objectionable," Lamar scoffed at the "certain stratum of the Negro group [that] has long howled and raved at the producers and Negro actors who appeared in the closing sequences of the film story, claiming it showed the Negro in an unfavorable light." Lamar chided these ostensibly ultra-sensitive viewers, coolly observing that

> like anything else, it's all in the way one views a thing. If it be the purpose of going to a motion picture theatre to be entertained, then *Tales of Manhattan* is good entertainment. But if a person goes to the theatre as if going to a church, or a school, then that person is doomed for disappointment in seeing the picture.[25]

Lamar's mocking tone was evoked in a photo-caption standalone that appeared in the *Defender* a few months later: a publicity shot of Robeson and Ethel Waters holding the cash-laden coat that was *Tales'* centerpiece, beneath the somewhat irreverent header "This Irked Paul Robeson."[26]

Yet for other African American viewers, the irony of Robeson performing in such a capacity was bitter indeed. Three of California's Black newspapers, the *California Eagle,* the *Los Angeles Sentinel,* and the *Los Angeles Tribune,* were lukewarm to cold in their reactions. The *Eagle* had printed enthusiastic puff pieces about the film's casting and production; one such piece anticipated that Robeson's "ability plus skill should make a hit combination," another called the anthology film "the most unique movie to be made in Hollywood."[27] But after *Tales of Manhattan* was released, the *Eagle* ran little more than related advertisements for the film, and reported only neutrally on its seeming popularity, offering no commentary or assessment of the movie's content.[28] In a gesture of outright condemnation, the editors of the *Sentinel* and the *Tribune* picketed *Tales of Manhattan*'s August 1942 run at Los Angeles' downtown Loew's State Theatre, decrying the film's hackneyed depictions of impoverished, religious African Americans. The *Tribune*'s editor, Leon H. Washington, Jr., posited *Tales of Manhattan* as exemplary of his charge that "Hollywood is the most vicious, race baiting, jim-crow, propaganda disseminating agency in America . . . . Every theatre goers [sic] is acquainted with the Hollywood version of the Negro as a shiftless, carefree, crapshooting, boisterous gin-drinking ante-bellum, clownish Uncle Tom or Aunt Dinah."[29] Likewise, Marian Freeman, writing back east in the *New York Amsterdam News*, asserted that the film's Black cast "let us down," and that

> it is difficult to reconcile the Paul Robeson, who has almost single-handedly waged the battle for recognition of the Negro as a true artist, with the "Luke" of this film. Robeson's impressive and passionate indictment of reactionary influences in the field of art has, no doubt, been largely responsible for the high respect in which he is held. His acceptance of this role, that of a simple minded, docile sharecropper, leads one to wonder whether Robeson is abandoning his lot as a martyr, though he hasn't exactly starved, for an easier path. Why must our greatest stars of music and stage be forever relegated to humiliating roles . . . . Why can't our stars make some concerted effort to raise the standards, and refuse, in no uncertain terms, offers of this type?[30]

Paul Robeson was the usual exception to the rule of Black cinematic marginalization, the man to whom "the show" legitimately belonged—at least sometimes—in the 1930s. Nevertheless, Robeson was relegated to the second-class, colored section of *Tales of Manhattan* in every meaningful way. His billing—along with Ethel Waters and "Rochester"—comes at the very end of the list of the film's stars, "in order of appearance." Theirs is also the only story that does not take place in the film's urbane Manhattan setting. (Apparently the hoodlums have their airborne crisis while their Mexico-bound plane is in flight over the stock cinematic Southland.) And even as the sequence's expressionistically barren and stark mise-en-scène underscores the poverty and misery in which Luke, Esther, Reverend Lazarus, and the rest of the sharecropping community live, it also lends a simplistic, two-dimensional flavor to their circumstances, especially in comparison to the fully realized visuals of the "Manhattan" scenes that precede them. The racially and geographically segregated vignette gives Robeson, Waters, and Rochester the very last crack at the film's central symbol, the now tattered, multiply-mended, scorched, hand-me-down tailcoat (however enriched it is with illicit loot).

As Judith Weisenfeld observes, "*Tales of Manhattan* . . . relied heavily on conventional Hollywood interpretations of the simplicity of black religious thought and on common visual tropes that have traditionally connected religious practice to the social and political subordination of African Americans."[31] Robeson biographer Scott Nollen echoes Weisenfeld, noting that

> every possible cliché is loaded into the scene as the black folks dance, sing gospel songs, praise the Lord, and generally shuck and jive all over the place. Even Grandpa (Clarence Muse) . . . crawls from his cot to claim $25 for his "coffin . . . with wheels on it, so I can roll right through the Pearly Gates."[32]

The visual of gleeful, grateful Blacks who unrestrainedly celebrate the tattered suitcoat's small fortune of forty-three thousand dollars as "more money than there is in the whole world" is uncomfortably reminiscent of the *L.A. Times'* condescending characterization of Hattie McDaniel and the Black Los Angeles actors' colony as merry dependents on Hollywood's second bests and discards.[33] The reality of the 1930s as a decade in which African American actors and actresses competed strenuously for the most meager of the movie industry's crumbs was far less droll a picture than either the *Times* or *Tales of Manhattan* conjured up.

The problematics of Blackness and stardom so prototypically established in the 1930s have never faded completely, even as the extremes of the racial prejudice of the early twentieth century have diminished and transformed. At the end of his "Time to Stop Now, Actors" plea, Langston Hughes expressed a common notion among African American race men and women, suggesting that the best hope for better roles for the Negro was in motion pictures that centered upon the lives of heroic and historical Blacks like Sojourner Truth, Phyllis Wheatley, George Washington Carver, and even Emperor Haile Selassie.[34] One might legitimately argue that Black stardom only began to achieve something like parity in the mainstream when Black actors had the credentializing power of these sorts of roles as part of their star personae. However, thirty-plus years would pass before this sort of casting, scripting, and producing of roles occurred on any highly visible or regular basis.

Walter White's hopes for Lena Horne, while not entirely frustrated, were nevertheless short-lived. Excepting her starring roles in the Black-cast musicals *Cabin in the Sky* and *Stormy Weather* (both in 1943, at the apex of White's campaign), Horne was largely relegated to making brief musical cameo appearances in Hollywood films. Her performances typically had little to do with a movie's plot, and could easily be edited out to cater to the tastes of Southern censors. As Horne herself observed,

Hollywood producers and directors were wholly unsure what to do with her, and while "they didn't make me into a maid . . . they didn't make me into anything else either. I became a butterfly pinned to a column singing away in Movieland."[35] Despite White's declarations about Horne's potential to diversify the African American cinematic image, her listing in the 1945 *Academy Players Directory* designated her a "character and comedienne," not a "leading lady" or even an "ingénue." It was a description that could have easily referred to Louise Beavers or Hattie McDaniel.[36] The notion that the "right" Black actress was all that Hollywood lacked missed the point of the industry's race problem entirely; it is not difficult to understand why so many of the movie industry's African American old settlers took offense to Horne's arrival.

And indeed, Paul Robeson's turn as *Tales of Manhattan*'s sharecropper, Luke, demonstrated how deeply entrenched the stock iconography of Black servility really was in the 1930s, especially if one takes seriously the claims of film historians like Charles Musser, who contend that *Tales*' leftist production team, along with Robeson himself, intended "to evoke a progressive, collective spirit that was at the heart of the Popular Front in the United States."[37] While the notion of Black folk qua folk clearly carried symbolic utility for such a political and ideological project, the film ultimately reproduced the same ironclad "praise-de-Lawd, whaw-whaw-whaw, boss" casting for African Americans that Langston Hughes would lament in the *Chicago Defender* a year later.[38] Even Musser concedes that in the context of the six-part narrative of *Tales of Manhattan,* in which "sophisticated white characters ruminate on the differences between appearance and reality," Robeson and the sharecroppers "become simple, naïve 'folk.'"[39]

Perhaps, in its attempt at a progressive representation of race, *Tales of Manhattan* provides an apt summation of the way that the 1930s established the centrality of roles as markers of the limits of the white cinematic imagination. After all, even *Imitation of Life*'s tragic Peola, upon having successfully passed for white, is discovered doing nothing more glamorous or even interesting than working as a shop girl at a soda fountain. Passively sitting and smiling to herself, making change and selling cigars, it becomes clear that Peola's purloined whiteness does not impel her to dream very far beyond a servility that her life as a wealthy Black heiress would have made wholly unnecessary. But such a moneyed, leisurely Peola lay entirely beyond the ken of the film industry's white story and screenplay writers. Limited casting and roles served as technical boundaries, fundamentally precluding any resemblance between Black Hollywood film stardom and the industrial and cultural significance of white stardom as a phenomenon of this period.[40]

James Baldwin makes it clear that roles are central to the vexed relationship between Black folk and stardom when he writes, in a prescient piece of theorizing about the nature of stardom from *The Devil Finds Work,* that

> the distance between oneself—the audience—and a screen performer is an absolute: a paradoxical absolute, masquerading as intimacy. No one, for example, will ever really know whether Katharine Hepburn or Bette Davis or Humphrey Bogart or Spencer Tracy or Clark Gable—or John Wayne—can, or could, really act, or not, nor does anyone care; acting is not what they are required to do . . . . One does not go to see them act: one goes to watch them *be.* One does not go to se Humphrey Bogart, *as Sam Spade:* one goes to see Sam Spade, *as Humphrey Bogart . . .*[41]

Even as Baldwin imagines the actor's role as absorbed and eclipsed by the star persona, the prerequisite for ample expression and elaboration of that persona is a leading role—Sam Spade provides the opportunity for us to see Humphrey Bogart *be*-ing. The star's masquerade of intimacy lies in the audience's belief that they "know" Hepburn, Gable, or Bogart well enough to know what it looks like (and what it doesn't) when they "be" on the screen. Baldwin goes on to make the even more interesting assertion that

> *no one,* I read somewhere, a long time ago, *makes his escape personality black.* That the movie star is an "escape" personality indicates one of the irreducible dangers to which the moviegoer is exposed: the danger of surrendering to the corroboration of one's fantasies as they are thrown back from the screen.[42]

Baldwin deploys his cutting prose largely at the expense of white readers here, for it is most explicitly white fantasies of racial superiority that Hollywood films and stars function so tirelessly to support and corroborate. But his notion that "no one . . . makes his escape personality black," however apocryphally he may credit it, arguably delimits the parameters of Black stardom in very precise terms. To imagine the star signifying fundamentally as an escape personality suggests that the essence of stardom is its aspirational quality for the viewer; that part of watching stars "be" is to imagine one's own parallel *be*-ing alongside them, as them. It is a conception of stardom that jibes very clearly with Baldwin's activism on behalf of Black people as an essayist, playwright, novelist, and race man. In *The Devil Finds Work,* he discusses his loathing for

Stepin Fetchit and Willie Best and Manton [sic] Moreland . . . [because] it seemed to me that they lied about the world I knew, and debased it, and certainly I did not know anybody like them—as far as I could tell; for it is also possible that their comic, bug-eyed terror contained the truth concerning a terror by which I hoped never to be engulfed.

Neither their debased humor nor their concealed terror are anything upon which the escape personality of a star can be made, because no viewer, whether white or Black, would want to escape as such a person.

Baldwin's declaration creates a far neater cleavage between the problematic stars of the 1930s and "real" stars like Katharine Hepburn or Clark Gable than do my own formulations in *Stealing the Show*. There is something to be said for the equation he calculates here, especially because his emphasis on escape and fantasy highlights the emotional and psychological uses to which spectators put films and stars. But even as the kinds of stardom that many contemporary Black actors have been able to achieve look more appealing as escape or aspiration—and are arguably more "real"—they nevertheless continue to carry many of the same burdens borne by their Black cinematic antecedents, and to likewise be caught in spaces between stealing the *show* and stealing the *shoat*. Stars like Denzel Washington, Halle Berry, Will Smith, and Viola Davis are routinely called upon by some African American viewers to defend roles or performances construed as defamatory or damaging to the race as a whole. Meanwhile, the legacy of controversial Oscar nominations and wins for roles that arguably fall into familiarly stereotyped territory likewise continues apace. The role, as the essential component of mainstream Black cinematic presences, continues to be determined largely in absence of African American creatives and executives, often with predictable outcomes, even in the face of expansion in the real political, social, and cultural circumstances of Black people in the United States.

Yet the thirties revealed the determination and agency of African Americans as both performers and as audiences, to be engaged in or by the business of show in defiance of decidedly more substantial odds and obstacles. Lincoln "Stepin Fetchit" Perry's wholehearted embrace of the kind of excessive lifestyle associated with stardom is telling in its expression of belief in *Hollywood* as a potential escape route, at least from the financial limits that typically bound Black life in the early twentieth century. Hattie McDaniel's intentional use of the flawed public platform that *Gone with the Wind* provided her, to advance a stance that by turns opposed, defended, and complicated "Mammy" suggests her apprehension of the complex public space she occupied, as even a minor, "supporting" star. Likewise Bill "Bojangles" Robinson's careful manicuring of his public persona demonstrated his shrewd understanding of what a mainstream audience would accept from him, even as aspects of his onscreen and offscreen performances catered to Black people specifically. And Louise Beavers and Fredi Washington's unprecedented acclaim and visibility in *Imitation of Life* carried a powerful foreshadowing of why Black stars could and would matter to Black audiences in the future. For their part, African American audiences demonstrated an intention to seek and find their images in the mainstream, the resilience to claim aspects of themselves from mere fragments, and ultimately, the will to demand something more from Hollywood's representations.

Notes

INTRODUCTION

1. Lawrence Levine, *Black Culture and Black Consciousness: Afro-American Folk Thought from Slavery to Freedom* (Oxford: Oxford University Press, 1977), 309.

2. Frederick Douglass, *My Bondage and My Freedom* (New Haven: Yale University Press, 2014), 153–54.

3. Levine, *Black Culture, Black Consciousness*, 310.

4. Jacqueline Stewart, *Migrating to the Movies: Cinema and Black Urban Modernity* (Berkeley: University of California Press, 2005), 73–74.

5. Toni Morrison, *Beloved* (New York: First Vintage International Edition, 2004), 224.

6. Ibid., 225.

7. Theodore Dwight Weld, *American Slavery as It Is: Testimony of a Thousand Witnesses* (Chapel Hill: University of North Carolina Press, 2011), 70.

8. Langston Hughes, "The Negro and American Entertainment," in *The Collected Works of Langston Hughes*, vol. 9, *Essays on Art, Race, Politics, and World Affairs,* ed. Christopher De Santis (Columbia: University of Missouri Press, 2002), 452. Quoted in Donald Bogle, *Toms, Coons, Mulattoes, Mammies, and Bucks: An Interpretive History of Blacks in American Films,* 3rd ed. (New York: Continuum Publishing, 2000), 37. Hughes's essay originally appeared in *The American Negro Reference Book,* ed. John P. Davis (Englewood Cliffs: Prentice-Hall, 1966), 826–49.

9. Bogle, *Toms, Coons, Mulattoes, Mammies and Bucks,* 36.

10. John Scott, "Picture-Stealers More in Demand than Costly Stars," *Los Angeles Times,* April 7, 1935, A1.

11. Ibid.

12. Ibid.

13. Loren Miller, "Uncle Tom in Hollywood," *The Crisis* 41, no. 2 (November 1934): 329.

14. Arthur Knight, "Star Dances: African American Constructions of Stardom, 1925–1960," in *Classic Hollywood, Classic Whiteness,* ed. Daniel Bernardi (Minneapolis: University of Minnesota Press, 2001), 404.

15. Thomas Cripps, "The Myth of the Southern Box Office," in *The Black Experience in America,* eds. James Curtis and Lewis Gould (Austin: University of Texas Press, 1970).

16. James Baldwin, *The Devil Finds Work: An Essay* (New York: Dial Press, 1976), 104–5.

17. The capitalized "S" in the word *Signify* here invokes Henry Louis Gates's seminal theory of Signifyin(g) as an African American vernacular tradition, cultural practice, and literary trope. (Gates patterns his graphical alteration of the word after Jacques Derrida's neologism *différance.*) In fine, Gates's concept references an intertextual mode of African American authorship and performance that "functions as a metaphor for formal revision." To Signify, from Gates's perspective, is to repeat with a critical, even oppositional difference that challenges meaning at the level of the *signifier* itself. For the generation of problematic African American stars considered here, it is the key signifier of stereotypical performance that is potentially complicated or altered. See Henry Louis Gates, *The Signifying Monkey: A Theory of African American Literary Criticism* (London: Oxford University Press, 1988).

18. The "stair dance," one of Robinson's hallmarks, showcased his upright tapping style by featuring him tapping percussively up and down a staircase; the dance is discussed in greater detail in chapter 2.

19. Richard Dyer, *Heavenly Bodies: Film Stars and Society* (London, Basingstoke: MacMillan Education, 1986), 67–69.

20. I borrow the structure of the subsequent analysis and the suggestion of racialized discourses from Richard Dyer's chapter on Paul Robeson in his 1986 study *Heavenly Bodies.* As such, I also borrow Dyer's disclaimer with respect to the generality and potential for exceptions to my theorizing. He writes, "in speaking of different, white and black perspectives, I don't imply that black people saw him [Robeson] one way and whites the other. What I want to show is that there are discourses developed by whites in white culture and by blacks in black culture which made a different sense of the same phenomenon, Paul Robeson. There is a consistency in the statements, images, and texts produced on the one hand by blacks and on the other by whites that makes it reasonable to refer to black and white discourses even while accepting that there may have been blacks who have thought and felt largely through white discourses and vice versa." Richard Dyer, "Paul Robeson: Crossing Over," in *Heavenly Bodies,* 67.

21. Anna Everett, *Returning the Gaze: A Genealogy of Black Film Criticism, 1909–1949* (Durham, NC: Duke University Press, 2001), 180.

22. See Victoria Sturtevant, "But Things Is Changin' Nowadays an' Mammy's Gettin' Bored: Hattie McDaniel and the Culture of Dissemblance" *The Velvet Light Trap* 44 (1999): 68–79; Jill Watts, *Hattie McDaniel: Black Ambition, White Hollywood* (New York: Amistad, 2005), 6–10, 23; Carlton Jackson, *Hattie: The Life of Hattie McDaniel* (Lanham, NY: Madison Books, 1990),

2; Charlene Regester, *The African American Actresses: Struggles for Visibility, 1900–1960* (Bloomington: Indiana University Press, 2010), 154.

23. Anna Everett puts this clearly when she asserts that "the black press was founded on a principle of protecting and promoting its vested interest in the accomplishments of African Americans." Everett, *Returning the Gaze,* 193.

24. Clarence Muse, "What's Going on in Hollywood," *Chicago Defender,* December 23, 1939, 21. The alternation between all-caps and lowercase is Muse's own idiosyncratic style, which appears in all of his columns.

25. Clarence Muse, "The Dilemma of the Negro Actor," Los Angeles, 1934, 5. Self-published pamphlet, from a speech given to the California Art Club in 1929.

26. Ibid., 17

27. "Hattie McDaniel: The Landmark of an Era," *New Journal and Guide,* March 9, 1940, 8.

28. Ibid.

29. The *Journal and Guide* had advanced an analogous response almost exactly a decade earlier in its description of the 1929 Black-cast film *Hallelujah* as "an entering wedge with which to pry open some doors of opportunity." "Hallelujah," *Norfolk New Journal and Guide,* April 5, 1930, 12.

30. "Hattie McDaniel: The Landmark of an Era," 8.

31. Everett, *Returning the Gaze,* 249.

32. Robert M. Farnsworth, "Introduction," *Caviar and Cabbage: Selected Columns by Melvin B. Tolson from the* Washington Tribune, *1937–1944,* ed. Robert M. Farnsworth (Columbia: University of Missouri Press, 1982), 4.

33. Ibid., 1. Tolson led the celebrated all-Black debate team from Wiley College chronicled in the 2007 film *The Great Debaters* (dir. Denzel Washington, Weinstein Company) and wrote a weekly column called "Caviar and Cabbage" for the *Washington Tribune* from 1937 until 1944.

34. Melvin Tolson, "*Gone with the Wind* Is More Dangerous than Birth of a Nation," in Farnsworth, ed., *Caviar and Cabbage,* 215.

35. Ibid., 213.

36. Melvin Tolson, "The Philosophy of the Big House," in Farnsworth, ed., *Cabbage and Caviar,* 221–22.

37. Ibid., 222.

38. Muse, "The Dilemma of the Negro Actor," 17.

39. Don Ryan, "Yoohoo! Hi'ya, Hattie!" *Los Angeles Times,* Feb. 11, 1940, 3.

40. Ibid.

41. Ibid.

42. Ibid., 3, 8.

43. Sturtevant, "But Things Is Changin' Nowadays an' Mammy's Gettin' Bored," 70.

44. Ryan, "Yoohoo! Hi'ya, Hattie!" 8.

45. Ibid.

46. Jimmie Fidler, "Jimmie Fidler in Hollywood," *Los Angeles Times,* December 20, 1939, 15.

47. Ibid.

48. Ibid.

49. Baldwin, *The Devil Finds Work*, 105.

50. Cathy Klaprat, "The Star as Market Strategy: Bette Davis in Another Light," in *The American Film Industry*, ed. Tino Balio, rev. ed. (Madison: University of Wisconsin Press, 1985), 351–76.

51. Adrienne McLean, "Stardom in the 1930s," in *Glamour in a Golden Age: Movie Stars of the 1930s*, ed. Adrienne McLean (New Brunswick: Rutgers University Press, 2011), 6.

CHAPTER 1: HATTIE MCDANIEL

1. Jill Watts, *Hattie McDaniel: Black Ambition, White Hollywood* (New York: Amistad, 2005), 6–10, 23.

2. Ibid., 27.

3. Ibid., 28.

4. Ibid.; Carlton Jackson, *Hattie: The Life of Hattie McDaniel* (Lanham, New York: Madison Books, 1990), 2.

5. Watts, *Hattie McDaniel: Black Ambition, White Hollywood*, 42–46.

6. Charlene Regester's important work *African American Actresses: The Struggle for Visibility, 1900–1960* provides a specifically gendered analysis of the careers of McDaniel and others (Bloomington: Indiana University Press, 2010).

7. See Evelyn Brooks Higginbotham, "The Politics of Respectability," chapter 7 in *Righteous Discontent: The Black Women's Movement in the Black Baptist Church*, 1880-1920 (Cambridge, MA: Harvard University Press, 1994), 185-229. I owe a debt of thanks to my research assistant, Jocelyn Szczepaniak-Gillece, for her own insightful scholarship on film and monumentality.

8. Watts, *Hattie McDaniel*, 166; Judy Cameron and Paul J. Christman, *The Art of* Gone with the Wind: *The Making of a Legend*, (Upper Saddle River, NJ: Prentice Hall, 1991), 44.

9. Medora Perkerson, "Seeing 'GWTW' Picture was an 'Experience' to Margaret Mitchell," *Atlanta Journal*, December 17, 1939; Letter from Margaret Mitchell to Hattie McDaniel-Crawford, dated May 12, 1941, Margaret Mitchell Family Papers, Hargrett Rare Book and Manuscript Library. Both quoted in *The Scarlett Letters: The Making of the Film* Gone with the Wind (New York: Rowman and Littlefield, 2014), 317.

10. Jimmie Fidler, "Jimmie Fidler in Hollywood," *Los Angeles Times*, Dec. 20, 1939, 15.

11. Edwin Schallert, "*Gone with Wind* Thrills Throng," *Los Angeles Times*, Dec. 29, 1939, 13.

12. *Variety* and Selznick quotes appear in Watts, *Hattie McDaniel*, 168, 173.

13. Steve Wilson and Robert Osborne, *The Making of* Gone with the Wind, (Austin: University of Texas Press, 2014), 202.

14. Even when Melanie and Scarlett are dressed in mourning, at the beginning of the film, after the death of Charles Hamilton (Scarlett's husband and Melanie's brother), they carry white handkerchiefs embroidered in black.

15. Regester, *African American Actresses*, 154.

16. Schallert, "*Gone with Wind,*" Dec. 29, 1939, 13; Regester, *African American Actresses,* 152.

17. *Webster's Third New International Dictionary* (Springfield: Merriam-Webster, 1993), s.v. "cipher."

18. Melvin B. Tolson, "The Philosophy of the Big House," in *Caviar and Cabbage: Selected Columns by Melvin B. Tolson from the* Washington Tribune, *1937–1944,* ed. Robert M. Farnsworth (Columbia: University of Missouri Press, 1982), 221.

19. Grace E. Hale, *Making Whiteness: The Culture of Segregation in the South, 1890–1940* (New York: Vintage, 2010), 99.

20. Elizabeth Fox-Genovese, *Within the Plantation Household: Black and White Women of the Old South* (Chapel Hill: University of North Carolina Press, 1988), 292.

21. Margaret Mitchell, *Gone with the Wind* (New York: Warner Books, 1993), 25.

22. Watts, *Hattie McDaniel,* 166.

23. Higginbotham, *Righteous Discontent,* 185–229.

24. Joan Marie Johnson, "'Ye Gave Them a Stone:' African American Women's Clubs, the Frederick Douglass Home, and the Black Mammy Monument," *Journal of Women's History* 17, no. 1 (2005): 63.

25. Schallert, "*Gone with Wind* Thrills Throng," 13. References for epigraphs in this section: Letter from Hattie McDaniel to David O. Selznick, dated December 11, 1939, quoted in Jill Watts, *Hattie McDaniel: Black Ambition, White Hollywood* (New York: Amistad Press, 2007), 177. Hortense J. Spillers, "Mama's Baby, Papa's Maybe: An American Grammar Book," *Diacritics* 17, no. 2 (Summer 1987), 65.

26. David Blight, *Race and Reunion: The Civil War in American Memory* (Cambridge, MA: Belknap Press of Harvard University Press, 2001), 79.

27. See Kimberly Wallace Sanders, *Mammy: A Century of Race, Gender, and Southern Memory* (Ann Arbor, MI: University of Michigan Press, 2009); M. M. Manring, *Slave in a Box: The Strange Career of Aunt Jemima* (Charlottesville: University Press of Virginia, 1998); and Micki McElya, *Clinging to Mammy: The Faithful Slave in Twentieth-Century America* (Cambridge, MA: Harvard University Press, 2007).

28. Manring, *Slave in a Box: The Strange Career of Aunt Jemima,* 115.

29. Ibid.

30. McElya, *Clinging to Mammy,* 2.

31. Blight, *Race and Reunion,* 287.

32. Catherine Clinton, *The Plantation Mistress: Woman's World in the Old South* (New York: Pantheon Books, 1984), 200.

33. Cheryl Thurber, "The Development of the Mammy Image and Mythology," in *Southern Women: Histories and Identities,* eds. Virginia Bernhard, Betty Brandon, Elizabeth Fox-Genovese, and Theda Perdue (Columbia: University of Missouri Press, 1992), 91.

34. Ibid., 92.

35. Herbert Gutman, *The Black Family in Slavery and Freedom, 1750-1925* (New York: Vintage, 1977), 632.

36. Johnson, "'Ye Gave Them a Stone,'" 71.

37. Quoted in ibid.

28. Bruce E. Baker, "How W.E.B. DuBois Won the United Daughters of the Confederacy Essay Contest," *Southern Cultures* 15, no.1 (Spring 2009): 70.

39. Johnson, "'Ye Gave Them a Stone'" 78.

40. Micki McElya, "Commemorating the Color Line: The National Mammy Monument Controversy of the 1920s," in *Monuments to the Lost Cause: Women, Art and the Landscape of Southern Memory,* eds. Cynthia Mills and Pamela Simpson (Knoxville: University of Tennessee Press, 2003), 207.

41. "For and against the 'Black Mammy's Monument,'" *The Literary Digest,* April 28, 1923, 48.

42. Quoted in ibid., 212.

43. "Another Suggestion for the 'Mammy' Monument,"" *Baltimore Afro-American,* March 30, 1923.

44. Ibid.

45. "Since Statues Seem to Be All the Rage, Suppose We Erect One: A White Daddy," *Chicago Defender,* April 21, 1923, 12.

46. "Dead Mammy Cries," *Baltimore Afro-American,* March 9, 1923, 13.

47. Johnson, "'Ye Gave Them a Stone,'" 73.

48. Hallie Q. Brown, "The Black Mammy Statue," *National Notes,* April 1923, 3–4, quoted in ibid., 74–75. Johnson helpfully points out Brown's Biblical reference to Matthew 7:9–10: "You parents—if your children ask for a loaf of bread, do you give them a stone instead? Or if they ask for a fish, do you give them a snake? Of course not!" (New Living translation).

49. Johnson, ""Ye Gave Them a Stone,"" 76.

50. *Literary Digest* 28, 48.

51. The Palmer Institute was a boarding school that Brown founded in 1902 with the financial assistance of Alice Freeman Palmer, the president of Wellesley College. Although the school began as an industrial and vocational institute, Brown continually augmented and upgraded its offerings, first providing instruction through grade school, then through high school. She ultimately provided students with teacher training at the Institute's junior college as well. Carolyn Wedin, "Brown, Charlotte Hawkins," in *Encyclopedia of African American History, 1896 to the Present: From the Age of Segregation to the Twenty-first Century,* ed. Paul Finkelman (Oxford: Oxford University Press, 2009), 290–92.

52. Robert Fay, "Brown, Charlotte Hawkins," in *Africana: The Encyclopedia of the African and African American Experience,* 2nd ed., ed. Kwame Anthony Appiah and Henry Louis Gates (Oxford: Oxford University Press, 2005).

53. Quoted in McElya, *Clinging to Mammy,* 192.

54. McElya, "Commemorating the Color Line," 215.

55. Mary B. Poppenheim, Maude Blake Merchant, and Ruth Jennings Lawton, *The History of the United Daughters of the Confederacy,* vol. 1 (1938; reprint, Richmond: United Daughters of the Confederacy, 1994), 49.

56. Ibid., 92.

57. Josep Lluis Sert, Fernand Leger, Siegfried Giedion, "Nine Points on Monumentality," in Siegfried Giedion, *Architecture, You and Me* (Cambridge, MA: Harvard University Press, 1958), 48–51.

58. "The Need for a New Monumentality" was written as an accompanying article enlarging upon the ideas set forth in "Nine Points."

59. Siegfried Giedion, "The Need for a New Monumentality," in *New Architecture and City Planning,* ed. Paul Zucker (New York: Books for Libraries Press, 1944), 555.

60. Giedion, "The Need for a New Monumentality," 550.

61. W. Barksdale Maynard, "The Greek Revival: Americanness, Politics and Economics" in *American Architectural History: A Contemporary Reader,* ed. Keith Eggener (London: Routledge, 2004), 132, 137–38. John Michael Vlach, *Back of the Big House: The Architecture of Plantation Slavery,* Fred W. Morrison Series in Southern Studies (Chapel Hill: University of North Carolina Press, 1993).

62. Maynard, "The Greek Revival," 134, 138.

63. Mitchell, *Gone with the Wind,*

64. Helen Taylor, *Scarlett's Women: Gone with the Wind and Its Female Fans* (New Brunswick: Rutgers University Press, 1989), 86. In a letter to Ed Sullivan dated January 7, 1939, David O. Selznick sought to explain and perhaps justify the choice of Vivien Leigh as Scarlett by explaining that "a large part of the South prides itself on its English ancestry." Rudy Behlmer, ed., *Memo from David O. Selznick* (New York: Modern Library, 2000), 205.

65. Mitchell, *Gone with the Wind,* 1024.

66. Sert, Leger, and Giedion, "Nine Points on Monumentality,"48.

67. Regarding the popularity of Bowers's *The Tragic Era,* see Gary Gallagher, *Causes Won, Lost, and Forgotten: How Hollywood and Popular Art Shape What We Know about the Civil War* (Chapel Hill: University of North Carolina Press, 2008), 49.

68. Sanders, *Mammy,* 2.

69. "*Gone with the Wind* Presents Dramatic Work of State U.D.C.," *The Atlanta Constitution,* December 24, 1939, 9M.

70. Letter to Katharine Brown, November 28, 1939, in Behlmer, ed., *Memo from David O. Selznick* (New York: Modern Library, 2000), 259.

71. Watts, *Hattie McDaniel,* 168. In Ralph Jones's "Silhouettes" column in the December 9, 1940 *Atlanta Constitution,* just a few days before the festivities were to begin, Jones wrote in a true southern style of politely feigned chagrin, "I am somewhat regretful that Hattie McDaniel, the Negro woman who played the role of 'Mammy' in *Gone with the Wind* can't be here for the big anniversary premiere on Thursday night. In the first place, we'd all like to meet her and tell her just how fine we thought her performance. In the second, because I'll bet Hattie would have had a grand time here."

72. Jackson, *Hattie,* 35; Leonard J. Leff, "The Search for Hattie McDaniel," *New Orleans Review* 10, no. 2–3 (Summer/Fall 1983), 92–93.

73. Blight, *Race and Reunion,* 4.

74. Gallagher, *Causes Won, Lost, and Forgotten,* 45.

75. ""Melanie,' Laurence Olivier, David O. Selznick Arrive,"*Atlanta Constitution*, December 14, 1939, 1.

76. Herb Bridges, Gone with the Wind: *The Three-Day Premiere in Atlanta* (Macon, GA: Mercer University Press, 1999), 41.

77. Atlanta History Center Album, *Gone with the Wind* Premiere Festivities, Atlanta History Photograph Collection, VIS.170.1788.001, http://album .atlantahistorycenter.com/store/Products/80263-gone-with-the-wind-movie-premiere-festivities.aspx.

78. McElya, "Commemorating the Color Line," 207.

79. "An Oscar for Hattie," *The Atlanta Constitution*, March 2, 1940, 6.

80. Quoted in Kimberly Wallace Sanders, "Southern Memory, Southern Monuments, and the Subversive Black Mammy," (lecture, Nov. 13, 2008), www.southernspaces.org/2009/southern-memory-southern-monuments-and-subversive-black-mammy#sthash.XrvRiR35.dpuf.

81. Letter from Margaret Mitchell to Katharine Brown, February 14, 1937, *Margaret Mitchell's* Gone with the Wind *Letters*, ed. Richard Harwell (New York: Macmillan Publishing, 1976), 120.

82. Ibid., 119–20.

83. Ibid., 119.

84. Quoted in Jackson, *Hattie*, 37.

85. Ibid., 40

86. Watts, *Hattie McDaniel*, 161.

87. In another column, Myrick certainly suggested as much, claiming that "Hattie McDaniel has played a Mammy so long in the picture *Gone with the Wind* that she is being a Mammy in real life." She claimed that McDaniel had been "Mammying" to her and Clark Gable, making up a tonic for their colds "that was made up according to an old formula which Hattie got from her mother." Quoted in Jackson, *Hattie*, 45.

88. Edward J. Thomas, *Memoirs of a Southerner: 1840–1923* (Savannah: n.p., 1923), 40.

89. Tony Horwitz, "The Mammy Washington Almost Had," *The Atlantic*, May 31, 2013, www.theatlantic.com/national/archive/2013/05/the-mammy-washington-almost-had/276431/.

90. Donald Bogle, *Bright Boulevards, Bold Dreams: The Story of Black Hollywood*, 1st ed. (New York: One World Ballantine Books, 2005), 136.

91. "Hattie McDaniel: The Landmark of an Era," *New Journal and Guide*, March 9, 1940, 8.

92. Selznick files, Inter-Office Memo from Selznick to L. V. Calvert, cc. Daniel O'Shea, March 25, 1940. This initiative on Selznick's part likely had to do with the fact that SIP was not one of Hollywood's acknowledged major studios (the "Big Five," as they are known, were MGM, Loews, RKO, Warner Brothers, and Fox) and was generally somewhat more resourceful and innovative about drawing in audiences and revenue. Even though SIP was the principal production company for *GWTW*, the film was produced in association with major studio MGM, and was released and distributed by both MGM and Loew's.

93. Behlmer, ed., *Memo from David O. Selznick*, 180.

94. Letter, John G. Turner to David O. Selznick, June 26, 1941; Letter, Claude A. Barnett to Donald [sic] O. Selznick, June 18, 1940; Ransom Center, Selznick Collection. In June 1940, when McDaniel was invited to appear on the program, she was on a road tour promoting *Gone with the Wind* on behalf of SIP, and initially CBS was informed that the conflict would prohibit her appearance. However, SIP executive Ray Klune wrote to executive vice president Daniel O'Shea with Selznick's backing, encouraging him to work out the timing issues, and to make certain that McDaniel would be available for the appearance. He attached to his memo a timely clipping from *Time* magazine, a brief article on *Wings Over Jordan* that described *Wings* as an extremely popular program which appealed to a Black listenership. The *Time* reporter noted that the show "attracts 5,000 letters a week, [and] is heard via short wave all over the world. A five-minute spot is reserved on every *Wings Over Jordan* program for a talk by a distinguished U.S. Negro on how the white and colored races can best get along together." As a result of her acclaim in *Gone with the Wind*, McDaniel was the "distinguished U.S. Negro" that the program was seeking to have its audiences hear. SIP interoffice memo, dated June 21, 1940, to Daniel O'Shea from Ray Klune; SIP interoffice memo, dated July 6, 1940, to Miss Rickman from Daniel O'Shea, Ransom Center, Selznick Collection; "Wings Over Jordan," *Time*, June 10, 1940, 71.

95. Henry Louis Gates and Anthony Appiah, "Wings Over Jordan," in *Africana: Arts and Letters: An A-to-Z Reference of Writers, Musicians, and Artists of the African American Experience* (Philadelphia: Running Press, 2005), 582.

96. "Speech for Sunday, July 7, 1940 broadcast of *Wings Over Jordan*, for Miss Hattie McDaniel, Los Angeles California/Negro Star of *Gone with the Wind* and winner of the 1939 Academy Motion Picture Award for the best supporting actress," David O. Selznick Collection, Harry Ransom Center, University of Texas at Austin.

97. Rosetta E. Ross, "Tubman, Harriet," in *African American National Biography*, eds. Henry Louis Gates, Jr., and Evelyn Brooks Higginbotham (Oxford: Oxford University Press, 2008). The Underground Railroad was a network of people and way stations that helped direct and transport African American slaves out of the South into the free North.

98. Kate Clifford Larson, *Bound for the Promised Land: Harriet Tubman* (New York: One World/Ballantine, 2004), 160–63. Tubman would also become an admirer and friend of the martyred insurrectionist John Brown. During his life, he had sought her out, in the hope that she would lead his planned revolt at Harper's Ferry, West Virginia. But for an onset of illness and a change of the planned date of the raid, Tubman would have been present (and might perhaps have changed the outcome of that mission).

99. Nell Irvin Painter, "Truth, Sojourner," *Black Women in America*, 2nd ed., ed. Darlene Clark Hine (Oxford: Oxford University Press, 2005).

100. Ibid.

101. Ibid.

102. Though Charity Still's name is less well known today, she and her husband were included in a list of pre–Civil War "Black Heroes" discussed as

possible subjects for a historical biopic in a 1939 Associated Negro Press (ANP) article touting a project being considered by Million Dollar Productions, a minor league production company that often collaborated with black directors and actors to produce films designed to appeal to African American viewers. Since the studio had "decided to produce a series of pictures built around actual facts of the Negro in history," according to the ANP, its research department was looking into the stories of important African Americans whose lives might make films directed at black audiences to compare with films like *The Life of Louis Pasteur* (1936) and *The Life of Emile Zola* (1937). Charity and Peter Still were joined luminaries like Sojourner Truth, Frederick Douglass, Nat Turner, and Crispus Attucks. "Black Heroes Film Subject," *New York Amsterdam News,* May 6, 1939, 21.

103. Rodger C. Henderson, "Still, William," in *Encyclopedia of African American History*, 205–6.

104. Ibid.

105. Tolson, "The Philosophy of the Big House," in Farnsworth, ed., *Cabbage and Caviar*, 221.

106. Rosetta E. Ross, "Tubman, Harriet," in *African American National Biography*.

107. "Mammies in Films O.K.'D: Hattie McDaniel Takes up the Cudgels in Defense of 'Low Rating Role.'" *New York Amsterdam News,* May 20, 1939, 21.

108. Darlene Clark Hine, "Rape and the Inner Lives of Black Women in the Middle West: Preliminary Thoughts on the Culture of Dissemblance," *Signs* 14 no. 4 (Summer 1989): 915.

109. Watts, *Hattie McDaniel,* 162.

110. Victoria Sturtevant, "But Things Is Changin' Nowadays an' Mammy's Gettin' Bored: Hattie McDaniel and the Culture of Dissemblance," *The Velvet Light Trap* 44 (Fall 1999): 69.

111. Ibid., 70.

112. Higginbotham, *Righteous Discontent*, 194.

113. Johnson, ""Ye Gave Them a Stone,"" 64.

114. Ibid., 63.

115. Ibid., 64.

116. Wanda A. Hendricks and Dorothy Salem, "National Association of Colored Women," in *Black Women in America,*.

117. See Deborah Gray White, *Too Heavy a Load: Black Women in Defense of Themselves, 1894–1994* (New York: Norton, 1998); Dorothy Salem, *To Better Our World: Black Women in Organized Reform, 1890–1920* (Brooklyn: Carlson, 1990).

118. Johnson, ""Ye Gave Them a Stone,"" 66.

119. Ibid., 65; Quotation from Sharon Harley, "A Study of the Preservation and Administration of 'Cedar Hill': The Home of Frederick Douglass," (Washington, D.C.: Frederick Douglass National Historic Site, 1987), 56.

120. "Mammies in Films O.K.'D: Hattie McDaniel Takes up the Cudgels in Defense of 'Low Rating Role,'" *New York Amsterdam News,* May 20, 1939, 21.

121. "Mammies in Films O.K.'D," *New York Amsterdam News*, May 20, 1939, 21.

122. Ibid.

123. Don Ryan, "Yoohoo! Hi'ya, Hattie!" *Los Angeles Times*, Feb. 11, 1940, 3; "Speech for Sunday, July 7, 1940 broadcast of *Wings Over Jordan*, for Miss Hattie McDaniel, Los Angeles California/Negro Star of *Gone with the Wind* and winner of the 1939 Academy Motion Picture Award for the best supporting actress," David O. Selznick Collection, Harry Ransom Center, University of Texas at Austin.

124. There was also significant overlap between the leadership of the two organizations; for example, Nannie Helen Burroughs, one of the WC's founders, and its corresponding secretary for more than a decade, also served as the chair of the NACW's Anti-Lynching Committee and as a regional president of the NACW.

125. Nannie Burroughs, "Straight Talk to Mothers," quoted in Higginbotham, *Righteous Discontent*, 202–3.

126. Higginbotham, *Righteous Discontent*, 205.

127. Ibid., 207.

128. Ibid., 208.

129. Ibid., 185.

130. "Mammies in Films O.K.'D," *New York Amsterdam News*, May 20, 1939, 21.

131. Marcia G. Synnott, "Burroughs, Nannie," in *African American National Biography*.

132. Quoted in Higginbotham, *Righteous Discontent*, 213.

133. Ibid., 212–13.

134. Jackson, *Hattie*, 24.

135. See Ruby Berkley Goodwin, "Negro Pioneers in the Field of Sound Movies," *The Pittsburgh Courier*, May 4, 1929, A1; "When Stepin Fetchit Stepped into Fame," *The Pittsburgh Courier*, city edition, July 6, 1929, 13; and "The Little Busybody Who Got a 'Break,'" *The Pittsburgh Courier*, city edition, Oct. 19, 1929, A1.

136. Lawrence C. Ross, Jr., *The Divine Nine: The History of African American Fraternities and Sororities* (New York: Kensington, 2001), 276.

137. Founded in 1922 by seven African American women who were education students at Butler University in Indiana, Sigma Gamma Rho is the only black Greek letter organization to be established at a predominantly white institution. In 2010, the sorority established the "Hattie McDaniel Breast Cancer Awareness" program, and committed its membership to honoring McDaniel's legacy and commemorating her death from breast cancer in 1952 by "raising awareness of breast cancer prevention and treatment through workshops and partnerships." Sigma Gamma Rho Sorority website, www.sgrho1922.org/october-initiatives.

138. Ross, *The Divine Nine*, 325.

139. The Lincoln Memorial concert was arranged behind the scenes by the NAACP's Walter White, First Lady Eleanor Roosevelt, and Secretary of the Interior Harold Ickes. Allan Keller, *Marian Anderson: A Singer's Journey* (Champaign: University of Illinois Press, 2002), 195–97.

140. Russell Freedman, *The Voice That Challenged a Nation: Marian Anderson and the Struggle for Equal Rights* (New York: Clarion Books, 2004), 39.

141. Ibid., 45.

142. Ibid., 47–48.

143. McElya, "Commemorating the Color Line," 211.

144. Quoted in Russell Freedman, *The Voice That Challenged a Nation*, 59.

145. Ibid., 65.

146. Spillers, "Mama's Baby, Papa's Maybe," 65.

CHAPTER 2: BILL ROBINSON AND BLACK
CHILDREN'S SPECTATORSHIP

1. James Haskins and N. R. Mitgang, *Mr. Bojangles: The Biography of Bill Robinson* (New York: William Morrow, 1988), 41.

2. Jake Austin and Yuval Taylor, *Darkest America: Black Minstrelsy from Slavery to Hip Hop* (New York: WW Norton, 2012), 65; and Mark Knowles, *Tap Roots: The Early History of Tap Dancing* (Jefferson, NC: McFarland, 2002), 121.

3. Marshall and Jean Stearns, *Jazz Dance: The Story of American Vernacular Dance* (New York: Schirmer Books, 1968), 180–81.

4. Knowles, *Tap Roots*, 238.

5. *Variety* Staff, "In Old Kentucky," *Variety Movie Reviews* 1:47 (1935), Film and Television Index, EBSCOhost.

6. Constance Valis Hill, *Tap Dancing America: A Cultural History* (Oxford: Oxford University Press, 2010), 65.

7. Ibid., 63. Mark Knowles makes a claim similar to Hill's, asserting that Robinson "kept the rhythm swinging while he danced up on the balls of his feet. Previously, jig and clog dancers had danced with their heels off the ground but did not swing the rhythm, and buck dancers, such as King Rastus Brown, who did swing the rhythm, danced flat-footed." Knowles, *Tap Roots*, 239.

8. Rob Roy, "Race Stage, Movie Stars, Praise Late Will Rogers," *Chicago Defender*, August 24, 1935, 6.

9. Karen Orr Vered, "White and Black in Black and White: Management of Race and Sexuality in the Coupling of Child-Star Shirley Temple and Bill Robinson," *The Velvet Light Trap* 39 (Spring 1997): 56.

10. Ibid., 52–65.

11. Shirley Temple Black, *Child Star: An Autobiography* (New York: McGraw-Hill, 1988), 90.

12. Temple does not provide substantiation for this pronouncement in her biography, and I can find no archival corroboration for the correspondence between Griffin and Sheehan that she references. But her assertion is interesting in the way that it underscores the incongruous power dynamics between the white child who ultimately "knew" these circumstances, and the African American adult who never mentioned any such story of origin.

13. Ann duCille, "The Shirley Temple of My Familiar," *Transition* 73 (1997): 10–32. See also Vered, "White and Black in Black and White."

14. Robin Bernstein, *Racial Innocence: Performing American Childhood from Slavery to Civil Rights* (New York: NYU Press, 2011), 8.

15. Haskins and Mitgang, *Mr. Bojangles,* 224.

16. Gaylyn Studlar, *Precocious Charms: Performing Girlhood in Classical Hollywood Cinema* (Berkeley: University of California Press, 2013), 78–79.

17. Oddly, Studlar's chapter on Temple in *Precocious Charms* includes a familiar still photo of Robinson and Temple holding hands (taken from *The Little Colonel*), while at the same time leaving Robinson completely out of its discussion of the sexualized dimension of Temple's performances.

18. *The Little Colonel,* DVD, dir. David Butler (1935; Los Angeles: 20th Century Fox, 2006).

19. Donald Bogle, *Toms, Coons, Mulattoes, Mammies, and Bucks: An Interpretive History of Blacks in American Films* (New York: Continuum, 1986), 13.

20. Studlar, *Precocious Charms,* 73.

21. Haskins and Mitgang's biography discusses Robinson's sporting in terms of his gambling and his extramarital affairs with other women, as well as his hot temper and the gold-plated gun—a gift from the New York City police force—that he regularly carried. The latter of these is testified to in a 1929 article from the *Amsterdam News* about Robinson angrily firing his gun "in the air" at theatrical producer Irvin Miller, "'Bojangles' Fires at Irvin C. Miller," *The New York Amsterdam News,* July 17, 1929, 1–2.

22. See for instance, Floyd Snelson's obituary comments about Robinson in "Snelson Pays Tribute To 'Greatest' Tap Dancer," *New York Amsterdam News,* December 3, 1949, 14.

23. This film in fact marked the song's introduction; it would be popularized one year later by Louis Prima.

24. The trio of children appearing in this sequence are three of the "Cabin Kids," a family singing, dancing, and acting group that appeared onscreen and in voice work in nearly two dozen movies in the 1930s.

25. For another example, consider Porgy's happy-go-lucky "I Got Plenty O' Nuthin" in Dubose Heyward and the Gershwin brothers' *Porgy and Bess.*

26. Alyn Shipton, *Fats Waller: The Cheerful Little Earful* (New York: Continuum, 2002).

27. Hill, *Tap Dancing America,* 63.

28. Here I quote Charles' Eckert's classic analysis of Shirley Temple from the essay "Shirley Temple and the House of Rockefeller." One might certainly argue that Robinson's melding of elements of both childlike play and philanthropy in his star persona produces very similar effects to Temple from Eckert's perspective. So much of Eckert's analysis focuses upon paradoxes and tensions (work/play; need/abundance; possession/sharing), anticipating Richard Dyer's theorizing of the black body as a representational "site of remembering and denying the inescapability of the body in the economy." See Charles Eckert, "Shirley Temple and the House of Rockefeller," *Jump Cut,* no. 2 (1974): 1, 17–20; and Richard Dyer, *Heavenly Bodies: Film Stars and Society* (New York: St. Martin's Press, 1986).

29. Gregory Bateson, quoted in Richard Schechner, *Performance Studies: An Introduction* (New York: Routledge, 2013), 92.

30. Richard Dyer explores this idea in *Heavenly Bodies:*

31. Hill, *Tap Dancing America*, 166.

32. Haskins and Mitgang, *Mr. Bojangles*, 21.

33. Haskins and Mitgang, *Mr. Bojangles*; David Hadju, *Lush Life: A Biography of Billy Strayhorn* (New York: Farrar, Straus and Giroux, 1996), 117–18; and Cholly Atkins and Jacqui Malone, *Class Act : The Jazz Life of Choreographer Cholly Atkins* (New York: Columbia University Press, 2001). According to the club's charter, the Copasetics was established as "a social, friendly benevolent club. Its members pledge themselves to do all in their power to promote fellowship and strengthen the character within their ranks." While the Copasetics began as a social club primarily for Black tap dancers, under the leadership of the club's second president, Billy Strayhorn, the Copasetics evolved into an athletic and energetic performing group. In turn, the influence and impact of the Copasetics would become substantial; its members would sustain the art of tap through the "lull" years of the 1950s (a period that arguably commenced with Robinson's death itself) and help to usher the form back into the spotlight with the rise of variety and performance television in the 1960s. See Hill, *Tap Dancing America*; *Great Feats of Feet: Portrait of a Jazz Tap Dancer*, dir. Brenda Bufalino (American Tap Dance Foundation, 1977; Alexander Street Press Dance in Video Online Collection, 2008); and Jennifer Dunning, "Ernest Brown, Last Member of the Original Tapping Copasetics, Dies at 93," *New York Times*, August 25, 2009.

34. "Greatest Tap Dancer Making Good in Movies," *New York Amsterdam News*, July 6 1935, 11.

35. Rusty E. Frank, *Tap!: The Greatest Tap Dance Stars and Their Stories, 1900–1955*, rev. ed. (New York: Da Capo Press, 1994), 72.

36. See Toni Morrison, "Rootedness: The Ancestor as Foundation" in *Black Women Writers, 1950–1980*, ed. Mari Evans (New York: Anchor Doubleday, 1984); Farah Jasmine Griffin, *Who Set You Flowin': The African American Migration Narrative* (Oxford: Oxford University Press, 1996); and Michael Awkward, "'Unruly and Let Loose': Myth, Ideology, and Gender in Song of Solomon," *Callaloo* 13, no. 3 (Summer 1990): 482–98.

37. Ted Poston, "The Cats Are Cynical over New Tree, Jack," *New York Amsterdam News*, November 10, 1934, 1; "Rockefeller Gives Land For Harlem Playground," *Chicago Defender*, December 11, 1937, 5; "Play Spots in Harlem," *Atlanta Daily World*, July 3, 1937, 8; and City of New York Department of Parks and Recreation, Historical Signs, http://mobile.nycgovparks .org/?id = 8250.

38. Earl J. Morris, "Morris Interviews 'Bojangles'; Learns He Is Real Race Man," *The Pittsburgh Courier*, July 31, 1937, 21.

39. Haskins and Mitgang, *Mr. Bojangles*, 213.

40. Mel Watkins, *On the Real Side: A History of African American Comedy from Slavery to Chris Rock* (Chicago: Lawrence Hill Books, 1994), 232.

41. Quoted in Watkins, *On the Real Side*, 233.

42. "Benefit Is Planned," *The Pittsburgh Courier*, June 28, 1930, A6; George Gregory, "Playground Sports," *Chicago Defender*, August 15, 1931, 9; "Bill Robinson, Dancer, Aids Kids [to] Keep Cool," *Chicago Defender*, August 15, 1931, 10; "Bill Robinson Plays Host at Kiddies' Party," *Chicago Defender*,

July 24, 1937, 11. William Brashler, *Josh Gibson: A Life in the Negro Leagues* (New York: Harper and Row, 1978), 13.

43. Associated Negro Press, "Bill Robinson Thinks about 'Feet' When Dancing, He Admits in Coast Interview," *Atlanta Daily World*, April 3, 1935, 2.

44. Toni Morrison, *The Bluest Eye* (New York: Holt, Rinehart and Winston, 1970), 19.

45. Manthia Diawara, "Black Spectatorship: Problems of Identification and Resistance," in *Black American Cinema*, ed. Manthia Diawara (New York: Routledge Press, 1993), 211.

46. bell hooks, "The Oppositional Gaze: Black Female Spectators," in *Black American Cinema*, 295.

47. Jacqueline Stewart, *Migrating to the Movies: Cinema and Black Urban Modernity* (Berkeley: University of California Press, 2005), 100.

48. Dialogue transcribed from Pearl Bowser and Bestor Cram, *Midnight Ramble: Oscar Micheaux and the Story of Race Movies*, PBS series *The American Experience*, dir. Rocky Collins (1994). Similar accounts can be found in published interviews with Jeffries, such as Drew Jubera, "Pioneer Film Cowboy: 'I am colored, and I love it,'" *The Atlanta Journal-Constitution*, July 25, 2008; also Sam Sherman, *Legendary Singing Cowboys* (New York: Friedman/Fairfax Publishers, 1995). Parenthetically, though notably, Jeffries's account is complicated by his revelation, later in life, that he had spent much of his life "passing" for black for all intents and purposes. The Drew Jubera interview cited above provides more detail about this fascinating aspect of Jeffries's complex cinematic identity.

49. James Forman, *Our Movie-Made Children* (New York: Macmillan, 1935), 278; and Paul G. Cressey, "A Social Setting for the Motion Picture," reprinted in Garth Jowett, *Children and the Movies: Media Influence and the Payne Fund Controversy* (Cambridge: Cambridge University Press, 1996), 183–85.

50. See Matthew Bernstein, "*Imitation of Life* in a Segregated Atlanta: Its Promotion, Distribution, and Reception," *Film History* 19, no. 2 (2007): 152–78; Arthur Knight, "Searching for the Apollo: Black Moviegoing and its Contexts in the Small Town U.S. South," in *Explorations in New Cinema History: Approaches and Case Studies*, ed. Richard Maltby, Daniel Biltereyst, and Philippe Meers (Oxford: Wiley Blackwell, 2011); Charlene Regester, "From the Buzzard's Roost: Black Movie-going in Durham and Other North Carolina Cities during the Early Period of American Cinema," *Film History: An International Journal* 17, no. 1 (2005): 113–24; and Gregory Waller, *Main Street Amusements: Movies and Commercial Entertainment in a Southern City, 1896–1930*, (Washington, D.C., Smithsonian Institution Press, 1995).

51. Thanks are due to my colleague and friend Nick Davis for pointing me toward White's instructive work.

52. Patricia White, "On Retrospectatorship," in *Uninvited: Classical Hollywood Cinema and Lesbian Representability* (Bloomington: Indiana University Press, 1999), 196.

53. Formal memoir and autobiography are sources in which the authors very explicitly reconstruct and narrativize themselves for their readers. Moreover, in certain cases, they do so specifically while considering issues of race and/or

gender in hindsight, from the vantage of a "present self" who considers a "past self" from a distance. I also realize that this small selection of memoirs is both self-conscious and self-selecting, and that these personal histories are considered significant because of their authors' adult accomplishments and status. Yet the discussion of film and film performers occurs in these accounts in a way that is usefully indirect, in that the accounts are wholly disinterested in the use to which I put them here.

54. Teresa deLauretis, *The Practice of Love: Lesbian Sexuality and Perverse Desire* (Bloomington: Indiana University Press, 1994), 285.

55. Stewart, *Migrating to the Movies*, 101.

56. Ruth Brown and Andrew Yule, *Miss Rhythm: The Autobiography of Ruth Brown* (New York: Donald I. Fine Books/Dutton, 1996), 14.

57. Ibid., 4.

58. Ibid. One might speculate that Brown's status as a native of Robinson's home state, Virginia, added to her sense of identification with him as role model and star.

59. Calvin Hernton, "Chattanooga Black Boy: Identity and Racism," in *Names We Call Home: Autobiography on Racial Identity*, eds. Becky Thompson and Sangeeta Tyagi (New York: Routledge, 1995), 141.

60. Ibid., 145.

61. The exception is Eartha Kitt, who did not appear in that film.

62. Given the standard "raggedy pickaninny" style-marking of African American children in films of this era, it is worth noting that all of these children are neatly attired, the boys in collared shirts, pleated trousers, and sweaters, the girls sporting dresses and grosgrain ribbons in their braided pigtails.

63. A photograph of Robinson rehearsing his time-step duet with this lovely little girl graces the cover of this book. I found her proud, sweetly beaming smile completely transcendent; even more compelling is her iconic, show-stealing, not-Shirley-Temple-ness. Sadly, though not surprisingly, neither she nor any of the children who appeared with Robinson in *Stormy Weather* received screen credit for their poignant performances, and despite extensive and ongoing research (up to the last possible moment before this book's publication), I have been unable to discover any of their names.

64. Knight strongly identifies his concept with the 1938 Black-cast musical *The Duke Is Tops,* starring Ralph Cooper, and also featuring (a young) Lena Horne. Whereas the plot of *Stormy Weather* poses Bill Williamson as needing Selina Roger's assistance to make his career fly, in *The Duke Is Tops,* Horne is cast as up-and-comer Ethel Andrews, whose boyfriend Duke Davis (Cooper) temporarily sacrifices his own stake in the couple's stage act to help Ethel make it as a "single" onstage. In both cases, the film's couples discover that they entertain better together than apart, and importantly, that they entertain best of all when they are together at the center of grand shows that showcase a variety of talented African American acts.

65. Jackie Stacey, *Star Gazing: Hollywood Cinema and Female Spectatorship* (London: Routledge, 1994), 64-65. My own family's anecdotes about segregated spaces within white theaters carry a similar charge—these are stories about the commonly segregated balconies or "buzzard roosts" of the early

twentieth century, stories in which the older generation of my family remember themselves as children gleefully throwing popcorn or candies onto the heads of unsuspecting white moviegoers.

66. Stewart, *Migrating to the Movies*, 94; Constance Valis Hill, *Brotherhood in Rhythm: The Jazz Tap Dancing of the Nicholas Brothers* (New York: Cooper Square Press, 2002), 43.

67. Quoted in Hill, *Brotherhood in Rhythm*, 48.

68. Display ad from the *Baltimore Afro-American*, November 1, 1930, 9.

69. Stewart, *Migrating to the Movies*, 101.

70. Adrienne Kennedy, *People Who Led to My Plays* (New York: Theatre Communications Group, 1987), 82.

71. Mel Watkins, *Dancing with Strangers: A Memoir* (New York: Simon and Schuster, 1998), 57.

72. Ibid, 41–44. Watkins uses "countrifying" as a humorous counterpoint to the word *gentrifying*.

73. Ibid., 58.

74. bell hooks, *Black Looks: Race and Representation* (Boston: South End Press, 1992), 162.

75. Watkins, *Dancing with Strangers*, 48.

76. DuCille, "The Shirley Temple of My Familiar," 20.

77. Ibid., 21.

78. Shearon A. Lowery and Melvin L. DeFleur, *Milestones in Mass Communication Research: Media Effects* (Upper Saddle River, NJ: Pearson, 1995); Gary Cross, *Kids' Stuff: Toys and the Changing World of American Childhood* (Cambridge, MA: Harvard University Press, 1999), 103–4; and Paula S. Fass, ed., *The Routledge History of Childhood in the Western World* (Abingdon: Routledge, 2013), 445.

79. White, "On Retrospectatorship," 196.

80. Dick Gregory, *Nigger: An Autobiography*, with Robert Lipsyte, 1st ed. (New York: Dutton, 1964), 40.

81. Ibid., 39.

82. Ibid.

83. Ibid..

84. Ibid.

85. Diawara, "Black Spectatorship: Problems of Identification and Resistance," *Black American Cinema*.

86. Gregory, *Nigger: An Autobiography*, 39.

87. Jane M. Gaines, *Fire and Desire: Mixed-Race Movies in the Silent Era* (Chicago: University of Chicago Press, 2001).

88. James Baldwin, *The Devil Finds Work: An Essay* (New York: Dial Press, 1976), 4.

89. Ibid., 7.

90. Ibid.

91. Ibid., 6.

92. Martin Shingler and Christine Gledhill, "Bette Davis: Actor/star" in *Screen* 49, no. 1 (Spring 2008): 67–76; and Cathy Klaprat, "The Star as Market Strategy: Bette Davis in Another Light," in *The American Film Industry*, rev. ed.,

ed. Tino Balio (Madison: University of Wisconsin Press, 1985), 361. Shingler and Gledhill (like Klaprat) note Davis's 1934 appearance in *Of Human Bondage* as the watershed at which Warner Brothers "abandoned its attempt to market her as yet another platinum sexy blonde," and shifted her publicity with stories like the "Universal Train Story." This myth, which circulated in fan magazines, claimed that "when Davis first went to Hollywood, Universal sent a representative to meet her at the train station. But the man saw no one who resembled a glamorous movie actress so Bette went unrecognized and unmet. Another version recalls that Carl Laemmle, Jr., the head of Universal, considered Davis 'about as attractive as Slim Summerville' (a skinny, homely comedian)."

93. See, for instance, Richard Dyer's chapter on Judy Garland in *Heavenly Bodies*.

94. White, "On Retrospectatorship," 201.

95. Maya Angelou, *I Know Why the Caged Bird Sings* (New York: Bantam Books, 1970), 3, 2.

96. Ibid., 4.

97. Ibid., 117.

98. Ibid., 114.

99. Ibid., 118–19.

100. Ibid., 58.

101. Ibid., 59.

102. Ibid., 115.

103. When the two children eventually did come to live with their Mother Dear, she realized that given her long absence from their childhoods, they could not be expected to call her "Mama" or "Mother," and asked them to choose the name by which they would refer to her. Led by Maya's choice, the two children called their mother "Lady," because "You are beautiful and you don't look like a Mother." See Maya Angelou, *Mom and Me and Mom* (New York: Random House, 2013) 17–18, 32.

104. Mary Desjardins, "Not of Hollywood: Ruth Chatterton, Ann Harding, Constance Bennett, Kay Francis, and Nancy Harding," in *Glamour in a Golden Age: Movie Stars of the 1930s,* ed. Adrienne McClean (Rutgers: Rutgers University Press, 2011), 19.

105. Ibid., 42–43.

106. Baldwin, *Devil Finds Work*, 3.

107. Haskins and Mitgang, *Mr. Bojangles,* 300.

108. *Ted Mack and the Original Amateur Hour,* dir. Lewis Graham, Kultur International Films, 1949.

CHAPTER 3: LOUISE BEAVERS AND FREDI WASHINGTON

1. *Chicago,* dir. Rob Marshall, 113 min, Miramax Films, 2002. Quotations taken from screen dialogue.

2. Richard Dyer, *Heavenly Bodies: Film Stars and Society* (London, Basingstoke: Macmillan Education, 1986), 17.

3. Beavers starred in the melodrama *Rainbow on the River* (Bobby Breen/Sol Lesser Productions, 1936) as "'Toinette," a former slave raising the orphaned son

of the white family that owned her before the Civil War. Despite her intentions to keep and raise the boy, he is taken away, to be reunited with the northern branch of his family. But by the film's end 'Toinette and her ward are reunited when she is employed by the northern family to be his "nurse." Washington was featured in the melodrama *One Mile from Heaven* (Twentieth Century Fox, 1937), cast alongside Bill Robinson as her love interest. Washington plays "Flora Jackson," a seamstress raising a young white child as her own, essentially "passing" the child for black. When the mother and daughter are "discovered" by a cub reporter seeking to exploit a human interest story, the daughter is returned to her mother, a former chorus girl whom Flora knew and believed dead. In the end, the child's mother, who has married a rich banker in the meantime, hires Flora as the child's nurse. These oddly similar plots seem intent on recreating something of the sensationalism of *Imitation of Life,* particularly in their casting of that film's black principals as mothers of white children.

4. A number of film and literary scholars (Valerie Smith, Cheryl Wall, Miriam Thaggert, Susan Courtney, and others) have observed the ways in which Delilah and Peola essentially perform critical emotional work for the benefit of Bea and Jessie, the assumed centers of *Imitation of Life.* See Valerie Smith, *Not Just Race, Not Just Gender: Black Feminist Readings* (New York: Routledge, 1998); Cheryl Wall, "Fannie Hurst and Zora Neale Hurston in 'Real' Time," paper presented at Imitating Life: Women Race and Film, 1932–2000, Princeton University, September 23, 2000; Miriam Thaggert, "Divided Images: Black Female Spectatorship and John Stahl's *Imitation of Life.*" *African American Review* 32, no. 3 (1998): 481–91; and Susan Courtney, *Hollywood Fantasies of Miscegenation: Spectacular Narratives of Gender and Race* (Princeton: Princeton University Press, 2004).

5. Andre Sennwald, "The Screen Version of Fannie Hurst's *Imitation of Life,* at the Roxy," *New York Times,* Nov. 24, 1934.

6. Norbert Lusk, "News and Gossip of Stage and Screen, *Imitation of Life* Winner at Box Office," *Los Angeles Times,* Dec. 2, 1934.

7. "New Films Reviewed: Keith Memorial *Imitation of Life,*" *Boston Globe,* Dec. 8, 1934.

8. Byron "Speed" Reilly, "Universal Casts Louise Beavers in Feature Role," Associated Negro Press (*Pittsburgh Courier*), Nov. 17, 1934; Ric Roberts, "*Imitations [sic] of Life* Is Great Negro Picture," *Atlanta Daily World,* Dec. 7, 1934; Harry Levette, "*Imitation of Life* Is Possible Best Seller," *Chicago Defender,* Dec. 15, 1934; Hilda See, "Race Actors Steal *Imitation of Life,*" *Chicago Defender,* Jan. 12, 1935.

9. Quoted in Donald Bogle, *Bright Boulevards, Bold Dreams: The Story of Black Hollywood,* 1st ed. (New York: One World Ballantine Books, 2005), 148–49.

10. *New York Times,* "Screen Notes," Nov. 27, 1934.

11. Earl Morris, "Fredi Washington, *Imitation of Life* Repeat at the 'Met.'" *Pittsburgh Courier,* Feb. 23, 1935; "Harlem Theatre," *New York Amsterdam News,* Jan. 26, 1935; "A Sensation in Harlem," *New York Amsterdam News,* Jan. 26, 1935.

12. Matthew Bernstein and Dana F. White, "*Imitation of Life* in a Segregated Atlanta," *Film History* 19, no. 2 (2007): 161.

13. Bernstein and White, 158.

14. Sam Staggs, *Born to Be Hurt: The Untold Story of* Imitation of Life (New York: St. Martin's Press, 2009), 345. See also "Make Special Trailer for Immitation," [*sic*] *Chicago Defender*, Sept. 7, 1935, 9.

15. Linda K. Fuller, "Beavers, Louise," in *African American National Biography*, eds. Henry Louis Gates, Jr., and Evelyn Brooks Higginbotham, (Oxford: Oxford University Press, 2008).

16. James Snead, *White Screens, Black Images: Hollywood from the Dark Side* (New York, London: Routledge, 1994); Norma Manatu, *African American Women and Sexuality in the Cinema* (Jefferson, NC: McFarland, 2003); Donald Bogle, *Brown Sugar: Eighty Years of America's Black Female Superstars* (New York: Da Capo Press, 1980).

17. Bogle, *Bright Boulevards*, 138.

18. David Krasner, "*Shuffle Along* and the Quest of Nostalgia," in *A Beautiful Pageant: African American Performance Theater and Drama in the Harlem Renaissance, 1910–1917* (New York: Palgrave Macmillan, 2002), 261.

19. James Weldon Johnson, *Black Manhattan* (New York: Da Capo Press, 1991), 217–18; "*Hot Chocolates* in 75th Performance," *Chicago Defender*, August 31, 1929, 7; Nardy, "Stage Stuff," *Chicago Defender*, July 9, 1927, 6.

20. Stephen Bourne, "Obituary: Fredi Washington," *The Independent*, July 4, 1994; Cheryl Black, "Looking White, Acting Black: Cast(e)ing Fredi Washington," *Theatre Survey* 45, no. 1 (May 2004), 23–25.

21. Bessye Bearden was the mother of celebrated African American artist Romare Bearden, herself an activist and community leader. She also served as the *Defender's* New York editor from 1927 to 1928. Bessye Bearden, "Fredi Washington Wed's Duke's Trombonist: Stage's Prettiest Star Signs a Mate," *Chicago Defender*, August 19, 1933.

22. Noliwe Rooks, *Hair Raising: Beauty, Culture, and African American Women* (New Brunswick, NJ: Rutgers University Press, 1996), 34–35.

23. Jayna Brown, *Babylon Girls: Black Women Performers and the Shaping of the Modern* (Durham, NC: Duke University Press, 2008), 219–34.

24. Martin Duberman, *Paul Robeson* (New York: Alfred A. Knopf, 1989), 168; see also Scott McGee and Jeff Stafford, "The Emperor Jones," Turner Classic Movies, accessed June 2003, www.tcm.com/this-month/article/24065|24068/The-Emperor-Jones.html.

25. Anna Everett, *Returning the Gaze: A Genealogy of Black Film Criticism, 1940–1949* (Durham, NC: Duke University Press, 2001), 221.

26. Ibid.

27. Karen M. Bowdre, "Passing Films and the Illusion of Racial Equality," *Black Camera* 5, no. 2 (Spring 2014): 25.

28. The next time a Black actor would be cast in a major motion picture in a "passing" role was Lonette McKee's turn in the 1984 film *The Cotton Club*. McKee plays "Lila Rose Oliver," a light-skinned Black chorus girl in 1920s Harlem who decides to pass for white. Meanwhile, independent films like *Lost Boundaries* (1949), exploitation movies like *I Passed for White* (1960), as well as major studio productions like *Pinky* (1949), Douglas Sirk's remake of *Imitation of Life* (1959), and even the 2003 film *The Human Stain*, all cast white actors in leading roles as Blacks passing for white.

29. Courtney, *Hollywood Fantasies of Miscegenation*, 165.

30. In 1935, the African American newspaper the *New York Age* carried a letter from a group of Black college students at Oberlin, who decried the unreality of the Peola character based chiefly on this very scene. With the disdain of true cosmopolites, they pointed out that, after all, Harlem was just a stone's throw away from Peola, and declared that they did not "care to try to explain a colored girl in the city of New York . . . who (we are led to suppose) is well supplied with funds, spending her evenings hanging around a basement staircase trying to catch a glimpse of the 'white folks' party. Imagine such a thing in New York!" "The *Age* Readers Forum," *New York Age*, March 9, 1935.

31. Sterling Brown, "Once a Pancake," in *A Son's Return: Selected Essays of Sterling A. Brown*, ed. Mark Sanders (Boston: Northeastern University Press, 1996), 287–91. This essay originally appeared in the March 1935 edition of *Opportunity*.

32. Darlene Clark Hine, "Rape and the Inner Lives of Black Women in the Middle West," *Signs* 14, no. 4 (Summer 1989): 912–20.

33. Indeed, it is a tribute to Louise Beavers's acting abilities that she, a Cincinnati native and California transplant, delivers the line as naturally and believably as she does.

34. "Popular Character Artist at Local Theatre: Louise Beavers Here Again at Loew Houses," *New York Amsterdam News*, Sept. 21, 1935, 7.

35. Ellen Scott's fine essay "More Than a 'Passing' Sophistication" provides a powerful and extended analysis of Fredi Washington and Claudette Colbert's similar costuming, build, and carriage in *Imitation of Life*, and makes a persuasive argument that "while the narrative insists that Peola is black, the film's visuals—accented by cross-cutting—suggest an indelible comparability between her and Bea." Ellen Scott, "More than a 'Passing' Sophistication: Dress, Film Regulation, and the Color Line in 1930s American Films," *Women's Studies Quarterly* 41, nos. 1 and 2 (Spring/Summer 2013): 73. Relatedly, Valerie Smith notes that *Imitation*'s "emotional logic sets up an analogy between the white mother [Bea] and the black daughter [Peola] . . . [with Peola's] rejection of her mother's love . . . shown to be analogous to what is seen as Bea's neglect of her daughter, Jessie . . . [Peola's] punishment is designed to teach both her and Bea a lesson." Smith, *Not Just Race, Not Just Gender*, 49–50.

36. Ruth Feldstein, *Motherhood in Black and White: Race and Sex in American Liberalism, 1930–1965* (Ithaca: Cornell University Press, 2000), 20.

37. Of course, Delilah's emotional distress is made both poignant and somewhat ironic in this context, given that African American women regularly lived through being separated from their children during the era of American slavery.

38. Louis Lautier, "Louise Beavers Wouldn't Use Epithet in *Imitation of Life*," *Baltimore Afro-American*, March 2, 1935.

39. Given Delilah's temperament, this comment registers as a surprising (unconscious?) criticism of Bea who has "sent" her own daughter away to boarding school.

40. Cherene Sherrard-Johnson insightfully suggests that "Peola represents black desire for white privilege and a kind of repression of sensual expression; despite her beauty, there is no love match for her." Cherene Sherrard-Johnson,

Portraits of the New Negro Woman: Visual and Literary Culture in the Harlem Renaissance (New Brunswick: Rutgers University Press), 99.

41. Snead, *White Screens, Black Images*, 4, 47.

42. Ibid., 68–73.

43. Henry Louis Gates, "The Trope of the New Negro and the Reconstruction of the Image of the Black," *Representations* 24 (Fall 1998): 130–31.

44. Ibid., 131, 143.

45. Sherrard-Johnson, *Portraits of the New Negro Woman*, xviii.

46. Rooks, *Hair Raising*, 26.

47. I use Maxine L. Craig's term "pigmentocracy" here to denote the significance of skin color hierarchy within African American communities. See Maxine Leeds Craig, *Ain't I a Beauty Queen: Black Women, Beauty, and the Politics of Race* (Oxford: Oxford University Press, 2002).

48. Sherrard-Johnson, *Portraits of the New Negro Woman*, 7.

49. Fred Daniels, "Fredye [*sic*] Washington May Talk Herself out of the Movies," *Chicago Defender*, April 28, 1934, 9.

50. Toward the late 1930s, *The Crisis* began to showcase more men on its covers, men whose skin color offered a range of shades, unlike the "cover girls" who preceded them.

51. All five of the performers discussed in this book were subject to this practice in African American newspapers. It was typical enough that activist Loren Miller harshly decried the practice in the pages of *The Crisis*. Loren Miller, "Uncle Tom in Hollywood," *The Crisis* 41, no. 2 (November 1934): 329.

52. In teaching *Imitation of Life*, I have jokingly referred to these advertisements as the "prizefight" images, in that they evoke the spatial relationship of "X vs. Y" so often established in advertisements for boxing contests.

53. Crane and Co. advertisement, *St. Louis Palladium*, January 31, 1903, 4. Rooks, *Hair Raising*, 26.

54. "Screen King and Movie Queen Gain Fame Overnight," advertisement, *Topeka Plain Dealer*, March 15, 1930, 5.

55. This is not to say that Black men did not benefit from the privileges that light skin bestowed; however, the link between light skin and beauty was pronounced enough to make Black men's clout and currency less dependent upon it, as attractiveness is generally less relevant as a source of power for men under patriarchy, irrespective of race.

56. Another Palmer's advertisement is even more unambiguous in its assertion that, for Black women at least, achieving a light skin is essential to attaining beauty and "success." A ad in the style of a multipanel comic that appeared in the Nov. 23, 1935 edition of the *Pittsburgh Courier* carried the headline "Twin Girls Show How to Lighten the Skin." By using identical twins "Nancy" and "Ella," the advertisement builds in the "before and after" conceit, as twin Nancy uses Palmer's skin success, and "Three Days Later," is asked out to the dance by a young man. When she asks her suitor "about somebody for Ella," he responds with a blunt "Sorry, honey no one likes Ella, she's too dark," in a panel that depicts a distraught Ella in the background. The next panel features a drawing of Nancy embracing and comforting Ella, and remarking "See Ella I told you to use Palmer's Skin Success," and the dispirited Ella responding

"Allright [*sic*] Nancy, now I'll try it." The advertisement enacts a pointed inversion; in *Imitation of Life,* mother Delilah comforts daughter Peola because of the anguish caused by Peola's light skin, while Palmer's has sister Nancy comfort her twin Ella because of the anguish caused by Ella's dark skin. And while Peola's despair in *Imitation* is evidently insuperable, Ella's is avoidable by the simple application of the Palmer's product. The cartoon ends with a double wedding for Nancy and Ella, who both get themselves married to "handsome men." The men are also light-skinned, though they are presented as such seemingly without having had to undergo any cosmetic labor or alteration. Given the currency of light skin as a class signifier irrespective of gender, we may imagine that Nancy and Ella's success via Palmer's inheres in their ability to marry "up" the economic ladder. The comic strip format and the conceit of "twins" allows for repeated side-by-side comparisons of Nancy and Ella along the lines of their desirability and success, and to this end, Nancy is depicted as lighter skinned than Ella from the very first panel in which we are introduced to them. It is only in the double wedding of the last panel, after both women have lightened their skins with Palmer's, that they become "identical."

57. Lena Horne, advertisement for Dr. Fred Palmer's Skin Whitener, *Chicago Defender,* May 25, 1935.

58. Advertisement for Elsner's Pearl Cream, *New York Amsterdam News,* April 2, 1930, 6.

59. Advertisement for Marlé Bleaching Lotion, *New York Amsterdam News,* January 15, 1930, 5.

60. Vere Johns, "In the Name of Art: *Imitation of Life,*" *New York Age,* Jan. 19, 1935, 4.

61. Fay M. Jackson, "Fredi Washington Strikes New Note in Hollywood Film," *Pittsburgh Courier,* Dec. 15, 1934.

62. Thaggert, "Divided Images," 490.

63. Jackson, "Fredi Washington Strikes New Note"

64. Johns, "In the Name of Art: *Imitation of Life.*"

65. Ibid.

66. E. Washington Rhodes, "Greatest Condemnation of Prejudice in America Seen in *Imitation of Life,*" *Philadelphia Tribune,* Feb. 14, 1935.

67. Ibid.

68. Her review was reprinted in other African American newspapers. For instance, the *Portland Advocate* reran the review a week later under the headline "Fannie Hurst Picture Portrays Vivid Story."

69. Bernice Patton, "Critics Weep at the Premiere of *Imitation of Life,*" *The Pittsburgh Courier,* Dec. 8, 1934, A9.

70. Bogle, *Bright Boulevards, Bright Dreams,* 135. See also Staggs, *Born to Be Hurt,* 343.

71. Patton, "Critics Weep."

72. Ibid.

73. Everett, *Returning the Gaze,* 194–96, 225.

74. Ibid., 228.

75. William Lee, "Louise Beavers in Pittsburgh," *Chicago Defender,* March 23, 1935.

76. Donald Bogle, *Toms, Coons, Mulattoes, Mammies, and Bucks: An Interpretive History of Blacks in American Films* (New York: Continuum, 1996), 57.

77. Brown, "Once a Pancake," 289.

78. Bogle, *Toms, Coons, Mulattoes, Mammies, and Bucks,* 57.

79. Levette, "*Imitation of Life* Is Possible Best Seller," 9.

80. See "Business and Professional Folk Are in Film," *California Eagle,* Sept. 7, 1934, 6; "300 Work in Death Scene of New Film," *Los Angeles Sentinel,* Sept. 20, 1934; Fay Jackson, "Fay Writes of Hollywood Dope," *Atlanta Daily World,* Oct. 23, 1934, 2.

81. Many African American newspapers featured regular sections about the doings of African American fraternal and lodge societies. The funeral scene caused at least some white viewers consternation. Robert Gaylord, a California-based officer of the U.S. Grand Encampment of Knights Templar wrote Joseph Breen of the MPAA to complain about the "display ... of a procession of negroes in Knights Templar uniform at the funeral ceremony of a negro mammy." He closed his letter declaring his hope that Breen would act to "remedy a display which every Mason naturally resents." Gaylord received a response from none other than Universal production manager Carl Laemmle, who apologized profusely and identified himself "as a Mason who prides himself on a serious, sincere, and generous acceptance of his Masonic obligations .... no one can possibly regret more than I that this unfortunate scene was permitted to creep into the picture." Robert B. Gaylord to Joseph Breen, January 8, 1935 and Carl Laemmle to Robert Gaylord, January 23, 1935, both in MPAA Collection, Margaret Herrick Library, Academy of Motion Picture Arts and Sciences.

82. Susan Courtney has suggested that Delilah's spectacularity and prominence in the film stems from Universal's need to tether the racially illegible body of Peola to an unequivocal signifier of blackness, even to the extent that Delilah's body obscures or conceals Peola's. She discusses the Production Code Administration's extreme apprehension about the film being made primarily in terms of the way that Peola as a character "confounded the PCA's ability to discern racial identity" and "perpetually threatened to unmask race as itself ... a cultural fiction in which we are asked to believe which has no natural life of its own." Courtney, *Hollywood Fantasies of Miscegenation,* 143.

83. See "Louise Beavers Believes Talkie Roles Misunderstood," "Star Dust," and "Louise Beavers at Apollo," *Baltimore Afro-American,* February 23, 1935; Louis Lautier, "Louise Beavers Wouldn't Use Epithet in *Imitation of Life,*" and "Louise Beavers in Person at Apollo," *Baltimore Afro-American,* March 2, 1935; William Smallwood, "Louise Beavers in D.C.; Tells of Movie Stars She Knows," "Many Think Academy Should Recognize Work of Louise Beavers," "Always Do Your Best, Miss Beavers Tells D.C. Pupils," and "Players Fete Louise Beavers," *Baltimore Afro-American,* March 9, 1935.

84. "Louise Beavers Believes Talkie Roles Misunderstood," *Baltimore Afro-American,* February 23, 1935.

85. Lautier, "Louise Beavers Wouldn't Use Epithet," *Baltimore Afro-American,* March 2, 1935.

86. Levette, "*Imitation of Life* Is Possible Best Seller," *Chicago Defender,* Dec. 15, 1934.

87. Joseph I. Breen to Harry Zehner, July 20, 1934, and Robert Cochrane to Joseph I. Breen, July 27, 1934, both in MPAA Collection, Margaret Herrick Library, Academy of Motion Picture Arts and Sciences.

88. Beavers's claim also anticipated a later, more widely publicized assertion made by Hattie McDaniel with respect to *Gone with the Wind* in 1939.

89. "Always Do Your Best, Miss Beavers Tells D.C. Pupils," *Baltimore Afro-American*, March 9, 1935.

90. Indeed, both Bunche and Beavers were transplanted Californians as teenagers. Beavers had come from Cincinnati to Pasadena, and Bunche's family moved from Detroit to nearby Los Angeles. Interestingly, another attendee at the luncheon was Daisy Brown, wife of Sterling Brown—the author of the scathing "Once a Pancake" article in *The Crisis*.

91. "A Constant Reader," "*Afro* Readers Say: Disgraceful Screen Example," and Rothall Gardner, "*Afro* Readers Say: *Imitation of Life* Certainly Irked this Reader Plenty," *Baltimore Afro-American*, February 9, 1935.

92. Dorothy Doleman, "*Afro* Readers Say: Credit to Louise Beavers," *Baltimore Afro-American*, March 16, 1935; Marie Alexander, "*Afro* Readers Say: Bitter Pill for Washington Movie-Goer," *Baltimore Afro-American*, March 23, 1935.

93. George Hall, "'The Inside'—Louise Beavers," *Philadelphia Tribune*, March 14, 1935, 1.

94. Ibid.; "Philadelphia Welcomes Lovely Louise Beavers," *Philadelphia Tribune*, March 21, 1935, 6; and "The A. Drews Entertain for Miss Beavers," *Philadelphia Tribune*, March 21, 1935, 6.

95. Brown, *Babylon Girls*, 236–37.

96. Fay Jackson, "Fredi Washington Hands Hollywood Lemon," *Press* (*Atlanta Daily World*), April 15, 1934, 7; see also "Uptown Fredi Gives the Lowdown on Hollywood," *Pittsburgh Courier*, April 14, 1934;

97. "Fredi Washington Signed for Miscegenation Film Role: Famed Actress Is Given Part," *Atlanta Daily World*, May 30, 1934, 2.

98. "Fredi Washington Has Problem Not Bared in *Imitation*," *Pittsburgh Courier*, March 2, 1935.

99. Ibid.

100. Ibid.

101. After McKinney's leading role in MGM's 1929 Black-cast musical *Hallelujah!*, the studio signed her to a five-year contract. Yet over the term of her employment, she appeared in minor roles in only two movies; as a hotel manager in *Safe in Hell* (1931), and in a small cameo as herself in *Reckless* (1935); she also dubbed songs for Jean Harlow in the latter film. Like many other African American performers of the early twentieth century, McKinney found greater popularity and acceptance in Europe, where she worked steadily as a club and cabaret singer and dancer, using the title "The Black Garbo." She also had a small but memorable part in the 1949 film *Pinky*, a film which ironically starred white actress Jeanne Crain in the role of a black woman who passes for white in the North, but must confront her past when she returns to the South. McKinney plays Rozelia, a Black southern character who angrily "outs" Pinky when she attempts to pass. Stephen Bourne, *Nina Mae McKinney: The Black*

Garbo (Oklahoma: Bear Manor Media, 2011), 19–37; Jonette O'Kelley Miller, "McKinney, Nina Mae," in *African American National Biography.*

102. Smith, *Not Just Race, Not Just Gender,* 35–36.

103. Sherrard-Johnson, *Portraits of the New Negro Woman,* 101, 77.

104. Clifford MacKay, "Going Backstage with the Scribe," *The Chicago Defender,* Jan. 19, 1935, 8.

105. "Part in *Imitation* Is Not Real Me, Says Fredi: NO 'IMITATION,'" *Chicago Defender,* Jan. 19, 1935, 9.

106. Earl Conrad, "American Viewpoint: To Pass or Not to Pass?" *Chicago Defender,* June 18, 1945.

107. Previously, the closest Washington had come to this sort of admission of what was effectively "passing" behavior was in a 1935 interview with the *Baltimore Afro-American,* in which she conceded that she did not "bother about hanging a sign over my shoulders warning people of my race or explaining apologetically what I am. You can see how utterly absurd that would be. I simply act naturally." See L. Herbert Henegan, "*Imitation of Life* White Folks' Play, Says Film Star," *Baltimore Afro-American,* Feb. 9, 1935.

108. Washington made her last film, *One Mile From Heaven,* in 1937. She continued to act in such stage productions as *Lysistrata* and *Mamba's Daughters.* She was also politically active, helping to cofound the Negro Actors Guild, a professional organization formed to help Black performers fight discrimination in the entertainment business. Regina V. Jones, "Washington, Fredi," in *African American National Biography.*

109. Conrad, "To Pass or Not to Pass?"

110. See *YouTube,* http://youtu.be/GVMFYDBxZr4; *The Internet Archive,* https://archive.org/details/ImitationOfLife1934Trailer_458; and *Turner Classic Movies,* www.tcm.com/mediaroom/video/103654/Imitation-of-Life-Trailer-for-Colored-Audiences-.html. Turner is the only one of the sites noted here to indicate that this was not the "regular" *Imitation* trailer, and that it was made specifically for Black audiences' viewership.

CHAPTER 4: LINCOLN PERRY'S "PROBLEMATIC STARDOM"

1. Arthur Knight, "Star Dances: African American Constructions of Stardom, 1925–1960," in *Classic Hollywood, Classic Whiteness,* ed. Daniel Bernardi (Minneapolis: University of Minnesota Press, 2001), 387–88.

2. Ibid.

3. Ibid., 404.

4. Of the group of actors explored in this book, Lincoln Perry's case is distinguished by the significance of his screen name. "Step and fetch it" is, after all, a command. The name's comedic reference to servitude and slavery is directly emblematic of the white supremacist dynamics in which Perry was obliged to traffic as a "problematic star" of this era. That being said, in the perceptions of the broader American public, Lincoln Perry hardly existed: Stepin Fetchit was the name by which Perry and his persona were widely known, disseminated, and celebrated. Given that (and despite my inclination to show Perry the personal courtesy of referring to him by the name given him at birth), this chapter

absolutely oscillates between addressing him as Lincoln Perry and Stepin Fetchit, treating them sometimes as if they were two different people. I do this both to acknowledge Perry's own agency in fashioning, perfecting, and publicizing Stepin Fetchit, and to advance this chapter's (and this book's) overall concern with stardom as a culturally constructed phenomenon. As the following pages attest, Perry recognized that by and large, Stepin Fetchit's appeal was based upon a preconceived notion of Blackness that made little if any room for Lincoln Perry the man. As such, for the most part, I use "Lincoln Perry" in instances to do with the actor's intended ownership, creation, promotion, and styling of a star persona and a performance aesthetic, as well as in discussions of his contractual agreements and connections with studios. I use "Stepin Fetchit" when talking about the star and character who appeared in Hollywood films, and publicity reports, and in other offscreen contexts that rely uncritically upon the contours of the Stepin Fetchit persona for their meaning.

5. Perhaps the most infamous of the texts to find Perry "guilty" is the 1968 CBS made-for-television documentary *Black History: Lost, Stolen, or Strayed*, discussed later in the chapter. But the two extant biographies of Perry, Champ Clark's slim *Shuffling to Ignominy: The Tragedy of Stepin Fetchit* (New York: iUniverse: 2005), and Mel Watkins, *Stepin Fetchit: The Life and Times of Lincoln Perry* (New York: Vintage, 2005), attempted to recuperate and vindicate the actor, underscoring the putatively subversive aspects of his performance and persona.

6. Ossie Davis, "Stepin Fetchit" in *Life Lit by Some Large Vision: Selected Speeches and Writings* (New York: Atria Books, 2006), 164. Davis made the tribute in 1981 on the "Hollywood Heroes" episode of *Ossie and Ruby!*, an anthology series that he and wife Ruby Dee hosted for two seasons on PBS.

7. See Ryan Jay Friedman, *Hollywood's African American Films: The Transition to Sound* (New Brunswick, NJ: Rutgers University Press, 2011); Arthur Knight, *Disintegrating the Musical: Black Performance and American Musical Film* (Durham, NC: Duke University Press, 2002); and Alice Maurice, *The Cinema and Its Shadow: Race and Technology in Early Cinema* (Minneapolis: University of Minnesota Press, 2013).

8. King Vidor, quoted in Alice Maurice, "'Cinema at Its Source:' Synchronizing Race and Sound in the Early Talkies," *Camera Obscura* 17, no. 1 (2002): 36.

9. Ibid., 44.

10. Rosalind Shaffer, "All-Colored Casts Invade Hollywood," *Chicago Tribune*, Dec. 9, 1928, 17.

11. Friedman, *Hollywood's African American Films*, 28.

12. J. F. H., "At the Movies this Week: *The Broadway Melody*, with Bessie Love and Anita Page," *The Baltimore Sun*, April 2, 1929, 5.

13. Robert Benchley, "*Hearts in Dixie*: The First Real Talking Picture," *Opportunity*, April 1929, 122.

14. Elizabeth Goldbeck, "Step Tells All," *Motion Picture Magazine*, July 1929, 76.

15. Ibid.

16. Frantz Fanon, *Black Skin, White Masks*, trans. Richard Philcox, rev. ed. (New York: Grove Press, 2008), 86.

17. Richard Dyer, *Stars*, new ed. (London: British Film Institute, 1998), 20.

18. Scott Eyman, *The Speed of Sound: Hollywood and the Talkie Revolution, 1926–1930* (Baltimore: Johns Hopkins University Press, 1999), 270.

19. "Who's Who of Talkie Stars," *Film Weekly*, Nov. 18, 1929, 44. His entry reads: "Negro. Musical comedy star, well known as the original singer of 'Old Man River' in *Showboat*. Talkies include *Fox Movietone Follies* and *Big Time*."

20. Knight, "Star Dances," 389–90.

21. "Actor Too Proud to Work in Films with Own Race," *Chicago Defender*, Dec. 29, 1928.

22. Ibid.

23. Maurice Dancer, "'I Didn't High-Hat Colored Players,' Answers Fetchit," *Pittsburgh Courier*, Feb. 2, 1929.

24. Knight, "Star Dances," 398.

25. Biographer Mel Watkins notes that Perry's father was himself a traveling vaudevillian, and that young Lincoln greatly admired his raffish style and his performance ability. Watkins, *Stepin Fetchit*, 12–16.

26. Ibid., 29.

27. Ibid.

28. Ibid., 61.

29. Bosley Crowther, "The Screen," *New York Times*, May 15, 1939; Herbert Howe, "Troubadour ob de Lawd," *New Movie Magazine*, June 1935, 32.

30. Michel Chion, *The Voice in Cinema*, trans. Claudia Gorbman (New York: Columbia University Press, 1999), 47.

31. Constance Rourke, *American Humor: A Study of the National Character* (Talahassee: Florida State University Press, 1959), 82.

32. Herbert Howe, "Stepin's High Colored Past," *Photoplay*, June 19, 1929, 31, 125.

33. Howe, "Troubadour ob de Lawd," 58.

34. New York Public Library for the Performing Arts, Stepin Fetchit clips, c. Dec. 1940, unidentified newspaper source. Quoted in Watkins, *Stepin Fetchit*, 63.

35. Perry gave this interview when he was in Boston, appearing in a production of the musical comedy *Three after Three*.

36. Maurice, "Cinema at Its Source," 33.

37. Chion, *The Voice in Cinema*, 102.

38. Ibid., 103. Emphasis in original.

39. Ibid., 95.

40. Watkins, *Stepin Fetchit*, 12.

41. There was even a somewhat hyped public disagreement between dramatic actor Lionel Barrymore and comic actor Eddie Cantor about whether or not Fetchit was Williams's equal. The venerable Barrymore asserted that Stepin Fetchit was as funny, if not funnier than Bert Williams. Cantor refuted the claim publicly and somewhat vocally.

42. See Charles Bowen, "Bert Williams or Stepin Fetchit Which Was the Greater Comedian?" *The Baltimore Afro-American*, Jan. 27, 1934, 21; Henri de la Tour, "Lionel Is No Judge at All: For He Places Stepin Fetchit above the Late Bert Williams as Comic," *The New York Amsterdam News*, Dec. 13, 1933, 7.

43. He and another man are actually witnessing a couple of chicken thieves dividing up their haul, but the sinister graveyard setting prompts a wild misinterpretation of what they see.

44. This routine is also sometimes referred to as "Incomplete Sentence." It is identified that way on YouTube, for instance, where a number of examples of Moreland and Carter's performances of the routine can be found.

45. The eponymous protagonist of the Charlie Chan films was played by three successive white actors in "yellowface." The first was Warner Oland, who was succeeded after his death in 1938 by Sidney Toler. Toler appeared as Chan until his death in 1946; thereafter the role was performed by Roland Winters.

46. *The Scarlet Clue*, dir. Phil Rosen (MGM, 1945). This and other indefinite talk routines between Moreland and Carter are currently available online at http://youtu.be/6bIyMBSx5Qo.

47. Knight, *Disintegrating the Musical*, 110.

48. Though Tommy Chan is one of Charlie Chan's thoroughly Americanized progeny, it seems that part of the humor in this interchange is intended at his expense, in reference to his racial difference from both the assumed white viewing audience and from Moreland and Carter. The notion of their unintelligibility is heightened by the presence of a visually "foreign" onlooker who symbolizes both his own otherness and theirs as well. Through the use of reaction shots of Tommy, the film implicitly compares the incomprehensibility of Moreland and Carter's conversation to the "inscrutability" of the speech of Chinese immigrants (like Charlie Chan) and their American-born children (like Tommy).

49. Watkins, *Stepin Fetchit*, 15.

50. Contracts between Fox West Coast Theaters, Fox Film Corporation, and Stepin Fetchit dated July 1928, November 1928, July 1929, and August 1933. Fox Legal Files, "Stepin Fetchit" Folder FLXR-861, Arts Special Collections Department, University of California at Los Angeles.

51. Perry was rehired by Fox in August 1933, under a contract far less generous than his first in the late 1920s. When the studio fired him in 1929, he was making $750 per week, and was halfway into a contract that would have ultimately paid him double that salary had he stayed. When he returned some four years later, he was re-signed at an introductory salary of $200 per week, on a contract that topped out at $750 per week. Perry's six-month raises were scheduled at $50 per period. His documented salary refutes the frequently repeated myth of Stepin Fetchit as an early Black millionaire. Fox Legal Files, "Stepin Fetchit" Folder FLXR-861, Arts Special Collections Department, University of California at Los Angeles.

52. Dyer, *Stars*, 18. Though Dyer makes a careful distinction between the terms "publicity" and "promotion," I use them fairly interchangeably here, in large part because of the widespread industrial use of the term "publicity" to mean what Dyer defines as "promotion." See also Tino Balio, *Grand Design: Hollywood as a Modern Business Enterprise, 1930–1939* (Berkeley: University of California Press, 1996); Cathy Klaprat, "The Star as Market Strategy: Bette Davis in Another Light," in *The American Film Industry,* ed. Tino Balio, rev. ed. (Madison: University of Wisconsin Press, 1985); Mia Mask, *Divas on Screen: Black Women in American Film* (Urbana-Champaign: University of Illinois

Press, 2009); Charlene Regester, *The African American Actresses: Struggles for Visibility, 1900–1960* (Bloomington: Indiana University Press, 2010); Arthur Knight, "Star Dances," in Bernardi, *Classic Hollywood, Classic Whiteness*; Anna Everett, *Returning the Gaze: A Genealogy of Black Film Criticism, 1909–1949* (Durham, NC: Duke University Press, 2001); Gaylyn Studlar, *This Mad Masquerade* (New York: Columbia University Press, 1996) and *Precocious Charms* (Berkeley: University of California Press, 2013); Richard Decordova, *Picture Personalities: The Emergence of the Star System in America* (Urbana-Champaign: University of Illinois Press, 2001); Christine Gledhill, *Stardom: Industry of Desire* (London: Routledge, 1991); and Jeanine Basinger, *The Star Machine* (New York: Vintage, 2009).

53. Dyer, *Stars*, 10, 17.

54. John C. Moffitt, "Mr. Fetchit in Kansas City," *New York Times*, Feb. 24, 1935, X5.

55. Letter dated November 25, 1929 from Sol Wurtzel to Stepin Fetchit; serial memoranda of 1929 from Fox casting director David Todd to Jack Gardner detailing Stepin Fetchit's refusal to report to the studio daily at 9:30 am, dated Nov. 19, Nov. 27, Dec. 2, Dec. 3, Dec. 18, and Dec. 19; memo dated Dec. 19, 1929, from Jack Gardner to William Crawford, attached to undated, unidentified newspaper clipping announcing "'Stepin Fetchit' is Arrested, Charged With Intoxication"; letter of termination from Sol Wurtzel to Stepin Fetchit dated December 20, 1929. Fox Legal Files, "Stepin Fetchit" Folder FLXR-861, Arts Special Collections Department, University of California at Los Angeles.

56. Although I explain my divided references to "Lincoln Perry" and "Stepin Fetchit" along the theoretical lines described in note 4, the hallmark of stardom is an inevitable messiness that precludes a neat separation between "the star" and "the person." My use of Stepin Fetchit's proper name in the "Prodigal Perry discourse" concept highlights this messiness. Besides being memorably alliterative, the phrase "Prodigal Perry" also invokes Perry's agency as Fox's contracted actor. His individual acts of willful resistance against his employers at Fox frequently relied upon a slippage between "himself" and the Stepin Fetchit persona, one which he attempted to use to his own benefit. For example, among his breaches at the studio in the 1920s was his manifest defiance of executives' demand that he present himself at the studio daily at 8:30 A.M., to be on hand in case there was work for him. Perry's refusal to do so was drawn out, passive-aggressive, and markedly Stepin-Fetchit-esque: he had a phone installed in his apartment at Fox's expense, and informed his handler at the studio that he would call in, instead of reporting in person. Despite being told that this practice was unacceptable, he continued to call in daily, then began having his chauffeur call the studio *for* him. Although Fox's public marketing of him as their wayward prodigal was based on far higher-profile affairs and scandals, this particular power struggle was ongoing in the weeks and days before he was finally fired. It is exemplary of Perry's layered, slippery use of the Stepin Fetchit persona, in its simultaneous embrace of Hollywood extravagance, resistance of seemingly unfair or exploitative industrial demands, and wryly cynical invocation of stereotypical motifs—in this case, of "laziness." Ultimately, even as Fox's publicity reports gloated over the change that taken place in their erst-

while, problematic star, this discourse of transformation was vulnerable to the public appeal of Stepin Fetchit's immutability.

57. Robert Burkhardt, Fox Publicity Report 5890, Stepin Fetchit Biographical File, Margaret Herrick Library, Academy of Motion Picture Arts and Sciences, Beverly Hills.

58. Morris Dickstein, *Dancing in the Dark: A Cultural History of the Great Depression,* (New York: W. W. Norton, 2010), 215–44.

59. Fox Publicity Report 5893, and Color Biography of Stepin Fetchit, Stepin Fetchit Biographical File, Margaret Herrick Library, Academy of Motion Picture Arts and Sciences, Beverly Hills. This report declares that Stepin Fetchit "made a dozen pictures and a barrel of money. Became the studio pest—was never on hand when he was wanted. Became so unreliable that the Hollywood⋅ ax was dropped on his black and unsuspecting neck and he found himself a penniless ex-star."

60. Richard Dyer, "Paul Robeson: Crossing Over," in *Heavenly Bodies: Film Stars and Society* (London, Basingstoke: Macmillan Education, 1986), 138–39. Emphasis in original.

61. Burkhardt, Fox Publicity Report 5890, Stepin Fetchit Biographical File, Margaret Herrick Library, Academy of Motion Picture Arts and Sciences, Beverly Hills, California.

62. Declaration of $35,000 Bankruptcy for Stepin Fetchit dated October 1933; October 29, 1934, Statement of Moneys Paid out by Fox Film Corporation on Account of Stepin Fetchit; Interoffice memo dated February 11, 1935, from Kenneth Chantry. Fox Legal Files, "Stepin Fetchit" Folder FLXR-861, Arts Special Collections Department, University of California at Los Angeles.

63. See Ronald L. Davis, *The Glamour Factory: Inside Hollywood's Big Studio System* (Dallas: Southern Methodist University Press, 1993), 144.

64. For example, Perry turned the rooftop of his Los Angeles home into a kind of outdoor recreation room and took to throwing lavish parties there. He irreverently dubbed his rooftop paradise "Harlemwood," and Fox's publicity department ran wild with the story, describing Harlemwood as the symbol of Stepin Fetchit's philosophy that "work kills the soul," and explaining that he intended it as a haven for "tired blacks" who might take advantage of the opportunity to rest and be bathed "in watermelon juice, or the juice of other fresh fruits in season." Miles, Fox Publicity Report, 1936, Stepin Fetchit Biographical File, Margaret Herrick Library, Academy of Motion Picture Arts and Sciences, Beverly Hills.

65. Ed Guerrero, "The Black Image in Protective Custody: Hollywood's Biracial Buddy Films of the Eighties," in *Black American Cinema,* ed. Manthia Diawara (New York: Routledge, 1993), 237–47. Various scholars have argued for the Fetchit-Rogers pairing as a cinematic progenitor of the black-white buddy films that flourished in the 1980s and 1990s. See, for example, Donald Bogle, *Toms, Coons, Mulattoes, Mammies, and Bucks: An Interpretive History of Blacks in American Films* (New York: Continuum, 1996); and Watkins, *Stepin Fetchit.*

66. *Judge Priest,* dir. John Ford (Fox Film Corporation, 1934).

67. Ibid.

68. Peter Stowell, *John Ford* (Boston: Twayne Publishers, 1986), 6.

69. Eileen Creelman, "The New Talkies: Will Rogers in *Life Begins at 40* and *The Case of the Curious Bride*," *New York Sun*, April 5, 1935, 32.

70. A scene in which Stepin Fetchit's character is nearly lynched was ultimately cut from the film. Original Script, *Judge Priest*, Fox Script Collection, University of Southern California Film Special Collections, Los Angeles.

71. Watkins, *Stepin Fetchit*, 178.

72. "Stepin Fetchit Resumes Screen Career With Fox," *New York Evening Post*, March 3, 1934, 11.

73. "Hobnobbing in Hollywood: With Grace Kingsley," *Los Angeles Times*, Oct. 18, 1933, A7.

74. Tino Balio, *Grand Design: Hollywood as a Modern Business Enterprise, 1930–1939* (Berkeley: University of California Press, 1996), 18–20.

75. Ibid., 19.

76. Ben Yagoda, *Will Rogers: A Biography* (Tulsa: University of Oklahoma Press, 2000), 306. Fox itself went into receivership at exactly this time, and would go from being "Fox Film Corporation" to "Twentieth Century Fox" in the fall of 1935 as the result of a successful but very necessary merger with Twentieth Century Corporation.

77. "Fetchit Returns," *New York Times*, Nov. 26, 1933, X5. The wisecracking writer of this piece almost appeared to be stumping for a position writing publicity for Fox. She clearly took creative license into her own hands, especially given that Dora Perry, Lincoln Perry's mother, died in 1914, more than a decade before Stepin Fetchit became a Hollywood phenomenon.

78. "Stepin Fechet [*sic*] Reinstated by Former Bosses: Barrymore Lauds Work; More About *Follies;* Amusement," *The Washington Post*, Dec. 6, 1933, 10.

79. A sampling of Cohen's stories from the *Saturday Evening Post* in the 1930s provide clearcut examples: "Snakes Alive," May 16, 1931; "Among those Presents," March 7, 1931; and "Deft and Dumb," May 27, 1933.

80. Watkins, *Stepin Fetchit*, 178.

81. Harry Levette, "Stepin Fetchit Is Sure Movies Rule," *The Chicago Defender*, Dec. 23, 1933, 5.

82. See Charlene Regester, "Stepin Fetchit: The Man, the Image, and the African American Press," *Film History* 6, no. 4 (Winter 1994): 507.

83. Harry Levette, "Stepin Fetchit Signs Contract for Long Term," *Philadelphia Tribune*, Aug. 31, 1933, 12.

84. Watkins, *Stepin Fetchit*, 119.

85. "Can Lazy Bones Stepin Fetchit Come Back?" *Afro-American*, Feb. 3, 1934, 21.

86. Louis Lautier, "Capital Spotlight: Stepin Fetchit Reforms," *Baltimore Afro American*, June 9, 1934, 3.

87. Ibid. In the *Post* article, the uniforms were described as a cross between "a Swiss admiral and the Emperor Jones."

88. Ibid.

89. Ironically the African American newspaper *The Pittsburgh Courier* referred to this benefit as a part of its "Crusade for Self-Respect." The well-known enmity between the two performers may have some of its roots in this encounter; Robinson was known to be judgmental about professional matters

in particular, and, as Perry's elder, he was no doubt disgusted by his dissipation and foolishness onstage.

90. Burkhardt, Fox Publicity Report 5901, Stepin Fetchit Biographical File, Margaret Herrick Library, Academy of Motion Picture Arts and Sciences, Beverly Hills.

91. Regester, "Stepin Fetchit," 507.

92. Watkins, *Stepin Fetchit,* 195.

93. Donald Crafton, *Shadow of a Mouse: Performance, Belief, and World-Making in Animation* (Berkeley: University of California Press, 2012).

94. Bogle, *Toms, Coons, Mulattoes, Mammies, and Bucks,* 69–77.

95. Yuval Taylor and Jake Austen, *Darkest America: Black Minstrelsy from Slavery to Hip Hop* (New York: W. W. Norton, 2012), 135–36.

96. Watkins, *Stepin Fetchit,* 150.

97. Yet it was Mantan Moreland who would make the most of the Charlie Chan franchise, appearing as Chan's chauffeur "Birmingham Brown" in more than a dozen films between 1944 and 1949. It should be noted that Moreland appeared as Brown with the second Charlie Chan actor, Sidney Toler. Stepin Fetchit had appeared with the first, Warner Oland.

98. Watkins, *Stepin Fetchit,* 198.

99. See Joseph McBride's interview, "Stepin Fetchit Talks Back," *Film Quarterly* 24, no. 4 (Summer 1971): 20–26.

100. Harry Levette, "Gossip of the Movie Lots," *Philadelphia Tribune,* Oct. 6, 1938, 13.

101. Watkins, *Stepin Fetchit,* 151.

102. Walter Benjamin, "The Work of Art in the Age of Mechanical Reproduction," in *Illuminations: Essays and Reflections,* ed. Hannah Arendt (Berlin: Schocken, 1969), 221.

103. Schechner, *Performance Studies: An Introduction* (New York: Routledge, 2013), 29.

104. "Stepin Fetchit, Now 68 and 50 Yrs. in Show Biz, in re Ofay Audiences," *Variety,* Sept. 27, 1961, 1, 64.

105. Henry T. Sampson, *That's Enough, Folks! Black Images in Animated Cartoons, 1900–1960* (Lanham, MD: Scarecrow Press, 1998).

106. Crafton, *Shadow of a Mouse,* 102.

107. Ibid., 23.

108. Sampson, *That's Enough, Folks,* 87.

109. Knight, "Star Dances," 404.

110. Christopher P. Lehman, *The Colored Cartoon* (Amherst: University of Massachusetts Press, 2009), 42.

111. One might reasonably discern a connection between the curly blonde girl doll and Shirley Temple, although her blindness (she is led by a toy seeing-eye dog) makes this association somewhat discomfiting, since so much of Temple's persona is predicated on her being able-bodied. In any case the little sailor boy doll has more of the spunk and "can-do" spirit that are Temple's hallmarks.

112. She is very like the mammy ragdolls that were popular in the 1930s, such as the "Beloved Belindy" doll popularized by Johnny Gruelle's "Raggedy Ann and Andy" stories, comic strips and dolls of the nineteen teens, twenties,

and thirties, or the Aunt Jemima Rag Doll that was offered as a promotion for Aunt Jemima pancake flour from the 1900s until the 1950s.

113. The late Marlon Riggs's 1986 film *Ethnic Notions* makes the cultural connection between distinct historical representations of black people and the ideological uses to which such images were put, especially during slavery and in the wake of Reconstruction.

114. Lehman, *The Colored Cartoon,* 44.

115. Crafton, *Shadow of a Mouse,* 119.

116. Roland Barthes, *Camera Lucida: Reflections on Photography,* trans. Richard Howard (New York: Hill and Wang, 1982), 20.

117. Note that the camera "pans" right to show six white stars in sequence: John Barrymore, Hugh Herbert, Constance Collier, Marlene Dietrich, George Raft, and Ned Sparks. Each one of them is eating peas with a knife, in a distinctive style that matches or makes fun of their onscreen personality.

118. David Graver, "The Actor's Bodies," *Text and Performance Quarterly* 17, no. 3 (1997): 229.

119. Homi K. Bhabha, "The Other Question: Stereotype, Discrimination and the Discourse of Colonialism," in *The Location of Culture* (New York: Routledge, 2004), 110.

120. McBride, "Stepin Fetchit Talks Back," 22.

121. McBride, "Stepin Fetchit Talks Back," 22.

122. Howe, "Troubadour ob de Lawd," 58.

123. Knight, "Star Dances," 389–90.

124. Audre Lorde, "The Master's Tools Will Never Dismantle the Master's House," in *Sister Outsider: Essays and Speeches* (Freedom, CA: Crossing Press, 2007), 111.

125. Ibid., 112.

126. Eric Lott, *Love and Theft: Blackface Minstrelsy and the American Working Class* (New York: Oxford, University Press), 6. See also Jason Richards, "Imitation Nation: Blackface Minstrelsy and the Making of African American Selfhood in Uncle Tom's Cabin," *Novel: A Forum on Fiction* 39, no. 2 (Spring 2006): 204–20; and David Roediger, *The Wages of Whiteness: Race and the Making of the American Working Class* (Brooklyn: Verso, 1999).

127. Bhabha, "The Other Question."

CONCLUSION

1. Langston Hughes, "Here to Yonder: Time Now to Stop, Actors," *Chicago Defender,* March 13, 1943.

2. Ibid.

3. Walter White to Lowell Mellett, Dec. 24, 1941, NAACP files, microfilm, Manuscript Division, Library of Congress.

4. Thomas Cripps, *Making Movies Black: The Hollywood Message Movie from World War II to the Civil Rights Era,* (Oxford: Oxford University Press, 1993), 35.

5. Walter White to Will Hays, February 4, 1942, NAACP files, microfilm, Manuscript Division, Library of Congress.

6. Clarence Muse, "Muse Presents Other Side of Film Picture," *Pittsburgh Courier,* Sept. 12, 1942, 20.

7. Walter White, "Statement to the Negro Public, Particularly in Los Angeles," Sept. 19, 1942, in records of NAACP, Library of Congress. Quoted in Thomas Cripps, *Slow Fade to Black: The Negro in American Films, 1900–1942* (Oxford: Oxford University Press, 1977), 387.

8. Letter from Hattie McDaniel to the Commanding Officer of the U.S. War Department, dated July 26, 1945, NAACP files, Manuscript Division, Library of Congress; and Letter from Hattie McDaniel to T. L. Griffith, dated January 20, 1956, NAACP files, Manuscript Division, Library of Congress.

9. Victoria Sturtevant, "But Things Is Changin' Nowadays an' Mammy's Gettin' Bored: Hattie McDaniel and the Culture of Dissemblance," *The Velvet Light Trap* 44 (Fall 1999): 77.

10. Letter from Almena Davis to Walter White, dated April 21, 1942, with accompanying, undated column "How 'bout This?" from the *Los Angeles Tribune.* In the Papers of the National Association for the Advancement of Colored People, Part 17: National Staff Files, 1940–1955, microfilm, Northwestern University.

11. Charlene B. Regester, *Black Entertainers in African American Newspaper Articles,* vol. 2, *An Annotated and Indexed Bibliography of the* Pittsburgh Courier *and the* California Eagle, *1914–1950* (Jefferson, NC: McFarland, 2010), 475.

12. Kenneth Robert Janken, *White: The Biography of Walter White Mr. NAACP* (New York: The New Press, 2003), 266.

13. Cripps, *Making Movies Black,* 36.

14. Donald Bogle, *Toms, Coons, Mulattoes, Mammies, and Bucks: An Interpretive History of Blacks in American Films* (New York: Continuum, 1996), 138–39.

15. Janken, *White,* 272.

16. Douglass Churchill, "Screen News Here and in Hollywood: Paul Robeson Will Appear in *Tales of Manhattan* after Absence of Five Years," *New York Times,* Aug. 29, 1941, 13.

17. Release and premiere date information from the American Film Institute catalog entry for *Tales of Manhattan,* http://www.afi.com/members/catalog/DetailView.aspx?s=&Movie=27496.

18. See "Paul Robeson Quits Pictures in Disgust; Hits Parts Given Race," *Chicago Defender,* Oct. 3, 1942, 21; Wendell Green, "Hollywood out for Him, Says Paul Robeson: Singer Regrets Role in *Tales of Manhattan,*" *Atlanta Daily World,* Oct. 12, 1942, 2; "Robeson Adds Protest to *Tales of Manhattan* Film," *Baltimore Afro-American,* Sept. 5, 1942, 10.

19. "Robeson Hits Hollywood: Says 'Old Plantation Tradition' Is 'Offensive to My People,'" *New York Times,* Sept. 23, 1942, 28.

20. "Robeson Replies to Critics of *Tales of Manhattan,*" *Pittsburgh Courier,* Sept. 5, 1942, 21.

21. "Robeson Quits Movies Because of Offensive Role," *Boston Globe,* Sept. 23, 1942, 17.

22. "Robeson Is Chided for Stand," *Pittsburgh Courier,* Oct. 24, 1942, 21.

23. Billy Rowe, "Writer of Colored Sequence in *Tales* Interviewed by Rowe," *Pittsburgh Courier,* Oct. 31, 1942, 20.

24. With their national "Double V" campaign, the *Courier's* editors urged African Americans to contribute fully to the war effort, while simultaneously calling on the U.S. government to do all it could to make genuine freedom and equality a reality for every citizen, regardless of race. The *Courier's* "Double V" logo became a fad throughout African American communities in the 1940s; it was intended as an unmistakable symbol "that the specter of German, Italian, and Japanese fascism abroad did not negate the damage caused by American racism at home." Todd Steven Burroughs, "Pittsburgh Courier," in *Encyclopedia of African American History, 1896 to the Present: From the Age of Segregation to the Twenty-first Century*, ed. Paul Finkelman (New York: Oxford University Press, 2008), 235–36.

25. Lawrence Lamar, "Here's *Tales of Manhattan*; See If You Think It Objectionable," *Chicago Defender*, Oct. 31, 1942, 20.

26. "This Irked Paul Robeson," *Chicago Defender*, Jan. 30, 1943, 18.

27. "Paul Robeson," *California Eagle*, Sept. 18, 1941, 4b; "Rochester, Robeson Waters in *Tales of Manhattan*," *California Eagle*, Nov. 13, 1941, 3.

28. Advertisement for *Tales of Manhattan*, *California Eagle*, Aug. 6, 1942, 2; "*Tales of Manhattan* Opens Today," *California Eagle*, Aug. 6, 1942, "*Tales of Manhattan* Held Over," *California Eagle*, Aug. 13, 1942, 2.

29. Lawrence F. LaMar, "Coast Citizens Picket House Using Film, *Tales Of Manhattan*," *Chicago Defender*, Aug. 22, 1942, 22. Leon H. Washington quoted in "Another Group Speaks on the Question Negroes in Pictures [*sic*]," *Chicago Defender*, Sept. 19, 1942, 20.

30. Marian Freeman, "Paul Robeson, Ethel Waters Let Us Down," *New York Amsterdam News*, Aug. 15, 1942, 15.

31. Judith Weisenfeld, *Hollywood Be Thy Name: African American Religion in Film, 1929–1949* (Berkeley: University of California Press, 2007), 167.

32. Scott Allen Nollen, *Paul Robeson: Film Pioneer* (Jefferson: NC, McFarland, 2010), 148.

33. Eddie "Rochester" Anderson's Reverend Lazarus character makes this assessment about the sum to his congregation as they decide what to do with the money that is left after everyone has been given an honest share. Don Ryan, "Yoo-Hoo! Hiya, Hattie!" *Los Angeles Times*, Feb. 11, 1940, 3.

34. Hughes ends his "Time Now to Stop, Actors" column with a paragraph listing these and other highly respectable "suggested roles."

35. Quoted in Bogle, *Toms, Coons, Mulattoes, Mammies, and Bucks*, 127.

36. Pamela Wojcik notes this listing of Horne as exemplary of the "unwritten rule that an African American ... actor cannot be a lead," Pamela R. Wojcik, "Typecasting," in *Movie Acting: The Film Reader*, In Focus: Routledge Film Readers (New York: Routledge, 2004), 184. Oddly, the *Academy Players Directory* listing makes no mention of Horne's singing talents.

37. Charles Musser, "Paul Robeson and the End of His 'Movie' Career," *Cinémas: Journal of Film Studies* 19, no. 1 (2008): 147–79. In this essay, Musser argues persuasively for a reassessment of *Tales of Manhattan*, one that reads its finale intertextually against Black-cast theatrical and film productions. Citing such instances as the implicitly Communist sentiment of Paul Robeson's inspirational speech, as "Luke," to his rapt community; the film's depiction of Black people with the agency and character to handle and share such a large sum of

money responsibly; and the characterization of African American religion as potentially political and revolutionary, Musser contends that the shantytown sequence sounded a pointed rejoinder to representations in *The Green Pastures* (1936, dirs. Marc Connelly and William Keighley, Warner Bros.) and especially to the popular Broadway version of *Cabin in the Sky*.

38. Hughes, "Here to Yonder: Time Now to Stop, Actors."

39. Musser, "Paul Robeson and the End of His 'Movie' Career," 167.

40. The problematics of limited casting persist to the present, even as a minimal flourishing of Black television roles in the 2014–15 season aroused concern for "displaced" white actors and actresses. See Nellie Andreeva, "Pilots 2015: The Year of Ethnic Castings—About Time or Too Much of Good Thing?" Deadline Hollywood, March 24, 2015, http://deadline.com/2015/03/tv-pilots-ethnic-casting-trend-backlash-1201386511/.

41. James Baldwin, *The Devil Finds Work: An Essay* (New York: Dial Press, 1976), 29–30.

42. Ibid., 30. Italics in original.

Selected Bibliography

ARCHIVES AND SPECIAL COLLECTIONS

Amistad Research Center, New Orleans

Arts Special Collections, University of California Los Angeles

Atlanta History Center, Atlanta

Auburn Avenue Research Library, Atlanta

Beinecke Rare Book and Manuscript Library, Yale University, New Haven, CT

Connecticut Historical Society, Hartford, CT

David O. Selznick Collection, Harry Ransom Center, University of Texas at Austin

Fox Scripts Collection, Cinematic Arts Library, University of Southern California, Los Angeles

George Eastman House, Rochester, NY

George P. Johnson Negro Film Collection, Department of Special Collections, University of California at Los Angeles

Hatch-Billops Collection, New York

Margaret Herrick Library, Academy of Motion Picture Arts and Sciences, Los Angeles

Motion Picture, Broadcasting and Recorded Sound Division, Library of Congress, Washington, D.C.

NAACP Files, Manuscript Division, Library of Congress, Washington, D.C.

Warner Brothers Archive, University of Southern California, Los Angeles

Will Rogers Memorial Museum, Claremore, OK

BOOKS AND ARTICLES

Abel, Richard, and Rick Altman, eds. *The Sounds of Early Cinema.* Bloomington: Indiana University Press, 2001.

Alexander, Karen. "Fatal Beauties: Black Women in Hollywood." In *Stardom, Industry of Desire,* edited by Christine Gledhill. London: Routledge, 1991.

Allen, Robert, and Douglas Gomery. *Film History: Theory and Practice.* New York: Knopf, 1985.

Altman, Rick. *Film/Genre.* London: British Film Institute, 1999.

Anderson, Lisa. *Mammies No More: The Changing Image of Black Women on Stage and Screen.* New York: Rowman and Littlefield, 1997.

Angelou, Maya. *I Know Why the Caged Bird Sings.* New York: Bantam Books, 1970.

Appiah, Anthony, and Henry Louis Gates, eds. *Africana: Arts and Letters.* Philadelphia: Running Press, 2004.

Atkins, Cholly, and Jacqui Malone. *Class Act: The Jazz Life of Choreographer Cholly Atkins.* New York: Columbia University Press, 2001.

Awkward, Michael. "'Unruly and Let Loose': Myth, Ideology, and Gender in *Song of Solomon.*" *Callaloo* 13, no. 3 (1990): 482–98.

Baker, Bruce E. "How W.E.B. DuBois Won the United Daughters of the Confederacy Essay Contest." *Southern Cultures* 15, no. 1 (Spring 2009): 69–81.

Baker, Houston A., Manthia Diawara, and Ruth H. Lindeborg, eds. *Black British Cultural Studies: A Reader.* Chicago: University of Chicago Press, 1996.

Baldwin, James. *The Devil Finds Work: An Essay.* New York: Dial, 1976.

———. *The Fire Next Time.* New York: Dial, 1963.

Balio, Tino. *The American Film Industry.* Madison: University of Wisconsin Press, 1985.

———. *Grand Design: Hollywood as a Modern Business Enterprise, 1930–1939.* Berkeley: University of California Press, 1996.

Barthes, Roland. *Camera Lucida: Reflections on Photography,* translated by Richard Howard. New York: Hill and Wang, 1982.

Basinger, Jeanine. *The Star Machine.* New York: Vintage, 2009.

Bates, Beth Tompkins. *Pullman Porters and the Rise of Protest Politics in Black America, 1925–1945.* Chapel Hill: University of North Carolina Press, 2001.

Baudry, Jean-Louis. "Ideological Effects on the Basic Cinematographic Apparatus." In *Narrative, Apparatus, Ideology: A Film Theory Reader,* edited by Philip Rosen, 286–98. New York: Columbia University Press, 1986.

Bean, Annemarie, James V. Hatch, and Brooks McNamara, eds. *Inside the Minstrel Mask: Readings in Nineteenth-Century Blackface Minstrelsy.* Hanover: University Press of New England, Wesleyan University Press, 1996.

Behlmer, Rudy, ed. *Memo from David O. Selznick: The Creation of* Gone with the Wind *and Other Motion Picture Classics, as Revealed in the Producer's Private Letters, Telegrams, Memorandums, and Autobiographical Remarks.* New York: Modern Library, 2000.

Benjamin, Walter. *Illuminations: Essays and Reflections.* Edited by Hannah Arendt. Berlin: Schocken, 1969.

Benjamin, Walter, and Michael William Jennings. *The Writer of Modern Life: Essays on Charles Baudelaire.* Cambridge, MA: Harvard University Press, 2006.

Bernardi, Daniel, ed. *The Birth of Whiteness: Race and the Emergence of U.S. Cinema.* New Brunswick: Rutgers University Press, 1996.

———. *Classic Hollywood, Classic Whiteness.* Minneapolis: University of Minnesota Press, 2001.

Bernstein, Matthew, and Dana White. "*Imitation of Life* in a Segregated Atlanta: Its Promotion, Distribution, and Reception." *Film History* 19, no. 2 (2007): 152–78.

Bernstein, Robin. *Racial Innocence: Performing American Childhood from Slavery to Civil Rights.* New York: New York University Press, 2011.

Bhabha, Homi K. *The Location of Culture.* New York: Routledge, 1994.

Black, Cheryl. "Looking White, Acting Black: Cast(e)ing Fredi Washington." *Theatre Survey* 45, no. 1 (2004): 19–40.

Black, Shirley Temple. *Child Star: An Autobiography.* New York: McGraw-Hill, 1998.

Blight, David. *Race and Reunion: The Civil War in American Memory.* Cambridge, MA: Belknap Press of Harvard University Press, 2001.

Bobo, Jacqueline. *Black Women as Cultural Readers.* New York: Columbia University Press, 1995.

Bogle, Donald. *Bright Boulevards, Bold Dreams: The Story of Black Hollywood.* New York: One World Ballantine Books, 2005.

———. *Brown Sugar: Eighty Years of America's Black Female Superstars.* New York: Da Capo Press, 1980.

———. *Heat Wave: The Life and Career of Ethel Waters.* New York: HarperCollins, 2011.

———. *Toms, Coons, Mulattoes, Mammies, and Bucks: An Interpretive History of Blacks in American Films.* New York: Continuum, 2000.

Bordo, Susan. *Unbearable Weight: Feminism, Western Culture, and the Body.* Berkeley: University of California Press, 2003.

Boskin, Joseph. *Sambo: The Rise and Demise of an American Jester.* New York: Oxford University Press, 1986.

Bourne, Stephen. *Black in the British Frame: Black People in British Film and Television 1896–1996.* London: Cassell, 1998.

———. *Elisabeth Welch: Soft Lights and Sweet Music.* Lanham, MD: Scarecrow Press, 2005.

———. *Nina Mae McKinney: The Black Garbo.* Oklahoma: Bear Manor Media, 2011.

Bowdre, Karen M. "Passing Films and the Illusion of Racial Equality." *Black Camera* 5, no. 2 (Spring 2014): 21–43.

Bowers, Claude R. *The Tragic Era: The Revolution after Lincoln.* New York: Houghton Mifflin Harcourt, 1957.

Brashler, William. *Josh Gibson: A Life in the Negro Leagues.* New York: Harper and Row, 1978.

Bridges, Herb. *Gone with the Wind: The Three-Day Premiere in Atlanta.* Macon, GA: Mercer University Press, 1999.

Brooks, Daphne. *Bodies in Dissent: Spectacular Performances of Race and Freedom, 1850–1910.* Durham: Duke University Press, 2006.

Brown, Jayna. *Babylon Girls: Black Women Performers and the Shaping of the Modern.* Durham, NC: Duke University Press, 2008.

Brown, Ruth, and Andrew Yule. *Miss Rhythm: The Autobiography of Ruth Brown.* New York: Donald I. Fine Books/Dutton, 1996.

Brown, Sterling. "Once a Pancake." *A Son's Return: Selected Essays of Sterling A. Brown.* Edited by Mark Sanders. Boston: Northeastern University Press, 1996.

Butler, Jeremy G. *Star Texts: Image and Performance in Film and Television.* Contemporary Film and Television Series. Detroit: Wayne State University Press, 1991.

Butters, Gerald R. *Black Manhood on the Silent Screen.* Lawrence: University Press of Kansas, 2002.

Cameron, Judy, and Paul J. Christman. *The Art of* Gone with the Wind: *The Making of a Legend.* Upper Saddle River, NJ: Prentice Hall, 1991.

Campbell, Edward D.C., Jr. *The Celluloid South: Hollywood and the Southern Myth.* Knoxville: University of Tennessee Press, 1981.

Carbado, Devon, ed. *Black Men on Race, Gender and Sexuality: A Critical Reader.* New York: New York University Press, 1999.

Carbine, Mary. "'The Finest Outside the Loop': Motion Picture Exhibition in Chicago's Black Metropolis, 1905–1928." *Camera Obscura* 8, no. 2 23 (1990): 9–42.

Carby, Hazel. *Race Men.* Cambridge, MA: Harvard University Press, 1998.

Childress, Alice. *Like One of the Family: Conversations from a Domestic's Life.* Boston: Beacon Press, 1986.

Chion, Michel. *The Voice in Cinema.* Translated by Claudia Gorbman. New York: Columbia University Press, 1999.

Clark, Champ. *Shuffling to Ignominy: The Tragedy of Stepin Fetchit.* New York: iUniverse, 2005.

Clark-Lewis, Elizabeth. *Living in, Living Out: African American Domestics in Washington, D.C., 1910–1940.* Washington, D.C.: Smithsonian Institution Press, 1994.

Clinton, Catherine. *The Plantation Mistress: Woman's World in the Old South.* New York: Pantheon Books, 1984.

Clinton, Catherine, and Michelle Gillespie, eds. *The Devil's Lane: Sex and Race in the Early South.* Oxford: Oxford University Press, 1997.

Cooper, Ralph, with Steve Dougherty. *Amateur Night at the Apollo: Ralph Cooper Presents Five Decades of Great Entertainment.* New York: Harper-Collins, 1990.

Courtney, Susan. *Hollywood Fantasies of Miscegenation: Spectacular Narratives of Gender and Race.* Princeton: Princeton University Press, 2004.

———. "Picturizing Race: Hollywood's Censorship of Miscegenation and Production of Racial Visibility through *Imitation of Life.*" *Genders* 27 (1998).

Cowan, William T. "Plantation Comic Modes." *Humor* 14, no. 1 (2001): 1–24.

Crafton, Donald. *Shadow of a Mouse: Performance, Belief and World-Making in Animation.* Berkeley: University of California Press, 2012.

Craig, Maxine Leeds. *Ain't I a Beauty Queen: Black Women, Beauty, and the Politics of Race.* Oxford: Oxford University Press, 2002.

Crenshaw, Kimberlé, Neil Gotanda, Gary Peller, and Kendall Thomas, eds. *Critical Race Theory: The Writings That Formed the Movement.* New York: The New Press, 1995.

Cressey, Paul G. "A Social Setting for the Motion Picture." In *Children and the Movies: Media Influence and the Payne Fund Controversy,* edited by Garth Jowett. Cambridge: Cambridge University Press, 1996

Cripps, Thomas. *Black Film as Genre.* Bloomington: Indiana University Press, 1978.

———. *Making Movies Black: The Hollywood Message Movie from World War II to the Civil Rights Era.* Oxford: Oxford University Press, 1993.

———. "The Myth of the Southern Box Office." In *The Black Experience in America,* edited by James Curtis and Lewis Gould. Austin: University of Texas Press, 1970.

———. *Slow Fade to Black: The Negro in American Films, 1900–1942.* Oxford: Oxford University Press, 1977.

Cross, Gary. *Kids' Stuff: Toys and the Changing World of American Childhood.* Cambridge, MA: Harvard University Press, 1999.

Davis, Ossie. *Life Lit by Some Large Vision: Selected Speeches and Writings.* New York: Atria Books, 2006.

Davis, Ronald L. *The Glamour Factory: Inside Hollywood's Big Studio System.* Dallas: Southern Methodist University Press, 1993.

Decordova, Richard. "The Emergence of the Star System in America." *Wide Angle* 6, no. 4 (1985): 4–13.

———. *Picture Personalities: The Emergence of the Star System in America.* Urbana-Champaign: University of Illinois Press, 2001.

deLauretis, Teresa. *The Practice of Love: Lesbian Sexuality and Perverse Desire.* Bloomington: Indiana University Press, 1994.

Dent, Gina, ed. *Black Popular Culture: A Project by Michele Wallace.* Seattle: Bay Press, 1992.

Desjardins, Mary. "Not of Hollywood: Ruth Chatterton, Ann Harding, Constance Bennett, Kay Francis, and Nancy Harding." In *Glamour in a Golden Age: Movie Stars of the 1930s,* edited by Adrienne McClean. New Brunswick, NJ: Rutgers University Press, 2011.

Diawara, Manthia. "Black Spectatorship: Problems of Identification and Resistance." In *Black American Cinema,* edited by Manthia Diawara. New York: Routledge Press, 1993.

———, ed. *Black American Cinema.* New York: Routledge, 1993.

Dickstein, Morris. *Dancing in the Dark: A Cultural History of the Great Depression.* New York: W. W. Norton, 2010.

Dormon, James H. "Shaping the Popular Image of Post-Reconstruction American Blacks: The 'Coon Song' Phenomenon of the Gilded Age." *American Quarterly* 40, no. 4 (December 1988): 450–71.

Douglass, Frederick. *My Bondage and My Freedom.* New Haven: Yale University Press, 2014.

Duberman, Martin. *Paul Robeson.* New York: Alfred A. Knopf, 1989.

DuCille, Ann. "The Shirley Temple of My Familiar." *Transition* 73 (1997): 10–32.

Dyer, Richard. *Heavenly Bodies: Film Stars and Society*. London, Basingstoke: MacMillan Education, 1986.

———. *The Matter of Images: Essays on Representation*. New York: Routledge, 1993.

———. *Only Entertainment*. New York: Routledge, 1992.

———. *Stars: New Edition, with Supplementary Chapter and Bibliography by Paul McDonald*. London: British Film Institute Publishing, 1998.

———. *White*. New York: Routledge, 1997.

Eckert, Charles. "Shirley Temple and the House of Rockefeller." *Jump Cut* 2 (1974): 1, 17–20.

Edwards, Paul Kenneth. *The Southern Urban Negro as a Consumer*. New York: Prentice-Hall, 1932.

Eisnach, Dwight, and Herbert C. Covey. *What the Slaves Ate: Recollections of African American Foods and Foodways from the Slave Narratives*. Santa Barbara: Greenwood, 2009.

Ellison, Ralph. "The Shadow and the Act." *Shadow and Act*. New York: Vintage, 1972.

Everett, Anna. *Returning the Gaze: A Genealogy of Black Film Criticism, 1909–1949*. Durham, NC: Duke University Press, 2001.

Eyman, Scott. *The Speed of Sound: Hollywood and the Talkie Revolution, 1926–1930*. Baltimore: Johns Hopkins University Press, 1999.

Fanon, Frantz. *Black Skin, White Masks*. Translated by Richard Philcox. New York: Grove Press, 2008.

Farnsworth, Robert M, ed. *Caviar and Cabbage: Selected Columns by Melvin B. Tolson from the* Washington Tribune, *1937–1944*. Columbia: University of Missouri Press, 1982.

Fass, Paula S., ed. *The Routledge History of Childhood in the Western World*. London: Routledge, 2013.

Fauset, Jessie Redmon. *Plum Bun: A Novel without a Moral*. New York: Frederick A. Stokes, 1929.

Feldstein, Ruth. *How It Feels to Be Free: Black Women Entertainers and the Civil Rights Movement*. Oxford: Oxford University Press, 2013.

———. *Motherhood in Black and White: Race and Sex in American Liberalism, 1930–1965*. Ithaca: Cornell University Press, 2000.

Ferber, Edna. *Show Boat: A Novel*. Garden City, NY: Doubleday, Page and Company, 1926.

Finkelman, Paul, ed. *Encyclopedia of African American History, 1896 to the Present: From the Age of Segregation to the Twenty-First Century*. New York: Oxford University Press, 2009.

Fleetwood, Nicole. *Troubling Vision: Performance, Visuality and Blackness*. Chicago: University of Chicago Press, 2011.

Foner, Eric. *A Short History of Reconstruction, 1863–1877*. New York: Harper and Row, 1990.

Forman, James. *Our Movie-Made Children*. New York: Macmillan, 1935.

Fox-Genovese, Elizabeth. *Within the Plantation Household: Black and White Women of the Old South*. Chapel Hill: University of North Carolina Press, 1988.

Frank, Rusty E. *Tap! The Greatest Tap Dance Stars and Their Stories, 1900–1955*. New York: Da Capo Press, 1994.

Frederickson, George. *The Black Image in the White Mind: The Debate on Afro-American Character and Destiny, 1817–1914*. Hanover, NH: Wesleyan University Press, 1971.

Freedman, Russell. *The Voice That Challenged a Nation: Marian Anderson and the Struggle for Equal Rights*. New York: Clarion Books, 2004.

Friedman, Ryan Jay. *Hollywood's African American Films: The Transition to Sound*. New Brunswick, NJ: Rutgers University Press, 2011.

Gabbard, Krin. *Black Magic : White Hollywood and African American Culture*. New Brunswick, NJ: Rutgers University Press, 2004.

Gabler, Neal. *An Empire of Their Own: How the Jews Invented Hollywood*. New York: Anchor, 1989.

Gaines, Jane M. *Fire and Desire: Mixed-Race Movies in the Silent Era*. Chicago: University of Chicago Press, 2001.

Gallagher, Gary. *Causes Won, Lost, and Forgotten: How Hollywood and Popular Art Shape What We Know about the Civil War*. Chapel Hill: University of North Carolina Press, 2008.

Gates, Henry Louis. *The Signifying Monkey: A Theory of African American Literary Criticism*. Oxford: Oxford University Press, 1988.

———. "The Trope of the New Negro and the Reconstruction of the Image of the Black." *Representations* 24 (Fall 1998): 129–55.

Gates, Henry Louis, and Evelyn Brooks Higginbotham, eds. *The African American National Biography*. New York: Oxford University Press, 2008.

Gavin, James. *Stormy Weather: The Life of Lena Horne*. New York: Atria Books, 2009.

Giedion, Siegfried. *Architecture, You and Me*. Cambridge, MA: Harvard University Press, 1958.

———. "The Need for a New Monumentality." In *New Architecture and City Planning*, edited by Paul Zucker. New York: Books for Libraries Press, 1944.

Gilman, Sander L. *Difference and Pathology: Stereotypes of Sexuality, Race, and Madness*. Ithaca: Cornell University Press, 1985.

Gledhill, Christine, ed. *Home Is Where the Heart Is: Studies in Melodrama and the Woman's Film*. London: British Film Institute, 1987.

———, ed. *Stardom: Industry of Desire*. London: Routledge, 1991.

Goings, Kenneth. *Mammy and Uncle Mose: Black Collectibles and American Stereotyping*. Bloomington: Indiana University Press, 1994.

Gomery, Douglass. *The Coming of Sound*. London: Routledge, 2004.

———. *The Hollywood Studio System: A History*. London: British Film Institute, 2005.

———. *Shared Pleasures: A History of Movie Presentation in the United States*. Madison: University of Wisconsin Press, 1992.

Gomery, Douglass, and Robert Allen. *Film History: Theory and Practice*. New York: McGraw-Hill, 1985.

Goodwin, Ruby Berkley. *It's Good to Be Black*. Carbondale: Southern Illinois University Press, 2013.

Gosselin, Adrienne Johnson. "Racial Etiquette and the (White) Plot of Passing: (Re)Inscribing 'Place' in John Stahl's *Imitation of Life.*" *Canadian Review of American Studies* 28, no. 3 (1998): 47–67.

Gottschild, Brenda Dixon. *The Black Dancing Body: A Geography from Coon to Cool.* New York: Palgrave Macmillan, 2003.

Graver, David. "The Actor's Bodies." *Text and Performance Quarterly* 17, no. 3 (1997): 221–35.

Gregory, Dick, with Robert Lipsyte. *Nigger: An Autobiography.* New York: Dutton, 1964.

Griffin, Farah Jasmine. *Who Set You Flowin'?: The African American Migration Narrative.* New York: Oxford University Press, 1996.

Gubar, Susan. *Racechanges: White Skin, Black Face in American Culture.* Oxford: Oxford University Press, 1997.

Gue, Randy. "'It seems that everything looks good nowadays, as long as it is in the flesh & brownskin': The Assertion of Cultural Difference at Atlanta's 81 Theater, 1934–1937." *Film History* 8, no. 2 (1996): 209–18.

Guerrero, Ed. "The Black Image in Protective Custody: Hollywood's Biracial Buddy Films of the Eighties." In *Black American Cinema,* edited by Manthia Diawara, 237–47. New York: Routledge, 1993.

———. "Black Stars in Exile: Paul Robeson, O. J. Simpson, and Othello." In *Paul Robeson: Artist and Citizen,* edited by Jeffrey C. Stewart. New Brunswick: Rutgers University Press, 1998.

———. *Framing Blackness: The African-American Image in Film.* Philadelphia: Temple University Press, 1993.

Hadju, David. *Lush Life: A Biography of Billy Strayhorn.* New York: Farrar, Straus, and Giroux, 1996.

Hale, Grace E. *Making Whiteness: The Culture of Segregation in the South, 1890–1940.* New York: Vintage, 2010.

Hall, Stuart. "Culture, the Media and the 'Ideological Effect.'" In *Mass Communication and Society,* edited by James Curran, Michael Furevich, and Janet Wallacott. London: Edward Arnold, 1977.

———. "What Is This 'Black' in Black Popular Culture?" *Social Justice* 20, no. 1–2 (1993): 104–14.

Hammonds, Evelyn. "Black (W)holes and the Geometry of Black Female Sexuality." *Differences: A Journal of Feminist Cultural Studies* 6, no. 2–3 (Summer–Fall 1994): 126–45.

Hansen, Miriam. *Babel and Babylon: Spectatorship in American Silent Film.* Cambridge, MA: Harvard University Press, 1991.

Hardy, Sarah Madsen, and Kelly Thomas. "Listening to Race: Voice, Mixing, and Technological 'Miscegenation' in Early Sound Film." In *Classic Hollywood, Classic Whiteness,* edited by Daniel Bernardi. Minneapolis: University of Minnesota Press, 2001.

Haskins, James, and N. R. Mitgang. *Mr. Bojangles: The Biography of Bill Robinson.* New York: William Morrow, 1988.

Hark, Ina Rae, ed. *Exhibition: The Film Reader.* New York: Routledge, 2001.

Harwell, Richard, ed. *Margaret Mitchell's* Gone with the Wind *Letters.* New York: Macmillan Publishing, 1976.

Hernton, Calvin. "Chattanooga Black Boy: Identity and Racism." In *Names We Call Home: Autobiography on Racial Identity*, edited by Becky Thompson and Sangeeta Tyagi, 139–55. New York: Routledge, 1995.

Higginbotham, Evelyn Brooks. *Righteous Discontent: The Black Women's Movement in the Black Baptist Church, 1880–1920*. Cambridge, MA: Harvard University Press, 1994.

Hill, Constance Valis. *Brotherhood in Rhythm: The Jazz Tap Dancing of the Nicholas Brothers*. New York: Cooper Square Press, 2002.

———. *Tap Dancing America: A Cultural History*. New York: Oxford, 2010.

Hine, Darlene Clark. "Rape and the Inner Lives of Black Women in the Middle West: Preliminary Thoughts on the Culture of Dissemblance." *Signs* 14, no. 4 (Summer 1989): 912–20.

———, ed. *Black Women in America*. New York: Oxford University Press, 2005.

Hirschhorn, Clive. *The Universal Story*. New York: Crown Publishers, 1983.

Hogan, Lawrence. *A Black National News Service: The Associated Negro Press and Claude Barnett, 1919–1945*. Rutherford, London: Associated University Presses, 1984.

hooks, bell. *Black Looks: Race and Representation*. Boston: South End Press, 1992.

———. "The Oppositional Gaze: Black Female Spectators." In *Black American Cinema*, edited by Manthia Diawara. New York: Routledge Press, 1993.

Horne, Lena, with Richard Schickel. *Lena*. New York: Limelight, 1986.

Hughes, Langston. "The Negro and American Entertainment." *The Collected Works of Langston Hughes*. Vol. 9, Essays on Art, Race, Politics, and World Affairs. Edited by Christopher De Santis. Columbia: University of Missouri Press, 2002.

Hunter, Tera W. *To 'Joy My Freedom: Southern Black Women's Lives and Labors after the Civil War*. Cambridge, MA: Harvard University Press, 1997.

Hurst, Fannie. *Imitation of Life: A Novel by Fannie Hurst*. New York: Harper and Brothers, 1933.

Jackson, Carlton. *Hattie: The Life of Hattie McDaniel*. Lanham: Madison Books, 1990.

Janken, Kenneth Robert. *White: The Biography of Walter White, Mr. NAACP*. New York: The New Press, 2003.

Jenkins, Henry. *What Made Pistachio Nuts?: Early Sound Comedy and the Vaudeville Aesthetic*. New York: Columbia University Press, 1992.

Jerome, V. J. *The Negro in Hollywood Films*. New York: Masses and Mainstream, 1950.

Jewell, K. Sue. *From Mammy to Miss America and Beyond : Cultural Images and the Shaping of U.S. Social Policy*. New York: Routledge, 1993.

Jewell, Richard. *The Golden Age of Cinema: 1929–1945*. Hoboken: Wiley-Blackwell, 2007.

Johnson, James Weldon. *Black Manhattan*. New York: Da Capo Press, 1991.

Johnson, Joan Marie. "'Ye Gave Them a Stone': African American Women's Clubs, the Frederick Douglass Home, and the Black Mammy Monument." *Journal of Women's History* 17, no. 1 (2005): 62–86.

Jones, Jacqueline. *Labor of Love, Labor of Sorrow: Black Women, Work and the Family, from Slavery to the Present*. New York: Vintage Books, 1985.

Kaplan, E. Ann. *Looking for the Other: Feminism, Film, and the Imperial Gaze*. New York: Routledge, 1997.

Keller, Allan. *Marian Anderson: A Singer's Journey*. Urbana-Champaign: University of Illinois Press, 2001.

Kennedy, Adrienne. *People Who Led to My Plays*. New York: Theatre Communications Group, 1987.

Kerr, Paul, ed. *The Hollywood Film Industry: A Reader*. London, New York: Routledge and Kegan Paul in association with the British Film Institute, 1986.

King, Barry. "Stardom as an Occupation." In *The Hollywood Film Industry: A Reader*, edited by Paul Kerr. London, New York: Routledge and Kegan Paul in association with the British Film Institute, 1986.

King, Wilma. "The Mistress and Her Maids: White and Black Women in a Louisiana Household." In *Discovering the Women in Slavery: Emancipating Perspectives on the American Past*, edited by Patricia Morton, 82–106. Athens: University of Georgia Press, 1996.

Kisch, John, and Edward Mapp. *A Separate Cinema: Fifty Years of Black Cast Posters*. New York: Noonday, 1992.

Klaprat, Cathy. "The Star as Market Strategy: Bette Davis in Another Light." In *The American Film Industry*, edited by Tino Balio. Madison: University of Wisconsin Press, 1985.

Klotman, Phyllis R. *Frame by Frame*. Vol 1, *A Black Filmography*. Bloomington: Indiana University Press, 1997.

Knight, Arthur. *Disintegrating the Musical: Black Performance and American Musical Film*. Durham, NC: Duke University Press, 2002.

———. "Searching for the Apollo: Black Moviegoing and its Contexts in the Small Town U.S. South." In *Explorations in New Cinema History: Approaches and Case Studies*, edited by Richard Maltby, Daniel Biltereyst, and Philippe Meers, 226–42. Oxford: Wiley Blackwell, 2011.

———. "Star Dances: African American Constructions of Stardom, 1925–1960." In *Classic Hollywood, Classic Whiteness*, edited by Daniel Bernardi, 386–414. Minneapolis: University of Minnesota Press, 2001.

Knowles, Mark. *Tap Roots: The Early History of Tap Dancing*. Jefferson, NC: McFarland, 2002.

Krasner, David. *A Beautiful Pageant: African American Performance Theater and Drama in the Harlem Renaissance, 1910–1917*. New York: Palgrave Macmillan, 2002.

Kreuger, Miles. *Show Boat: The Story of a Classic American Musical*. Oxford: Oxford University Press, 1977.

Landay, Eileen. *Black Film Stars*. New York: Drake, 1973.

Larsen, Nella, and Carla Kaplan. *Passing: Authoritative Text, Backgrounds and Contexts, Criticism*. Norton Critical Edition. New York: W. W. Norton and Co., 2007.

Larson, Kate Clifford. *Bound for the Promised Land: Harriet Tubman*. New York: One World/Ballantine, 2004.

Leab, Daniel J. *From Sambo to Superspade: The Black Experience in Motion Pictures*. Boston: Houghton, 1975.

Leff, Leonard J. "The Search for Hattie McDaniel." *New Orleans Review* 10, no. 2–3 (1983): 91–98.

Lehman, Christopher P. *The Colored Cartoon*. Amherst: University of Massachusetts Press: 2009.

Levine, Lawrence. *Black Culture and Black Consciousness: Afro-American Folk Thought from Slavery to Freedom*. Oxford: Oxford University Press, 1977.

———. *The Unpredictable Past: Explorations in American Cultural History*. Oxford: Oxford University Press, 1993.

Lorde, Audre. "The Master's Tools Will Never Dismantle the Master's House." *Sister Outsider: Essays and Speeches*. Freedom, CA: Crossing Press, 2007.

Lott, Eric. *Love and Theft: Blackface Minstrelsy and the American Working Class*. New York: Oxford University Press.

Lowery, Shearon A., and Melvin L. DeFleur. *Milestones in Mass Communication Research: Media Effects*. Upper Saddle River, NJ: Pearson, 1995.

MacCann, Richard D. *The Stars Appear*. Metuchen: Scarecrow Press, 1992.

Maltby, Richard, Melvyn Stokes, and Robert C. Allen, eds. *Going to the Movies: Hollywood and the Social Experience of Cinema*. Exeter: Exeter University Press, 2008.

Manatu, Norma. *African American Women and Sexuality in the Cinema*. Jefferson, NC: McFarland, 2003.

Manring, M.M. *Slave in a Box: The Strange Career of Aunt Jemima*. Charlottseville: University Press of Virginia, 1998.

Marks, Carole. *Farewell—We're Good and Gone: The Great Black Migration*. Bloomington: Indiana University Press, 1989.

Martin, Michael T. *Cinemas of the Black Diaspora: Diversity, Dependence, and Oppositionality*. Detroit: Wayne State University Press, 1996.

Mask, Mia. *Divas on Screen: Black Women in American Film*. Urbana-Champaign: University of Illinois Press, 2009.

———, ed. *Contemporary Black American Cinema: Race, Gender and Sexuality at the Movies*. New York: Routledge, 2012.

Massood, Paula J. *Black City Cinema: African American Urban Experiences in Film*. Philadelphia: Temple University Press, 2003.

Maurice, Alice. *The Cinema and Its Shadow: Race and Technology in Early Cinema*. Minneapolis: University of Minnesota Press, 2013.

———. "'Cinema at Its Source:' Synchronizing Race and Sound in the Early Talkies." *Camera Obscura* 17, no. 1 (2002): 31–72.

May, Lary. *The Big Tomorrow: Hollywood and the Politics of the American Way*. Chicago: University of Chicago Press, 2000.

Maynard, W. Barksdale. "The Greek Revival: Americanness, Politics, and Economics." In *American Architectural History: A Contemporary Reader*, edited by Keith Eggener, 132–42. London: Routledge, 2004.

Mayne, Judith. *Cinema and Spectatorship*. New York: Routledge, 1993.

McBride, Joseph. *Searching for John Ford: A Life*. New York: St. Martin's Press, 2001.

———. "Stepin Fetchit Talks Back." *Film Quarterly* 24, no. 4 (Summer 1971): 20–26.

McElya, Micki. *Clinging to Mammy: The Faithful Slave in Twentieth-Century America.* Cambridge, MA: Harvard University Press, 2007.

———. "Commemorating the Color Line: The National Mammy Monument Controversy of the 1920s." In *Monuments to the Lost Cause: Women, Art, and the Landscape of Southern Memory,* edited by Cynthia Mills and Pamela Simpson, 203–19. Knoxville: University of Tennessee Press, 2003.

McLean, Adrienne L. *Being Rita Hayworth: Labor, Identity, and Hollywood Stardom.* New Brunswick, NJ: Rutgers University Press, 2004.

———, ed. *Glamour in a Golden Age: Movie Stars of the 1930s.* New Brunswick, NJ: Rutgers University Press, 2011.

Means Coleman, Robin R. *Say It Loud! African-American Audiences, Media, and Identity.* New York: Routledge, 2002.

Mitchell, Margaret. *Gone with the Wind.* New York: Warner Books, 1993.

Morrison, Toni. *Beloved.* New York: First Vintage International Edition, 2004.

———. *The Bluest Eye.* New York: Holt, Rinehart, and Winston, 1970.

———. *Playing in the Dark: Whiteness and the Literary Imagination.* New York: Vintage, 1993.

———. "Rootedness: The Ancestor as Foundation." In *Black Women Writers, 1950–1980,* edited by Mari Evans. New York: Anchor Doubleday, 1984.

Morton, Patricia, ed. *Discovering the Women in Slavery: Emancipating Perspectives on the American Past.* Athens: University of Georgia Press, 1996.

Mulvey, Laura. "Afterthoughts on 'Visual Pleasure and Narrative Cinema' Inspired by *Duel in the Sun.*" *Framework* 15–17 (1981): 12–15.

———. *Visual and Other Pleasures.* Bloomington: Indiana University Press, 1989.

Murray, James P. *To Find an Image: Black Films from Uncle Tom to Super Fly.* New York: Bobbs-Merrill, 1973.

Muse, Clarence. "The Dilemma of the Negro Actor." Self-published pamphlet, 1934, from a speech given to the California Art Club in 1929.

Musser, Charles. "Paul Robeson and the End of His 'Movie' Career." *Cinémas: Journal of Film Studies* 19, no. 1 (2008): 147–79.

Myrick, Susan. *White Columns in Hollywood: Reports from the* Gone with the Wind *Sets.* Edited by Richard Harwell. Macon, GA: Mercer University Press, 1994.

Naremore, James. *Acting in the Cinema.* Berkeley: University of California Press, 1990.

Nesteby, James R. *Black Images in American Films, 1896–1954: The Interplay between Civil Rights and Film Culture.* Washington: University Press of America, 1982.

Noble, Peter. *The Negro in Films.* London: Skelton Robinson, 1948.

Nollen, Scott Allen. *Paul Robeson: Film Pioneer.* Jefferson, NC: McFarland, 2010.

Null, Gary. *Black Hollywood.* Secaucus, NJ: Citadel Press, 1975.

Patterson, Lindsay, ed. *Black Films and Film-Makers.* New York: Dodd, Mead, 1975.

Peiss, Kathy. *Hope in a Jar: The Making of America's Beauty Culture.* New York: Metropolitan Books, Henry Holt and Company, 1998.

Petty, Miriam J. "'Doubtful Glory': 1930s Hollywood and the African American Actor as Star." PhD diss., Emory University, 2004.

———. "Passing for Horror: Race, Fear, and Elia Kazan's *Pinky.*" *Genders* 40 (2004): n.p.

Pines, Jim. *Blacks in Films: A Survey of Racial Themes and Images in the American Film.* London: Studio Vista, 1975.

Polan, Dana B. *Scenes of Instruction: The Beginnings of the U.S. Study of Film.* Berkeley: University of California Press, 2007.

Poppenheim, Mary B., Maude Blake Merchant, and Ruth Jennings Lawton. *The History of the United Daughters of the Confederacy.* Vol. 1. Richmond: United Daughters of the Confederacy, 1994.

Regester, Charlene. *The African American Actresses: Struggles for Visibility, 1900–1960.* Bloomington: Indiana University Press, 2010.

———. *Black Entertainers in African American Newspaper Articles.* Vol. 1, *An Annotated Bibliography of the* Chicago Defender, *the* Afro-American (Baltimore), *and the* New York Amsterdam News, *1910–1950.* Jefferson, NC: McFarland, 2002.

———. *Black Entertainers in African American Newspaper Articles.* Vol. 2, *An Annotated and Indexed Bibliography of the* Pittsburgh Courier *and the* California Eagle, *1914–1950.* Jefferson, NC: McFarland, 2010.

———. "From the Buzzard's Roost: Black Movie-Going in Durham and Other North Carolina Cities during the Early Period of American Cinema." *Film History: An International Journal* 17, no. 1 (2005): 113–24.

———. "Stepin Fetchit: The Man, the Image, and the African American Press." *Film History* 6, no. 4 (Winter 1994): 502–21.

Reid, Mark. *Redefining Black Film.* Berkeley: University of California Press, 1993.

Richards, Jason. "Imitation Nation: Blackface Minstrelsy and the Making of African American Selfhood in *Uncle Tom's Cabin.*" *Novel: A Forum on Fiction* 39, no. 2 (Spring 2006): 204–20.

Richards, Larry. *African American Films through 1959: A Comprehensive, Illustrated Filmography.* Jefferson, NC: McFarland Press, 1998.

Roach, Joseph R. *It.* Ann Arbor: University of Michigan Press, 2007.

Robinson, Cedric J. *Forgeries of Memory and Meaning: Blacks and the Regimes of Race in American Theater and Film before World War II.* Chapel Hill: University of North Carolina Press, 2007.

Rodowick, David N. "The Difficulty of Difference." *Wide Angle* 6, no. 3 (1984): 16–23.

Roediger, David. *The Wages of Whiteness: Race and the Making of the American Working Class.* Brooklyn: Verso, 1999.

Roffman, Peter, and Jim Purdy. *The Hollywood Social Problem Film: Madness, Despair, and Politics from the Depression to the Fifties.* Bloomington: Indiana University Press, 1981.

Rogin, Michael. *Blackface, White Noise: Jewish Immigrants in the Hollywood Melting Pot.* Berkeley: University of California Press, 1998.

———. *Ronald Reagan: The Movie.* Berkeley: University of California Press, 1987.

Rooks, Noliwe. *Hair Raising: Beauty, Culture, and African American Women.* New Brunswick, NJ: Rutgers University Press, 1996.

Ross, Karen. *Black and White Media: Black Images in Popular Film and Television.* Cambridge: Polity, 1996.

Ross, Lawrence C. *The Divine Nine: The History of African American Fraternities and Sororities.* New York: Kensington, 2001.

Rourke, Constance. *American Humor: A Study of the National Character.* Tallahassee: Florida State University Press, 1959.

Rubin, Martin. "Mr. Ford and Mr. Rogers." *Film Comment* 10, no. 1 (January-February 1974): 54–57.

Russell, Kathy, Midge Wilson, and Ronald Hall. *The Color Complex: The Politics of Skin Color among African Americans.* New York: Anchor Books, 1993.

Salem, Dorothy. *To Better Our World: Black Women in Organized Reform, 1890–1920.* Brooklyn: Carlson, 1990.

Sampson, Henry T. *That's Enough, Folks! Black Images in Animated Cartoons, 1900–1960.* Lanham, MD: Scarecrow Press, 1998.

Sanders, Kimberly Wallace. *Mammy: A Century of Race, Gender, and Southern Memory.* Ann Arbor: University of Michigan Press, 2009.

———, ed. *Skin Deep, Spirit Strong: The Black Female Body in American Culture.* Ann Arbor: University of Michigan Press, 2002.

Sanders, Mark A., ed. *A Son's Return: Selected Essays of Sterling A. Brown.* Boston: Northeastern University Press, 1996.

Schatz, Thomas. *The Genius of the System: Hollywood Filmmaking in the Studio Era.* Minneapolis: University of Minnesota Press, 2010.

———. *Hollywood Genres: Formulas, Filmmaking, and the Studio System.* Philadelphia: Temple University Press, 1981.

Schechner, Richard. *Performance Studies: An Introduction.* New York: Routledge, 2013.

Scott, Ellen. "More than a 'Passing' Sophistication: Dress, Film Regulation, and the Color Line in 1930s American Films." *Women's Studies Quarterly* 41, no. 1–2 (Spring/Summer 2013), 60–86.

Sherman, Sam. *Legendary Singing Cowboys.* New York: Friedman/Fairfax, 1995.

Sherrard-Johnson, Cherene. *Portraits of the New Negro Woman: Visual and Literary Culture in the Harlem Renaissance.* New Brunswick, NJ: Rutgers University Press, 2007.

Shingler, Martin, and Christine Gledhill. "Bette Davis: Actor/Star." *Screen* 49, no. 1 (Spring 2008): 67–76.

Shipton, Alyn. *Fats Waller: The Cheerful Little Earful.* New York: Continuum, 2002.

Sklar, Robert, and Charles Musser. *Resisting Images : Essays on Cinema and History.* Philadelphia: Temple University Press, 1990.

Smith, Valerie. *Not Just Race, Not Just Gender: Black Feminist Readings.* New York: Routledge, 1998.

―――. *Representing Blackness: Issues in Film and Video.* New Brunswick, NJ: Rutgers University Press, 1997.

Snead, James. *White Screens, Black Images: Hollywood from the Dark Side.* New York: Routledge, 1994.

Sollors, Werner. *Neither Black nor White yet Both: Thematic Explorations of Interracial Literature.* New Oxford: Oxford University Press, 1997.

Sorlin, Pierre. *The Film in History: Restaging the Past.* Totowa: Barnes and Noble Books, 1980.

Spillers, Hortense J. "Mama's Baby, Papa's Maybe: An American Grammar Book." *Diacritics* 17, no. 2 (Summer 1987): 64–81.

Stacey, Jackie. *Star Gazing: Hollywood Cinema and Female Spectatorship.* London: Routledge, 1994.

Staggs, Sam. *Born to Be Hurt: The Untold Story of* Imitation of Life. New York: St. Martin's Press, 2009.

Staiger, Janet. *Interpreting Films: Studies in the Historical Reception of American Cinema.* Princeton: Princeton University Press, 1992.

―――. "Seeing Stars." *The Velvet Light Trap* 20 (1983): 10–14.

―――, ed. *The Studio System.* New Brunswick, NJ: Rutgers University Press, 1995.

Stearns, Marshall, and Jean Stearns. *Jazz Dance: The Story of American Vernacular Dance.* New York: Schirmer, 1968.

Stewart, Jacqueline. *Migrating to the Movies: Cinema and Black Urban Modernity.* Berkeley: University of California Press, 2005.

Stewart, Jeffrey, ed. *Paul Robeson: Artist and Citizen.* New Brunswick, NJ: Rutgers University Press, 1998.

Stowell, Peter. *John Ford.* Boston: Twayne Publishers, 1986.

Streible, Dan. "The Harlem Theatre: Black Film Exhibition in Austin, Texas: 1920–1973." In *Black American Cinema,* edited by Manthia Diawara, 221–236. New York: Routledge, 1993.

Studlar, Gayln. *Precocious Charms: Stars Performing Girlhood in Classical Hollywood Cinema.* Berkeley: University of California Press, 2013.

―――. *This Mad Masquerade: Stardom and Masculinity in the Jazz Age.* New York: Columbia University Press, 1996.

Sturtevant, Victoria. "'But Things Is Changin' Nowadays an' Mammy's Gettin' Bored': Hattie McDaniel and the Culture of Dissemblance." *The Velvet Light Trap* 44 (Fall 1999): 68–79.

Taylor, Clyde. "The Ironies of Palace-Subaltern Discourse." In *Black American Cinema,* edited by Manthia Diawara, 177–99. New York: Routledge, 1993.

Taylor, Helen. *Scarlett's Women: Gone with the Wind and Its Female Fans.* New Brunswick, NJ: Rutgers University Press, 1989.

Taylor, Yuval, and Jake Austen. *Darkest America: Black Minstrelsy from Slavery to Hip Hop.* New York: W. W. Norton and Company, 2012.

Thaggert, Miriam. "Divided Images: Black Female Spectatorship and John Stahl's *Imitation of Life.*" *African American Review* 32, no. 3 (1998): 481–91.

Thomas, Edward J. *Memoirs of a Southerner: 1840–1923.* Savannah: n.p., 1923.

Thurber, Cheryl. "The Development of the Mammy Image and Mythology." In *Southern Women: Histories and Identities*, edited by Virginia Bernhard, Betty Brandon, Elizabeth Fox-Genovese, and Theda Perdue, 87–108. Columbia: University of Missouri Press, 1992.

Toll, Robert. *Blacking Up: The Minstrel Show in Nineteenth Century America*. New York: Oxford University Press, 1974.

Turner, Patricia. *Ceramic Uncles and Celluloid Mammies: Black Images and Their Influence on Culture*. New York: Anchor Books, 1994.

Vered, Karen Orr. "White and Black in Black and White: Management of Race and Sexuality in the Coupling of Child-Star Shirley Temple and Bill Robinson." *The Velvet Light Trap* 39 (Spring 1997): 52–65.

Vlach, John Michael. *Back of the Big House: The Architecture of Plantation Slavery*. Chapel Hill: University of North Carolina Press, 1993.

Walker, Alexander. *Stardom: The Hollywood Phenomenon*. New York: Stein and Day, 1970.

Waller, Gregory. "Another Audience: Black Moviegoing, 1907–1916." *Cinema Journal* 31, no. 2, (1992): 3–25.

———. *Main Street Amusements: Movies and Commercial Entertainment in a Southern City, 1896–1930*. Washington, D.C.: Smithsonian Institution Press, 1995.

Watkins, Mel. *Dancing with Strangers: A Memoir*. New York: Simon and Schuster, 1998.

———. *On the Real Side: A History of African American Comedy from Slavery to Chris Rock*. Chicago: Lawrence Hill Books, 1994.

———. *Stepin Fetchit: The Life and Times of Lincoln Perry*. New York: Vintage, 2005.

Watkins, S. Craig. *Representing: Hip Hop Culutre and the Production of Black Cinema*. Chicago: University of Chicago Press, 1998.

Watts, Jill. *Hattie McDaniel: Black Ambition, White Hollywood*. New York: Amistad, 2005.

Weisenfeld, Judith. *Hollywood Be Thy Name: African American Religion in Film, 1929–1949*. Berkeley: University of California Press, 2007.

Weld, Theodore Dwight. *American Slavery As It Is: Testimony of a Thousand Witnesses*. Chapel Hill: University of North Carolina Press, 2011.

White, Deborah Gray. *Ar'n't I a Woman?: Female Slaves in the Plantation South*. New York: Norton, 1985.

———. *Too Heavy a Load: Black Women in Defense of Themselves, 1894–1994*. New York: Norton, 1994.

White, Patricia. *Uninvited: Classical Hollywood Cinema and Lesbian Representability*. Bloomington: Indiana University Press, 1999.

White, Shane, and Graham J. White. *Stylin': African American Expressive Culture from Its Beginnings to the Zoot Suit*. Ithaca, NY: Cornell University Press, 1998.

Wilderson, Frank B. *Red, White, and Black: Cinema and the Structure of U.S. Antagonisms*. Durham, NC: Duke University Press, 2010.

Wiley, John Jr., ed. *The Scarlett Letters: The Making of the Film* Gone with the Wind. New York: Rowman and Littlefield, 2014.

Williams, Carla. "Naked, Neutered, or Noble: The Black Female Body in America and the Problem of Photographic History." In *Skin Deep, Spirit Strong: The Black Female Body in American Culture,* edited by Kimberly Wallace-Sanders. Ann Arbor: University of Michigan Press, 2002.

Williams, Linda. *Playing the Race Card: Melodramas of Black and White from Uncle Tom to O.J. Simpson.* Princeton: Princeton University Press, 2002.

Williams, Raymond. *Marxism and Literature.* Oxford: Oxford University Press, 1977.

Wilson, Steve, and Robert Osborne. *The Making of* Gone with the Wind. Austin: University of Texas Press, 2014.

Witt, Doris. *Black Hunger: Food and the Politics of U.S. Identity.* New York: Oxford University Press, 1999.

Wittke, Robert. *Tambo and Bones: A History of the American Minstrel Stage.* Durham, NC: Duke University Press, 1930.

Wojcik, Pamela R., ed. *Movie Acting: The Film Reader.* New York: Routledge, 2004.

Woll, Allen. *Black Musical Theatre: From "Coontown" to "Dreamgirls."* Baton Rouge: Louisiana State University Press, 1989.

Wright, Richard. *Native Son.* New York: Harper and Brothers, 1940.

X, Malcolm, and Alex Haley. *The Autobiography of Malcolm X.* New York: Grove Press, 1965.

Yacowar, Maurice. "An Aesthetic Defense of the Star System in Films." *Quarterly Review of Film Studies* 4, no. 1 (1979): 39–52.

Yagoda, Ben. *Will Rogers: A Biography.* Tulsa: University of Oklahoma Press, 2000.

Index

Salon" (*La Revue des lettres et des arts*, 1st May 1908; *Pr2* 105-106).

In *The Cubist Painters*, Apollinaire uses the term "metamorphosis", which had already appeared in the Picasso chapter, to describe Braque's sudden transformation in 1908. Indeed the word "revolution", applied once to Picasso, occurs twice in the Braque chapter. Braque is recognised as one of the two instigators of radical artistic renewal, second only to Picasso. These revolutionaries are also, however, presented as heirs to a long and prestigious tradition of artistic innovation and creativity, a tradition betrayed by the conservative citadel of the rue Bonaparte, the Paris Academy of Fine Arts. This art no longer has a social function, is not burdened with a political, moral or religious message. Neither is it avant-garde in the sense of being "ahead of its time". Despite their innovatory appearance, these fragmentary works in fact reflect contemporary experience, and Braque's Cubism is "in tune with the society in which it is developing."

The reference to Braque's "inventiveness" recognises his introduction of the housepainter's simulated wood effect into Cubism, and then stencilled lettering in late 1911 (though in the Picabia chapter, Apollinaire credits only Picasso with "precisely copied lettering"). Braque made the first Cubist constructions in paper in late 1911 or spring 1912, began mixing sand with oil paint in August 1912 (a technique adopted by Picasso two months later), made the first *papier collé* in September 1912. He was so inventive that Picasso called him "Wilbourg", after aviation pioneer Wilbur Wright.

Apollinaire highlights Braque's application of craft and trade techniques, such as simulated wood, vigorously extending the vocabulary of painting, proving that great art can grow from simple things. This is a fundamental element in the aesthetic of the poet who invented the "conversation poem", made from fragments of everyday speech, and who in 1917 would state that the artist or writer can always "start from an everyday event, so a falling handkerchief may for the poet be the lever with which he will lift a whole universe" ("The New Spirit and the Poets", *Pr*2 951). A reference to the late sixteenth/early seventeenth-century poet and theorist Malherbe crops up here because he famously promoted the literary use of clear, everyday language.

Reference to the "tender beauty" and "the pearly sheen" of Braque's paintings is taken from the Preface to his November 1908 exhibition catalogue. Braque's Cubism, like Picasso's, despite its emphasis on the formal over the chromatic, on the conceptual over the retinal, was not as austere as is often claimed, and as muddy reproductions may suggest. Apart from the ludic dimension which often marked the rivalry between Picasso and Braque, high Cubism also had its sensual dimension. This 1908 observation seems particularly appropriate to later works by Braque, such as those of summer and autumn 1911, where a rich but restrained palette produced majestic compositions in myriad facets of silver and dark gold.

In private correspondence, Apollinaire may once or twice have backtracked on Braque.[3] In *The Cubist Painters*, however, he declares his unqualified support. He suggests that Braque's inventiveness is backed up by solid, dependable, down-to-earth